JEWISH IDENTITY IN AN
AGE OF IDEOLOGIES

JEWISH IDENTITY IN AN AGE OF IDEOLOGIES

Jacob B. Agus

FREDERICK UNGAR PUBLISHING CO.

NEW YORK

Copyright © 1978 by Frederick Ungar Publishing Co., Inc.
Printed in the United States of America
Designed by Irving Perkins

Library of Congress Cataloging in Publication Data

Agus, Jacob Bernard, 1911–
Jewish identity in an age of ideologies.

Bibliography: p.
Includes index.
1. Judaism—History—Modern period, 1750–
2. Jews—Identity. 3. Judaism—Germany—History.
4. Judaism—Relations—Christianity. I. Title.
BM195.A35   296′.094   76–14230
ISBN 0–8044–5018–8

To Dr. William Raffel
of blessed memory (1908–1976)
Physician and friend

Contents

Preface

This work discusses the various challenges to Judaism and the Jewish people posed by the great intellectual movements in the modern world and the responses of Jewish thinkers. The period covered extends from the Emancipation to the present day.

When theology ceased to dominate the minds of men, the age of ideologies was begun, especially in continental Europe. One ideal or another was projected as the supreme standard by which all else was to be judged. We may now be living in a "post-ideological" age, in the sense that we have gradually become aware of the limitations of all ideologies. Every ideal is like the beam of a flashlight, illuminating a cone of space and deepening the darkness around it. The mystery of life is too complex to be understood from any one vantage point. It is to be hoped that we have now learned to shun one-sidedness and to strive for an all-harmonizing perspective, but we know that each of the ideologies discussed here is relevant to our quest for self-understanding. In this sense, each ideology is a contemporary reality.

The self-image of the Jewish people was deeply affected by the ebb and flow of ideologies in the western world. Jewish consciousness at any one time is determined by the reaction to contemporary challenges as well as by the continuity of tradition. We tend to interpret our literary and cultural heritage in the light of the influences and concerns that affect our thought and life. Hence, our self-image is peculiarly sensitive to changes in our intellectual climate, the variations of which cannot but put into question one or another aspect of Jewish identity.

European ideologies were in effect Christian "heresies," since the Christian faith formed the intellectual background of the western nations. Each ideology, in transforming the Christian heritage, modified as well the image of the Jew and the philosophy of Jewish history that are implicit within the Christian tradition. And the ambivalence within the Christian world of the Jewish image—at once the bearer of the Promise and of the "curse"—was often carried over into the secular ideologies.

Mass movements are caused by the coincidence of diverse forces. In addition to their own inner logic, ideologies serve to rationalize and to orient emergent social forces. And in the European world, Jews were not only a historical reminder but a vital, socioeconomic factor, especially in the large cities.

By setting the diverse philosophies of Jewish thinkers within the perspectives of the contending ideologies of their time, I hope to cast light on the central themes of modern Judaism. It is my belief that the view of western culture from the Jewish viewpoint will also illuminate the shadowy underside of modern ideologies, an aspect that is so often overlooked. Specifically, I focus attention on the intellectual roots of the diverse images of the Jew, which, in their popular form, were at times decisively instrumental in determining the tragic course of modern Jewish history. There was a direct connection between the ethereal dialectic of philosophers and historians on the one hand, and the coarse propaganda of malicious demagogues on the other. I trust, therefore, that this volume will prove helpful in dissipating the smog of anti-Jewish prejudice, which in our day has been so lethal.

Attention is centered in this volume largely but not exclusively on the ideological scene in Germany, since the firestorm of the Holocaust originated in that country.

The Appendix offers some of Professor Arnold J. Toynbee's letters to me. In his *Study of History* Toynbee challenged Jewish thinkers to reexamine their self-image and their conception of Jewish destiny, especially in connection with the establishment of Israel. As a critic and a friend of Toynbee's I kept up a correspondence with him. The twelfth volume of his *Study* contains excerpts from my letters and his overly kind description of my role as a Jewish consultant. In view of the tremendous impact of the Toynbee controversy in Jewish circles, his letters should arouse special interest. Mrs. Veronica Toynbee kindly consented to their publication. My responses to these letters and others, are contained in my books *The Meaning of Jewish History* and *Dialogue and Tradition* and within the text of this volume.

Finally, may I thank all those who assisted and encouraged me during the preparation of this work: the officers, directors, and leaders of Beth El Congregation, Baltimore; the staff members of the congregation; my colleagues at Temple University and Dropsie University, where I have taught courses on the themes of this volume; the librarians at Dropsie and at the Myerhoff library of the Baltimore Hebrew College; my publisher, Frederick Ungar, whose understanding and vision guided me in completing this volume; and, not least, my family, whose affection and love are the chief marks of God's blessings in my life.

This work is addressed to all thoughtful men and women who know that an unexamined identity cannot lead to a great destiny.

J.B.A.

I. *A New Kind of Christian-Jewish Disputation*

Ever since Christianity was born, a dialogue has been under way between its followers and the defenders of Judaism. Since both Jews and Christians interpreted every aspect of life in terms of their respective central beliefs, this dialogue expanded in time to include nearly every phase of culture. In essence, the same arguments have been repeated, as if every generation were called upon to justify its position anew. But there were always fresh nuances, reflecting the particular bias of the age. Most of the time the antagonists were not present in the flesh, only in the imagination of the disputant. Yet a debate of some sort, even against the ghost of a contestant, has been going on since the Christian branch grew out of the ancient stem of Judaism.

For Christians this dialogue is inescapable, since it is enshrined in the New Testament. Jesus is represented in the Gospels as debating either with Pharisees or with "Jews." In the Synoptic Gospels he speaks as a Jewish teacher, not only when he agrees with his interlocutors, but also when he condemns with impassioned intensity the Pharisaic leaders of the people. At times he speaks in the style of the biblical prophets, hurling his rebuke at the people in thunderbolts of holy wrath. At times he poses a challenge or responds to a question in the style of the rabbis themselves. In the Gospel of John, the debate turns into a cosmic duel between the source of light and the children of darkness. There the argument on earth is conceived as a shadowy replica of the metaphysical struggle in the heavens. Every affirmation of the Christian faith is stated by God Himself, through His Son.

1

By the same token, Jewish opposition appears to be only the tip of the iceberg of Jewish depravity. The disputants do not speak to each other; they shout and declaim or rather, sing out their convictions.

To be sure, even in the darkest ages of history there were occasional glimpses of humanity and rational piety. May it not be that God employs diverse instruments to establish His Kingdom on earth? Thus, Rabban Gamaliel the Elder tells his colleagues in the Sanhedrin that the Christian community may well be "of God," playing its role in the divine scheme of redemption (Acts 23:9). And James, head of the mother church in Jerusalem, allows that there may be two communities of the faithful—a Jewish one consisting of "those who are zealous for the Law" and a Gentile one consisting of those who abide only by the Noachian commandments (Acts 15; 1–29).

In the course of history, however, the mediating positions between the loyal Jews and the Gentile Christians were destroyed. The fall of Jerusalem was, perhaps, the decisive event in this polarization. Increasingly, the Jewish image in the Christian tradition was demonized. No longer was the Jew a human antagonist, but a minion of Satan, rejected and accursed. The Hebrew Bible was not an expression of Jewish life, but a record of the Jewish fall from grace, to be read as a warning for future generations. The prophets and psalmists had been "Christians before Christ," forever fighting against the pernicious spirit of Judaism. Jews studied the Torah and the prophets with all the passion of their souls, but a veil was draped over their minds and hearts that they might not grasp its true meaning. From beginning to end, the Old Testament was a tissue of myths, oracles, and metaphors, foreshadowing the career of Christ on earth. The true meaning was plain to all, save accursed heretics and Jews.

In Catholic Europe, heretics were ruthlessly persecuted and condemned to death. However, Jews, the worst heretics of all, were generally permitted to live albeit under severe restrictions. They were regarded by the Church as a special case, a paradoxical mystery, at once divine and demonic, since "they were beloved for the fathers' sakes" (Romans 11;28) and at the same time minions of Satan. Accordingly they were allowed to occupy a marginal position in society, a precarious one of degradation and humiliation, in which they might atone throughout historic time for the infinite sin of "deicide."

This medieval image of the Jew, in all its fantastic imagery, persists in the minds of millions down to our day. It is deeply imbedded in the folk imagery of most European nations. And it is capable of being infinitely varied by subtle minds. Its one invariant feature is the metaphysical uniqueness of the Jew; he is different from all other human beings in a cosmic, existential sense. His history and his destiny must be understood not in human terms but in the light of his special status in the divine scheme of things. It took the genius of Shakespeare in his "Merchant of Venice" to call attention to the basic dehumanization in the Christian image of the Jew.

Into the modern age the Christian-Jewish disputation has continued but in more diverse and subler forms. A portion of the population continues to live in spirit within the mythological world of medievalism, and even enlightened people move uneasily between the poles of rationality and fantasy. All too often the underworld of ancient myths can be easily detected beneath the facade of contemporary rhetoric. In the modern world, individual Jews have come to play so central and powerful a role that no intellectual movement could afford to ignore them. As in Greek legends ancient ghosts acquired fresh life when they were given libations of blood, so the myths of antiquity have been reborn in modern times through interaction with contemporary conflicts. At times, the underpinning of medieval mythology is banished to the limbo of the unconscious; at times belief in it is passionately denied, and sincerely so, yet its impetus endures even in movements that are consciously anti-Christian. The Holocaust perpetrated by the Nazis was consciously anti-Christian and nihilistic; yet it was made possible by the massive momentum of medieval folk-antisemitism and by the fantastic mythology that grew for centuries under the aegis of the Church.

The Jew, for his part, has not always responded overtly and publicly to the challenge of Christians. Rabbinic literature contains only rare and scattered replies to the arguments of contemporary Christians. Ever since the banishment of Jewish Christians from the synagogues in the last decade of the first century, the rabbinic tradition virtually ignored the spectacular expansion of the Church. Talmudic literature attained its final form in Babylonia, where there were very few Christians. The Palestinian *Midrashim* were composed in the fifth and sixth centuries, when Jewish preachers could refer only indirectly and by the way of parables to the dominant Christian faith in the Byzantine empire. In addition, the inner exposition of the Jewish faith did not require that account be taken of the emergence of Christianity. While the Church defined itself by reference to the Synagogue, the Synagogue did not feel called upon to define itself by any references to the Church.

Yet it would be wrong to conclude that the Jews of the medieval world ignored the challenge of Christianity. How could they fail to think about it? Believing that the hand of God was seen in history, they could not but assign some role to the Church in the divine plan for redemption. Maimonides stated explicitly that both Islam and Christianity are instruments employed by God to spread His teaching and prepare the world for redemption. Some French rabbis taught that Christians do not belong in the category of idolators that the Talmud describes, but in that of the Noachian semi-converts. Certainly whenever Jews pondered their destiny they could not help wondering at the uniqueness of their fate—on the one hand, their message was accepted, at least in part, by Christians to the north and by Moslems to the south; on the other hand, they, the bearers of the message, were scorned and persecuted. Their faith in their heritage, however, was reinforced by the steadily mounting evidence of its universal appeal, and their determination to survive, despite all detractors, was strengthened by the doctrinal and practical faults they found in the religions of their neighbors.

So, although genuine face to face dialogues rarely took place in the ancient and medieval worlds, Jews and Christians could not but agonize over their relations to one another.

Between Traditionalists and Philosophers

The public life of Moses Mendelssohn, 1729–86, was a living demonstration of the Jewish-Christian dialogue. He was an outstanding philosopher, read and admired by the intellectuals of Germany. Residing in Berlin, the capital of Prussia, he was generally regarded as the leading Jew of his day. As such, he was challenged by believing Christians, on the one hand and by enlightened philosophers, on the other hand. The first challenge was directed at him by Johann Caspar Lavater, 1741–1801, a Swiss pastor and popular author, who had translated a work by the French historian, Bonnet, detailing the evidences of Christianity. Lavater sent a copy of that book to Mendelssohn, with a letter asking that he either refute the "proofs" offered by Bonnet or consent to their validity and convert to Christianity. Presumably, Jews had not been convinced in the past of the truth of Christianity because they had willfully closed their minds to its message. As "children of the devil," (John 8; 44) they would not listen to the truth. But Mendelssohn, as a philosopher, was trained to be open-minded. Hence, the challenge.

Here the traditional position of the Christian protagonist is clearly revealed. First, he does not put his own faith on the line. Like Augustine, he affirms his belief *ab initio* and then proceeds to find justifications for it. He believed in order to understand. His faith does not grow out of his own efforts to comprehend the mysteries of existence. So, the Catholic catechism defines faith as follows: "Faith is a gift of God infused into our souls, by which we firmly believe all those things which God has revealed to us."

Lavater and his colleagues did not ask, if faith is God's gift transcending our understanding, may not God in His Wisdom devise different patterns of belief for different people? If faith is not founded on rational proofs, why marshal those proofs? To the "enlightened" Jews of Berlin, miracles reported in the Gospels do not prove that Jesus was a divine being, any more than the miracles told of Hasidic saints. Mendelssohn repeated an idea that is emphasized in medieval Jewish philosophy. The Jews believed in Moses not because they were impressed by his miracles, but because they were persuaded by the cogency of his teachings. The belief that God could offer to men only one pathway of salvation is itself non-rational. As Mendelssohn pointed out again and again, the doctrine of religious exclusiveness is the one irrefutable proof of the falsehood of a faith, for it imputes rank injustice to God.

Second, eagerness to convert, or missionary zeal, is characteristic of the Christian protagonist's position. In itself, this zeal is laudable. People should share their treasures with others. But this eagerness is combined with a stigmatization of the faith of the non-Christian, judging it to be inferior, or inadequate for salvation, or false. During the Enlightenment, when the intellectuals came to realize the folly and futility of the wars of religion, any such denigration of a historic faith was manifestly contrary to the spirit of the times. After the Protestant Reformation called into question some of the central institutions of the medieval faith, how could they in turn wield the sword of exclusiveness against Jews?

Third, to men of enlightenment, be they Jews or Christians, it is the turning of one's heart and mind to God that counts, not the rituals, or ceremonies, whereby devotion is expressed. In this light, there is need for all of us to be converted to a deeper spirituality. The *mizvot* of the heart are infinite in number and in degrees of outreach, as Bahya Ibn Pakuda reminds us. Hence, conversion, in Jewish hope, is conceived as an inner transformation, a keener grasp of truth, a deeper love, a more determined consecration to "deeds of loving kindness." The spiritual convert may continue to practice the rites of his ancestral faith, while the essence of the true faith lives within him. So the messianic future includes the hope for a universal conversion, in this spiritual sense, while diverse faiths and peoples will continue to cherish their own individual identities.

In this sense, a true dialogue is indeed a call for conversion, but it is neither one-sided nor concerned with externals. Along these lines, Mendelssohn replied to Lavater both directly and through his active correspondence with many friends. "The internal religion of the Jews contains no other precepts than those of the Religion of Nature." As to the external expressions of faith, they are inevitably entangled with the history of a particular group—hence, they cannot be purely rational. "But, this I know, that no external religion can be universal."[1]

Lavater shared the widespread prejudice among Christians that Jews practice some form of desecration of the image of Jesus and that they continually abuse his name. How surprised was he to encounter in Moses Mendelssohn "a beautiful person," wise and tolerant, who extolled Jesus as a great teacher and a moral personality. Mendelssohn had to disabuse Lavater and his confreres of the notions that Jews curse the name of Jesus or that they reject his ethical teachings:

"It is an ingrained prejudice of your coreligionists that the Jews, all of them, incessantly slander the religion of the Christians and its founder, and thereby a great many things are conveniently explained in dogmatics, and much that is both irreligious and unrational is thereby justified in ordinary life."[2]

As to the distinction that Jews make between the ethical teachings of Jesus amd the dogmas concerning his divinity, Mendelssohn wrote:

I also know many a Jew, who, like me, go a step further, and basing themselves upon the statements of Christian testimonies (for, I repeat, we have no reliable Jewish ones) acknowledge the innocence and moral goodness of that founder's character, yet do so on the clear condition
   (1)   that he never meant to regard himself as equal with the Father,
   (2)   that he never proclaimed himself as a person of divinity,
   (3)   that he never presumptiously claimed the honor of worship,
   (4)   that he did not intend to subvert the religion of his fathers.[3]

The concept of the Religion of Nature suggests the influence of Rousseau, whose description of the Vicar of Savoy was then extremely popular. Rousseau's *profession de foi*, in his book *Emile*, describes true religion as a synthesis of feeling, conscience, and intelligence. "God has given us conscience to love the good, reason to know it, freedom to choose it." Rousseau's famous hymn to conscience anticipated the moral philosophy of Kant.

Conscience! Conscience! divine instinct, immortal and celestial guide of an ignorant and limited, but intelligent and free being; infallible judge of good and evil, that makes man like unto God: It is you who make the excellence of his nature and the morality of his actions; without you I feel nothing in me that lifts me above the beasts except the sad privilege of straying from error to error with the help of an understanding without rule and a reason without principle.

The manifold evils of society were man-made, not inevitable

products of our natural endowment. "Man is born free, yet, he is everywhere in chains."

It is important to note that Rousseau, unlike Voltaire and other contemporary philosophers, excoriated the Christian authorities for their oppression of Jews.[4]

Mendelssohn's claim that the Religion of Nature was identical with the central teachings of Judaism was challenged in an anonymous pamphlet. "Does not the Torah of Moses ordain the punishment of death for any number of offenses against the prescribed rituals? Does Mendelssohn, then, consider himself to depart from the laws of Judaism, or does he view religion as an evolving phenomenon, constantly continued, altered and improved?"[5]

Actually, Mendelssohn had ample justification within the Jewish tradition for the notion of a Religion of Nature and for the distinction between "internal" and "external" religion. The notion of "spiritual converts," that is, Gentiles who accept the central principles of monotheistic faith and ethics, without adopting the Jewish "external" ritual, goes back to the pre-Christian period of Judaism. "Spiritual converts," participating in Synagogal worship, were numerous in the far-flung Jewish Diaspora in the Roman Empire.[6] Maimonides maintained that the divine mandate to convert the pagans to "the true faith" is fulfilled when they accept "the seven Noachian laws." Furthermore, Maimonides distinguished between laws of "first intention," such as the injunction to love God and to practice compassion, and laws of "second intention," such as the regimen of sacrifices in the Holy Temple.[7] Laws of "second intention" were instituted in order to meet certain specific historical needs. Maimonides distinguished also between ideas that are true in themselves and "necessary ideas," that is, ideas that serve to bind the community together, providing a viable organism for the maintenance and dissemination of the true faith.[8]

To be sure, Maimonides maintained that pagans are obliged to accept these Noachian principles on the ground that they are contained in the revelation granted to Moses.

Whoever accepts the seven *mizvot* and observes them conscientiously belongs in the category of the "pious among the nations of the world" and shares in *olam haba*, the world to come. This is true, however, only if he accepts them and observes them because the Lord commanded them in the Torah, informing us through Moses, our teacher, that all the descendants of Noah were so commanded previously. But if he observes them because of his own reasoning, he is not a *ger toshav*. And he is not counted among "the pious of the nations," and not among their sages.[9]

In another version, the last phrase reads "but among their sages."[10] Spinoza quoted this passage from Maimonides, attributing it to "the Jews" generally.[11]

Mendelssohn pointed out that Maimonides had no textual justification in the Talmud for his qualification. Therefore, Mendelssohn concluded, Maimonides's position was only a personal opinion, not an integral part of Jewish teaching.

Possibly, Maimonides was impelled to adopt his formally dogmatic position because he saw the entire Judeo-Christian-Moslem world of thought set against a pagan world that he knew only from literature. Christians as well as Moslems were, in his view, disseminators of the scriptural world view.[12] Without the impulse deriving from the Torah, we cannot decide whether the world is created or not. This basic doctrine "should be accepted without proof because of prophecy."[13] His reference to Christians as idolators[14] was purely legalistic, having to do with the difference between reverencing and worshiping icons. For the law in question to apply, it was sufficient if someone *might* overstep the subtle boundary line. Maimonides's deeper view is expressed in the famous Responsum concerning a would-be Christian convert, in which he asserts that "God looks to the Heart."

The fifteenth-century Jewish philosopher, Joseph Albo, developed the concept of a God-given faith still further, allowing that several true, divinely revealed faiths may coexist at any one time. While the historic forms of true religion are many and diverse, adapted to the varying cultural contexts of their adherents, its essential core is one and the same. It consists of faith in the One God, His revelation of the laws of morality, and His Providence.[15]

To be sure Joseph Albo did not agree that the medieval, Inquisition-ridden Christianity of his day was consonant with the principles of a true faith. For that matter, did not the philosophers of the Enlightenment similarly condemn the horrendous perversion of the teaching of Jesus by their contemporary narrow-minded minions of the Church? In the modern world of his time, Mendelssohn argued, both Judaism and Christianity needed to divest themselves of the ugly rags and tatters of superstition and return to the pristine purity of their God-given faiths. Indeed, Christianity and Judaism today may be compared to "two pyramids of which the apices are exactly alike, but from then downward they vary in a great many respects."[16] Each apex is founded on its own traditional pyramid, and the lower one descends from the intellectual elite to the masses and from reason to emotion, the more the pyramids diverge in pattern and structure.

As a son of the Enlightenment, Mendelssohn thought in terms of individuals rather than groups. As "thinking reeds," human beings are expected to make use of their rational faculties in order to seek and find salvation. God, Who is just, did not fail to endow every individual with the gifts of intelligence and conscience, sufficient to lead him to salvation. Religion means literally that which binds, the bond between man and God, and, in essence, that bond is the capacity to reason and to judge. So Mendelssohn was bitterly opposed to any suggestion for the preservation or the reconstitution of Jewish autonomy. He took strong exception to the recommendation of his own friend, Christian Dohm, who authored an epochal work calling for the improvement of the civil status of Jews, that the Jewish community be given the right to impose discipline within its own ranks and to expel recalcitrant members. As an advocate of the Jewish cause, Dohm argued that "they may be allowed to bind their members amongst themselves by a voluntary covenant, to have their disputes judged and decided by their own laws."[17]

Through the centuries, Jewish people had insisted on the right to judge their own members in any agreement that they made with the rulers of the land. Generally, they had been taxed as a unit, and the burden of taxes had then been distributed by a committee of lay and rabbinic leaders. Internal discipline in religious as in communal matters had been maintained by means of the *herem*.[18] Spinoza was the most famous of all who fell under the interdiction of the *herem* because of his heretical views.

To Mendelssohn, the very thought of renewing the *herem* was an abomination. Religion must not resort to coercion. "True divine religion arrogates no dominion over thought and opinion, it knows no other force than that of winning by argument."[19] Since a religious community does not possess coercive powers by nature, a voluntary covenant cannot create such rights, "any more than cultivation can create a flower, where there was no natural seed."[20] Civil and criminal law should be applied without any regard to the religion of the litigants.

It is in this eagerness to eliminate the vestiges of communal self-government that Mendelssohn definitely and defiantly broke with the organic tradition of Judaism. The medieval ghettoes preserved intact the historical traditions of Judaism. The Talmud and the Codes of Jewish law embrace the whole of life in the fine meshes of the selfsame law, making no distinction between ritual and civil ordinances. In the Yeshivot, the scholars argued from the same premises in cases of civil litigations, of family purity, of Nazarite abstention, and of the scapegoat sent into the wilderness on Yom Kippur. Rabbis were generally preoccupied with the problems of commercial law rather than with any other phase of the tradition, and it was considered an act of treachery for businessmen to bring their litigations to non-Jewish courts. Looking ahead to the new order of freedom, Mendelssohn argued that a unitary society cannot permit separate, self-segregating enclaves. On the altar of freedom, he was eager to sacrifice the entire edifice of Jewish civil and criminal law as well as every other remnant of autonomy.

In contrast, Maimonides had been acutely conscious of the organic nature of the Jewish community. To him the purpose of the *mizvot* was communal as well as personal—that is, designed to maintain the kind of community that is suitable for the emergence of saintly philosophers.[21] True, the philosopher pursues his own path to God; he distinguishes between the *mizvot* of primary significance and the true ideas, on the one hand, and the communal disciplines and inevitable popular beliefs, on the other hand; he meditates in solitude on the love of God, pursuing the *via negativa*, determining what is not God, and the *via eminentia*, contemplating the marks of His excellence in creation and in Torah. In the end, he attains a state of religious ecstasy, when Divine Providence envelops him like a protective cloud. But this ecstatic union is only a stage in the life of the saintly philosopher. He must go beyond this state and reinvolve himself in the mundane concerns of the community.[22]

To Maimonides, the nature and content of the Jewish community was fixed and immutable. The children of Abraham, Isaac, and Jacob pledged themselves at Sinai to accept the covenant. Individuals from among the Gentiles joined them in the course of time. Such individuals should be welcomed at all times with open arms, for while Israelites are children of Abraham, the righteous proselytes are "children of God." Saintly and philosophical individuals may also emerge in the non-Jewish world and attain the highest levels of ethical and religious perfection. But Maimonides did not doubt that there was but one divinely ordained community and that this community was destined to regain its own land, eliminate all idolatry from it, and then proceed to impose the "true religion," at least in its internal sense, on all men. Characteristically, the order of redemption, as Maimonides saw it, is for the Jewish people to regain its land first, rebuild the Holy Temple, and bring back the dispersed from among the nations. Only when these national goals have been fulfilled will the redeemed people of Israel proceed to redeem the rest of mankind. To be sure, this sequence of events was presented by Maimonides with two reservations—first, that no one really knows how the process of messianic redemption will unfold; second, that this process will not be a sudden, supernatural manifestation, but that it will take place within the context of the laws of nature as they have been fixed in the six days of creation. Thus Maimonides prepared the way for an evolutionary and naturalistic interpretation of the messianic hope.[23]

Mendelssohn built on the Maimonidean vision, but with a radical reordering of priorities—the free, universal society, based on the rights of the individual, may well emerge in the early stages of redemption. A new community of the "enlightened" will shake itself loose from the grip of ancient hatreds. The historic faiths will be purified from all that is unworthy of a Religion of Nature. Jews as individuals will share in building this universal society. Ultimately, the land of Israel will once again become the possession of the people of Israel. The messianic hope, then, will be fulfilled first in its universalist-ethical dimension. The beginning of redemption for Jews is "but simply a period when they will be more humanely treated in the lands in which they dwell and put on an equality with the rest of the inhabitants." Then, with the advance of international amity, "the Israelites will gradually retrieve their rank as a nation."[24]

Thus Mendelssohn anticipated the approach that was subsequently adopted by Jewish liberals and socialists: the establishment of the universal, free society must come first; the complete fulfillment of Israel's national hopes, if they are still tenable at that time, will follow as a matter of course, as a natural consequence of the age of perfection. And this universal society must be built by a coalition of enlightened, emancipated individuals who constitute in effect a new, all-embracing brotherhood.

Yet Mendelssohn, in contrast to later liberals and socialists, was a thoroughly observant Jew. Did he then depart from the tradition in his vision of redemption? Did the Torah impose "walls of iron" around the children of the Covenant, which prevent them from joining with others in building the great society?[25] To be sure, there were various ordinances calculated to impede the natural process of social intercourse between Jews and their neighbors. And there was the mental attitude of the chosen people, insofar as this attitude was constantly nurtured by the biblical imagery of "a nation that dwells alone, and is not counted among the peoples" (Numbers 23:9).

Mendelssohn countered the first challenge by the claim, which was attested to by his own achievements, that it is possible to be loyal to the Law in every respect and yet be part of the emergent society of the enlightened. Furthermore, he maintained, the forbidding ramparts of the Law are gradually lowered in practice, if not in theory. Such prohibitions as the use of Gentile wine, for instance, are now obsolete.[26] As to cultural differences, modern Jews progressively divest themselves of the peculiarities of speech, dress, and economic specialization. Whatever is incompatible with the dawning sense of universal brotherhood will gradually wither and fade away. These observances were historic accretions, by no means part of the essential structure of the Covenant, which was designed to promote the love of God and the love of man.

As to the second challenge, Mendelssohn argued that the notion of belonging to the chosen people implies neither arrogance nor exclusiveness, but simply the spirit of obedience to a divinely imposed body of laws. In his German writings, he addressed himself to a society that accepted the Holy Bible as the basis of its own ideological structure. But while Christians were aware of their own emergence from the Dark Ages and of standing on the threshold of a new era, they persisted in seeing the Jews of their own day as a strange, petrified relic of the ancient people of the Old Testament. Christians must realize that even as they are no longer identical with the apostolic community of Jerusalem, Jews are no longer identical with the ancient biblical community, save that they continue to be obligated by the same basic Torah-law. This law was revealed at Sinai to the community as a whole in a unique manner so dramatic that it cannot be revoked except by God, and by Him only, in a similar, dramatic, and absolute fashion. Every Jew adds to his consciousness of humanity the remembrance of the revealed Sinaitic legislation, to which he remains subject, as an individual, so long as that legislation has not been superseded.

Mendelssohn refuted the Christian claim that this law had been annulled by the birth of Christianity. He pointed out that even the Synoptic Gospels fail to sustain this claim. Jesus lived and preached as a Jew (Matthew 23:2, 3; 5:17, 7:24–27; Mark 1:44).[27] But, whether or not loyalty to the law runs counter to Christian dogmatics, it certainly is fully in accord with the universal Religion of Reason. For the Jew does not substitute the precepts of the law for the demands of reason, but he *adds* these precepts to the principles of a Religion of Reason. Furthermore, there is an organic relationship between the *mizvot* and the rational essence of religion. The practical precepts articulate the theory of faith, just as speaking and writing give expression to our thoughts. The entire body of Jewish observances is a form of writing through deeds, articulating and reinforcing the essential principles of monotheism. Thus the purpose of the *mizvot* is to make the monotheistic faith a living reality in the hearts and minds of the children of the Covenant. And there is nothing irrational in the observance of these external precepts, though they are *non-rational*, having been dictated by God to Moses. As to why God did not impose similar obligations on Gentiles, Mendelssohn pointed out that Providence employs diverse ways in guiding the historical evolution of different nations. So long as He provided for all people what they needed for salvation, through the gifts of conscience and reason, we cannot complain about the plurality of cultural and ceremonial devices with which He supplemented His essential revelation. In the case of the Jewish people, this supplemental revelation was the revealed law. Christians cannot question that this revelation had taken place, since their own faith is ultimately founded on the Old Testament. If the foundation of a building is shaky, one does not run for safety to the upper stories.

Like Spinoza, Mendelssohn insisted that the revelation at Sinai consisted not of doctrines but of laws that were meant to establish the Jewish polity. But while Spinoza inferred from this circumstance that the laws became invalid when the Jewish polity was destroyed,[28] Mendelssohn distinguished between the communal and the personal precepts. The communal precepts were indeed no longer valid, since the biblical constitution in which religion and government were merged together was a unique, divinely instituted experiment. Its singularity is affirmed in Scripture. After the breakup of the biblical polity, religion and government were intended to go their separate ways—religion directing its efforts to man's inner nature and employing only instruments of persuasion, and government directing its attention to the external actions of people and employing methods of coercion. Mendelssohn concurred with Spinoza that a free society should separate religion from the state, but unlike Spinoza, he insisted that the personal precepts of the revealed law remained the special obligation of Jewish people. Thus the Jew is bidden to share in the building of a universal culture while remaining subject to a special body of divine legislation.

In view of his living in a Christian society, however, among people who are dedicated to a culture and a philosophy that are intimately associated with a religious heritage of their own, why cannot the Jew accept the practical rites of Christianity as a supplement to his philosophical faith? It is at this point that the impact of

Mendelssohn's interpretation becomes clear. Practical precepts are indeed consonant with a Religion of Reason, but dogmatic injunctions, ordering the mind to accept as true this or that irrational belief, are utterly incongruent with a rational faith. The central rites of Christianity are inseparable from their roots in a body of dogmas, which must be accepted on faith. On the other hand, in the entire Torah, Mendelssohn pointed out, there is no commandment imposing any beliefs on the Israelites. The dignity of man consists in his freedom to seek truth and to distinguish between good and evil. Man cannot surrender his intelligence and his conscience without ceasing to be human. Man's freedom is "the image of God" within him. Even God does not intrude into the inner sanctuary of man's soul. According to the Talmud, "everything is in the power of heaven, save the fear of heaven" (Berochot 33b). How could He, Who is the Source of Wisdom and Goodness, restrict and frustrate the faculties of the human personality by making salvation dependent on quasi-magical formulae?[29]

It follows that although Judaism adds *nonrational* ceremonies to the Religion of Reason, these "external" *mizvot* are not indispensable for salvation. Christianity, or Christian theology, in all its orthodox forms is essentially *irrational*. It may still serve as a Religion of Reason for its own constituents, who, as they become philosophers, modify its dogmas privately in order to preserve its essential, ethical-spiritual impetus. But official Christianity, glorying in its paradoxes, cannot serve in the same capacity, openly and universally—that is, in the Germany of Mendelssohn's day—so long as it remains unreconstructed, weighted down by dogmas that the free mind of man utterly repudiates. To be sure, man's reason points to its own limitations. Hence, "the fear of God is the beginning of wisdom" (Ps. 3; 10). But although man acknowledges a transrational mystery, he cannot succumb to irrationalism without surrendering his freedom, his essential, human, and divine dignity.

Mendelssohn's assertion that Judaism does not require the acceptance of beliefs was repeated throughout the nineteenth century by detractors as well as by defenders of the Jewish faith. The defenders pointed to Judaism's essential rationality, while the detractors asserted that Judaism was not a religion at all, since it did not aim to achieve a mystical communion between God and Man, requiring only the rote performance of certain deeds.

We need to take account of the special context in which Mendelssohn's argument was made. First, the Religion of Nature, to Mendelssohn, was a warm, full-blooded theism, in which the sentiments of the Psalmists acquired fresh and vibrant meaning—it is significant that Mendelssohn completed a sensitive translation of the Book of Psalms. Reason, to him, included that tissue of rational and moral arguments that leads to a firm assurance of the Divine Presence, of man's immortality, of the role of Providence and the freedom of will. Spinoza's pantheism, which denies human freedom, was to him an aberration. And the deism of the French Voltairians was a cynical abomination. He admired Rousseau's description of the faith of the Vicar of Savoyard. In his innocent age, people could hardly conceive of the enormities that were perpetrated a decade or so after his death in the name of the Goddess of Reason. Thus Mendelssohn included an existential "fear of God" and an impassioned love of Him within the Religion of Nature that he deemed to be purely rational. His religion included faith in the sense of trust in God's faithfulness, a trust that was common to both Judaism and Christianity. What he rejected was the blind, dogmatic beliefs that were blatantly irrational.[30]

In his recent *Jewish Philosophy in Modern Times*, Nathan Rothenstreich contends that "by subsuming religion under law and ethics Mendelssohn reduced Judaism to dimensions that satisfy the moral mind but not the religious temper."[31] But as we have noted, Jewish law, to Mendelssohn, was God-given—hence, charged with a special aura. Also, he was doubtless familiar with Leibnitz's distinction between the three stages of law—preventive of wrongdoing, affirming positive obligations for the common good, and instilling piety. Mendelssohn regarded Jewish law, in its particularistic areas, as falling within the second and third stages. And as to "the religious temper," no one can read the *Morgenstuden* without feeling the resonance of Mendelssohn's vibrant piety.

Second, Mendelssohn did not reject belief in those theses that are inferred by human reason. He was after all a disciple of Maimonides, who formulated the Thirteen Principles of Faith, beginning each one with the phrase "I believe with perfect faith." His disciples in the next generation did not hesitate to include these principles in their manuals and catechisms. For all but one of the Thirteen Principles of Faith are inferences of reason, affirming the existence of God and His Providence and the truth of the Sinaitic revelation, which was attested by the collective experience of the Jewish people. The only irrational Principle of Faith is the one affirming the resurrection of the dead, which many Maimonidean disciples interpreted in the sense of immortality of the soul.[32]

Third, every historical faith implies belief in a sacred tradition of interpretation, and Judaism was no exception. The character and extent of the authoritative tradition, however, might be disputed. In the first century, debate centered on the validity of the Pharisaic Oral Law; the authority of the Talmud was questioned by the Karaites, a sect founded at the beginning of the eighth century. To Maimonides, the authoritative chain of tradition continued down to the compilation of the Babylonian Talmud by Rabina and Rav Ashi (ca. A.D. 500). He rejected, therefore, the claims of the Babylonian Geonim (589–1038 c.e.) to speak as heads of "the great Sanhedrin and the small one." Among the authoritative Geonim between the Talmud and his own day he mentions those of Spain and France, along with those of Babylonia.[33]

The prevailing belief in the Yeshivot of Central Europe affirmed the continuity of the Holy Spirit down to the authors of the *Shulhan Arukh*, in the sixteenth century. The Kabbalists added a whole series of fresh revelations, including those of Rabbi Simon bar Yohai of the second century, the presumed author of the Zohar, and Rabbi Isaac Luria, of the sixteenth century, whose disciples instituted a number of new rites in the practice of the faith.[34] In the lifetime of Moses Mendelssohn, there raged a bitter debate between the Hasidim and the Mithnagdim of Poland and Lithuania, concerning the range and authority of the Holy Spirit in their day. Both sides accepted the authority of the revelations accorded to Rabbi Isaac Luria.[35]

We can hardly doubt that Mendelssohn wanted to introduce some basic reforms in Jewish life in order to further the process of integration, and that he consciously aimed to minimize the area of rabbinic authority. Living in a Protestant country, he found it natural to appeal to the authority of Scripture rather than to that of a living tradition. In regard to biblical exegesis, he found ample justification in Jewish commentaries for a non-literal, non-fundamentalist approach. In this area, as in so many others Maimonides had shown the way by laying down the rule "The gates of interpretation are not closed to us"("Guide" II, 25).

In sum Mendelssohn was called on to justify his Jewish loyalties by believing Christians and by the philosophers in his circle. He accepted the philosophers as brothers in spirit, asserting that the principles of modern theism coincided with the essential teachings of Judaism. As against the Christian challenge, he responded with the weapons of philosophy—the rejection of any theory of exclusive salvation as unworthy of a just God, and the repudiation of any shackles on the human mind in the shape of irrational dogmas, rejecting the charge of deicide directed against the Jews, as an utter absurdity, and opposing the involvement of the external trappings of religion in the realm of political affairs as a grave fallacy. In the process of enlarging the scope of philosophy within Jewish life and in the policy of governments, Mendelssohn became the champion of a new humanism. He could uphold the Jewish side of the debate because of his achievements as a philosopher and as a humanist. In turn, the spirit of humanism could not but lead to new esthetic and ethical norms for the modification and transformation of Jewish life in the emerging, free society.

Two consequences of Mendelssohn's position are particularly worth noting. First, the repudiation of the corporate status of the Jewish community. In the debates on Jewish emancipation, following the French Revolution, the prevailing position of both Jews and Gentiles called for the enfranchisement of Jews as individuals, not as a closed corporation or caste. Jewish spokesmen willingly surrendered any claims for communal autonomy and submitted in all but purely religious matters to the civil authorities of the state. In the Assembly of Notables and in the Paris Sanhedrin, the Jewish representatives affirmed their eagerness to conclude a covenant with Gentiles, joining in the "fraternity" of the emerging nations of

Europe. For generations, and in spite of recurring setbacks, Jews considered modern humanism as the common ground on which they and the "enlightened" Gentiles could build together.[36]

The other historic consequence of the Mendelssohnian position was to impoverish the rich complex of Jewish loyalties and to transform it into a commitment to intellectual liberalism. The closest disciple of Mendelssohn, David Friedländer, (1750–1834), wrote a letter to Pastor Teller, a leading Protestant clergyman in Berlin, offering to bring a number of Jewish families into his church providing they would not be required to accept the Christian dogmas. Friedländer acknowledged that the severe restrictions to which Jews were then subject in Prussia accounted in part for this decision to join the prevailing faith. But, then, no financial or social blandishments have in the past induced Jewish people to give up their faith. To Friedländer, however, the sole obstacle to a Jewish-Christian fusion was the irrational dogmatism of the Church. And these dogmas could be allegorized, in theory at least. As to the obligations of Jewish law, many laymen had begun to disregard them.

In fact, it was the widespread violation of Jewish dietary and Sabbath regulations that induced the mid-nineteenth-century Reform leaders to base Jewish loyalty on the truth and relevance of the central ideas of Judaism rather than on the particular precepts of Jewish law. To be sure, they were still operating, in the synagogues at least, with the traditional pattern of symbols and rituals, but they could no longer assume that the prescriptions of rabbinic law governing personal life were indeed observed by their laymen. In contrast to the age of Mendelssohn, they had to contend against philosophers and historians, as well as believing Christians, in order to make room for the vital ideas of Judaism.

In German Jewry, it was the emergence of the nineteenth-century Conservative movement of Zechariah Frankel and Heinrich Graetz that led to a renewed appreciation of Jewish law as the historic embodiment of the Jewish spirit. In the middle of the nineteenth century the ideas of Savigny and other legal historians had prepared the way for an understanding of legal institutions as the distinctive expressions of a nation's soul, marking the evolution of its historic character.

In nineteenth-century France, Joseph Salvador (1796–1873) called attention to the social idealism that was embodied in the legislation of the Torah. If the liberals in Europe had to contend frequently against the Church in order to extend the horizons of liberty, equality, and fraternity, these ideals formed the living nucleus of Pentateuchal legislation. In Salvador's view, the mission of Judaism consisted not in the "purity" of its monotheistic ideals, but in the historic impetus of its ethical-social laws. The Jewish faith poses a continuing challenge to all Christian denominations, reminding them of the common task in every generation to hasten the establishment of a just and all-embracing society here on earth.

Mendelssohn was sustained in his intellectual position by the German Enlightenment (*Aufklärung*), which was basically religious and reverent toward the heritage of the past. His *Phaedo*, a demonstration of the immortality of the soul, was received with acclaim by the German public, which was well disposed to a Platonic line of reasoning. His lifelong friend, Gotthold Ephraim Lessing, was a brave champion of rationality in religion, but unlike Voltaire, he was not an iconoclast. On the contrary, he cautioned his followers to treat the old faith with humility and reverence.

> Take care, more capable individual, when you paw the ground and are aglow on reaching the last page of the first primer (the Jewish-Christian revelation!). Take care not to let your weaker school-fellows feel what you are sensing or already beginning to see. Until these weaker school-fellows have caught up with you, turn back the pages of this primer again, and find out whether what you take to be the result of mere expressions of method, makeshifts of the teaching system, is not perhaps something more.[37]

This reverence for tradition characterized Mendelssohn as well. He never forgot the third element in Micah's summation of the essence of piety, "to walk humbly with the Lord." Thus he wrote: ". . . our reasonings can never free us from the strict obedience we owe to the law."[38]

Lessing agreed with Mendelssohn that "natural religion" is the substance and "revealed religion" cannot add more than methods, instruments, or mnemonic devices to the basic core of the Religion of

Nature: "The best positive or revealed religion is the one containing the fewest conventional additions to natural religion and least limits the good effects of natural religion."[39]

Lessing was more inclined than Mendelssohn to believe in the inevitable development of mankind toward a higher, universal faith. But the two friends were equally dedicated to the belief that the reasoning faculty of the human mind is itself the supreme expression of the Divine Will. Therefore, God cannot possibly demand dogmatic faith in a non-rational proposition, much less an irrational one. It is the very endeavour to seek truth that is divine. These famous words of Lessing's reflect Mendelssohn's basic approach as well:

> If God were holding all the truth that exists in his right hand and in his left just the one ever-active urge to find the truth, even if attached to it were the condition that I should always and forever be going astray, and said to me, "Choose!" I should humbly fall upon his left hand and say, "Father, give! Pure truth is surely only for Thee alone."[40]

Mendelssohn was profoundly disturbed and angered by the charge of F. H. Jacobi that Lessing was really a Spinozist. Jacobi himself had come to champion the position that reason was a weak reed, which was incapable of sustaining a theistic and ethical world view. Religion and morality must be based on faith. Those who lack faith are bound to drift toward the abyss of materialism or pantheistic naturalism. Jacobi challenged Mendelssohn directly. And Mendelssohn felt that Jacobi's message was only a sophisticated way of restating Lavater's original challenge. Blind faith is certain to lead men back to medievalism. If faith, not reason, be indeed the one foundation of both ethics and religion, how can we avoid the horrors of religious fanaticism?

Several decades after the death of Mendelssohn, even non-orthodox Jewish thinkers such as S. L. Steinheim could embrace the Halevian position and argue in behalf of revelation as a nonrational source of faith and morals. But Mendelssohn was extremely wary of "enthusiasm" and fanaticism. In his *Morgenstunden* and in his posthumous missive to the friends of Lessing, he maintained first that Spinozism could be interpreted in a theistic sense. He wrote of a "purified Spinozism." Did not Spinoza himself lay down core principles of faith, which express the essence of an enlightened faith? Spinoza's rejection of Judaism was based on nonphilosophic grounds.[41] Secondly, Mendelssohn argued that pure reason needs to be "oriented" by moral feeling if it is to serve as the foundation of a theistic faith. He called for the aid of *sensum communis*, or common sense. Perhaps Mendelssohn had in mind the Maimonidean tradition in the "Guide"—that training in moral principles and in the life of piety were prerequisites to the use of reason in the realm of pure speculation. Perhaps he recalled Maimonides's principle in the opening of his "Code"—that the love of God is one with the quest for the understanding of God. In any case, he insisted on fidelity to "pure, authentic reason." And the fervor of his insistence was due in no small measure to his intuitive conviction that an upsurge of romanticism would pose a deadly challenge to the Jewish people in particular, and to humanist values in general.[42]

In contrast to Lessing and the liberals, the Christian traditionalists maintained that the Jews were not ready for emancipation. Their corporate character prevented Jews from becoming integrated into the emergent states of Europe. In the Christian view, Judaism is an ethnic community, "of the seed of Abraham," in which sovereignty belongs to an earthly Messiah, or to a messianic pretender, since the "true Messiah of Israel" had already come. The Jews of their day were seen by the Christian traditionalists as petrified fossils of the Zealots and the Pharisees in the New Testament who contended against Jesus and his apostles. It was difficult enough for them to accept the changes occurring in their own faith communities, owing to the irresistible pressures of the modern mentality. All the more difficult was it for them to recognize the surge of vitality in the Jewish community, which was gradually transforming the ancient and medieval concepts of Jewish identity and messianic redemption.

On the threshold of emancipation, the ardor of Jewish messianism was unfocused and disoriented. It was poised and ready to move into several different channels. It could turn toward a humanistic goal, or toward the establishment of a Jewish state. It could be emptied of vital content. In isolated enclaves of tight Orthodoxy, it continued to retain its supernaturalistic and mystical dimensions, along with the feeling of an imminent Eschaton, expected tomorrow if not sooner. Actually each of these interpretations of messianism was embraced by diverse segments of the Jewish community in the modern world.

Insofar as the Christian image of the Jew is concerned, the old messianic hope loomed as a forbidding barrier to Jewish integration. This point was raised by the German historian, Michaelis, in his critique of Dohm's book, and by many others in Germany and France. Mendelssohn's reply was as follows:

> The hope to return to the land of Israel is irrelevant to the life of Jews as citizens of their respective countries. Human nature impels one to love the land in which he lives in freedom, and if his religious doctrines interpose any obstacles, he assigns to them a place in his worship and liturgy, without according them any real significance in his daily life.[43]

In other words, the messianic hope is likely to become vestigial, just as the dogma of the Second Advent became peripheral and inconsequential in the life of the vast majority of Christians. A similar reply was given by Comte de Mirabeau, who spent some time with Mendelssohn in Berlin.[44] It is interesting to observe that Mendelssohn, in keeping with his philosophical rationalism, followed the lead of Maimonides in stripping the messianic hope of all supernaturalism and stating it in a nationalistic version:

> I believe that the children of Abraham, Isaac, and Jacob will not always live outside the borders of their land and scattered among the nations, but that the Lord will raise for them in the time known to Him alone a prince Messiah from the House of David who will make them a free people as in ancient times and will reign over them in the land of their fathers.[45]

Mendelssohn's willingness to allow the supernatural aspects of the messianic hope to become a desiccated formula, or a metaphor for the blend of humanistic and nationalistic aspirations, was not shared by the Orthodox leaders of his day or of future generations. The Hasidic movement, which exploded with elemental force in the southern provinces of Poland during his lifetime, was profoundly messianic in character. The Mithnagdim (opponents), led by the Gaon Elijah of Vilna, were similarly persuaded that "the footsteps of the Messiah" had already been heard. In the following generation, when many Jews acclaimed the French Revolution and Napoleon as messianic deliverers, the Hasidic Zaddik of Lublin regarded Napoleon as a kind of anti-messiah, the chief figure in the apocalyptic wars of God and Magog.[46]

The Talmud asserts "there is no session in the house of study without some innovation." Similarly, we may assert that no genuine dialogue occurs without some modification of the positions of the debaters. Mendelssohn contested Maimonides's interpretation that the category of "saints among the nations" requires an acceptance of the truth of Mosaic revelation. While he respected the erudition and authority of Rabbi Jacob Emden, he took issue with the latter's endorsement of Maimonides's restriction. As Altmann put it: "The ideal Judaism to which Mendelssohn aspired possessed a kind of Platonic reality for him."[47] He was prepared to admit that the Talmud contained some ugly distortions of the Torah.

Mendelssohn asserted, in his response to Lavater, that Judaism is not interested in any missionary activity, that it is even inhibited by its laws from disseminating its teaching among the nations. We can allow for the fact that Mendelssohn was driven to this untrue position by the persistent challenge of Christian missionary efforts. Nevertheless, his argument is unhistorical and contrary to the traditional hope. The Reform leaders, in the middle of the nineteenth century, rejected Mendelssohn's thesis and proclaimed it to be the Jewish "mission" to convert all men to the doctrines of "ethical monotheism." Mendelssohn's assertion that only the laws of Judaism were revealed, and that these laws were intended for Jews only, did not elevate the value and sanctity of the ritual *mizvot*, since a parochial revelation could not be of the same rank as a universal one. Also the act of revelation at Sinai was inevitably interpreted in the nineteenth century as a continuing process of inspired legislation. It was therefore historicized and relativized. This devaluation of the ritual as mere ceremonialism is inevitable in a philosophical version of Judaism. It implies also a relativization of the actual practice of the Jewish faith. It cannot be allowed the claim of being exclusively true, or even uniquely significant. Mendelssohn anticipated this development when he wrote, "The Jewish faith is best for us, but it is not the best absolutely. Which is the best form of worship for other nations? Who knows? Perhaps the Lord gave them guidance through their understanding or by means of prophets."[48]

Mendelssohn, and several of his Christian friends, looked forward to a basic revision of Christian doctrine, whereby its exclusivistic ardor would be curbed and its irrationalism modified. It seemed to him that the Unitarians and some English Deists represented the "wave of the future." Of the Christian Unitarians, he wrote in a letter to Bonnet, "I must confess to you honestly that this religious party seems to me to belong more to Judaism than to the really dominant Christian faith." He could look forward to a closer approach of Judaism and Christianity in the future, perhaps even a convergence.[49]

Nationalistic Dissent

The response of Mendelssohn to the challenges of Christianity, philosophy and the emergent nation-states of Europe was itself challenged not only by the builders of Reform Judaism and the ideologists of political Zionism, but also by the pre-Zionist nationalists, to whom Perez Smolenskin (1840–85) belonged. Smolenskin spoke for the Maskilim ("enlightened") of the Pale of Settlement in Russia, who lived in massive enclaves, spoke Yiddish, and wrote in Hebrew. He argued in behalf of radical modifications of the traditional way of life, especially the liturgy of the Synagogue and the curriculum of the elementary schools. He sought to break down the inner walls of the ghetto and to foster effective communication between the Jewish people and their neighbors. Yet his opposition to Mendelssohn was based on the latter's identification of the Jewish heritage as basically religious. Smolenskin considered Judaism to be the product of "the spirit of the nation." The Jewish people were a "people of the spirit" (am horuah), and it was their mission to demonstrate the validity and viability of national communities that are held together solely by cultural and spiritual bonds. Like the romantic nationalists of the nineteenth century, he considered religion to be a most important component of Jewish culture, but only a component. The overriding bond is that of national culture, and a viable culture requires a large measure of self-government or national autonomy. Hence the chief target of Smolenskin's critique of Mendelssohn was the latter's willingness to surrender the corporate status of limited self-government that Dohm was willing to grant to Jewish citizens.[50]

Indeed, in France and Holland, following the French Revolution, the Jewish liberals pressed for complete individual emancipation, while the Orthodox pleaded for the limited freedom of a recognized corporate status. Similarly, the Gentile liberals echoed the sentiments of the French politician, Clermont-Tonnerre: "To the Jews as individuals, everything; to the Jews as a nation, nothing." On the other hand, the reactionaries and antisemites resisted the plea for total emancipation and pressed for the continuation of the medieval corporate status of Jewry, with possibly a few economic concessions.[51]

Smolenskin's program was elaborated and deepened by the great Jewish historian Simon Dubnow (1860–1941). In theory, the concept of cultural nationalism was recognized in the Treaty of Versailles, which included the recognition of ethnic minority rights in the constitutions of the states of central Europe. In practice, these guarantees were largely disregarded. But even in theory, it is doubtful that modern Jews prefer to be self-governing in civil matters when they are offered equality and the chance to share the obligations and privileges of an open society. As they broke out of the medieval shell and began to participate more fully in the cultural life of the western world, they began to turn away from the ideal of communal self-government, especially if it included an element of cultural, religious, or philanthropic coercion. The so-called Jewish values—reverence for learning, patterns of worship, and works of charity—belong to the realm of freedom, in which individuals choose to participate in one or another activity, as they please and on their own terms.

From the experience of Jewish communities in the lands of freedom, we may conclude that Mendelssohn was more right than his critics—in spite of the pressures of central bureaucracies and nationalist ideologists, Jewish people do prefer individual freedom to a corporate, self-governing status. However, even in lands of freedom the sentiment for collective self-government and self-discipline attains at times a fairly high pitch. In response to external challenges, such as the plight of a segment of world Jewry or the danger to the survival of Israel, Jewish philanthropic agencies take on temporarily the appearance of governing bodies—but not for long. As soon as the danger passes, they revert to their voluntaristic character.

Existentialist Dissent

In our own day, Arthur A. Cohen articulated the resentment of an existentialist against the rationalistic position of Mendelssohn. Cohen sees Jewish history as the intersection between two curves— the supernatural and the natural. We sin against the God of history, he maintains, when we define the status of Jewry in terms of general European culture. The Jew is unique in a metaphysical sense, not merely in the sense that all historical communities are unique. His destiny must be understood in the light of messianism, as an immediate concern, a waiting and an acting, as if our age were poised on the razor's edge between the "fallen" world and "the Kingdom of God." The attitude of Cohen, irrational though it be, is actually a direct continuation of the pre-modern conviction of both Jews and Christians.[52] But what the ancients and the medievalists accepted in simple faith, Cohen affirms as "an existential dogma." (p. 5) It is "existential" because "without it there is nothing I consider *ultimately* relevant or meaningful to believe." And it is a "dogma" in the sense of an "evocation of meaning."

"Without the command to sustain one's supernatural vocation (that is, the belief that God has called the Jew to Himself) to call oneself a Jew is but a half-truth—a mere designation without meaning."

Cohen reflects an intellectual posture that is not uncommon in our distraught generation, shocked as we have been by the incredible agony of the holocaust on the one hand, and the exaltation of the rise of Israel on the other hand. The irrevocability of the Covenant has been established, as a historical fact—Jews were gassed by the modern Satan, whether or not they accepted their role as children of the God of Israel. The pre-moderns believed in God, Torah, and the special destiny of Israel, in this order of logical primacy. Some of the post-moderns believe in the mystery of Israel's destiny primarily, with commitment to Torah and faith in God as vague and tenuous implications. In Cohen's view, Mendelssohn, standing at the gate of the modern world begging for entrance, is the symbol of the modern Jew's fatal mistake. Thus he writes:

> The modern Jew who succeeded the age of Mendelssohn was a European according to nature and history, and a Jew according to God. Henceforward one's culture was that of one's nation and language, and one's faith was directed toward a God no longer covenanted to a specific people. It is no surprise that the earliest reformers—Israel Jacobson, Jacob Herz Berr, Abraham Geiger, and Samuel Holdheim—should have rejected a personal messiah, denied the centrality of the Land of Israel, abandoned the Hebrew language, and transformed the historical monotheism of tradition into ethical monotheism. The messianism of the classic Jew disappeared and the new European messianism—culture, emancipation and equality—were substituted. Mendelssohn made credible to Europe the existence of a rational Judaism and the possibility of the de-Judaized Jew.[53]

As we have pointed out, Mendelssohn did not give up the messianic dream, but he assumed that the universal aspects of "the Kingdom of God" might well be realized prior to the fulfillment of Jewish ethnocentric ambitions. The traditional spectrum of the messianic vision included both national and all-human goals, as well as a truly super-human, transcendent radiance.

Mendelssohn was attacked in his lifetime by Sonnenfels (1732–1817), a Jewish convert to Roman Catholicism, a "de-Judaized Jew." In fact, Altmann concludes that "Mendelssohn wrote his *Jerusalem* in the mistaken belief that he was replying to Sonnenfels."[54] Sonnenfels argued that Mendelssohn had virtually given up the Jewish faith when he rejected all kinds of religious compulsion. "If it be possible, without detriment to unalloyed

Judaism, to abolish churchly privileges (i.e., the right of excommunication), which is based upon positive Mosaic laws, why should it be impossible to cancel, for the nation's benefit, mere rabbinic measures of late vintage, which create such detrimental barriers between Jews and Christians? One more step and you have become one of us."[55]

Mendelssohn was in favor of making many changes in Jewish observance. He was optimistic on this score, just as he was generally confident that sound reason will triumph everywhere. But he was not willing to allow the Jewish individual to be subject to the coercion of the rabbis. Spinoza had written that one may not surrender his inner freedom without violating his humanity. Mendelssohn agreed. Generally, he cautioned his followers to be ever community minded. It is one thing, however, to respect prevailing opinion and to cooperate freely with the members of one's community; it is quite another to submit one's mind to the dictates of others. Judaism respects the freedom of the mind; hence, in Mendelssohn's view, the Torah never commands "Thou shalt believe." Judaism is "revealed legislation," but the laws are intended to safeguard freedom, not to crush it.

H. J. Schoeps, a scholar and an existentialist, maintains that Mendelssohn cut out "the heart of Judaism; *the living God,* who without consideration for reason and 'ability to gain agreement' (which *Morgenstunden* VII defines as the highest form of suitability), has acted in the history of this nation.[56] In other words, the core of Jewish consciousness is the awareness of God's direct action in Jewish history.

There is no doubt that Mendelssohn was a man of deep piety, a *homo religiosus*, for whom God was a powerful, living presence. If he avoided the historical argument, such as "He who took you out of the land of Egypt" (Genesis 32;4), it is precisely because historical events are not self-explanatory. Theology does not spring full-grown from the mouths of canons, or of mass graves. The opponents of Moses interpreted the Exodus by crediting its wonders to the Golden Calf. Philosophy must provide the standpoint and the standards for the interpretation of history, not vice versa. Mendelssohn had to contend every day against the presumption of Christians to infer the depravity of the Jews and the falsehood of their faith from the circumstance of their dispersion among the nations.

A Twentieth Century Disputation

It was easy enough for narrow-minded Christians in Mendelssohn's day to beat the Jew with one hand, and with the other point to the moral "Behold, the witnesses of God." If today, following the holocaust and the rise of Israel, the "mystique" of Jewish history has been revived, it is instructive to note how this line of reasoning looked during World War I, when two most gifted friends took up the Jewish-Christian Argument in a famous correspondence.

The debate between the young Franz Rosenzweig and Eugen Rosenstock-Huessy may be studied as a counterpoint to the dialogues in which Mendelssohn was engaged. It was highly praised as most revealing. H. J. Schoeps extols it with the greatest enthusiasm: "This dialogistic correspondence may be put forward as the purest form of Judeo-Christian dialogue ever attained, perhaps even for ages to come."[57]

The debate took place in 1916, when both men served in the German army. Rosenstock-Huessy had been converted to Christianity at the age of sixteen. Rosenzweig had also contemplated conversion, but he determined to make this crucial decision as a Jew, not a pagan. Hence, his search for the full significance of being a Jew within the stream of European history. Both had arrived at the need of recognizing the transcendent in personal life and in history. Both had come to reject the liberal version of religion, be it Jewish or Christian. Leo Baeck's "The Essence of Judaism" was as unacceptable to them as Adolf Harnack's "The Essence of Christianity." Both had moved the Jewish-Christian dialogue from the rational sphere to the domain of the transrational, the course of revelation in history. As Rosenstock-Huessy phrased it, fifty years later:

Franz and Eugen came to agree on the futility of the shilly-shallying academic shibboleths of their day—objectivity, humanism, and the so-called enlightenment. They agreed that real people can be Jews or Christians, but they may not play the roles of "Benjamin Franklin" or "Thomas Paine," at least not for long, since there can be no common sense—certainly no good sense shared in common—among men who are content to be ciphers, dealing in generalities and platitudes.[58]

The confrontation, a century and a half after the Mendelssohn-Lavater exchange, was based precisely on the rejection of the Religion of Nature of the Enlightenment. The young debaters explored an existential approach, based on personal experiences and on the mysterious course of history. Rosenstock-Huessy wrote of "speech-thinking" and the "I-Thou" event long before Buber and Rosenzweig did. As he saw it, God takes the initiative. "The soul must be called *Thou* before she can ever reply *I*, before she can ever speak of *us* and finally *it*. Through the four figures *Thou, I, We, It*, the Word walks through us. The Word must call our name first."[59]

From this vantage point, it is indeed amazing to note how the medieval Christian's stereotyped images of the Jew were insinuated into Rosenstock-Huessy's dialectic: (1) the Jews "always crucify again the one who came to make the word true"; (2) "With all the power of their being they set themselves against their own promises"; (3) "the image of Lucifer"; (4) Israel's "naive way of thinking that one has won inalienable rights in perpetuity against God"; (5) "you (Jews) have no aptitude for theology, for the search for truth, any more than for beauty"; (6) the Jew strives too hard just to live; (7) the "Jew dies for no country and no cause"; (8) the reliance of the individual Jew is "on the number of his children." To sum up, the Jew "is a paragraph of the Law. *C'est tout*."[60]

These stereotypes come naturally to those who view the Jew in history from the Christian viewpoint. Rosenzweig, at that time groping for a way back to Judaism, saw virtually the same picture:

This practical way, in which the theological idea of the stubbornness of Jews works itself out, is *hatred of the Jews*. You know as well as I do that all its realistic arguments are only fashionable cloaks to hide the single true metaphysical ground: that we will not make common cause with the world-conquering fiction of Christian dogma . . . and putting it in a popular way: that we have crucified Christ, and believe me, would do it again every time."[61]

Not content with providing a metaphysical root for antisemitism, the young Rosenzweig, with the boundless fervor of a neophyte, maintained that the "metaphysical basis" of the Jewish attitude to Christians consists of three articles: "(1) that we have the truth, (2) that we are at the goal and (3) that any and every Jew feels in the depths of his soul that the Christian relation to God, and so in a sense, their religion, is particularly and extremely pitiful, poverty-stricken, and ceremonious."[62]

With all this mutual contempt, "metaphysically grounded," Rosenzweig went on to say, the Jew still feels that his own fulfillment lies in goading the Christians to complete their task. The Jew bursts like a rude intruder into Christian assemblies, crying out "the *Eschaton* is not yet here." He works "as a ferment on Christianity and through it on the world."[63] The Jew is not intimidated by the price he must pay in isolation and suffering. Rosenzweig even echoed the Nazi stereotype of the Jew as a parasite. "For you may curse, you may swear, you may scratch yourself as much as you like, you won't get rid of us, we are the louse in your fur. We are the internal foe; don't mix us up with the external one!"

In his later writings, Franz Rosenzweig's philosophy of Judaism was ripened and mellowed. He must not be judged by the above quotations from his years of agonized searching. But the debate as it stands is a historic record of the shape the Jewish-Christian argument assumes when it departs from the common ground of reason and religious humanism. The alternative to the Mendelssohnian approach consists in a preference for unreason and for the seductive half-truths that appeal to a group's "pooled pride." It is formulated through the positioning of private "mysteries" against private "mysteries," barriers of contempt against towers of scorn, providing a metaphysical blanket of justification for ancient lies, and multiplying hatred in the world.

The young Rosenzweig's reference to Jewish contempt for Christianity was based in part on the literature of the Romantic rebellion against the Jewish emancipation at the beginning of the twentieth century. It certainly reflects neither the standard Orthodox view nor that of the modernists. Mendelssohn championed, all his life, not only tolerance of other faiths but also a deep appreciation of the wisdom of Providence in providing diverse historical embodiments of the same Religion of Nature. This is also the import of Lessing's drama *Nathan the Wise*, in which Nathan is modeled on Mendelssohn.

In turn, Mendelssohn derived his basic approach to the Jewish-Christian Dialogue from the elitist philosophy of Maimonides, in whose famous parable the saintly philosophers in all historical monotheistic communities come closer to "the throne of the king" than the naive Talmudists, who simply follow the law.[64] The philosopher, however, must not detach himself from his historic community and must supplement his solitary meditations by active concern for the problems of the community.[65]

Still, he knows that within each of the monotheistic communities the differences among individuals are far greater than those among the several historic forms of monotheism.

Rosenzweig was probably familiar with the rejection of the Mendelssohnian approach by the Jewish thinkers of the Reform period. In his later years, Abraham Geiger (1810–1874) had become convinced that Christianity, Protestant as well as Catholic, was inevitably reactionary.[66] Judaism, in his own interpretation of its dynamic essence, was allied with the unfolding spirit of the age, while Christianity was incurably antirationalist in philosophy, antiliberal in politics, and antiprogressive in social legislation. Salvador, living in France, had arrived at a similar conclusion. His book, *Paris, Rome, Jerusalem*, takes Paris to be the city of the French Revolution, announcing the credo of modern man. Catholic Rome symbolizes the counterrevolution, assigning the ideals "liberty, equality, and fraternity" to an ethereal, heavenly realm and thereby removing them effectively from the earthly domain of social and political struggle. Jerusalem represents the ideal synthesis of a this-worldly faith and the humanist vision of a free, utopian society.

Philosophically, Rosenzweig had become an existentialist rebel against the shallowness of rationalism. Eager to discover the roots of his own faith, he began to devour Judeo-German philosophical literature. Among the Romantics he found echoes of a supreme, impassioned pride. From the liberals, he absorbed resentment against the reactionary social policies of the Church.

Rosenzweig lived at a time when the impassioned chauvinism of the Teutons rejected any Jewish contribution to German literature and philosophy as being essentially "un-Germanic." It is enough to read the poignant autobiography of Jakob Wassermann (1873–1934) to recognize the depth of despair that tormented those Jewish intellectuals who shone as the brightest stars in the cultural sky of Germany.

> It is in vain to keep faith with them, be it as cofighters or as citizens. They say—he (the Jew) is a Proteus, he can do everything.
>
> It is in vain to help them knock off the chains of slavery from their bodies. They say—he will surely make profit out of the deal.
>
> It is in vain to counter any poison; they brew it afresh.
>
> It is vain to live for them and to die for them; they say—he is a Jew.[67]

In reaction against the swelling tide of inhuman hatred, the young Rosenzweig concurred in the antisemitic premise and agreed that he could only do "hack's work" in Christian Europe and that the Jewish share "in the life of the peoples can only be *clam, vi, precario* ("secret, perforce, precarious"—expressions in Roman law)"[68] Here, then, is a complete reversal of the Mendelssohnian position.

We need hardly state our disagreement with the manic rhetoric in this correspondence, which reflects the newly found passions of existentialism. For us the debate is paradigmatic of the perverse posturing that is all too often the alternative to a dialogue based on the liberal plane of religious humanism.

Between the Mendelssohn-Lavater and the Rosenzweig-Rosenstock-Huessy debates, there emerged several tides of "Teutonomania," rising on occasion to the verge of collective self-deification. Germanic nationalism was from its beginning, in the Romantic period, infected with a resolute disdain for other nations and religions. No dialogue could possibly be meaningful with men who appealed to the "voice of blood."

Saul Ascher (1767–1822), one of the early Reform ideologists, was compelled to react against what he termed "*Germanomanie.*" A rationalist in the tradition of Mendelssohn, he defended the role of faith as a nonrational faculty of the individual in confrontation with the riddles of reality, but he drew the line against any kind of irrationalism. He opposed Mendelssohn's concept of "revealed legislation" and argued that the validity of ritual laws depends on their effectiveness in sensitizing the individual to the moral imperatives of society.

In his day, however, the argument shifted from religious dogmatics to racial narcissism. His book, *Germanomanie* (Leipzig, 1815), a critique of the excesses of Germanic nationalism, was burned at the Wartburg Festival of the *Deutsche Burschenschaft*. In his open letter to E. M. Arndt, he wrote: "So long as you build your constitution on Germanism, Christianity, and Original Language, treating as bastards humanity, cosmopolitanism, and the religion of reason, no reasoning world-citizen can react to you with faith and love."[69]

The organic unity of Germanic nationalism and the Protestant faith was stressed by a long line of ideologists from Schleiermacher to the Teutonic Christians of the Nazi era. In their search for the elusive qualities of the national soul, the Romanticists were impelled to distinguish between the genuine piety of their own "folk" and the faith of other nations. Indeed, Schleiermacher was "one of the first to show that the national character of any group of people was determined by all their customs, and that their version of the Christian faith was as much a national expression of the German people as their language or their folk-ways."[70]

Strangely, even Germanic atheists, who reduced Christian theology to a tissue of myths, could reconfirm their opposition to Judaism for its nonparticipation in the national mythology. David F. Strauss's *Leben Jesu*, which described the teaching of the Gospels as products of "the mythical consciousness" of the community, provided additional justification for the resentment of Jewish aloofness—they refused to dream in the same metaphors as their neighbors.

II. *In the Light of Philosophical Rationalism*

To the Jewish intellectuals of Mendelssohn's day, the champions of Enlightenment were the hope of the future. It was they who were expected to banish the dark shadows of medieval bigotry, restructure society along lines of freedom and justice, and assure the complete emancipation of European Jewry. Furthermore, according to the Maskilim ("enlightened ones"), the cause of Judaism, as well as the fate of the Jew, is dependent on the expanding horizons of the free human mind, since the Jewish faith is basically the religion of reason.

To be sure, even in Mendelssohn's generation, some of the outstanding knights of reason, such as Voltaire and Diderot in France and King Frederick II of Prussia, found it possible to mingle the venom of antisemitism with sharp barbs against the Church. But, these occasional anti-Jewish outbursts were out of phase with their general rational position and appeared to be merely personal aberrations, the lifeless vestiges of a dead past. Voltaire's scorn of the Jew was an incidental consequence of his frontal attack on the Church, since the entire Christian edifice was founded on the Old Testament. If the foundation is shattered, the upper stories are sure to crumble. Also, embittered atheists could not be expected to look with favor upon a people whose very existence was a demonstration of the supreme power of faith.[1] Voltaire and Diderot, however, could not but offer to Jews, as to other Europeans, the hope of salvation through the advance of the liberal philosophy. An enlightened religious philosopher was a natural ally to Voltaire, in spite of his cantankerous temper. In his reply to Isaac de Pinto's complaint about the anti-Jewish tone of some of his writings, Voltaire urged him and other enlightened Jews to become philosophers.[2]

Voltaire often wrote with tongue in cheek. In *The Philosophy of History* (1766), at the age of seventy-two, he pretended to respect the dogmas of the Church. He summarized the evils of ancient Jews (p. 192) and pointed to the malice of some of the Psalms (pp. 211–216). But the most characteristic passage is the one in which he calls attention to the theological uniqueness of the Jews—an assumption dear to Jewish romanticists, which is anathema to all rationalists, Jewish or Christian.

"But God who conducted them, God who tried and punished them, rendered that nation so different from all the rest of men, that we should view them with other eyes than those with which we look upon the rest of the earth, and not judge of these events as we do of common events."[3]

As we shall demonstrate abundantly in this volume, this axiom of Jewish metaphysical uniqueness, derived originally from the religious traditions of both Judaism and Christianity, was the cornerstone of modern antisemitism. Voltaire was an impassioned but inconsistent champion of reason.

The flat, one-dimensional rationalism of Voltaire was opposed by the equally popular philosopher, Jean-Jacques Rousseau, who, in his *Emile*, included a plea for the complete enfranchisement of the Jews.[4]

Immanuel Kant was a friend of Mendelssohn's and the most admired thinker in the liberal circles of Germany. His three critiques represent the high-water mark of reason in the modern world. His *Critique of Pure Reason* established that man can neither prove nor disprove the basic theses of metaphysics. His *Critique of Practical Reason* identified the "moral law" as the one metaphysical certainty in human awareness. On the basis of this law and the quest of a *summum bonum*, Kant reestablished the principles of religion that he had appeared to undermine in the first critique. God, he suggested, was implied in our consciousness of the "categorical imperative" and in the moral universe that it postulates. In his *Critique of Judgment*, Kant analyzed the phenomenon of purposiveness that we find in living things, concluding that there must be a metaphysical source of the two forces, the mechanical and the teleological. "We can however think an Understanding, which being not like ours, discursive, but intuitive, proceeds from the synthetic-universal (the intuition of the whole as such) to the particular—i.e. from the whole to the parts."[5]

The religious rationalism of Kant appeared to be thoroughly in harmony with the genius of Judaism. His monumental achievement in discovering the limits of speculative reason and focusing attention on the ontological implications of the categorical imperative was thoroughly in keeping with the major trend of Maimonides's philosophy. Maimonides set the arguments in behalf of creation over against those of the eternity of the universe and concluded that human reason is incapable of deciding between the two positions. Then, by an act of faith, he embraced the doctrine of *creatio ex nihilo,* "so that the Torah shall be possible."[6] Presumably it is our moral obligation to choose the path of divine service. So, too, Spinoza spoke of the truth of prophecy being based on "moral certainty."[7] The teleological argument is already stated in the Psalms (94: 9).

The closest affinity of Kant to Judaism, however, was his conception of the moral law as the bond between man and God. Kant rejected sentimentalism and the riot of fantasies. He established religion on the basis of morality, and he described the life of morality as being obedience to a universal law of "practical reason." At first it appeared that Judaism as the religion of lawfulness and of good deeds would be vindicated, through the labors of Kant, in its debate with Christianity, the religion of sentiment, irrational dogma, and fantastic imagery. Did not Moses Mendelssohn describe Judaism as the religion of reason, opposed to dogmatism and to any monopoly on salvation by a historic Church? But how distressed the Jewish intellectuals were when Kant's work on religion appeared! For in that diffuse and seminal work Kant opened a new front against Judaism, instead of acknowledging its worth as the religion of reason.

Kant's procedure was paradigmatic for the religious rationalists of the modern world. Consciously and deliberately, he provided an idealized interpretation of the Christian faith, revised in keeping with modern thought and purged of all archaic myths and rites, while he continued to view Judaism through unchanged traditional glasses as the background and foil of a sublimated Christianity. Kant considered it his duty to reshape the Christian heritage of his generation after the ideal pattern of a religion of reason, in order to give direction to the momentum of religious feeling and make it serve the ends of reason and morality. He agreed that "frequently, this interpretation may appear to be forced . . ."[8] but, then, it is not dishonest because subconsciously, the moral element is always at work. In evaluating Judaism, however, he forgot all about idealization and reverted to the reductionist tone of French rationalists.

So, in the interpretation of Christianity, he took the terms, Christ and Son of Man, to stand not for a historic person but for the concept of humanity. The dogmatic affirmation of Matthew (11:27) and John (14:6) that the Father can be sought only through the Son, Kant interpreted as a metaphor, a picturesque way of stating the rational thesis that we worship God when we love, adore, and work for humanity as a whole. When Jesus preached of the coming of the Kingdom of God, he had in mind, according to Kant, none of the eschatological visions of either the Old or the New Testament, but the reign on earth of universal reason and morality, "not according to a particular covenant. . ."[9] And when he asserted "the Kingdom of God is within you," he conveyed the message that the categorical imperative sounds the divine call within our breast.

But, since the Son of Man stands for mankind, does the logic of idealization require that his Jewish opponents be described as anti-humanistic? Kant thought so. Accordingly, he maintained that the Jews resisted the "good news" either because of their superstition or their excessive ritualism or their arrogant ethnicism. Narrow-hearted and narrow-minded, according to Kant, the Jews cherished the letter rather than the spirit of "the Law and the Prophets." The Pharisees, in particular, insisted that God be worshiped through external observances rather than through inner intention. And the Jews generally limited the saving grace of God to their own people, substituting their well-known clannishness for the love of all mankind. Thus Kant gave fresh currency to the medieval anti-Jewish stereotypes by the very process of transforming Christ into the prophet of modern humanism. Kant was certainly aware of the unhistoric character of his interpretation of the New Testament. Was he also aware of his distortion of historic Judaism? Possibly not. In all likelihood he expected that his modernized version of Christianity would be acceptable to the enlightened Jews of his day. In any case, Kant reinforced the historical perspective of his idealization by leveling the following strictures against the Jewish faith:

"First, all its commands relate morally to external acts."[10] Its percepts are not expressions of practical reason, but arbitrary enactments of so-called statutory law. In religion, all laws must arise out of reason legislating its own directives, but if man obeys a law imposed by others, he is not acting as a free, human being. A free, rational being follows the law, which is manifested in his own mind as universally binding— hence, he is "autonomous." He is enslaved to the past, to others, or to superstition, if he obeys merely statutory laws, which are to him "heteronomous." Religion is the recognition of all duties as divine commands."[11] In pseudo-religion, this relationship is reversed, and morally indifferent actions are treated as divine commands.

Second, he claimed, Judaism is this-worldly and materialistic. In the Old Testament, all rewards and penalties refer to terrestrial existence, not to the bliss of paradise and not to the torments of hell. "Furthermore, since no religion can be conceived of, which involved no belief in a future life, Judaism, which when taken in its purity is seen to lack this belief, is not a religious faith at all."[12] Reflecting the emergent discipline of biblical criticism, Kant believed that the Hebrew Bible does not teach the doctrine of immortality. This belief, as well as the doctrine that virtue is its own reward, was imported into rabbinic Judaism from the culture and philosophy of Hellenism, "for this otherwise ignorant people had been able to receive much foreign (Greek) wisdom. This wisdom presumably had the further effect of enlightening Judaism with the concept of virtue."[13]

In these passages, Kant reduced Judaism to what he presumed to be its state in the biblical period in its "purity," abstracting from it the ideas that emerged in the exilic and rabbinic periods. Furthermore, he disregarded the distinction between the secular orientation of the Stoic who extols virtue for its own sake and the rabbinic exhortation to serve God in love, without any expectation of reward.[14] Greek influence was certainly instrumental in stimulating the growth of Judaism. This circumstance was proof of the intellectual vitality of the Pharisees and their openness to the winds of doctrine in their day. Did not a first-century sage define the Wise Man as "the one who learns from all men?"[15] Why, then, define Judaism only in terms of those elements that are peculiar to it? But Kant was, after all, a child of his age. In his description of Judaism, Kant had in mind Mendelssohn's concept of Jewish law as being revealed legislation, ignoring Mendelssohn's claim that it was designed for the purpose of educating the people to understand and to follow the religion of reason. So by abstracting it from the rational-moral principles that constitute its living core, Kant stigmatized Jewish law as devoid of religious content.

> The Jewish faith was, in its original form, a collection of mere statutory laws, upon which was established a political organization. Judaism is really not a religion at all, but merely a union of a number of people who, since they belonged to a particular stock, formed themselves into a commonwealth under purely political laws, and not into a church; nay, it was intended to be merely an earthly state, so that were it possibly to be dismembered through adverse circumstances, there would still remain to it (as part of its very essence) the political faith in its eventual reestablishment (with the advent of the Messiah).[16]

This reduction of the grand messianic vision "to transform the world through the Kingdom of Heaven" into a mundane, secular, narrowly political ambition became a characteristic claim of the eighteenth-century opponents of Jewish emancipation. They preferred to see modern Jewry as a tribal clan rather than as a living faith. In their view, the living kernel of Judaism was an ethnic "will to live," and the trappings of religion were only the instruments of an inflamed survivalism. Like a turtle, the Jews transformed their religion into a hard shell, which they dragged along wherever they went and into which they retreated from a hostile world.

Thus we come to Kant's third stricture of Judaism: "Judaism fell so far short of constituting an era suited to the *church universal* . . . as actually to exclude from its communion the entire human race, on the ground that it was a special people, chosen by God for Himself."[17] Here again Kant's exclusion of the entire humanist dimension from

Judaism was intended to dramatize and to glorify the secession of Jesus and his followers from their ancestral faith.

Kant was certainly aware of the prophetic hope for the conversion of all mankind to the service of the One God (Isaiah 2:2; Micah 4:1; Zephaniah 3:9; Jeremiah 12:16; Isaiah 56:7). Doubtless, too, he was not unacquainted with the massive propaganda against idolatry of the Jewish Hellenists, culminating in the mighty philosophical achievements of Philo of Alexandria, the contemporary of Jesus. Nor, on the other hand, was he unfamiliar with the restrictive dogmas of the apostolic community, which, far from abandoning the concept of an elect community, actually narrowed its meaning by excluding from salvation those pagan monotheists who attended the synagogues, without undergoing full conversion, the so-called Fearers of the Lord, and asserting its own claim to be the new Israel. In Judaism, it will be recalled, the acceptance of the Seven Noachian principles was sufficient for salvation.

But Kant had a job to do in behalf of the liberating ideals of the Enlightenment. He had to idealize Protestant Christianity, enabling it to serve as the universal religion of reason. Catholicism was to him also a religion of ritual and "works" rather than a religion of faith and reason. Protestantism recaptured the genius of the original Christian community, which "completely forsaking the Judaism from which it sprang and grounded upon a wholly new principle, effected a thorough-going revolution in matters of faith."[18] The Sermon on the Mount, offering a critique of Judaism, marked, in his judgment, the inauguration of the new faith, in which the Son of Man stands for humanity.

> Suppose that all he (the Son of Man) did was done in the face of a dominant, ecclesiastical faith, which was onerous and not conducive to moral ends, (a faith whose perfunctory worship can serve as a type of all the other faiths) at bottom, merely statutory, which were current in the world at the time. Suppose further, we find that he had made this *universal religion of reason* the highest and indispensable condition of every religious faith whatsoever."[19]

Thus Kant offered a new interpretation of the meaning of

Christianity, one that was suited to the temper of the Enlightenment. In his view, the Church was just beginning to discover its true nature. To the question, which period in the life of the Church was best? he replied without hesitation: "I have no scruple in answering, 'the present.'"[20] But, while he labored nobly to transform the Christian Church, he felt no compunction in robbing Judaism of all spiritual content, reducing it to its peculiar, legalistic husk, that it might serve as the clannish and unlovely contrast for the humanist and spiritual illumination of the Protestant faith. Also, he lent the immense prestige of his name to the proposition, dear to the heart of Teutonic racists, that the spiritual grandeur of Christianity was a radical innovation, not an outgrowth of Jewish teaching.

We may confidently assert that Kant was not motivated by a personal anti-Jewish animus. But it was difficult for an eighteenth-century rationalist, aiming to transform the Christian faith, to do justice to the Jewish opponents of Christianity. He favored the attempt of the Friedländer group of Jewish intellectuals and businessmen to become part of a non-dogmatic Church. The survival of the Jewish people, he noted, was open to contrary interpretations. Some saw in it "proof of a special beneficent Providence, saving this people for a future kingdom on earth"; others saw in it "nothing but the warning ruins of a disrupted state, which set itself against the coming of the Kingdom of Heaven ... because it stiff-neckedly sought to create a political and not a moral concept of the Messiah."[21]

Again, he ignored the historical fact that the Jewish contemporaries of Jesus faced a concrete choice—whether or not to accept a particular person as a mysterious Divine Being who was soon to usher in the Day of Judgment, the resurrection of the dead and an earthly age of redemption. After all, "The Apostle to the Gentiles" cannot be accused of political narrowness or of sharing the views of the lesser disciples, who, Luke tells us, asked, "Lord will you at this time restore the Kingdom of Israel?" (Acts 1:6). Yet Paul's descriptions of the coming of Christ "with power" was surely known to Kant (I Corinthians 15: 51–58; I Thessalonians 4: 16–17; II Thessalonians 2:1). (Mathew's apocalypse is in Chapter 24.)

We can understand Kant's critique of Judaism as merely a

consequence of his eagerness to further the cause of the religion of reason in a Christian country. He attempted to wean people away from a naive faith in miracles or in the divinity of Christ or in the predestination of souls to either heaven or hell by divine grace with no regard to good or evil works. He even urged that while it may be desirable to teach children some form of prayer, it is necessary to shun petitional prayers, for "prayer as a means of winning divine grace is a superstitious illusion."[22]

Indeed, King Frederick II did not fail to rebuke Kant for his daring: "Our Most High Person has for a long time observed with great displeasure how you misuse your philosophy to undermine and debase many of the most important and fundamental doctrines of the Holy Scriptures and Christianity; how namely, you have done this in your book, "Religion within the limits of Reason Alone . . ."[23]

Each one of Kant's critiques of Judaism recurs again and again in European thought. His condemnation of the externality of the *mizvot* and their heteronomous character reflects the ancient polemic against Jewish legalism, as well as the Lutheran crusade against the Catholic Church and the pietist emphasis in his own upbringing.

It was not difficult for Jewish Kantians to rebut the critique of their philosophic master. God, Who lays down the law in the Covenant, is also the source of morality. So, in the rationalistic tradition, the commandments are ethical in essence and purpose; they are either disciplines intended to provide psychological and sociological reinforcement for the moral law, or they are embodiments of a moral purpose that is proven by the experience of generations, though it is not immediately self-evident to the limited perceptions of any one age. In this sense, the heteronomous laws of the Torah are accepted and obeyed by the Jewish worshipers as if they were autonomous. For the implication of the Covenant is the willingness to become "a partner of God" in "the improvement of the world through the Kingdom of the Almighty."

Furthermore, this idealization of Judaism was not a new hypothesis. It was rooted in the Talmud and Midrash. It was articulated explicitly and formulated in detail by Saadia and Maimonides.[24] Essentially the rationalistic Jewish tradition differs from Kant's own judgment in that it focuses on the religious feelings of humility, trust, awe and love, which are inherent in man's encounter with God. We cannot address God simply as an idea, "The Good, Whose Mercies are infinite," without acknowledging existentially our frailty and finitude. The prophet Micah defines God as the One Who tells man what is good—"to do justice, to love kindness and to walk humbly with thy God." The third component in Micah's definition is the religious dimension that provides the aid of a deep surge of dynamic feeling in behalf of the first two components of the good life. In his valiant struggle for the life of reason, Kant on occasion neglected to take account of the complex of feelings that comes into play when man becomes aware of his standing before God. Today, after two centuries of dubious moral progress, which were punctuated again and again by mass crimes in the name of high ideals, who can doubt that a dash of humility regarding man's moral perceptions is more than justified?

Kant's critiques played an important role in the emergence within Judaism of the Reform movement. As against the reverence of the Orthodox for every tittle of the law, the Reform leaders regarded the practices, which were not obviously moral and spiritual, as surplus baggage, which might be abandoned without regrets. In the heyday of classical Reform, nearly the entire body of distinctively Jewish practices was scorned as expendable, a hindrance to true spirituality because it was heteronomous. This tendency was countered in the course of time by two motivations—the recognition of the need for the symbolic expression of man's direct relation to God, and the awareness of the role of a historic tradition in preserving and creating spiritual values. As we shall see, two men, Lazarus and Cohen, both ardent Kantians, provided the best replies to Kant's criticism, a century or so after the appearance of *Religion within the Limits of Reason Alone*.[25] This contribution will be discussed later in this chapter.

Responses to Kant

Solomon Ludwig Steinheim (1789–1866) made his first contribution to Jewish thought as a critic of Kant and of religious rationalism generally. According to him religion cannot be woven out of the threads of logic or ethics. It derives from moments of revelation through which a unique self-contained realm of values is revealed. This body of revelation is authenticated by its inner resonance in feeling; yet it is subject to critical analysis. Revelation is "a source of knowledge of its own kind, altogether unique, and, therefore, its own validity."[26] The religious person employs inductive reasoning, since his starting point is given to him, by a series of revelations described in Scripture and authenticated in his own life. In his reflections, he reasons out the implications of that which was conveyed to him personally and to mankind collectively. Naturally, there must be a certain correspondence between the central core of biblical teaching and the experience of the man of faith.

In the second volume of his major opus, *Offenbarung*, printed in 1856, which he entitled *Glaubenslehre der Synagoge als exacte Wissenschaft* and which appeared twenty-one years after the first volume, Steinheim moved closer to a rationalistic position and labored to harmonize his views with those of Kant. The noumenal reality appears to us in different systematic structures—those of the physical world, those of ethics, and those of esthetics; so, too, a religious realm of ideas and values is given in revelation or in religious experience. Its core command is "be ye holy, for I, the Lord, am holy." (Lev. 18,1).

While holiness partakes of the quest of truth and of the qualities of harmony and love, it comprises a unique and all-shattering awareness of the Divine Presence. In holiness, man encounters a transcendent Being. Fragmentary echoes of the mystery of holiness are found in all the religions of mankind. But, in all its depth and power, we encounter it in the Holy Scriptures, where its power is a given fact. Layer after layer, the various documents of the Bible reflect the consequences of a mighty incursion of divine revelation.

Steinheim did not maintain that Scripture is literally the word of God. Holiness is, after all, a human phenomenon, man's reaction to the Divine Presence. So, in the moments of revelation, human and contingent elements are absorbed and patterned into enduring symbols and rituals. The sacrificial system, for instance, was obviously structured out of the forms of worship prevailing in ancient times. The core ideas of revelation are those that the phenomenal world can neither prove nor disprove. They are boundary concepts, virtually meaningless in mundane categories, yet all-important in endowing human life with meaning. They are the triad of freedom, creation, and God. These three ideas are essentially one, and the entire panoply of religious life must be weighed by reference to this triad.

In Steinheim's interpretation, the laws of religion cannot be condemned on the ground of being heteronomous, since in religion man freely yields his freedom in order to become God-like. The holiness of God looms as the goal of human life. It is man's task to become a free creator, or in the famous rabbinic phrase, to become "a partner in the work of creation." God labors through the processes of history in order to establish His Kingdom on earth. We join in his efforts when we accept freedom as the highest goal of the life of the individual and of society. Our role is passive, to surrender to His ends, but also active, to build the redeemed world of the future. For Jews, a special task has been set. The Holy Scriptures maintain that God had chosen the people of Israel as His instrument for the redemption of mankind. This assertion contradicts neither the laws of reason nor those of morality. History is inevitably particularistic, with different ethnic groups carrying the banner of progress at different times and in diverse fields, but its goal is the free and universal society. Thus the Jew observes the particular laws of the Torah as his contribution to the building of the all-embracing society of mankind, God's Kingdom. Jewish laws are therefore nationalistic in appearance but universal in intent.

Under Kant's influence, Steinheim rejected Mendelssohn's concept of revelation as divine legislation. He came close to Schleiermacher's position, especially in the first volume of his book, with the claim of a unique experience of the Divine Presence, an experience that could not be analyzed into ethical and esthetic components; but then, as his thought progressed, he came to shun the mysticism and irrationalism of those who based religion on "feeling" (*Gefühl*). Like Kant, he maintained that revelation can take the form only of ethical and social laws that articulate and guard the ideals of God, freedom, and creation.

It has been said that Kantianism became for Steinheim the essence of Jewish experience. Reason acknowledges its own limitations, according to Kant, making room for the incursion of the laws of ethics. But what Kant called practical reason was deepened by Steinheim to be progressive revelation. Steinheim maintained that a religion of reason can deal only with lifeless ideas—God as an abstraction and man as a mechanism. Reason can lead only to "bad monotheism," an abstract Deity. In true monotheism, God is encountered in our experience as a real personality; His presence is apprehended directly as a noumenal reality. And our awareness of God's transcendence makes it possible for us to recognize the noumenal character of the human soul. Though created, it is immortal, for it is not enclosed in the fetters of physical causality.

Living in an age when the science of history had come into its own, Steinheim introduced the notion of progressive development into the realms of ethics and revelation. He maintained that this phenomenal universe is breached from God's side through successive thrusts of revelation; from man's side through an expanding ethical conscience and the acceptance of perfect holiness as the ultimate goal of life.

Judaism contains the record of its growth and development in the Bible, Talmud, and subsequent literature. It unfolds in history from Abraham, to Moses, to the prophets, to the sages of the Talmud and Midrash, to the philosophers of the medieval and modern worlds. It does not depend on the uniqueness of one event, not even the Covenant of Sinai. As Steinheim saw it, Judaism was a compounding of a series of revelations, in which those which occurred earlier provided the tests and standards for subsequent revelations.

Kant, as we have seen, idealized Christianity and interpreted Judaism as a religion of external rites that remained essentially unchanged throughout history. Steinheim idealized Judaism and insisted on the invariant, fixed character of ancient Christianity. Thus he returned the compliment, as it were. The Christian faith, he asserted, was a blend of paganism and Judaism, or a bridge between them, if you will. He defined paganism as the understanding of the world in its own terms, apart from revelation.

Hence, the emphasis in Christianity on man's unfreedom, the worthlessness of man's righteousness, his predestination to redemption or perdition, his salvation through a blind acceptance of that which is "folly for the Greeks, a stumbling block to the Jews." As Christianity enters the modern world, it is certain to stress its Hebraic heritage ever more decisively.

Kant's second line of criticism consisted of two parts—the allegation that Judaism promises physical, or carnal, rewards for the good life, and that it was originally a pattern of tribal practices. The first point reflects a long tradition of Christian criticism of the messianic expectations of the Jews. Being materialistic and nationalistic, it was said, the Jews hoped for a Messiah who would redeem their nation from oppression and usher in an age of fantastic plenty for all mankind; therefore they proved incapable of comprehending the spiritual blessings and the universal implications of Jesus' message, "Lo, the Kingdom of God is within you" (Luke 17: 21).

In response to this line of criticism, Jewish traditionalists would point to the fact that the doctrine of immortality was implied in many of the Psalms, taught in the earliest sections of the Talmud, defended dialectically in Jewish medieval philosophy, and affirmed in the oldest Aramaic paraphrases of Scripture.[27] The exponents of Reform reinterpreted the Jewish religion in keeping with the principle of historical development. Growth is the mark of vitality. A living faith unfolds by way of creative responses to fresh challenges. And it is the divine nisus in itself that is holy, not the forms it assumes at various times. So in reference to the tribal origin of some practices, the Reform leaders pointed to the process of continuous reevaluation and transformation that was ceaselessly at work within Judaism. The story in Genesis of Abraham's willingness to sacrifice his son was paradigmatic of this progressive development. It tells how the sacrifice of children to Moloch, a practice that was well-nigh universal in the ancient Mediterranean world, was transmuted by Abraham or by his descendants into the feeling of inner devotion to God. The prophets and the sages were engaged in the work of spiritualizing the Jewish faith. Abraham Geiger (1810–1874) showed how the very text of the Scriptures revealed the traces of this ongoing process. Indeed, according to Geiger, the Sadducees in the time of

Jesus represented the priestly traditionalists, while the Pharisees, abused as hypocrites in the New Testament, were actually the party of spiritual progress and reform.[28]

To be sure, within the Pharisaic party, there was constant tension between those who searched for the inner meaning of the law and those who reveled in multiplying fresh structures and new hedges around it. The debate between Jesus and *some* Pharisaic teachers took place within the context of Pharisaic teaching and ideals, for Jesus was evidently a popular preacher who did not belong to the official academy, a "folk-Pharisee," though he castigated the policy and performance of the Pharisaic order (Matthew 23:2, 16:6; Luke 11:42, 12:1, 16:14; Acts 15:5, 23:6). The peculiar greatness of Judaism is evident in the fact that it encouraged the practice of self-criticism. The biblical prophets were the great reformers of their day, and their protests against the abuses of religion constitute the greatest treasure of the Jewish heritage. In the same way, Jesus' critique of false piety is an integral part of the Jewish tradition, as is demonstrated by the numerous parallels to his teachings in the Talmud and Midrashim. It was not the religion *of* Jesus that the Jewish leaders rejected, but the religion *about* Jesus—that is, the belief that in him the messianic hope was fulfilled and later, the notions of the incarnations of God in Christ, the Trinity, and the doctrine of transubstantiation.

Indeed, the Protestant critique of Catholicism was akin to the basic attitude of the rabbis in the first centuries of our era. The idea that the advent of the messianic era, and subsequently the world to come, is contingent upon penitence was stressed again and again in rabbinic literature. "All the *eschatons* have already, come to pass and redemption is now dependent only on the consummation of repentance"[29] The gates of repentance are open to all men, not merely Israelites. Indeed, the literature emphasizes that the Gentiles were more likely to repent in heart and soul than the Israelites. That is why the book of Jonah was read on Yom Kippur. "Said the prophet Jonah, 'I know that the nations are inclined toward repentance [literally, *krovai teshuvah*, "near to repentance"], I shall therefore preach to them and they will respond and repent.'"[30]

As to the materialistic metaphors of the messianic era, their function was, according to the Reformers, to stress the realistic nature of the redemptive process. It is to occur within the course of history, not in some mythical realm. It is to relate to actual men and women, not to ghosts floating in clouds. So the vision of a perfect age must include the elimination of disease and the overcoming of the manifold evils of society. There is nothing unspiritual in the quest of improving the physical lot of suffering humanity. On the contrary, to meet the physical needs of other people is what the love of neighbor is all about.

In keeping with the secular interpretation of messianism, the Reform theologians described the socio-political struggle of the liberals in nineteenth-century Europe as the contemporary equivalent of the prophetic call to prepare for the messianic Kingdom of God. Of particular interest is the messianic rhetoric of Leopold Zunz (1794–1886), the spiritual father of modern, critical Jewish scholarship, the so-called science of Judaism. He wrote: "Wherever justice, freedom, and harmony dwell together, there is the Kingdom of God."[31] Nahum Glatzer summarized Zunz's messianism in this way: "Indeed, in his mind, the vision of a new Europe had replaced that of a new Jerusalem in the messianic prophecies of classical Israel."[32]

In the nineteenth century, the biblical emphasis on the material implications of the messianic age turned out to be fully in line with the aggressive secularism of the emergent modern society. Some Jewish teachers gloried in the idea that "Judaism is not a religion at all," for the term *religion* had come to mean a mystical retreat from the world and an exaggerated concern with the anxieties of the individual.[33] With the progressive secularization of Jewish consciousness, the communal dimension was stressed more and more. The scientific study of Jewish history took the place of works of pious devotion. The dominant question in the age of emancipation was not the individual's quest for meaning but the nature and destiny of the Jewish people.

Thus we come to Kant's third critique. The Jewish doctrine of the chosen people was interpreted by Kant in the sense of excluding the rest of humanity; it was the great merit of the Christian Church that it opened wide the gates of salvation to all mankind. This critique is as erroneous as it is popular. The following considerations help us to see it in perspective.

The concept of humanity is basic in the Hebrew Bible. God is the Creator of all men, having endowed them with His image and having concluded His covenant with the children of Noah. The choice of Abraham and his descendants was made so "that all the families of the earth might be blessed through them" (Genesis 12:3). This all-human dimension was supplemented by the moral goal of this choice—"that they might keep the way of the Lord to do justice and righteousness" (Genesis 18:19). At Sinai, the Israelites submitted to another covenant, whereby they undertook to be "a people of priests and a holy nation" (Exodus 19:6). Now, the role of priests was to serve as teachers and custodians of the sacred tradition to the lay population. Israel was called "my first-born son" (Exodus 4:22), suggesting the image of humanity as one family, with God as the Father demanding that His first-born son live up to the responsibility of being *primus inter pares*. The great exilic prophet, Deutero-Isaiah, described the role of Israel in terms of the suffering servant (Isaiah 52:13–15, 53:1–12). The hope for the conversion of all men was sounded by several prophets in words of unforgettable beauty (Zephaniah 3:9; Zechariah 14:9; Isaiah 2:1–4, 42:6). In the Jewish liturgy of the High Holy Days, this hope is the basic theme—"that all of them [Gentiles] might become one association to do Thy Will with a perfect heart." Since all this was well known to Kant, how could he possibly regard Judaism as a faith that excludes mankind from salvation? Furthermore, Mendelssohn had called attention to the universalist outreach of Judaism and had laid down the rule that a religion was surely false if it excluded from salvation those who did not belong to it.

Presumably, we have here an example of a phenomenon that might be aptly termed "the Christian unconscious." Christian scholars had long maintained that the Pharisees had choked the Jewish faith by the chains of casuistry and legalism, so that its biblical grandeur had faded and shriveled. The expulsion of the non-Jewish women and their children by Ezra and Nehemiah signaled for them the beginning of this isolationist policy (Ezra 10; Nehemiah 13). And its tragic climax was reached when the Jewish leaders resisted Paul's claim that salvation was intended for Gentiles also. A cursory reading of the New Testament lends credence to this assumption (Acts 11:1, 13:46; Romans 3:39, 15:16; Ephesians 3:1–6).

On closer examination, however, we find that rabbinic Judaism had established a regular procedure for the acceptance of "righteous proselytes." It had also developed a large pool of semi-converts, or spiritual converts, who were not required to undergo any special sacrament of conversion.[34] Indeed, in the first century Judaism underwent a remarkable expansion, as we learn from Roman satirists, as well as from Philo and Josephus. Inasmuch as the rabbis allowed that the "righteous among the nations shared in the world to come," the biblical-rabbinic doctrine of Israel being a chosen people cannot be scorned as exclusive in character.[35]

In Judaism, the people Israel as a whole was chosen, but individuals were free to join it, in whole or in part (Jeremiah 15:5; Zechariah 2:15; Isaiah 57:6); in the Church, individuals were chosen through the Holy Spirit, and the Church as a whole was established as the sole agency of salvation. To be sure, the attitude of Jewish leaders toward the task of converting the Gentiles underwent great variations. There were times when Israel felt itself to be surrounded by enemies, "a lonely lamb among seventy wolves," kept alive by the beneficent providence of God. In such moments of distress and despair, people might be tempted to surrender their hope for the conversion of mankind to "the true faith," prior to the coming of the Messiah. Indeed, the gates of salvation were occasionally narrowed, under the impact of external persecution or internal mystical fantasies, but they were never closed.[36]

Does the concept of the chosen people imply a cosmic or metaphysical superiority? Is the special love of God for Israel, in the Hebrew Bible, manifested in special biological or physical qualities of the Israelites?

Doubtless, there were strong romantic and narcissistic trends in Jewish life, particularly in times of trouble. The chosenness of Israel could then easily be given an exceptionalist and even a racial twist. Innumerable passages, reflecting this mood of despair, can be cited. But in the classic eras of prophecy, rabbinism and philosophy, the Jews regarded themselves as the vanguard of humanity, custodians of a "light unto the nations" (Isaiah 42:6). We are familiar with the reason given by the Deuteronomist for God's choice—it was an arbitrary fiat of the Divine Will to direct His love to Israel (Deuteronomy 7:8). We know, too, that Spinoza and Mendelssohn insisted that there was nothing special about the Jewish people.

In the post-Napoleonic era, however, we encounter a revival of medieval mysticism and an increasing emphasis by Jewish exponents on the uniqueness of the Jewish people. Perhaps it was the nationalist awakening in western Europe at that time; perhaps it was the frustration of Jewish hopes for emancipation in Germany, following the defeat of Napoleon; perhaps it was the desire to halt the massive tide of desertion from the besieged ghettos. In any case, we find that Abraham Geiger, the leading exponent of Reform, interpreted Jewish uniqueness in terms of an inborn racial genius.[37] The theological dogma of the chosen people was understood by him to reflect a biological phenomenon. Individuals among all nations may vary in talent, but genius is a special capacity, higher by a quantum-jump than the normal range of talent, and dependent on the collective quality of a people, as a whole. So the ancient Greeks had a genius for art and beauty. Similarly, Geiger maintained, Israelites possess an inborn genius for religion. In his view, history attests this fact, since in a sea of paganism Israel alone produced a solitary island of monotheistic culture. For a millenium and a half, the pagan world continued to be unready for the lofty faith of monotheism. And when Paul undertook a mighty effort to convert the most advanced nations of antiquity, he had to compromise the austere demands of the Jewish faith, interposing a human-divine Savior between man and God and substituting for the muscular doctrine of free will, which requires constant exertion and vigilance, the fearful notion of man's inability to save himself from the fires of hell by deeds of goodness and penitence. The "good news" of the Savior was, after all, predicated upon the certainty of man's failure to achieve salvation through his own efforts to love God and to serve Him.

The foul fruits of mystical racism were not yet evident in the beginning of the nineteenth century, and rationalist Reform leaders such as Geiger made use of the sentiments of racism to reinforce Jewish pride and to stem the tide of assimilation. In contrast to

Mendelssohn, who followed the lead of Maimonides in working with the universal categories of rationalistic philosophy, Geiger and his followers followed the lead of the medieval romantic philosopher, Judah Halevi, who maintained that the Jewish people were uniquely endowed with a special genius for "the divine influence." Philosophers such as Aristotle might be able to conceive of the First Cause or the Prime Mover, but only prophets could enter into a meaningful communication with the Deity, and the Jewish people as a whole were the people of prophecy. So the term *the God of Israel* reflects this intimate and exclusive bond between God and His people.

Yet Halevi did not ignore the universalist outreach of the Jewish faith. His philosophy of Judaism is presented within the context of the historical conversion of the king of the Khazars to the Jewish religion. He conceived of humanity as forming one living organism, with the people of Israel being its heart. "Israel among the nations is like the heart among the organs, exceeding them in both healthfulness and sickness." This imagery allows that other faiths also fulfill important functions. In a beautiful metaphor, Halevi compares the three great faiths of monotheism to three branches of a tree that has grown out of the seed planted by God in the days of Abraham and later Moses. In the final analysis, the same seeds will ripen in all the three branches of this tree.[38]

The Kantian charge of Jewish legalism was taken to heart by the foremost thinkers of German Jewry. Accordingly, they responded to his challenge by idealizing, or reinterpreting their ancient faith in keeping with his principles of pure reason and practical reason. In this creative response, they found within the Jewish tradition an ample array of penetrating principles, which could be arranged in systematic form. The Jewish faith had encountered the challenge of Babylonian and Egyptian wisdom in the biblical period, of Hellenistic philosophy in the prerabbinic period, of Stoicism in the early centuries of our era, of modified versions of Aristotelianism and Platonism in medieval times. In all these cases, Jewish thought had responded by partially absorbing and partially rejecting the alien philosophies. For this reason, the Reform leaders of the nineteenth century could cite valid precedents for their position that Judaism was essentially a religion of reason. In their view the immense legalistic superstructure was either a pedagogic device, intended to train the people for the ethical life, or a means of protecting the community against the acids of disintegration. In either case, its validity is secondary, subject to reevaluation in every generation. As a matter of practice, the Reform leaders discarded most of the ancient laws.

The Conservative wing of the Reform movement emphasized "the positive-historical" aspects of Jewish law. In keeping with the nationalistic schools of law, such as that of Savigny, they argued that the historical unfolding of a nation's laws was the best guide to its authentic national spirit. And nationalism is the alter ego of religion. It is by sharing in the historic tradition of a community that we reach out to God. We cannot seek God, without seeking spiritual communion with our fellow-men, beginning with those who are closest to us.

Nationalistic philosophers ignore the fact that the sentiments of tribalism are quite capable of strangulating a living faith as well as vitalizing it. In the combination of nationalism and religion, the demonic and the divine are intertwined. There is no telling whether the resulting mixture will promote a narcissistic self-deification or an idealistic temper of dedication to universal values. In the case of Judaism, the sentiments of nationality and religion, rooted in the same soil, have been refined by the prophetic spirit and spiritualized by several millennia of struggle against ethnic pride and prejudice. Hence, the Conservatives contended, we may well utilize our rituals and laws to reinforce our faith, without awakening the slumbering ghosts of ethnic separatism and self-glorification.

The Conservatives were more concerned with the life of Judaism than with its message. They granted that viewed from the outside, the character of Judaism as a universal religion is obscured by legalistic impediments and nationalistic rhetoric, but they maintained that viewed from within, the ethnocentric–legalistic shell is seen as a protecting cover for the inner kernel of "ethical monotheism." Since the Conservative theologians were, in contrast to some of the Reform leaders, uninterested in converting Christians, the view from within was all that mattered to them. Christians need not convert to

58 JEWISH IDENTITY IN AN AGE OF IDEOLOGIES

Judaism, for the sake of salvation, since their faith too is a version of ethical monotheism.

Lazarus and Cohen

Moritz Lazarus's *Ethik des Judentums*, which appeared in 1898, is an excellent illustration of the Kantian interpretation of Judaism in Germany. In his preface, Lazarus disavowed the comparative method, though he was by profession an ethno-psychologist. He aimed to rise above disputations and polemics. "Naught of apologetics!—A purely objective statement was aimed at, and it must speak and act for itself."[39]

Yet, from our present perspective, there is no doubt that Lazarus was apologetic, in the best sense of that word—that is, he was constantly aware of the critical notions that were then in the air.

He asserted solemnly:

> I declare before God and man that I will not advance a thought in this work which I do not conscientiously believe was born of the spirit of Judaism. Whatever the Greeks and the Romans, and the philosophic and general literature of modern nations have taught me, may assert itself in my presentation as a shaping force. The subject matter I have drawn, to the best of my knowledge and belief, solely from Judaism and the Jewish spirit.[40]

Such an excess of protestation is itself proof of the apologetic mood. Furthermore, in the realm of thought, methodology and formulation are of the essence.

Indeed, we may ask, why deny the impact of western thought upon modern Judaism? Is not the sign of a vital faith precisely its capacity to respond creatively to fresh challenges? A careful reading of Lazarus's work will show it to be as sensitive to the spirit of classical German thought as it is reverent toward the Jewish tradition. Many an Aggadic passage is illuminated by him in a fresh and brilliant light. While the new interpretation may not be correct in terms of the canons of historical criticism, it is in accord with the Kantian method of idealization, whereby a living faith acquires fresh nuances by virtue of its own natural unfolding in a challenging new mental climate.

Actually Lazarus's work is a fine synthesis of Judaism and Germanic liberalism at the turn of the century. He described Jewish law as autonomous, in Kantian terminology—that is, it is the ethical, and only the ethical, that God wills.

> This, then, is the relation between divine law and human ethics: God is the lawgiver, but He did not promulgate the law as His pleasure or as an arbitrary or despotic command; and man is not to obey it as such. It is law for man, because he recognizes in God the prototype of all morality, because God is the creative force back of the moral order and moral purpose of the world. Moral law, then, is based, not upon some dogmatic conception of God, but upon the idea of His morality. Not God the master, but God the ideal of all morality is the fountainhead of man's moral doctrine.[41]

Lazarus's negations are not convincing. Of course, God is more than the ideal of morality. He is Creator and Father, in whom we find refuge and fulfillment, not merely our moral inspiration. Our relation to God includes the ethical dimension, but is not exhausted by it. And Judaism, as a historic faith, includes much more than the merely ethical.

Lazarus summed up the essence of Jewish ethics in this sentence, which Kant might have written: "Love of the morally good alone is the ethic of life; all else belongs to the technic of life."[42] Even more Kantian is the statement Lazarus presumed to find in the Midrash, "If you observe the Torah I shall regard it as if you had made yourselves" (Leviticus Rabba 35:7). Lazarus translated Torah as "the moral law," and he concluded, "as a moral agent, man is his own creator."[43]

Lazarus was generally justified in finding texts to support his exposition, but he is extremely selective, identifying as normative those fragmentary aspects of the tradition that fit into his scheme. He acknowledged obliquely utilitarian and dogmatic motifs: "Biblical language sometimes, it must be conceded, accommodates itself to the simple thought of the populace which by nature and by nurture has a leaning toward utilitarianism."[44] "It cannot be denied that many of the Talmud sages deferred with too great indulgence, to the naive simplicity of the people, who value every action according to its success."[45]

Lazarus's version of Jewish ethics conforms to the nineteenth-century rationalistic ideal, but it does not capture the inner tensions and even contradictions within the tradition. He spoke of the traditional regimen of conduct as being "at once a textbook of ethics and a theocratic code,"[46] but he did not discuss the fact that the religious motif of total obedience may on occasion conflict with the dictates of conscience.

He devoted a chapter to the theme "moralization is lawfulness," in which he extolled the moral virtue of obedience to the law of God.

"Obedience to his law is the noblest form of devotion to God. On a plane beyond mystical abstraction, superfine speculation, ecstatic emotionalism, obedience produces the pure, transparent atmosphere in which the spirit of morality has its being."[47]

True, but the law of God is revealed in "the still, small voice" of conscience as well as in the precepts of tradition. Was it the law of God to annihilate the Canaanites? Manifestly, it was the glory of classical prophecy to set the promptings of heart and mind above the priestly laws. "Purification consists in the subjection of all incentives to action by the formal element of obedience. In the call to Abraham, in whom 'all the nations of the earth' were to be blessed, the central idea is 'that he will command his children.' "[48] But, the import of his proof-text is distorted when it is quoted only in part. The verse goes on to say, "and they shall keep the way of the Lord to do justice and righteousness" (Genesis 18:18–19). God's way is identified with man's perception of the moral law, which is justice, and with the outreach of love and compassion, which is righteousness. But when Lazarus ignored the ritualistic and what Kant called the statutory portions of the law, he failed to deal with the actual problem of the opposition between the ethical conscience and the traditional law.

Lazarus took up the challenge of his contemporary, the philosopher Edouard von Hartmann, who maintained that theism is essentially incompatible with the autonomy of the moral principle. In reply, Lazarus pointed out that in Judaism absolute morality is one with the will of God, "because it is the moral principle in itself and absolutely, therefore, it is necessarily in God."[49] From our vantage point, Lazarus's answer is correct only in a modernized, rationalized faith, that is, so long as God's Being is deduced, à la Kant, from the categorical imperative. But in the actual, historical literature of Judaism, as in other historical faiths, it is pointless to ignore occasional contradictions between the religious and ethical motivations.

Lazarus took pains to distinguish the virtue of lawfulness from the vice of external legalism, on the ground that the former involves the fullness of devotion:

> Lawfulness as an ethical conviction means more than knowing the law with clear insight, more than bringing about its fulfillment with energy; it means embracing the Law with emotion, and being animated with the longing to see the Law attain to supremacy in the world and in ourselves, so that our whole life may be ordered, guided and enriched by its fulfillment.[50]

Again, we note the confusion between the moral law and that of the religious tradition. And when he goes on to assert, "the law is the profoundest, noblest, most pregnant reason for the existence of the community,"[51] we think of the famous principle of the rabbis, which implies the reverse order of ends and means—namely, "the Sabbath was given over to you, not you to it."

Lazarus gave an excellent account of one phase of Jewish ethics and law, but he overlooked the spontaneous and heroic aspects of Jewish piety—the vision of the Good Society in the "end of days" and the endeavor to share in its construction. He steered clear of the contemporary Eastern European religious phenomena, the fervor of the Hasidic movement and the austere self-criticism of the Mussar movement, though the masses of Jewry at the turn of the century were still predominantly Orthodox. At the same time, he ignored the secularist trends, the Zionist and the socialist, which transformed the ancient dream of the messianic era into a concrete program of national rebirth.

As a moralist and a Kantian, Lazarus was a universalist. Yet he reflected the upsurge of ethnic pride and the rising infatuation with the mystique of race at the turn of the century. He distinguished between the Indo-European and the Semitic psyches in regard to poetry. While the former deal with imaginary entities, "such things 'as nowhere and ne'er have been,' the Semitic peoples, especially the Jews, are far different."[52] "Their poetry is almost exclusively lyric-didactic, dealing not with the shapes of untrammeled fancy, not with the images of an unreal world, but with actual phenomena, with forms, characters, acts and religious movements of history." He cautioned the reader not against ethnic pride, but against an unjustified modesty.

"It would be false modesty and reprehensible to omit mention here of the circumstances that brought about the special excellence of the Jewish race."[53] There is no harm in dwelling on the special excellences of any historic group, providing its special faults are also taken into account.

In a word, Lazarus's *Ethics*, for all its loftiness and erudition, was marred by his ardent desire to paint a beautiful picture. If we make allowances for the necessity to counter the hostile judgments of antisemitic detractors, we recognize that his idealized version of Judaism is an impressive monument of modern Judaism at the turn of the century. His self-image as a Jew reflected the impact of both Kantian rationalism and modern ethnicism.

The most complete response to the Kantian critique of Judaism was offered by Hermann Cohen (1842–1918), founder of the "back to Kant" movement in German philosophy. But Cohen's response absorbed a variety of elements from the century of European, especially German, thought that intervened between him and Kant. His "critical" philosophy adopted from Hegel the notion of an unfolding Reason, culminating in an all-embracing Concept. From Comte and the school of positivists, he accepted the idea that complete understanding must assume the form of a mathematical equation. With Marx, he agreed that the goal of ethical action must be the creation of a social order of perfect equality and total fraternity. Yet the system of philosophy Cohen evolved was uniquely his own.

We cannot reach for the Absolute, Cohen contended, parting company with Hegel. Metaphysics is beyond our ken. We can only deal with human consciousness, as it evolves in accordance with its own laws. The consciousness of primitive man is overwhelmingly a mass of impressions, wild guesses, troubling fears, and savage lusts. But as cultural awareness lights up the confused mentality of primitive people, they become more and more conscious of certain coordinates of order in the fields of true knowledge, right action, and beautiful feelings.

If now we glance back at the whole travail of man, we can see the emergence of three "pure" directions of spirit—the quests for Truth, Goodness, and Beauty. Cohen was particularly concerned with the first two. In his logic, he shows how Reason aims at becoming totally self-sufficient, evolving its own mathematical and logical categories. "Reason is the organ of laws."[54] In his *Ethik des Reinen Willens* (1904), he arrived at the notion that the ultimate goal of history is the emergence of a messianic society, in which men and women will behave as if they were all part of one living, immortal organism. One for all, and all for one. This goal will not be reached through a bloody Armageddon, as in Marxism, but through the progressive translation of ethical insights into the laws of the state, in accord with the inner logic of Practical Reason. There are no sudden leaps in the realm of spiritual life. As the national conscience is refined and deepened, laws of social justice and compassion are enacted. The essential quality of the pure components of culture, in logic, in ethics, and in esthetics is lawfulness. So a state is constituted by the growth of reverence for the inner unfolding of the law; families are merged into tribes, tribes into nations. In turn, nations become states, and in line with this development, nation-states, he was certain, will become "ethical states" (Rechtstäte), providing equality of rights for all citizens. In due course, the states will become part of a federation of states, encompassing the whole of mankind. While the actual course of history may lag far behind this vision of redeemed humanity, we become aware of the ultimate goal, whenever the Pure Will asserts itself in our consciousness. The concept of messianic mankind is implied in all our ethical actions.

As in the case of Kant, Cohen's ethics lead to the idea of God. In Cohen's system, the idea of God appears at the dawn of ethical awareness and at its goal. What is it that makes us feel that we ought to trust the ethical imperative? The "ought" of our conscience implies a universal Ought, that relates to all men. We are impelled to view human life in the perspective of a transcendent purpose. We feel that we would be false to our true self, were we to ignore this ethical call. We respond to the categorical imperative, because we want to be true. Thus Cohen maintained that the deep sense of truthfulness (Wahrhaftigkeit) mediates between our deeper self and our culture-consciousness; it binds our conscious self to its roots in true Being. We want to be true neither to the physical world nor to our own empirical selves, but to the source of pure Being, that is, to God.

Truthfulness is deeper than logical coherence or ethical abstractions or esthetic principles; it appeals to our deeper self, in which these pure directions of spiritual life are rooted. In the last resort, then, Cohen asserted that the quests of Truth, Beauty and of Justice, which follow their respective lines of development in our experience, are one at their root, in the realm of true Being, in our spirit and in God. These coordinates of spirit also converge in their outreach toward the future, for the goal of ethics, the attainment of an all-embracing messianic society is guaranteed for us by the idea of God, Who is the source of the physical world and of the realm of purposes or values.

Like Kant, in the *Critique of Judgment*, Cohen assumed that the mathematical-mechanical physical order and the psychical teleological order of purposes have their source in God, the Supreme Intelligence.

Cohen's philosophy, then considers that the blooming confusion of immediate experience together with the totality of anthropological and sociological knowledge is so much raw material, which the human mind sorts out gradually and painfully, evaluating and ordering it in three directions of culture. Each direction is marked by the quality of lawfulness—esthetics, ethics, and logic following a similar curve of growth. All that is unscientific, mere opinions and sheer sentiments, are filtered out of "culture consciousness."

But, and this is his main point, culture is more real than unexamined experience. And at the peak of culture, as well as at its gate, stands the idea of God, which is the supremely real Idea. We encounter this Idea in our quest of Truth, which is the fountainhead of the three currents of culture, and in our assurance that the physical order of force and the ethical order of purpose are inwardly consistent. To Cohen, God is not the Absolute, nor is He comprised within the meshes of culture, but He represents the ultimate outreach of man's all-embracing quest for Truth, Goodness and Beauty. "The whole man out of his innermost self, out of all the directions of his consciousness, must bring forth the love of God."[55]

To come closer to Anglo–American philosophical terminology, we might rephrase Cohen as saying God is in the deepest integrity of our being when it is directed toward the ultimate values, and He is our assurance of their ultimate realization.

How does this conception of God enter into the history of religions? Cohen did not claim that his God-Idea is contained embryonically in the fears, anxieties, and impassioned longings, which generate the myths and rituals of primitives. But in the evolution of mankind, there comes a time when religion acquires "a share in reason." Does not science similarly emerge by slow and halting steps out of the fog of myth and magic? To be sure, Cohen was aware that the religion of reason, as he conceived it, is not yet completely unfolded, not even in modern Judaism. In plant life, the growing oak reveals the potentialities contained in the acorn. In human life, the ultimate shape of the religion of reason is beyond our ken. We may only sketch out its outline and extrapolate as best we can.

For Hegel, Christianity was "the absolute religion" in his own formulation, of course. Cohen rejected any such claim in behalf of Judaism. The religion of reason is evolving out of the efforts of diverse groups. "I do not assert that Judaism alone is the religion of reason."[56] But, he insisted, true religion had its primary origin in the religion of Israel. Biblical monotheism centers round the belief in the Unique God, a God who cannot be represented by any material image. For He is the Source, as well as the goal of all that we aspire to achieve. Our vast knowledge of cultures and faith contains no parallel to the remarkable course of biblical faith. It was easy enough for the great religions of antiquity to attain the world view of pantheism which celebrates "the sacredness of life," and the inner unity of all existence. In pantheism, which has indeed been reached in many parts of the world, the gods are assimilated to nature while in the biblical faith God is one and incomparable. He is sought through the diverse domains of spirit. It was the rare insight of the Hebrew prophets that identified God as the author of the moral order, the source of justice and compassion. He is revealed not in nature but in history, not in our animal existence but in our quest for spiritual perfection—"be ye holy, for I am holy."

How is this religion of reason generated? Cohen saw it as a process that curves around and above the straight tracks of ethics, the quest of justice. Religion arises out of the "category of the individual" but not in the existentialist sense. Franz Rosenzweig, who was Cohen's pupil for some years, began his book with the individual's anxiety in the face of death. "All cognition of the All originates in death, in the fear of death."[57] In contrast, Cohen's individual reaches the point of ethical sophistication at the point where his own death is no longer of consequence, because of his intense commitment to the conservation of ethical values. In our personal lifetime we may indeed fail to realize our ideals, but, he asks, can we possibly assert that the efforts of all who strive to advance the cause of humanity are doomed to frustration and failure?

Cohen argued that ethical people must not be overly concerned for their own life; instead their anxiety is focused on ethical ideals. Are man's ideals so many vain illusions, destined to fall into the dust like dry leaves in the autumn? The religion of reason is born when man discovers within himself the capacity to "correlate" himself to God, Whose Kingdom will be realized in the messianic era. Man's ideals and hopes are sustained when he learns to cling to God with all the passion of his soul, finding the meaning of his life in this total devotion. While man cannot expect to see the fulfillment of his ideals in his own lifetime, he may dare to hope that the little mite that he is able to contribute will not be lost. That which is divine within our strivings is eternal. In opposition to Spinoza, Cohen's ethical personality dares to believe that God loves him, as he loves God, for the Divine Purpose is fulfilled in the lives of those who set it above all their personal concerns.

Indeed, Cohen's correlation implies a polarity. While the man of faith must be ready to sacrifice his very life for the sake of God, he must also be aware of God's infinite love for his own existence. For if our own life be worthless, how can the life of any other individual be precious in our sight and in the sight of God? A messianic vision of history can easily lead to a totalitarian order, in which the rights of individuals are treated with Olympian disdain. Did not Marxism in Soviet Russia actually generate a despotic impatience with the rights and even the lives of many millions? To Lenin, Stalin, and their associates, it was axiomatic that the resplendent ideal of Communism is worth the sacrifice of several generations. Of what worth are so many living individuals when the shape of the future for all mankind is being forged by the hammer blows of history? In contrast, Cohen's man of religion sees every human being as an embodiment of infinite worth. He sees his neighbor not as a cipher, not as just another living being, but as a Thou whose life and destiny reflect the meaning of his own life and destiny. And if one's Thou is troubled the man of faith questions God insistently about the meaning of human suffering. In the domain of secular ethics, utilitarian philosophers may well set up the standard of "the greatest happiness of the greatest number." The devotees of Cohen's religion of reason must learn to supplement sociological generalization with an alert empathy for the individuals that need their help. God is not only in the universal ideal. He is also in the personal encounter between man and his neighbor. "Up until now the kind of human peculiarity inherent in the Thou has not been positively determined; apparently it is the *personality* that is brought to light more through the Thou than through the He. The He is more subject to neutrality, which makes it hardly distinguishable from the It . . ."[58]

Monotheism is a double-pronged commitment to God and the future of mankind, on the one hand, and to living individuals, on the other hand. We are bidden to reject neutrality or indifference to the suffering of the next man, whom we embrace as a fellow son of God, a fellow-man. While the purely ethical-rational response to the challenge of poverty may well be an increased determination to build the messianic society, the religious response is to identify in pity with the suffering neighbor. With Job we ponder the question, Why does God allow this poor man to suffer? With Job, too, we refuse to entertain easy answers. We dare not fall into the trap of the friends of Job who attributed his suffering to his guilt. Instead, we must identify ourselves with the sufferer; it is we, who confront God and confess our *sins*. And to face God, the source of spirit, is to realize our freedom. We can repent our sins, atone for them and achieve reconciliation with God. Man is a free being not because he can frequently do what he wills, but more deeply because he can will to transform his will. If God stands above and beyond the chains of necessity that hold nature in thrall, man correlated with God can rise above himself, as it were. This is the meaning of the Jewish ideal of *teshuvah* (return) which is the essence of a living faith, even though it is logically paradoxical.

> Thus, it is established beyond doubt that love, as religious love, begins with the love for man.
>
> Only now, after man has learned to love man as fellow-man, is his thought turned back to God, and only now does he understand that God loves man, and indeed loves the poor man with the same favor as He loves the stranger.[59]

In brief, it is not man's fear of death, but his compassion for the suffering of others and his fear of sin that generate the driving energy of the religion of reason. "But no other term designates the origin of the correlation between God and man more profoundly than the term 'compassion' "[60]

We must not imagine that Cohen's religion of reason is only a rational construct. In religion, it is man's whole being that comes into play. "The God of religion is never a theoretical concept only."[61] Cohen's religion is socially oriented. It stands as a corrective to his vision of the all-embracing society of the future. True, the man of ethics must drive himself to build an organismic socialist society, but at the same time, it is his obligation to see not masses, but so many *Thou's*, personalities representing the image of God, each being of infinite worth, and to train himself to be compassionate toward those who suffer. In his inner life, Cohen's man of faith blames himself for the sins, or failures of his day, disdaining the usual excuses—social forces, historical necessities, or other individuals and other classes. By his self-examination and repentance, man correlates himself ever more completely to the Unique God.

Cohen's God-Idea sounds abstract and remote, but then his philosophic method did not provide for a more earthy rhetoric. He assumed that the flesh and blood of human experience in all its pathos does indeed envelop the bare bones of theory. In his view, philosophy, like the blueprints of architects, draws limits and angles for buildings that are real enough. His God-Idea is indeed the ultimate goal of all love, even if in actuality mythical motifs and human, all too human, impulses usually flesh out the idealized outline of religion. His mind was formed in a happy and confident era, when the tender sentiments and ideals of the religion of reason could be regarded as the steel structure of the evolving universal faith of mankind. An inveterate idealist, he wrote as follows: "How is it possible to love an idea? To which one should retort, how is it possible to love anything but an idea? Does one not love, even in the case of sensual love, only the idealized person, only the idea of the person?"[62] "The love of man for God is the love of the moral ideal."[63]

> The ideas are archetypes of action. Pure love is directed only toward archetypes, toward models upon which pure and moral action can be established.
> The emulation [of God] must have its source in the whole unity of consciousness, in spirit and in feeling . . . all the powers of the soul have to merge into one common effort in this emulation of God.[64]

To return now to the Kantian challenge of Jewish ethnicism and legalism, Cohen invited us to inquire how did the religion of reason come down to us? Manifestly, it originated among the people of Israel. Biblical monotheism contains the essentials of the religion of reason, though it is also freighted with some popular and unworthy notions. The essence of the Jewish faith was articulated by the classical prophets, who transmuted the priestly heritage and national culture of their people. At this point, Cohen followed the lead of the great founders of the Reform movement.

Prophecy is the spiritual focus of Jewish creativity. "What is the distinguishing characteristic of the prophetic idea? It is the notion that religion and politics are inseparable."[65]

The prophets did not allow religion to be submerged by priestly sacramentalism or by other-worldly fantasies, nor did they permit the power-hungry kings to disregard the claims of conscience. The prophet is the perpetual protestor against the idolatries of politics. For God "looks to the poor and the lowly of spirit" (Isaiah 66,2). No reasons of state can justify the wrong done to even one person. We recall Eliyah's protest against King Ahab's acquisition of the vineyard of Naboth. At the same time, the prophet combats the kind of religion that caters to the sentiments of the rich and ignores the needs of the poor. Cohen's socialism, we recall, was balanced by his exaltation of compassion for the individual, who must not be crushed by the juggernaut of the totalitarian state.

Some Bible critics exaggerated the antagonism between the prophets and the masses of the people, representing the former as being literally "voices crying in the wilderness," perhaps even "Christians before Christ." Cohen pointed out that the prophets succeeded in imposing a monotheistic mold upon the protean spirit of the people. The national spirit became the foundation of the emergent structure of ethical monotheism. The natural feelings of ethnic pride and loyalty were sublimated and directed into the channels of a universal faith first by the prophets and then by their successors, the scribes.

> For these "scribes" were much rather speakers, as of old only the prophets and singers were. It was this national spirit, which intended to, and had to, carry through the homogeneous development of the original teaching. The Torah would have had only temporal value if this continuation had not been recognized as the continuous development of the fundamental national spirit.[66]

Within Judaism, the national spirit was hammered out in the pattern of prophecy—that is, the quest of a universal faith became the soul of the collective life of the Jewish people. So Jewish particularism was universal in essence, providing an example of the direction in which national spirits ought to develop. As the Jews, prodded by the prophets, poured their sublimated ethnic loyalty into the channels of love toward God and humanity, so the biblical faith calls upon every nation to achieve a similar transformation. Here we have a new application of the Kantian categorical imperative—nationalities should so act that their actions can become standards of action for all other nationalities. In other words, nationalism is not a morally self-justifying principle; it is compatible with the demands of faith only if it is thoroughly ethicized and spiritualized. To an ethical monotheist national feeling is the raw material, messianic humanity is the goal, and the function of a national culture is to generate the forms and instruments whereby the people might be summoned to contribute to the ultimate consummation.

We might say that, in Cohen's view, the Jewish people were chosen as *example*, rather than as *exception*, though he does not employ precisely this formulation. Thus he wrote: "God's love for Israel, no less than God's love for the poor, expresses God's love for the human race . . . that the election of Israel is in no way an exception, but is rather the symbolic confirmation of God's love for the human race."⁶⁷

The people of Israel, in Cohen's terminology, is an ideal concept, embracing all who commit themselves to the religion of reason. "The people of Israel, as God's servant, according to the Talmud, has already received in its bosom 'the pious of the peoples of the world.' "⁶⁸

Still, Cohen insists, Jewish people must maintain their actual, historic identity and resist the temptation to become simply an "invisible Synagogue." If individual Jews were to dissolve into the anonymous masses of their host countries, they would deprive the emergent religion of reason of a most fruitful resource. At this point, the utility of Jewish so-called legalism becomes evident.

The purpose of the various laws is twofold: to safeguard the nature of Jewish identity and to train people in reverence toward the laws of ethics. As instruments of Jewish identity, the laws of Torah serve to direct the feelings and memories of ethnicity into the channels of faith. As disciplinary measures, they are calculated to promote the virtues of faithfulness to the imperatives of ethics.

Cohen quoted from Kant's unpublished writings the latter's admission that Christian doctrines of faith might also be corrupted into mere statutory regulations. But, Cohen pointed out, Jewish laws

72   JEWISH IDENTITY IN AN AGE OF IDEOLOGIES

were not irrational, but rather nonrational, even if "some laws have
their basis in mythological prejudices, or are the result of concessions
to them."[69] Jewish law is formally heteronomous, but according to
its inner meaning, it is an autonomous expression of the individual's
desire to maximize his contribution to ethical monotheism, since no
virtue is as significant as that of reverence for law. "Even according to
Kant's teaching, man is not a volunteer of the moral law, but has to
subjugate himself to duty. Thus, the Israelite also must take the yoke
upon himself . . ."[70]

Cohen conceded that Jewish law can qualify as an instrument of
ethics only if it is interpreted in a flexible and dynamic sense, that is, in
the Reform tradition. Ritualistic laws are of secondary importance,
subject to modification and even suspension, in accordance with the
changing needs of the times. Otherwise, the law might become
dysfunctional, promoting Jewish self-segregation and encouraging
an inner withdrawal from general culture. Such a tragic drift toward a
ghetto of the spirit would lead inexorably to a disastrous cultural
impoverishment. "The real but also the only danger of the absolute
power of the law lies in this one-sidedness of the moral interest with
regard to culture."[71]

We must remember that Cohen interpreted the secular law of the
state as being not a static determination of what is right in society, but
as a continuous legislative process, reflecting the unfolding Pure Will
in the growing culture of the state. The ultimate goal of legislation is
the attainment of the all-embracing, organismic society of the future.
In the same way, he conceived of Jewish law as an ongoing process of
legislation. The law is not an end in itself but an educational-cultural
instrument. The ancient sages perceived this truth, however dimly.
He pointed out that according to the Talmud, the laws of the Torah
will cease to function in the messianic era, except for the Day of
Atonement, which symbolizes the inescapable need for self-criticism
and atonement. That is, the legal phase of Judaism will parallel in its
decline the so-called withering of the secular state, in socialist theory.

Cohen was even more opposed to Zionism than he was to a
legalistic Orthodox Judaism. As he saw it, the direction of historical
development was firmly set in the twentieth century toward the
evolution of pluralistic states, in which diverse nationalities will

cultivate their respective religious cultures. The emergence of political nationalism in nineteenth-century Europe he considered to be a tragic disaster. Not being a prophet, he indulged the consoling hope that it would prove to be only a passing infatuation. He questioned whether, with all the good will in the world, it was possible to apply the Wilsonian principle of the self-determination of nations in our industrial society. Nations should not seek to embrace all members of their ethnic community under one umbrella of sovereignty, or to exclude people of a different ethnic character from their state, since no political boundaries can be drawn that will be fair to all. Nationality as a cultural factor is of great educational value, but nationalism, as a political movement, is fraught with immense dangers.

It is the function of the Jewish people in Europe to demonstrate that the heritage of a nationality may be cultivated fruitfully in the service of religious faith and without any political ambitions. The Jewish example, Cohen was convinced, is in keeping with the manifest course of history.

> If we now return to the Jewish problem, then we recognize the backwardness of Zionism with regard to the concept of nation. If the isolation of the Jewish community remains necessary, then isolation in a separate state would be in contradiction to the messianic task of the Jews. Consequently, a Jewish nation is in contradiction to the messianic ideal.[72]

Cohen did not shut his eyes to the plight of the Jews in eastern Europe, allowing that a homeland was needed "for those who had none."[73] But, he was radically opposed to a Zionist ideology that would denigrate the dignity of Jewish life in the Diaspora and empty the messianic hope of any universalistic content. Of the two elements within Judaism—nationality and religion—he wrote: "We do not identify the two, but consider nationality to be an anthropological instrument for the continuation of religion."[74] "Without hope in 'messianic' humanity, there is for us no Judaism."[75]

He objected strenuously to the official Zionist line of propaganda in his day: "The Zionist style in its general literature confirms the prejudice of the Christians, that we don't have any piety, that our religion is only *Gloria gentis*."[76]

In his debate with Martin Buber concerning Zionism, he protested against the fact that "ghetto-consciousness" was esteemed by Buber as "the true spirit of Judaism," instead of being recognized for what it is in fact—an aberration, the consequence of external bigotry and hatred.[77]

While Buber extolled the virtues of the Jewish folk, Cohen maintained that ethical people should direct their loyalties to the state and the messianic future, not to the folk and the myths of the past. "In so far as I take part in the ideal Personality of the State, I assert true self-consciousness."[78]

In that famous exchange, which occurred before the I-Thou breakthrough in his life, Buber claimed that there were only two authentic forms of Judaism—Torah-true Orthodoxy and Zionism. Cohen replied that the classical prophets best represented the inner dynamic of Judaism. "The criterion is in our history, and the thread of our religious evolution is *prophetism*, which attains its climax in messianism . . . This religion of humanity is our modern Judaism."[79]

In keeping with the Kantian policy of idealization, he proceeded to reinterpret true Germanism, as he had reinterpreted the nature of Judaism. The essence of Germanic culture is not a narcissistic mysticism, à la the barbarous preachers of Teutonism. On the contrary: "The German Spirit is the spirit of classical humanity and of genuine world-citizenship. Which people had a Kant? The great men of German culture were one and all prophets of humanity."[80]

For a Jew to become truly part of the German nation-state, Cohen affirmed, it is not enough for him to be merely a law-abiding productive citizen. The Jew is impelled by his religious heritage to seek a deep and abiding empathy with German culture and life. He should so identify himself with the evolving spirit of the nation as to feel its pulse in his own breast. So he wrote: "I read Faust as a German revelation. And I feel this way, too, about Luther . . ."[81]

Cohen was by no means an exception in the lands of Germanic culture. His whole-souled identification with the classical and humanist currents in German thought was characteristic of the majority of the Jews in Germany and Austria. But he was ahead of his time in his ecumenical outreach. He maintained that historically the tension between Judaism and Christianity was creative. Did not

Hegel stigmatize the medieval age, when the Christian faith reigned supreme, as "the religion of the unfortunate consciousness?" The ascent from that dark period was in large part made possible by the revival of interest in the Hebrew Bible. In turn, modern Judaism was influenced by the ideals of the Enlightenment. The two forms of the religion of reason were mutually supportive in the task of overcoming the ever-fresh dragon-teeth of mythology and bigotry. As the Jew is no alien in the secular culture of Germany, he is no outsider to the Christian matrix of that culture.

> As it is offensive to proclaim an "either-or" of "Jew or German," so the attempt to coin the slogan, "Jew or Christian," must also be recognized as repulsive.
>
> And so too the frightening specter of alienism must disappear from the mind of the Jew, as if he were an alien in Christian culture or even in German Protestantism, since Deuteronomy has written its teaching in his heart.[82]

In this judgment, Cohen was thinking more of the future than of the past. Historical religions are needed to safeguard the sanctity of the individual in the emergent, organismic state. With all his optimism, he recognized that history sometimes takes wide and dangerous detours. Both the Jewish and Christian versions of the religion of reason provide resistance to the absolutist sway of ideologies; they serve to prevent the excesses of either nihilism or fanaticism.

Leo Baeck

The world of Hermann Cohen was swept away by the horrors of World War I and its aftermath. The hurricane of popular frenzy that agitated the German masses made the voices of reason all but inaudible. The brave ideals and delicate sentiments of the prewar period now seem to be fragile relics of a distant past. The brutal shouts of rabble-rousers appealed not to the minds of people but to their violent instincts. And the Jews, who had anchored their destiny in the realms of culture, of ethical ideals and humanism, found that their ideal homeland was shattered.

A goodly number of German Jews embraced the Zionist ideal and emigrated to Palestine in the half-dozen years between Hitler's seizure of power and the outbreak of World War II. Among those who stayed in Germany to the very end, fighting to preserve Jewish dignity even in the throes of certain annihilation, was Rabbi Leo Baeck of Berlin. By a strange oversight of the camp director, he emerged alive from the tortures of Theresienstadt, continuing to represent the heritage of liberal Judaism down to his death in 1956.

Hermann Cohen regarded Leo Baeck as his disciple and successor. Indeed, in the first English edition of his great work, *The Essence of Judaism* (1905), Leo Baeck described Judaism as the religion of reason *par excellence*. As against Adolf Harnack's *Essence of Christianity*, Baeck argued that Judaism was more compatible with humanism than any possible idealization of Christianity, since Christianity was inevitably bound up with dogmas concerning the unique metaphysical stature of a historical personality. As to Judaism, its ethnocentric limitations had already been transcended in its normative literature, according to Baeck. The term *Israel* is already used in some Midrashim as a metaphor for all men and women who turn to God in heart and soul. So, all the splendid laudations in rabbinic literature of God's love for Israel may be interpreted to refer to all mankind. Did not Philo already interpret Israel to mean, "He who sees God"? Similarly, the various laws of the Torah, insofar as they are esteemed to be valid today in liberal Judaism, are either moral precepts or moral disciplines. By retrojecting his own principles into ancient rabbinic literature, Baeck did for Judaism what Harnack had done for Christianity. Clearly and systematically Baeck set out to reinterpret the Jewish faith in keeping with this governing principle—normative Judaism is the highest level of idealization reached at any point in its sacred literature. And "the highest" was, to Baeck, the most humanistic.

However, as the dark tide of racist mysticism engulfed the European world, Baeck steadily moved away from the austere rationalism of Cohen. In his revised edition of *The Essence of Judaism*, which was published in 1923, he took account of the mystical component of the Jewish religion. In our encounter with the Supreme Being, he noted, we feel the power of mystery as well as the divine "thou shalt." While the content of the commandment evolves in keeping with the growing ethical sophistication of man, the sense of Mystery is never utterly dissipated. In our experience of holiness, it remains challenging, fascinating, and terrifying. We never outgrow our "creatureliness." However, in Judaism the Mystery serves only as background, and the import of the commandments is the never-ending task. In Christianity, on the other hand, the feelings of Mystery are cherished and cultivated, while the command "to transform this world into the Kingdom of God" is all but ignored.

As the hordes of Hitler began to dominate the streets of Germany, Baeck became more and more convinced that Christianity, in both its Protestant and Catholic versions, was morally bankrupt. The Lutheran pastors were content to preach of "long ago" and "in time to come" and of "the inner kingdom" and of an unearthly "heaven," but they did not dare to apply the divine command to the issues of the day. The prophetic component of German Christianity had been smothered, in his view, by St. Paul's emphasis on faith, by the pagan mystique of Teutonism, and by the so-called inwardness of Martin Luther; by the darkly romanticized "feeling" of Schleiermacher, by the individualistic existentialism of Kierkegaard—and, above all, by the embittered hostility of Germans to all things Jewish, including the Hebrew Scriptures.[83]

In a famous essay, "Romantic Religion," Baeck described Christianity as the religion of sentiment and mystery. In contrast, Judaism represented classical religion—that is, the faith that seeks to do justice to the whole of man's nature, his rationality and ethical ardor as well as his awareness of the Transcendent.

Baeck adopted Schlegel's definition of the romantic world view, namely, "one which treats sentimental material in a phantastic form."[84] Hence, the fanciful imagery of Christian theology. And in Lutheranism, it is not the fullness of a good life but the inner feeling of assurance that is cherished as proof of having been saved. Therefore, a persistent encouragement of a closed mind, impervious to the world and its mere facts. The romantic believer rejects all tremors of doubt with might and main. His passions and his faith must be shielded by high barriers of dogma. As a result the intellectual component of religion is reduced to the fantasies of imagination—"thinking is only a dream of feeling." The romantic loves not God but the feeling of dependence on Him, crying out, "accord me lovely illusions."[85] And the liturgy of romantic faith is designed to promote the feelings of possessing the Divine Being, rather than the ardor of dedication to His will. "Judaism is the classical religion, and Christianity compared with it, the romantic religion."[86]

The reason that Christianity, rather than Judaism, prevailed in the Hellenistic world was due neither to Jewish legalism nor Jewish particularism, but to the dominance of the Dionysiac mood in the first centuries of our era— ". . . the victory of Christianity was in reality this victory of romanticism."[87] In the mind of Paul, the mystery religions of antiquity, centering on the death and rebirth of a god, were blended with the prophetic heritage of Judaism. The synthesis that resulted "became victorious in a world which had become weary and sentimental; it became the religion for all those whose faint, anxious minds had darted hither and thither to seek strength."[88]

To be sure, Baeck was not so shaken by the rise of Nazism as to deny that within the long history of the Christian world the prophetic spirit of Judaism was reborn from time to time.

> It is therefore no accident that peoples with a live sense of independence have turned, consciously or unconsciously, toward the paths of classical religion—increasingly so as their sense of independence grew in strength. The history of Calvinistic, Baptist piety with its affinity to the Old Testament, its "legalistic" orientation, and its ethical stress on proving oneself, shows this clearly. And it was the same story wherever the social conscience stirred; it, too, had to effect this reversion, for it too, runs counter to romantic religion. The social conscience finds romantic religion repugnant because it is at bottom a religious egotism.[89]

As we read Baeck's essay today, we recognize that his perspective was thrown out of focus by his anguish at the failure of Christian leaders to resist the onslaughts of Nazism. A Cardinal Faulhaber might dare to protest against the denigration of the heroic figures of the Old Testament, but even he did not protest against the dehumanization of his Jewish neighbors. Few and far between were the Bonhoffers and the Niemöllers, who risked martyrdom in defense of their beliefs.

The religious leaders of Germany were clearly aware of the challenge of communism, but for the most part they were indifferent or even sympathetic to the Nazis, on the specious reasoning that "the enemy of my enemy is my friend." It is indeed disheartening that when the moment of truth arrived, the churches were found wanting. Some of them even detected a religious awakening in the upsurge of mass enthusiasm, in the abandonment of liberalism, and in the exaltation of the holy mystery of Teutonic blood.

So we cannot blame Baeck for his embittered denunciation of Christianity as romantic religion. At the same time, as we review the histories of Judaism and Christianity, we cannot deny that in both religions there coursed three currents—rationalism, romanticism, and mysticism. The spirit of modern humanism, like the dove Noah sent from his Ark, could hardly alight anywhere in Europe throughout the Dark Ages. Jewish romanticism was generally more ethnocentric than feeling-centered, and Jewish mysticism was more tradition-bound and esoteric than ecstasy-oriented. Making allowance for these differences, we may grant only differences in emphasis, at various times and among diverse individuals. With these reservations we may agree that on the whole, Judaism inclined toward the classical pole and Christianity toward the romantic pole.

But we must remember Baeck's liberal Judaism was no more representative of the whole of Jewish tradition than Harnack's "essence of Christianity" was of the total history of Christianity. Alexander Altmann points out that Baeck himself became steadily more and more mystical. Breaking with the tradition of German-Jewish scholarship, he immersed himself in the study of Kabbalah and Hasidism. In his view, Jewish mysticism remained oriented toward the good life here on earth; hence it did not suffer from the same stigmata as Christian mysticism. He interpreted the Kabbalistic doctrines in humanistic terms—the realm of the *Sefirot* were "moral potencies" and the Lurianic scattering of "divine sparks" was a symbolic affirmation of the goodness of all creation. We need hardly add that these judgments are instances of extreme idealization.[90]

In the book he began to write in Theresienstadt, Baeck moved over to the mystical position, insofar as the nature and destiny of the Jewish people were concerned.

As Altmann put it: "Leo Baeck's *This People* reverts to the old mystical understanding of Jewish existence. It reaffirms the uniqueness of the Jewish people in metaphysical terms."[91] Baeck spoke of the Jews as a metaphysical people.[92] Yet, even in that trying period, he continued to insist that the uniqueness of the Jewish people consisted precisely in the dedication of their collective existence to the ideal of messianic mankind.

> Every people is a question which God addresses to humanity; and every people, from its place, with its special talents and possibilities, must answer for its own sake and for the sake of humanity . . . This people, Israel, developed and grew in one millennium and formed the question that rests within it. It has kept arising ever again, through rebirths, in new epochs, for more than two millennia now. Through its prophets, its poets, its teachers, its righteous ones, Israel was able to learn how to listen to the question which God addressed to it. Its question proved, in Israel's experience, to be the deepest of all questions which live within and form humanity.[93]

We might paraphrase Baeck by saying the Jews were more different than other peoples because they were more committed to humanity. Their tradition and their destiny combined to make them "like all human beings, only more so."

In regard to the emergence of the State of Israel, Baeck wrote:

> Which voice will finally be decisive in the state, that of the enduring covenant, the pledge, the commandment? Or that of the coming and going day which promises something of utility? This people can never be permitted to look only at itself. It has life only when it looks outward, when it sees itself within humanity, when it holds to itself for the sake of humanity and to humanity for the sake of itself.[94]

To Jewish rationalists, the reality of the state of Israel will always be viewed in the light of Baeck's question. Unlike the romanticists with their "leaps of faith," liberals must be aware of the ambiguities inherent in every political situation. And Israel's stature, at this writing, twenty-eight years after its birth, is still shrouded by the dust storms of implacable hatred which surround it. After four bloody victories, the Israelis cannot feel that their Arab neighbors have finally consented to the very existence of their state. In politics, the things that make possible the life of the state come before the things that the life of the state makes possible.

III. *In the Perspective of German Romanticism*

The essence of romanticism is the exaltation of feeling.[1] In this sense, it appeared in the history of modern Europe as the countermovement to the rationalistic revolution. The increasing freedom of people, made possible by the dissolution of the rigid medieval society, encouraged poets and politicians to celebrate the inner dialectic of human feeling. In France, this phase of revolutionary ideology was best expressed by Rousseau, who called for a return to nature. "Man is born free, yet he is everywhere enslaved." Man's very attempt to develop the arts of civilization leads him by degrees to alienate himself from his natural environment and to become estranged from his own true being. In building the new society, the logic of feeling must be consulted as well as the abstract logic of reason.

Thus nationalism was born almost at the same time as democracy, with the former emphasizing the natural bonds of feeling among ethnic groups and the latter aiming to structure a society in which all individuals, regardless of faith or ethnic origin, would be treated alike. With the emergence of the nation-state as the political ideal, the romanticists focused attention on the sentiments of national unity, while the rationalists stressed the ideals of equality and of individual freedom. Of the three ideals on the escutcheon of the French Revolution, the romanticists gloried in the vague but exciting goal of fraternity, while the rationalists expatiated on the social virtues of liberty and equality.

Rousseau's "general will" is an intuitive awareness of the inner striving of the social organism as a whole. Gifted charismatic leaders

82

discover that will and awaken the people to recognize its implications. The general will is not the same as the will of all, which might be determined by way of a free election. It is not the counting of votes that matters, in the long run, but instinctive identification with the life of the republic, allowing a vote, if not a veto, to ancestors and posterity as well as to the living generation of adults. Thus, the seeds of totalitarianism were planted in the eighteenth century, even before the emergence of the democratic state. For totalitarianism is a function of organismic thinking, in which the nation is the source of all values. Rousseau postulated also "civil religion," designed to safeguard the full obedience of all citizens. This plea for unity was somehow associated with a hysterical condemnation of inequality, which appealed to the masses.

So close were the ideals of democracy and totalitarianism in the Enlightenment that Rousseau could be said to be the prophet of both movements. He has been rightly acclaimed as "the revolutionary thinker who first inscribed on the political banners of modern times the opposing slogans, both of democratic and totalitarian governments."[2]

The Jews who sought to become part of the new society demanded equality as their due and shared in the search of their contemporaries for a new society of freedom and justice, but the new ideal of fraternity posed special difficulties for them. They had been taught to regard all Jewish people as their brothers, who live in exile in "lands that are not theirs," awaiting the Messiah who will lead them back to their promised homeland. To be sure, the messianic kingdom will ultimately result in a universal society, "when all men will call upon God's Name and serve Him with a perfect heart." Then, Gentiles and Jews will become brothers indeed. But this ultimate consummation loomed at the end of the horizon. Mendelssohn and his followers argued that the fullness of the messianic era was indeed approaching. New bonds of brotherhood were presently being forged, and the Jews should share in this momentous transformation of erstwhile strangers, separated by history, blood, and faith, into one warm-hearted family. The age of emancipation was aglow with the radiance of hope.

Actually, even in the heyday of the French Revolution, serious doubts were raised as to the possibility of the Jews becoming truly brothers of the peoples of Europe, among whom they lived. The opponents of Jewish emancipation maintained that the Jews were not merely a religious community, but also a separate "nation." The force of this argument is not evident on the surface. After all, there were other nationalities in France—Basques, Italians, and Poles; yet, no one suggested that they be denied equal rights, much less that they be isolated in separate enclaves. But the national character of the Jew was believed to be *sui generis* in its scope, intensity, and mystery. If national feeling is the clue to Jewish survival, then it must be a mystical power of peculiar force, a kind of super-nationalism, bordering on the absolutist fanaticism of religious faith. How else, they argued, could one account for so tiny a minority resisting the many pressures of Church and state? Can a feeling of separatism so strong as to resist the solvent powers of the pagan Roman Empire and the universal sway of the Catholic Church permit the kind of emotional identification that the emergent national fraternity demands? Is there a mysterious, psychic gulf, perhaps even a metaphysical abyss, that separates the Jews from the European Christians? Did not classical historians such as Tacitus and a whole array of Christian theologians postulate such a mythological view of Jewish nature and destiny? Clearly the image of the Jew in Christian lands was covered by a veil of myth and mystery. And many Christians doubted the willingness and capacity of Jews to surrender their traditional identity on the altar of national unity.

The enfranchisement of the Jews by the French National Convention in 1792 was finally effected on the ground of the Rights of Man. As individuals the Jews could not be denied those rights that belonged to all men; however, their national, or communal, character was not recognized.

Well known is the formulation of the French statesman, Clermont-Tonnerre—"to the Jews as individuals, everything; to the Jews as a nation, nothing." The Abbé Grégoire, who led the fight for Jewish rights, discounted the practical significance of the messianic hope:

The prophecies which foretold the dispersion of Israel also pictured the

End of Days when their misfortune will end. But even if we truly remove all their chains before then, they will still remain without an altar (Hosea 3:4), since we do not intend to return Jerusalem to them.[3]

Elsewhere in the same pamphlet, he wrote of the land of Israel as "the land in which they were born and toward which they direct their vision, but which they will never see."

So the specter of Zionism was raised by the reactionaries at the dawn of the French Revolution and repudiated by the friends of Jewish emancipation.

Napoleon, impelled by a heroic sense of history, undertook to solve the Jewish Question once and for all. He convened the Assembly of Notables and later the Paris Sanhedrin and invited them to answer twelve questions. The underlying theme of the questions was precisely this issue—are the Jews willing so to interpret their tradition and so to order their lives as to become brothers of Frenchmen? The Paris Sanhedrin included some Orthodox, deeply learned, and renowned rabbis who saw nothing wrong in concluding "a new covenant with the nations."[4] Accordingly, its members concurred in a festive declaration asserting the eagerness of the Jewish people to become part of the "great nation."

The answers of the Sanhedrin referred frequently to the obligation of Jewish people to cultivate the feelings of fraternity with the Gentiles. They noted the doubts of "the men of France and Italy," as to whether the Jews in their midst regarded them as brothers, and declared that Jews are commanded by the holy Torah to regard Frenchmen and Italians as brothers, since they worship the God of the universe.

> For we are commanded to love and to help the inhabitants of these lands and to order our affairs toward them in the same manner as we do toward those who belong to our faith. [Ordinance 4]
>
> In respect of the love of neighbor, there is no qualification of faith. Hence, we are commanded to love them as friends and brothers, to visit their sick, to bury their dead and to assist their poor as we assist the Jewish poor. [Ordinance 5]
>
> In respect of the obligation to serve in the armed forces of the nation, Jewish soldiers are dispensed from their duty to observe their ritual laws if these conflict with their assignments. [Ordinance 6][5]

In this way, it seemed that the Jewish Question was solved. If, in the light of our present knowledge, we are tempted to minimize this achievement, let us recall that Napoleon was stigmatized as the Antichrist in the military bulletins of the leader of Russia's army, General Kutuzov, because of his according equal rights to Jews.

The hesitations of the French regarding the fitness of Jews for fraternity were multiplied in the case of the Germans. Since the nationalism of the Germans was forged in the fires of the Napoleonic Wars, it was from the beginning anti-French, repudiating the rationalism of the French Enlightenment, which included the emancipation of the Jews. The French Revolution had proclaimed the rule of reason, the rights of the individual, and the establishment of a new society that would not permit any religious discrimination because of religion. In their embittered scorn of all things French, many Germans were inclined to reject rationalism in general and to sink their roots in those vital currents of reality that reason cannot penetrate. They would reveal the organic logic of life that is impervious to the abstract understanding of the shallow peoples—the French, the English, and especially the Jews. As against the rational structure of a liberal democracy, they would continue the slow and ponderous evolution of an organic society, in which all classes are moved by one purpose that is sensed intuitively. Every man knows his station in life and the duties appertaining to that station.

In such an organic society, what place can any stranger have, least of all the Jew, who hails from afar and has always cherished the badge of alienism? Animated by a national soul that eludes the reach of mere reason, he may indeed consent to accept consciously certain conditions that can be formulated in a covenant; he can become part of the national organism only through a metamorphosis of body and soul whereby his subconscious feelings are completely reshaped.

But this inner, total transmutation—how can it ever be judged to have been completed? Thus an insuperable obstacle to Jewish emancipation was raised in Germany, even before the genesis of the mystique of racism.

German romanticism emerged in a series of tidal waves. Perhaps all the seminal ideas were formulated in the first decades of the nineteenth century, but their full impact was not felt before the unification of Germany in 1871. Let us recall that aspect of the movement that posed a special challenge to the exponents of the Jewish faith.

Religion is the articulation of metaphysical "feeling" (*Gefühl*). Schleiermacher inaugurated a new era in German Protestantism when he veered away from the religion of reason and pointed to a unique structure of feeling as the living substance of faith. It is possible for people to orient their feelings toward the Infinite and to sense their total dependence upon this living Whole. Indeed, the noble ideals and vital powers of a nation derive from this fundamental orientation. While philosophers can only speculate about the Absolute, the genuinely religious person experiences the overwhelming power of the Absolute in a shattering immediacy. Then he looks for ways to articulate his life-giving secret. He endeavors to express the inexpressible, to translate in objective and concrete terms that which is intensely subjective and ethereal. To this end, he may employ myths and symbols. How else can the ineffable be articulated? The narrow-hearted and superficial rationalists, however, cannot possibly comprehend the language of religious feeling. They will either take literally the myths and symbols of the religious ecstatic, accepting them blindly as so many dogmas and sacraments. Or they will reject his message totally, particularly if their minds are attuned only to material and practical goals.

In itself, Schleiermacher's message did not offer a challenge to Judaism. He had simply restated with remarkable eloquence the emotional-mystical phase of religion, reminding his contemporaries that religion was a living, endless quest of an eternal mystery, not merely so many beliefs or rites. Yet there were two special points in Schleiermacher's exposition that were of concern to Jewish people. First, his reservations about the contemporary Jews—they belonged with the "logical" French and the "mercenary" English in the category of alien outsiders whose sense of the Infinite has atrophied. In his view, direct apprehension of the Absolute is the mark of true greatness, and only Germans possessed this ability in its fullness. Second, in his exposition of Protestant Christianity, he naturally described Jesus as the man of metaphysical feeling *par excellence*, and by the same token, the Jews were inevitably cast in the role of the archetypal enemy, the shallow rationalist, the unfeeling egotist, the hypocritical fraud who delights in fooling others and ends in fooling himself. The argument between Jesus and the Pharisees was transferred from the realm of exegesis of ancient texts to the domain of psychology, and the supreme tragedy of the past was now seen as a perennial psychological drama in which the hollowness of Jewish character and its inescapable fate were foreshadowed.[6]

In a similar vein, Fichte delivered his famous addresses to the German nation, laying the foundation for the romantic philosophy of German nationalism.[7] Later, in his *Characteristics of the Nineteenth Century*, he expounded at great length an all-embracing philosophy of history. In the domain of universal history, two kinds of people were engaged in a perpetual struggle. And the psychological distance between them was deep and unbridgeable. The first were the people of "intuitive reason" (*Vernunft*). They have an inner sense of metaphysical truth, a serene harmony of values, reacting with silent moral certainty in any situation. They know the way because within their soul the Absolute is revealed. Yet in practical affairs, they may appear to be slow and stolid. In contrast, the men of "practical understanding" (*Verstand*) are quick and clever, eager to achieve success in the affairs of this world. Their shallowness, which makes them blind to the great issues of morality, serves as an advantage in mundane matters. When they venture into philosophy, they ignore the inner truths of metaphysics and present a distorted, superficial image of reality. They are good logic-choppers but devoid of insight. In political philosophy, they are individualists and liberals, operating with the rules of practical understanding, which is utterly incapable of grasping the intricacies of an organic society. The people of practical understanding are the cause of the ills of the time, Fichte concluded, and the millennium will arrive only when the people of intuitive reason attain their deserved place of honor in the international arena. Again, the Jews, along with the French and the English, were considered preeminently the people of practical understanding.

In general, the anti-Jewish posture of the German nationalists was part of a larger, more general anti-western stand.[8] Yet because the image of the Jew was so constantly associated with biblical and medieval mythology, it tended to become archetypical. The other enemies were only partially and temporarily demonic, but the Jew served in that capacity totally and irretrievably.[9]

Completely different in tone and direction was Herder, who is sometimes described, as is Goethe, as a classical author. He expounded the positive implications of the biological approach to peoplehood. In every people, God is revealed in some way. Through the study of its language, literature, and history, it is possible to comprehend the unique pattern of truths and values of any particular folk. In his first work on the philosophy of history he described each folk as a living organism, passing through the stages of genesis, maturity, and decline and generating its own unique values.[10] In his later work on the same theme he posited a unified humanity as the goal of history. Furthermore, he acknowledged that God is revealed through great individuals as well as through the culture of peoples. He projected a bright vision of a steady movement toward a universal culture, achieved by the contribution of diverse nationalities, but it is "a unity of concrete differences," not a grey amalgam.[11] In beautiful and eloquent prose, Herder demonstrated the infinite worth of every folk, since through it the divine goal of humanity is revealed. Every language embodies a kind of revelation, and the Hebrew language, as well as the poetry of the Old Testament, is particularly meaningful because the Bible contains the oldest philosophy of history. The relation of the best of pagan poetry to the Hebrew Bible is like chaff to wheat. The narration of Genesis should be read neither as literal truth nor as a body of primitive beliefs but as a poetic articulation of the wonder of life and the self-revelation of God in the spiritual growth of mankind.[12] But a folk can fail as well as succeed in making its contribution to the emergent universal culture of humanity. It might stop halfway, caught in a mood of self-adulation, and then fall by the wayside as a desiccated empty shell.

Herder's estimate of Judaism was ambivalent. On the one hand, he extolled the vitality of Hebraic culture. On the other hand, he criticized the resistance of Judaism to change and to the intermingling of its values with those of other peoples in the give and take of a free and universal society. As he saw it, the Jewish people "excelled neither in state-matters, nor in war, but least in science and art";[13]

however, it produced the idea of God, which, to his mind, is central to the emergent universal culture of mankind. This tremendous achievement was not without its drawbacks, since religious enthusiasm may preempt the creative powers of a nation and discourage scientific progress. Hebraic ardor for the service of God was, in Herder's view, responsible for the medieval fanaticism of the Church, especially its hostility to scientific research.[14] He may have been the first philosopher to describe the paralyzing effect of an unprogressive religion as being "like an opium of the spirit."[15]

Altogether, the impact of Herder's philosophy was felt in the direction of encouraging the folk aspects of the Jewish faith and welcoming its unique contributions to the emergent, many-faceted treasurehouse of mankind. As he saw it, Judaism was the reflection of the psyche of the Jewish people. At a time when Judaism was stigmatized for the remnants of nationalism that it fostered, Herder criticized the Jewish lack of zeal for national regeneration. He wrote:

> A people that failed in its education because it has never attained political maturity on its own soil and had therefore failed to acquire a true feeling for soil and freedom—almost from the beginning of its emergence it has been more like a parasitic plant on the stems of other nations, a race of cunning merchants spread over the face of the entire earth, which in spite of all kinds of oppression has never sought its own honor and dwelling, nor did it long for a fatherland of its own.[16]

How did Jewish thinkers restructure their self-image in response to the challenge of romanticism and its emphasis on folk feeling? The leaders of Reform and the Jewish liberals generally reacted against the upsurge of romanticism as a reversion to medieval bigotry. It is the rule of reason that will alone create the free society of the future. The dreamy veneration of feeling, ethnic or religious, can only take us back to the crippling fantasies and blinding follies of the Middle Ages. In the perspective of the Reform ideologists, Christianity is, in contrast to Judaism, the religion of sentiment and fantastic imagination. This is why the Christian faith teeters perpetually on the precipice, threatening to fall back into the seductive abyss of pagan mythology. Jewish rationalism is a stern opponent of the vagaries of dreamy sentimentalism. Its absolute rejection of mythology and its uncompromising rationality tend to pull the Christian community from the precipice of the abyss of paganism, reinforcing the Jewish component within the religious life of Christians. Accordingly, the Jewish liberals argued, it is the manifest mission of the Jewish faith to serve as the ferment of rationality within the emergent family of religions in the western world.

In order to fulfill this task, modern Judaism must purge itself of all the vestigial remnants of ancient folk culture and superstition. The time has come for the living kernel of Judaism to function freely for the benefit of mankind. To this end, the Jewish faith must undergo a reformation whereby the shell of observances, customs, and doctrines is discarded in order to uncover and revitalize the living kernel of religious rationalism. True, the protective shell of rigid legalistic tradition was needed in the dark centuries of medievalism, when society was not yet ready for an enlightened faith. But in the age of reason, the genius of Judaism need no longer be hidden from view.

Naturally, the Reformers did not always agree on the exact trajectory of the border between the national and the religious phases of Judaism. What of circumcision, the dietary laws, and the Sabbath? What of the messianic hope, the rebuilding of Zion, and the ingathering of the exiles?

And the Hebrew language—is it "the language of holiness" (*loshon kodesh*), or is it an expression of national loyalty? On the whole, the Reformers agreed that the Hebrew language cannot be regarded as indispensable for Jewish worship. This was the issue that caused Zechariah Frankel and his colleagues to secede from the Reform Conference and to form the Conservative movement.[17] As a language Hebrew was a national rather than a religious asset, especially in Protestant Germany. There was considerable disagreement in the formative period of the Reform movement on the extent to which the messianic hope needed to be purged of its national elements. Some wanted to eliminate the words *Zion* and *Jerusalem* from the Prayer Book. Others were content to retain the words but to endow them with fresh, contemporary, and universal significance. All the Reformers agreed that the essence of Judaism was not the code of laws, regulating the conduct of the faithful Jew, but the body of ideas that had been accumulated through the several millennia of Jewish history.

To identify these ideas and to study their consequences it was necessary to change the character of Jewish learning. The central question was no longer, what is the rule of the law in this or that instance? but, how did this or that law, or idea, or event come to pass? The overall problem was to explicate the full meaning of the monotheistic idea in history and in life. To this end, it was necessary to take account of the entire context of western intellectual and cultural history, revealing the full range of issues on which the world-view of ethical monotheism differed from that of paganism, in all its guises and disguises. Then, in the confrontation with Christianity, it was necessary to trace the lines of agreement and disagreement with the pure monotheistic idea. This vast, indeed endless undertaking, had to be carried out with scientific rigor, for it is only on the plane of reason and scientific research that Judaism and Christianity can find common ground. Hence, the new learning was called "science of Judaism" (*Wissenschaft des Judentums*); it was to provide objective reinforcement for the inner, subjective loyalties of Judaism.[18]

As we understand it today, a Jewish-Christian dialogue was implicit in the very idea of a science of Judaism. Living in a Christian world that was steadily being secularized, the old Bible-centered anti-Jewish ideology was indeed eroding, but as fast as the old ones were giving way, new ideologies were being built up to buttress the myths and fancies of ancient bigotry. The infrastructure of Christian prejudice was largely unconscious, and it projected in the public mind endless apologies for the massive, perverted hatred that could no longer be attributed to the spiteful curse of a loving God. Furthermore, apart from the bitter smog produced by ancient myths, Christianity and Judaism viewed from different angles the common biblical treasure, which both regarded as supremely holy and embraced in whole-souled love. But love is blind, or shall we say, one-sided? Hence, an inevitable dialogue, as the best minds in both camps sought to interpret the same heritage and contemplate it objectively, but from angles of vision that were driven apart by two thousand years of history.

As we noted earlier, the leading Reform philosophers rejected the romantic emphasis on personal feeling and folk-wisdom. In political philosophy, they thought in the liberal terms of citizen and state, as against the romantic terms of folk and national psyche. Yet they did accept the concept of race, which had not yet been corrupted by the inhuman mystique of proto-Nazism. Also some of them recognized the facts of organic growth in history and agreed that the process of Reform must be slow enough to suit the pace of change in the actual life of a historical community. But they could not make peace with what they considered to be the vestigial elements of Jewish tribalism and ritualism. The role of the Jew was to march in the cultural vanguard of mankind, not to be stagnant among the backward elements of the population.[19] In their Reformist ardor, they occasionally provided ammunition for the reactionary opponents of Jewish emancipation.[20]

As to the mystical stream of Jewish thought, the Reformers virtually rejected it out of hand on several grounds. While they acknowledged that Kabbalah is one of the strands of Jewish philosophy, along with those of rationalism and romanticism, they questioned its Jewish authenticity, on a purely monotheistic basis. For Kabbalistic speculation balanced uneasily on a razor's edge, as it were, between a radical acosmism and a virtual dualism, between an ecstatic pietism and a mythological Gnosticism. Furthermore, Kabbalah deepened immensely the gulf between the Jews and the rest of mankind and between the Torah and secular wisdom. It reveled in paradoxes that defied understanding, and it multiplied laws and customs. So, while in the intellectual isolation of eastern Europe Lurianic Kabbalah generated the eighteenth-century mystical mass movement of Hasidism, in the free atmosphere of the western world, Jewish mysticism was scorned among the Conservatives as well as the Reform ideologists. Heinrich Graetz, the leading historian, a Conservative, regarded Kabbalah as an alien, quasi-pagan plant in the Jewish vineyard and Hasidism as a base and degraded form of Jewish piety.[21]

Leopold Zunz, the leading historian and early Reformer, sought to stem the tide of anti-ceremonialism among his early colleagues and disciples. In 1840, he reintroduced the dietary laws in his home, believing that the symbols and rites of Judaism serve to train us in obedience to the will of God. "As sinful humans we all too often cast off those guides that, unbeknown to ourselves penetrate into our lives, urging us to observe commandments and duties, those rites that teach obedience to all who are willing."[22]

Zunz attacked bitterly those who deprecated the rite of circumcision: "As sign of the unity and eternal duration of Israel, a visible act of the transmission and inheritance of the divine law, its omission is decisive for the coming generation."[23] In a letter to Geiger, he asserted: "The criterion of the *religious*, can only be the *religious*—that which, in the stream of the living tradition, is generally accepted and esteemed."[24]

Zechariah Frankel, founder of the Breslau Rabbinical Seminary, sought to counter the ideology of Reform by the principle of fidelity to "the positive-historical" elements in the Jewish tradition. In addition to that of the Torah at Sinai, Frankel postulated a continuous process of revelation that operates within the Jewish community as a whole. Hence, it is the entire community, acting through its recognized leaders, that best reflects the divine will. "There is a kind of revelation also in the general consciousness of a religious community, which, so long as it is vital, enhances the living tradition. This form of revelation should be recognized as immediate and divine."[25]

This ongoing course of divine inspiration may be seen in all great historic faiths; it is progressive, humanistic, but also intuitive. In contrast to the medieval philosopher Judah Halevi, Frankel did not believe that only the Jews were endowed with an intuition for things divine. But he maintained that the unique pattern of religious feeling and ethical ideals, embodied in the institutions and practices of a people, reflects the divine nisus far more faithfully than the abstract cogitations of philosophers. Along with the romanticists, he esteemed the actual evolution of a nation's culture as the effects of Divine Providence.[26]

The Conservative and neo-Orthodox thinkers utilized many of the ideas of the romantic movement for the reinforcement of Jewish loyalty. They argued that one cannot separate the monotheistic content of Judaism from the historical forms it assumed any more than one can separate the soul from the body. Idea and ritual, ethical ardor and the pattern of daily services, inner devotion and the Hebrew language—all these elements have become one organism through the course of history and the agency of Providence. In religion it is the logic of feeling that matters. Hence, only minor changes in form may be allowed, changes that do not affect the process of organic growth within the tradition. With Savigny and the conservative school of thought that he founded, they held that the development of law is not a logical process but an organic one, mirroring the inner ideals of a society.

For the Conservatives also, the new science of Judaism was needed for practical as well as theoretical reasons. They agreed that Judaism was a living tradition, absorbing fresh ideas from the outside world and transforming them in keeping with its own genius. They shared in the conviction that traditional Torah-learning was insufficient, since it did not convey to the Jew an objective understanding of the place of his people in history. For the Jew the philosophic demand "know thyself" implies the study of every phase of Jewish life in the context of universal history.

The Conservatives accepted Herder's view of Judaism as a reflection of the Jewish national psyche. The character of Jewish nationalism was hammered out in the course of the centuries under the aegis of the monotheistic idea. Hence, every aspect of Jewish nationalism is inseparable from the vital current of the pure faith. Jewish worship in the European vernacular is inconceivable, except as additions to the Hebrew text of the liturgy. Zion and Jerusalem as geographic entities, not merely as symbols, belong to the essence of the messianic ideal. The attainment of messianic perfection must include the reestablishment of the Jewish people in their ancient homeland and some form of the ingathering of exiles. Yet the Zionist hope is no impediment to the fullest participation of Jewish people in the affairs of the European nation-states, since the messianic ideal is transhistorical, to be achieved through the agency of Providence.

In general, the romantic ideal of nationalism coincided with the double aspiration of Conservative-minded Jewish leaders. They were eager to deepen the feelings of Jewish ethnic identity, or peoplehood, as the surest way of strengthening the Jewish will to live. At the same time, they shared in the general desire to build a new and open society on the rational basis of the rights of man. Hence, in political matters they sided with the liberals, while in the realm of religious life they elaborated the romantic approach to folk-feeling. If the Germans were stirred by the mystique of Grimm's fairy tales, how much more can Jews find depths of meaning in their own legends, the Aggadot, created as they were by the psyche of a monotheistic people. Indeed, the entire life of the Jewish people could be read as one long commentary on the text of monotheism, and the text was unintelligible without the commentary.

Throughout the nineteenth century, the Conservative ideologists remained unsympathetic to Kabbalah and to its offspring, the Hasidic movement in eastern Europe. The Italian scholar and philosopher, Samuel David Luzzato (1800–1865) wrote a critical study of Kabbalah, suggesting that it was alien to the genius of Jewish monotheism.[27] At the turn of the twentieth century, however, Solomon Schechter, the founder of the Conservative movement in America, undertook a fundamental revision of this attitude. In a series of beautiful essays, he wrote appreciatively of the ideal of saintliness among the Kabbalists and the Hasidim.[28]

Perhaps the most typical romantic among the nineteenth-century Conservatives was the aforementioned Samuel David Luzzato. A renowned scholar and historian, he combatted vigorously what he considered to be the rationalistic distortion of the character of Judaism. Essentially, he argued, Judaism is not a religion of reason at all, but the "religion of compassion," with all the facets of life being seen through the perspective of an all-embracing sympathy. Compassion (*Hemlah*) is man's response to the felt presence of God, Who is conceived as the Compassionate One (*Hormahmon*). It endeavors to subjugate and control the natural impulses of men, which are variations of the basic instinct for self-preservation. Compassion is an echo in man's heart of God's will, His supernatural revelation.[29]

Luzzato saw two stages of supernatural revelation—the Abrahamite, directed to all men, and superimposed upon it the Mosaic, directed to the Jewish people. The former was carried into universal history through the agency of Christianity and Islam. The latter was designed both to reinforce Abrahamism and to perpetuate the Jewish people as the unfailing fountainhead of divine revelation. All of history could be seen as a struggle between Abrahamism, the philosophy of compassion, and Atticism, the arrogant assertion of man's intellectuality. We can leave it to Providence, working in its own mysterious ways, to assure the ultimate triumph of Abrahamism in the messianic era. But until that glorious consummation, it is the task of the Jewish people to assure its own survival as a people dedicated to Mosaism, preserving the kernel of divine revelation in behalf of all men.

The bright figure of Maimonides, which was idolized by Jewish intellectuals, was to Luzzato a negative signpost warning of a wrong turn in the course of Jewish scholarship. For Maimonides proudly introduced Hellenism into the inner sanctum of Jewish thought. Particularly in his interpretation of the "reasons for the commandments," Maimonides explained the purpose of all ritual observances in terms of general, ethical principles, applicable to the lives of all men. In Luzzato's view, Maimonides was guilty of overlooking the specific, unique worth of every facet of Jewish life. For example, he gave a historical explanation of the laws of sacrifice and the laws of purity—they were designed to counter the attraction of certain pagan practices. On this view, Luzzato argues, one might conclude that their pedagogical purpose has been fulfilled in our day. Maimonides himself did not draw this inference, but he maintained that the Holy Temple and all that took place within it was of secondary significance.[30] To Luzzato, the prime purpose of the temple cult in Jerusalem was to deepen the feelings of humble piety and to reinforce the awareness of God's love for His unique and holy people.

Like the romantics Luzzato saw intellectuality as the evil principle of history. It encouraged individuals and nations to alienate themselves from their cultural roots and to wander as unredeemed skeptics and cynics in a moral wasteland. Men in the Middle Ages may have been poor, but at least they were then humble and pious. Instead of welcoming the age of emancipation, Luzzato called for an "inner reform," whereby Jews would learn to recognize the vanity of modern idols. "Not emancipation is our good fortune but the perfect solidarity of our people, like the feelings of kinship, which knit a family together. This feeling is lost in the process of emancipation."[31]

Luzzato lived far from the great centers of Jewish life, where the issue of emancipation was a daily and bitter struggle. For this reason he could represent the recurrent mood of Jewish romanticism, which recoiled from the realities of a decayed degenerate Europe. Jewish romanticism imagined that all the ills of modern culture were due to sickly, shallow rationalism, which caused Jewish youth to forsake their heritage and to wander disconsolately as unwanted guests at the parties of strangers. Luzzato advised the renowned philanthropist, Moses Montefiore, not to offer scholarships to Jewish youths in Near Eastern countries to enable them to study in the great universities of western Europe—they would only be corrupted by the seductive temptations of modern city life. Instead, he counseled Montefiore to establish agricultural colonies in the land of Israel, where young Jews might be enabled to build an organic society permeated completely by the spirit of the Torah. To Luzzato, the culture of Europe was perverted; only by returning to their own land could Jews reestablish their own unique, God-ordained way of life. Long before Herzl, the modern Zionist ideal occurred spontaneously to many a romantic dreamer.

In the first half of the nineteenth century, the influence of German romanticism on Jewish Orthodoxy was most clearly exemplified in the work of Samson Raphael Hirsch (1808–1888). As a child of the Enlightenment, he believed that a new era of redemption had begun in 1789: the French Revolution was "one of those events in which God entered into history"[32] and the wave of revolutions in Europe in 1848 was an expression of "the light of God in the heart of man."[33] In addition to the revelation at Sinai, an "inner revelation" was deposited in the hearts of all men. This divine power is articulated in the quest of truth and justice and in the feeling of our dependence on the Supreme Being. It is not in man's abstract reasoning that the divine is revealed, but in the yearnings of man's heart and in the silent speech of nature.

But while God is revealed in physical nature and in human nature, the definitive revelation is contained in the Torah of Jewish people, the oral and written laws. Hirsch viewed Torah-revelation as a direct parallel to the revelation of God in the cosmos. Both are given to us as incontrovertible facts: we cannot deduce the laws and principles implicit in them by abstract reasoning. A genuine science of Judaism would parallel physical science, in his view, rather than the abstractions of philosophy and mathematics. With pre-Darwinian naïveté, Hirsch inferred from the beauty and harmony of nature the universal sway of love—"thus one glorious chain of love, of giving and receiving, unites all creatures; none is by and for itself, but all things exist in continued reciprocal activity—the one for the All; the All for the One."[34] All of nature testifies directly to the presence of God. In man, this testimony rises to the threshold of consciousness. "The law to which all powers submit unconsciously and involuntarily, to it shalt thou also subordinate thyself, but consciously and of thy own free will. 'Knowledge and freedom,' these words indicate at once the sublime mission and the lofty privilege of man."[35]

But in Hirsch's world, freedom does not mean the autonomy of man's mind and conscience, à la Kant, but man's willingness to play his part in the divine scheme of redemption, a part spelled out for the Jew in the Torah and the Talmud. As to the rest of mankind, Hirsch considered Christianity a divinely mandated religion for Gentiles, over and above the inner revelation that is granted to all men.

On the very eve of the exile (i.e. in the first century of our era), a branch left the parent tree, which was obliged to surrender largely the characteristics of the parent stem, in order to bring to the world, which had relapsed into polytheism, violence, immorality and inhumanity, the tidings of the existence of the All-One and of the brotherhood of man and his superiority to the beast, and to proclaim the deliverance of mankind from the bondage of wealth and lust-worship. Assisted greatly by this offshoot in rendering intelligible to the world the objects and purposes of Israel's election, the nation was scattered into the four quarters of the earth, unto all peoples and all zones, in order that in the dispersion it might better fulfill its mission."[36]

So the role of Christianity is to help prepare the way for the realization of Israel's mission. But Israel itself must fence itself off from the nations in order to proclaim fidelity to the One God.[37] In the wisdom of Providence, Israel was scattered among the nations, where, purged in "the school of suffering," it served as a witness of God. "Israel accomplished its task better in exile than in the full possession of good fortune. Indeed improvement and correction were the chief purposes of exile."[38]

Hirsch rejected the call of the early Zionists—Kalisher, Luzzato, Moses Hess and Graetz, for a return to Zion. He fought bitterly against the Reformers, enjoining his followers to secede from the organized Jewish communities that included Reform and Conservative people. He inveighed against Maimonides, who set reason up as the criterion for interpreting the Torah, and against the Kabbalists, whom he blamed for the rites of Judaism becoming for many people, "through misconception, a magical mechanism, a means of influencing or resisting theosophic worlds and anti-worlds."[39]

As a romanticist, Hirsch set speech above logic. On the assumption that Hebrew was the original tongue of mankind, he proceeded to interpret the Hebrew Bible by means of a "philosophical etymology."[40] Like Friedrich Schlegel (1772–1829), who coined this phrase, Hirsch sought to uncover the hidden truths in the sacred tongue. To this end, he disregarded the principles of linguistics and concentrated attention on the similarity of sounds. If Fichte could speak of German as an original tongue (*Ursprache*), why not plumb the depths of the language that the Lord Himself employed in creating the cosmos?[41]

In his commentary on the Five Books of Moses, Hirsch maintained that the universe was not only the best possible, but "the actual best," since it was the product of God's Will. Mankind was originally monotheistic (Genesis 1:1), but it then declined into polytheism (Genesis 4:2). Like Fichte, he saw the course of history as declining downward from a high peak and then slowly, painfully ascending up to another summit.

In Hirsch's view, however, the Torah is already at the highest possible peak of human achievement; hence, the people of Israel are situated at the goal toward which the nations are steadily rising. The goals of humanism in his day were stepping stones toward the redeemed humanity of the future, which he called *Yisroeltum*.

If it is to come to pass that the existence of this people is to be a second creation of God's in history, then this people can only come to be a nation by way of homelessness, of *galuth* (exile) and *gerut* (alienism) . . . The Abrahamic nation is to know nothing of these national institutions, is to have no national politics and no national economy.[42]

Secular nationalism was, to Hirsch, an abomination, possibly because he saw the evil outcropping of xenophobia in the 1880s. Far from describing the Torah as the national heritage of the Jewish people, he maintained that the Torah was imposed on them in order to demonstrate that there was no race that could not be molded by it. "The victory of godliness was to begin with the stubbornest race and the stubbornest soul." (Genesis 12:7). Even so, the course of redemption required that Jews leave their homeland, give up the struggle for power and pride, and become apostles of a penitent humanity.

To Hirsch, the glory of Jewish life in exile is that while Jews have often enough been victims, they have never been the victimizers. (Genesis 14:12) Hence, they could demonstrate the virtue of faithfulness. Indeed, Jews were not enjoined to believe *that* certain ideas were true, but to believe *in* God—that is, to put their trust in Him, utterly and without reservations. (Genesis 15:6) Hirsch's piety is reminiscent of Schleiermacher's feeling of total dependence. But while the Protestant theologian extolled the beauty of religious feeling, the rabbi glorified the performance of divine mandates as action-symbols of surrender to the divine will.

As we survey the writings of Samson Raphael Hirsch today, we recognize that he was a son of the German Romanticism which prevailed in his youth, almost as much as he was a product of the millennial Jewish tradition. His insistence on pursuing his idea, whithersoever it led, even to the verge of separatism from the community, his glorification of sentiment as well as his determined opposition to the resurgence of secular nationalism—these were all stamped with the seal of nineteenth-century ideologies. Yet the one guiding line in all his writings was fidelity to the Torah of Israel. The implacable opponent of alien influences was a child of his age, in his affirmations as in his negations.

IV. *Are the Jews "Ahistorical"?*

The history of the Jewish people presents a peculiar challenge to all historians of the western world. It is a history ambivalent in respect to time, space, religion, progress, and the emergent greater society. Here is a people whose roots go far deeper into the past than those of any other western people: their history is a miracle of survival. Yet if a people's life be measured in terms of power and polities, it lacked both dimensions during the major span of its life and it survived only in memories and dreams, or so it seemed to nineteenth-century observers. Dispersed in the lands of Europe, the Near East, and Northern Africa, it was still somehow, to itself and to its foes, a living reality, transcending political boundaries. As a religion Judaism molded the minds of millions; yet as a people, the Jews seemed to be the relic of a distant past.

So even an objective historian would encounter special difficulties in his efforts to include the Jewish people within the categories of a universal theory of progress. And it is most difficult to remain completely objective in the face of the many-faceted Jewish reality. Fundamentalist Christian historians found a ready-made categorization of Jewish history in the standard manuals and catechisms of their faith: the Jews had been chosen by God for the noblest mission, but they had proved unworthy; again and again, they rejected their own great men and capped their catalog of sins by their repudiation of the Son of God, whereupon they were condemned to the punishment of Cain—they were driven by a mysterious power to wander over the face of the earth, to be every-where homeless, uprooted, hated; only in the end of days, when they will acknowledge their sin and accept their Savior, will they find peace.

102

Since even anti-Christian historians were raised from childhood on this tissue of fables, they could not completely free themselves from this mythological miasma whenever they proceeded to write about Jews. Voltaire, for example, was educated in a Jesuit college, and the large library that he assembled reflected anti-Jewish hostility.

Furthermore, the champions of a new humanism found their inspiration in Imperial Rome and in the Stoic philosophy. But when Voltaire and his philosophical colleagues sought to escape from Christian fanaticism to what they thought to be the free atmosphere of classical, pre-Christian Europe, they discovered that even in that era Jews were the objects of disdain and hostility. Mighty Rome, which had established a universal society of peace, order, and religious tolerance, encountered endless difficulties in dealing with the Jews. Twice, the Roman legions devastated Palestine; yet, somehow, as Tacitus put it, "the conquered conquered their conquerors," imposing a version of their own faith upon the Roman Empire.

Classical authors such as Cicero, Juvenal, and Tacitus painted the Jews as a peculiarly disgusting people who refused to share in the universal tolerance of the pagan world. Tacitus was a particularly beloved author to the Germans, since in the nostalgic mood of the over-civilized dreaming of the simplicities of life among the "noble savages" of the forest, he had written an idealized and romanticized portrait of the primitive Teutons. Could the Germans doubt his description of the Jews as a people of religious zealots who were determined to shatter the gods of all other nations and infect them with their own peculiar fanaticism? In that ideal age of apparently universal concord, the Jews seemed to be the only holdouts, filled with a "hatred of mankind" (*odium generis humani*), and, as many a secularist historian saw it, they bequeathed their peculiar zealotry to the Christian Church, the rightful heir of the Roman Empire.

So whether a historian drew his inspiration from Christian sources or from the works of classical authors, he encountered a similar image of a hateful, self-isolating people, the victim of the historical repercussions of its own fanatical delusions and of the just retribution of its neighbors. In whichever literary direction modern historians moved, wavering between the claims of Christianity and classical secularism, they were likely to find reinforcement for a hostile view of the Jewish people. It required a bold and original mind to overcome these stereotypes.

Furthermore, historians were likely to be ideologists as they still are today, propagating a philosophy of public life for their contemporaries. As propagandists for a Christian state, they were naturally tempted to stigmatize the invariant non-Christian in their midst as the enemy. Or, as anti-Christian prophets of a totally secular society, they might be tempted to undermine the entire edifice of Christianity by attacking its Jewish foundations—Spinoza, who had set out to establish the outlines of a free and open society, described in the most scornful terms the Israelites of the biblical period.

Edward Gibbon's *Decline and Fall of the Roman Empire* was a brilliant effort to recreate the image of "the grandeur that was Rome." With consummate artistry, Gibbon brought to life the splendid saga of the ancient empire, which succeeded in overcoming the ethnic hatreds and the religious differences that drive nations apart. As is well known, he attributed the fall of the empire to two causes—barbarism and religion. It was Jewish zealotry in the shape of nascent Christianity, that captured the minds of the Roman proletariat and destroyed the martial spirit of the Roman legions.

To be sure, there is no evidence that Christian soldiers were less courageous than their pagan colleagues, nor that the numerous semi-converts of Judaism, the so-called fearers of the Lord, were unpatriotic. The converts to Judaism in the first century, whatever their number, were caught in a quandary only during the time when a war between Rome and Judea broke out. But then at the time of the Great Revolt (65–70 c.e.) Jewish soldiers in Agrippa's army fought on the side of Rome.

The so-called zealotry of Christianity, its endeavor to impose a uniform system of dogmas was by no means Jewish in inspiration. While Jews did impose their faith on the mixed population of Palestine during the first pre-Christian century, they limited their concern to the borders of the Holy Land. Outside its borders, Jewish propaganda was directed chiefly toward the abandonment of idolatry and the acceptance of the Noachian Laws.[1]

Hegel's philosophy of history posed a special challenge to Jewish thinkers. In his early essays on theological matters, Hegel gave expression to the common clichés regarding the Jewish people. At that time, he regarded all "positive" religions, the Jewish as well as the Christian and Moslem faiths, as clerical attempts to enslave the human mind.

As his own "dialectical" philosophy took shape, Georg Hegel (1770–1831) projected several powerful ideas that were to become part of the intellectual history of the western world. First, spirit is essentially dynamic, with the basic category of existence being the notion of becoming, which mediates between being and nonbeing. Hence, vitality and greatness are not found in static positions, however pure and lofty, but in movement and change. The principle of movement is negation, the inherent drive of any ideal, which leads by way of its own impetus first to its negation and then to a new idea.

Second, the true philosophy is the history of philosophy. To be sure, the history of philosophy does not consist in a series of portraits of diverse world views. Rather, it is the progressive unfolding of spirit, as it is represented in the great ideas of past ages; in each stage of its unfolding, the ideas of the preceding stage are comprehended and transcended. This entire course of development aims at the attainment of absolute freedom, in which the individual discovers his own identity with God.

Third, this quest of philosophy is the clue to the actual history of mankind. "The rational is the real." In history each idea brings about its own frustration and the emergence of a higher idea, which is really the synthesis of earlier affirmations and negations. So "the cunning of reason" (*List der Vernunft*) makes use of the passions of individuals to achieve its own progressive development. The account of the rise of man from Cain and Abel to the Napoleonic Wars appears to be a long and monotonous recital of brutal horrors, senseless wars, mass delusions and endless follies. Yet from a higher viewpoint, it is possible to see the unfolding of reason beneath the bloody conflicts. Freedom was achieved in ever greater measure, from the beginning of the biblical period to the present—freedom in religion, in culture, and in the constitution of the state.

Fourth, in religion man seeks communion with God, Who is grasped by means of constructs of the imagination (*Vorstellung*). The myths of primitive peoples reflect their enslavement to nature and tribal customs. As peoples rise on the ladder of freedom, their myths grow with them, reflecting the new reality. In the ancient Orient, only one man was free, the king. This political reality was adumbrated in the Olympian mythology and in the imaginative vitality of Greek culture. In the Hebraic faith, the One God represented absolute freedom, and His chosen people were totally enslaved to His will; the Jewish faith, therefore, sounded the high tones of sublimity, reflecting man's infinite distance from God. Hegel at times placed Judaism before Hellenic religion, as a lower stage, and at times after it, as a later stage. In either case, he described Christianity as the Absolute Religion, in which man becomes one with God. To be sure, the Catholic Church, according to Hegel, subverted the true meaning of the Gospels, and humanity was compelled to undergo the dark medieval period, which reflected "the unhappy self" of man. In his view, the Reformation of Luther and the rationality of Kant prepared the ground for the consummation of all phases of culture— in religion, in philosophy, in art, and in politics.

The dialectic of Hegel was an instrument of extreme plasticity as well as subtlety. It was not difficult for his disciples to employ their master's dialectic in a way that contradicted Hegel's own conclusions. As a matter of fact, soon after Hegel's death, his disciples split into opposing camps. The Right-Hegelians interpreted his philosophy as a total endorsement of the status quo in Protestant Prussia, where "freedom" meant the voluntary and total submission of the citizen to the power and glory of the "organic" state. And political conservatism went hand in hand at that time with religious conservatism. Hegel could be interpreted as a conservative in both fields. Did he not claim that Christianity was the Absolute Religion? Hegel's God was manifested in the career of great states as well as in great ideas. God stands' beyond the world and enters it through revelation and through the succession of power states. In fact, Hegel's magnificent achievements could be read as an endorsement of an authoritarian form of government as well as a demonstration of the truth of religion, à la the *Summa* of Thomas Aquinas.

In respect of religion, Hegel claimed that philosophy was the speculative unfolding of that which faith grasps in the immediacy of its feelings and creative imagination. "The Absolute Idea may be compared to the old man, who utters the same religious doctrines as the child, but for whom they signify his entire life. The child in contrast may understand the religious content. But, all of life and the whole world still exist outside it."[2] "Religion can exist without philosophy, but philosophy cannot exist without religion. For it encompasses religion."[3]

The Right-Hegelians argued that Hegel had established the inner unity of religious mysticism and the boldest flights of reason: " . . . the mystical, as synonymous with the speculative, is the concrete unity of those determinations that the understanding accepts as true only in the separation and opposition."[4] He had given philosophical meaning to the Christian dogma of the incarnation, as the unity of man and God. Since the incarnation was "necessary" for the unfolding of the life of God in human history, it could be regarded as a fact of history. Similarly, Hegel had given fresh meaning to the dogma of the Trinity in its speculative sense as being God in Himself, in the world, and in the spirit that unites them, and to the Trinity in its historical meaning as God in Himself, God becomes man, and the spirit. The bond between the two Trinities is love.

Hegel had dismissed the regnant school in German theology, that of Schleiermacher, with the caustic comment: " . . . if the feeling of absolute dependence is the essence of religion, then a dog would be the best Christian." But he had praised Luther as the one who had established religious freedom, which is the basis of political freedom. To Hegel, freedom is not the simple availability of alternatives for the individual but the congruence of man's will with the contemporary stage of the universal spirit. In his view, the French Revolution failed precisely because its thinkers and movers conceived of freedom in a purely secular way. But then the French had not experienced the glory of the Reformation, which brought God into the human heart. It is the state that makes possible the freedom of the individual, "in his inner life"—that is, in religion, art, and philosophy. Spirit is revealed in the life of the great power states, and "the morality of the individual man consists in knowing the duties of his station, and these are easy to know."[5]

Here, then, is a conservative Christian philosophy, articulated in terms of the most rigorous demands of reason. The nineteenth-century ideologies of a Christian state, which severely limited the role of Jews in public life, owed much to this Right-Hegelian philosophy. It was also a contributing factor to the Kultur-Kampf of the 1870s, which was directed against the Catholics. Their Germanism was imperfect and questionable, since they had not profited from the German revolution, that is, from Luther's Reformation. So, writing at the turn of the century, Adolf Harnack still identified Protestantism as the expression of Germanic genius.

> The question has often been raised whether, and to what extent, the Reformation was a work of the *German* spirit. But this much seems to me to be certain, that while we cannot, indeed, connect Luther's momentous religious experiences with his nationality, the results, positive as well as negative, with which he invested them display the German—the German man and German history. From the time that the Germans endeavored to make themselves really at home in the religion handed down to them—this did not take place until the thirteenth century onwards—they were preparing the way for the Reformation . . .[6]

The Left-Hegelians interpreted their master's teaching as implying the necessary dissolution of all historical religions. Since religion and politics are expressions of the same dynamic spirit, it is impossible to establish a truly free society, while the spirit of submission and slavery, implicit in Judaism and Catholicism, and residually even in Protestantism, continues to exert its hold upon the minds of a portion of the population. The Left-Hegelians interpreted the meaning of God in an immanentist sense—that is, God symbolizes the evolving spirit of man. As Ludwig Feuerbach (1804–1872) put it, "*homo hominem deus est.*" The ultimate stage of religious development is atheistic humanism, whose slogan might well be, "God is dead, now man is free."

Yet, the Left-Hegelians contended, it is not the individual person that is or can be free, in the French or English sense of this term. Since the spirit of humanity unfolds in the life of the state, it is the organic state, wherein the individual's interest and that of the state coincide, that becomes the embodiment of the Supreme Being. And this all-inclusive state does not tolerate any independent enclaves of any kind. "Truth is the whole," and any deviation from the whole is an intolerable heresy.

The absolutization of the state was an enduring legacy of Hegelianism. Many German historians assumed that it is through the great and dominant states that the World Spirit articulates its meaning; hence, states cannot be judged by any ethical standards. And all their policies, in war and peace, are related to a unique aspect of the Absolute. There is no room in this political perspective for any partial or contingent loyalties. Diverse subcultures must not participate in the life of the state. The English-American view of the political state as being the traffic officer of society, unobtrusive and impersonal, interfering as little as possible with the lives of the citizens and their ultimate concerns, was stigmatized by post-Hegelian writers as atomistic, shallow "manchesterism." No, the state is an all-inclusive, organic being, with all its parts reflecting the life of the whole. Even the inner reservations of citizens are treason, for the spirit of the state must govern the minds and hearts of its citizens, allowing no private islands of thought, sentiment, or action. The state does not merely impose external obligations upon its citizens. It demands of its sons that they internalize their duties as sacred, inviolate commandments. In a real, inner sense, religion and politics are inseparable. It is obvious that any such absolutist state would barely tolerate a community that cherished its own historic identity and its bonds of fellowship with people living in other countries.

If this logic sounds Stalinist, its beginnings and only its beginnings were already apparent in the generation of Bruno Bauer, Ludwig Feuerbach, and the young Karl Marx. The evolution of German historicism, which removed public policy from the restraints of the laws of morality, owed much to the Left-Hegelians. They abandoned the notion of Providence in history and insisted that every state generated its own values and moral standards. Unlike Kant, Hegel did not believe in a society of nations, and his brightest disciples tended to transform the ideal of the secular state into an all-devouring idol.

Judaism was challenged by both Right and Left Hegelianism. In the version of the Right-Hegelians, the new philosophy implied that whatever emerged later in time was best, especially if it could lay claim to a synthesis of all previous stages. Judaism had emerged in an early period, it was only a phase in the life of spirit, it could not claim to represent the totality of spirit; hence, it was a relic of the past, or to use the phrase Arnold Toynbee made popular in our day, a fossil.

Furthermore, the remnants of medievalism can only be removed by the silent subterranean processes of history, which transform society at a glacial, deliberate pace. Savigny and his school scorned the liberal movements of the West, including the progressive emancipation of the Jews, as artificial and harmful. We must not hurry history along in disregard of its natural, organic growth.

In the version of the Left-Hegelians, all historic religions were intolerable hindrances to the emerging free society. Judaism, as the foundation of both Protestantism and Catholicism, was a particularly good target of attack by the new atheists. For if the foundation is demolished, the superstructure will fall of its own account.

To the historian Bruno Bauer (1809–1882), Christianity was a form of intellectual slavery. The total rejection of Christianity is a pre-condition for social progress. "The terrorism of pure theory must clear the ground clean."[7] "Personal and social salvation can only be found through 'critical love' and the 'serenity of knowledge.' "[8] In his quest of an atheistic messianic age, Bauer opposed bitterly any relaxation of anti-Jewish laws.

The philosopher Ludwig Feuerbach, apostle of anthropomorphism, described Christianity as the alienation of man's true religion, which is the awareness of the sanctity of man, the I-Thou relation. He extolled the holiness of mankind, but he scorned Judaism on account of its entanglement with Jewish nationalism. Thus he wrote: "*The Israelitish religion is the religion of the most narrow-hearted egoism.* Even the later Israelites, scattered throughout the world, persecuted and oppressed, adhered with immoveable firmness to the egoistic faith of their forefathers."[9]

The response of Jewish thinkers to the double-pronged Hegelian challenge was based on the historic themes of Jewish philosophy: first, the emphasis on divine supremacy and God's creation of the cosmos out of nothing; second, the sanctity of the individual and his freedom; third, the limits of human understanding; fourth, the infinite evil of idolatry or paganism. While the Jewish thinkers learned much from the titans of philosophy of their day, they did not abandon the insights of their own philosophic tradition. And these ideals of their religious heritage afforded them a secure base from which they could resist the threatening embrace of the new Moloch and the resurgent idolatry of the folk, or the state. In turn, their subjective tradition was reinforced by their objective experience. Their position as outsiders in German culture enabled them to absorb its creative genius while rejecting its peculiar excesses, and to effect a synthesis between the ongoing stream of Jewish philosophy and the new approaches.

Of the three responses that we shall here consider, Samuel Hirsch (1815–1889) and Solomon Formstecher (1808–1889) were not as firmly embedded in the traditional soil of Jewish thought as Nahman Krochmal, who lived and worked in southern Poland, on the outer fringe of German culture and within the folk culture of eastern European Jewry.

The Jewish theologians Formstecher and Hirsch wrote as children of the nineteenth century, not as defenders of a pre-Christian religion. They challenged the Hegelians of both wings by their very modernity. Their Judaism was neither encased in a shell of dogmas nor frozen in unvarying customs. It was not in any sense a dated phase of the World Spirit. They were heirs of a philosophic tradition, which, with some interruptions and digressions into Kabbalah, continued to take account of contemporary challenges down to their own time. In fact, they believed that, beginning with Mendelssohn and the age of the emancipation, Judaism had entered a new age of self-knowledge and growth. Kant, it will be recalled, maintained that his own generation was the greatest age of Christianity. Similarly, the Reform Jewish philosophers set themselves the double task of idealizing the Jewish faith and demonstrating the truth of its creative core. Only in the new age of freedom, they believed, will the universal significance of Judaism be fully realized.

Hegel assumed that truth is the whole; hence, we may expect to find it only in the movement that aims to synthesize the totality of previous thought. Such a yardstick would hardly do justice to Judaism, which had rejected all forms of paganism. Throughout the ages, Judaism scorned the seduction of syncretism for the sake of pure, divine truth. Formstecher and Hirsch take religious truth to be the self-revelation of God in history, with the demands of ethics constituting the decisive standards of revelation. "He hath told thee, O Man, what is good" (Micah 6:8). This truth is universal in the sense that it accords with the conscience of humanity; furthermore, in the course of time it is certain to win universal assent.

Schiller postulated that the feeling of the beautiful leads to the core of reality. "There is no other way to make the man of the senses rational than to make him esthetic first."[10] The human imagination attains creativity and truth when it achieves a perfect balance between passion and form. In those moments of dynamic equilibrium, the "playful impulse" (*Spieltrieb*) manifests itself, corresponding to the playfulness of an animal, giving expression to the abundance of its vitality. Similarly, Hegel agreed with Schelling that the esthetic sense was the organon of metaphysical truth.

The Jewish philosophers could not but regard this emphasis on esthetics as a revival of the genius of Hellenism. In keeping with the thrust of prophecy and Kantian philosophy, they insisted that ethics was the vital essence of spirit. For them the basic polarity was between paganism and Judaism, corresponding to the polarity between Nature and Spirit. Man may either see himself in the light of Nature, or Nature in the light of himself. Within Nature, all events are organized in keeping with the inner chains of necessity. In the human spirit, freedom is the governing principle. Paganism saw man's life and destiny in the perspective of Nature. Hence, a plurality of gods was assumed, gods that lived in a carefree, "natural" way, contending against one another. Yet a blind, inexorable shadow of fate hangs over the gods, whose doom is certain and terrible. And fate is the reflection of the unvarying laws of nature. Paganism is either polytheistic, atheistic, or pantheistic. In each case, it sees evil as a cosmic force. It is grimly fatalistic, and in personal life it is either sensuous or ascetic. In either case, it assigns only a minor role to the demands of the moral life, to penitence and forgiveness.

Hellenism, or rather popular Hellenic religion, was the brightest expression of paganism in history. But the Greek philosophers leaned to the Jewish position. "When Anaxagoras and Socrates, and later

Plato, arrived at a concept of spirit, or deity independent of nature, they passed from paganism to Judaism."[11]

In this judgment, Formstecher followed the lead of the Hellenistic Jews, who saw the philosophers as their allies in the battle against paganism. Judaism asserts its belief in the One God, who stands above and beyond nature. Its basic axiom is *creatio ex nihilo*, a belief which draws a cosmic gulf between God and Nature. To be sure, God is also revealed partially in Nature as the World-Soul, but He remains transcendent to it. As the master of Nature, evil is included as an instrument in His grand design, but Satan is not an independent force. The free God reveals Himself continuously throughout history in ever greater thrusts toward freedom. Man is free to choose between freedom, the perfect unity of body and mind, and the slavery of the mind. Upon his choice as an individual, the realization of God's call depends. Spirit aims to overcome man's native paganism, to subdue man's body and soul to its own precepts, and to attain complete self-consciousness, in the course of history. But, it is either actualized or repudiated in the lives of individuals, not in the careers of states. Indeed, it is only the individualistic nineteenth century that made possible the full unfolding of the human spirit. The decisive turning point is in the passage from the pagan to the Jewish way of thinking.

Reviewing the course of Jewish history, Formstecher made the following points: While Egypt had achieved, under the leadership of Ikhnaton, a kind of physical monotheism, Moses taught the Israelites to accept ethical monotheism as their national faith. As Hegel taught, Spirit seeks to be articulated in the constitution and operation of a state. Moses proceeded to formulate in the Torah the constitution of a state, embodying his principles. The low state of religion in the early biblical period led King Solomon to build the Holy Temple. The system of sacrifices in the temple was a necessary phase in the evolution of the Spirit. But the very existence of a house of God posed the danger of idolatry: people might think that God was indeed imprisoned in His house. Hence, "the dialectical necessity" of the breakup of the Solomonic kingdom and the worship of the golden calves in Beth El and Dan. Later, when the mighty labors of the prophets had prepared the people for a nonpolitical existence, the kingdom of Israel was no longer essential for the life of Judaism, and it disappeared from history.[12] The prophets had done their work well. Their vision of a messianic state had made an earthly state superfluous.[13] So, the kingdom fell apart, as the shell bursts when the seed is ripe. Formstecher quoted approvingly the words of Jesus, "My Kingdom is not of this world." (Luke 17:21)

When the bright culture of Hellenism inundated the Near East, the very existence of Judaism was threatened, since the Greeks represented the highest pinnacle of paganism. In accordance with Hegelian "cunning of reason," the world-spirit in Judaism had to make some concessions in order to prevail. Accordingly, it adopted some Gnostic elements in its esoteric tradition, or what might be called proto-Kabbalah. Philo's concept of the Logos, of the "second god," of the Trinity and the rabbinic notion of the *Shechinah*, whereby God's Presence is personalized and brought close to the feelings of the people—all these are devices of the Spirit, that stoops in order to conquer. In fact, both Formstecher and Hirsch classified Philo as a marginal Jewish figure, who trotted out pagan ideas in a Jewish dress.[14]

Both Christianity and Islam became the instruments of the World Spirit in the subjugation of the pagan world. They made the kind of concessions to paganism that Judaism was unable to make because of its advanced monotheistic faith. In Christianity, pagan metaphysics was combined with the divine thrust of prophetic ethics. In Islam, the pagan elements are fatalism, blind belief, physical imagery of immortality, and a state of torpor generally. Accordingly, Formstecher pointed out, Christianity is best suited for the peoples of the north, Islam for the cultures of the south. But the same evolving Spirit, conveying its message through the course of reason in history, ordained that the Jewish people continue to follow their own pathway with absolute fidelity.[15]

Formstecher held that in the Christian world, the greatest forward thrust of the spirit was manifested in the Reformation, when the Jewish spirit triumphed over the residual vestiges of paganism in the Christian way of life. Thereafter, development was rapid. In the light of world history, it is evident that Christianity and Islam were given the mission of extensive dissemination of ethical monotheism, while the Jewish community was charged with the task of keeping the faith, in its purity, with absolute fidelity.

To fulfill its role, Formstecher believed that Judaism must undergo a Reform, in which its "protective armor" of rituals is abandoned. Required for survival in the dark ages of fanaticism and oppression, this regimen of *mizvot* is now a superfluous burden, which occasionally hides the true light of Judaism.

Manifestly, Formstecher's exposition, for all its brilliance, was one-sided. In his enthusiasm for the dynamic expansion of pure and practical reason, he scorned the emotional and imaginative phases of religion. In his eagerness to justify the role of Judaism as the religion of the future, he repudiated as pagan the feelings and symbols of God's nearness. The only role of faith was to make the leap from Nature-bound paganism to the life of the Spirit—that is, Judaism in its purity. The pattern of daily observances of the faith was to him expendable. Like so many of the early Reformers, he transformed the flesh and blood of Judaism into a pale ghost of reason, in order to meet the challenge of Christian life and thought. But as a philosopher of history, he had developed an alternative to the model of the course of history in the Hegelian theory of progress. Judaism represented, not the past, but the future of mankind. Judaism had removed itself from the pole of Nature and had taken its stand at the pole of Spirit, which is the goal of all history. The Jewish people as a whole, not merely the prophets and the philosophers, constitute the nucleus of the messianic age.

Humanity oscillates between the poles of Judaism and Paganism. It is the task of Christianity and Islam to convert mankind, while it is the special mission of the Jewish people to remain faithful to the dynamic essence of its own faith. The image of history is not that of a mighty river, draining the entire continent of humanity and leaving behind it some stagnant eddies, of which Judaism is one; but it is the image of two streams, one of which has found its way to the ocean directly, while the other meandered through the valley, draining it and fertilizing it, moving eventually toward the same delta. Formstecher suggested the image of the sun and its rays, permeating the darkness of the cosmos: the sun is the Jewish faith, and Christianity the rays issuing from it and illuminating the universe. This image became the focus of Franz Rosenzweig's brilliant exposition in his famous work *The Star of Redemption.*

Samuel Hirsch's philosophy of religion followed the same basic course as that of Formstecher in drawing the existential line between Judaism and paganism. With greater consistency than Formstecher, he condemned ancient Greek philosophy as well as Greek religion. He too assigned to Christianity the role of disseminating monotheism extensively throughout the world, and to Judaism the role of fidelity to the "intensive dimension of religion." Hirsch insisted that God is a live presence in Jewish piety, not simply a transcendent being, dwelling beyond the bounds of nature. True, the essence of Judaism is the recognition of God's lordship over nature. But, wherever man is present, there God is too. God does perform miracles, signaling His lordship. The biblical miracles are demonstrations of divine help in man's struggle to attain freedom. He is the source of human freedom; He is also the revealer of laws, whereby the Jews were kept from succumbing to paganism. While God does not interfere in man's free choice, He provides an educational regimen, the pattern of *mizvot*, whereby man is trained for freedom, and He intervenes in history in order to assure the eventual triumph of freedom.

Hirsch's concept of God was that of a living, transcendent reality, Who is independent of man's knowledge of Him. Hirsch combatted the Left-Hegelians and the pantheistic tendencies in Hegel's own philosophy, especially the notion of sin as a necessary stage in the unfolding life of the spirit. "Sin is not inevitable, though an ever-present possibility." For Hirsch, too, Jesus and his apostles were true to the inner dynamic of Judaism. Jesus taught that every Jew should realize in his own life the messianic destiny of the people as a whole, overcoming the inner Satan through an ethically heroic way of life.

The one error of Jesus, Hirsch maintained, was his fervent belief that the Kingdom of God was "at hand," but this error did not remove him from Judaism. On the contrary, it demonstrated the total earnestness of his devotion to the Jewish idea. Did not tides of pseudo-messianic expectancy engulf the Jewish world again and again? So Hirsch expounded the Gospels as one long and marvelous Midrash, interpreting the essence of faith. He concentrated attention especially on the Gospel of Matthew. Even the Last Supper was interpreted by Hirsch as a symbolic demand that Jesus' disciples follow his pathway to the glory of "sonship."[16]

Max Wiener summarized Hirsch's estimate of the unique role of Jesus in the divine plan for the education of the human race as follows:

> Jesus is absolutely Jewish; he belongs within the true faith of Judaism. He is and remains the ideal Jew. Hirsch does not content himself with demonstrating the agreement of fundamental ideas between Judaism and Jesus, but he proceeds to prove that the image of Jesus, in all its details, as transmitted by tradition, is fully in harmony with the Judaism of his time. He even interprets the belief in the resurrection of Jesus as a God-induced representation (*Vorstellung*) in the minds of the early apostles and disciples, in order that they might be inspired to disseminate his teachings. And, indeed, he lives actually in all those who wish to live as genuine Jews. Hirsch believed so strongly in the congruence of Jesus' personality with Jewish teaching that he regarded every deviation from this line in the Gospels as a later addition.[17]

But Paul's doctrine of original sin, of redemption through faith in "Christ crucified" and through baptism, was according to Hirsch, a concession to "unfreedom." The emergence of Protestantism was a giant step toward Judaism, to the point where the Protestant faith can no longer proselytize the pagan world as effectively as the Catholic Church, or so Hirsch believed. Still Judaism must keep itself apart, even from the Protestant faith.

Hirsch regarded the Jewish community as a living people, not merely a religious ecclesia. He considered the hope for the return to Palestine to be part of the living faith, though he disavowed the political dimension of national rebirth.[18]

The philosopher who responded most creatively to the challenge of the philosophy of progress was Nahman Krochmal (1785–1840). Rooted in the folk culture of eastern European Jewry and thoroughly familiar with the mystical as well as the rationalistic trends of Jewish thought, Krochmal produced a fascinating and stimulating philosophy of Jewish history that had the feel of reality for several generations of Jewish scholars. Working with genuine components of Jewish thought, he replicated the achievement of Hegel in fusing together three ideas: the absolute truth of Jewish monotheism; the rise and fall of the national culture in keeping with the dialectical evolution of the Jewish idea; and the art of self-understanding through self-criticism as being the call of Spirit. Krochmal embraced many ideas from the German and Italian philosophers of history, but he remained essentially within the ongoing streams of Jewish thought. In his work, ancient maxims of the Midrash acquired fresh and contemporary philosophic meaning.

Unlike his German confreres, Krochmal regarded Kabbalistic thought, in its early phases, as a genuine component of the authentic tradition, and he did not fail to make use of the paradoxical logic of Kabbalah, which seeks to bridge the gap between the One and the many, the spiritual and the material, the divine and the human. It is a logic of dynamic motion, rather than of static classification, and against the strictures of ordinary logic, it appeals to metaphysical reason, which is grasped intuitively.[19]

Krochmal sought to overcome the polarities and contradictions of life by elevating himself in thought to the ultimate source of the contending opposites. In the beginning is the unifying idea, and all polarizations result from the failure to comprehend it in its totality. This conception was probably suggested by the logic of Fichte and Hegel, but Krochmal saw this idea in the Kabbalistic *Sefiroh* of *Hochmoh*, Wisdom, which is the source of *Binah* ("understanding, recognizing distinctions") and *Da-ath* ("knowledge of the sensible world"). It proceeds from the whole to the parts, as against human, discursive, analytical logic, which reasons from the parts to the whole. Yet even in *Hochmoh*, man does not become one with God, since *Hochmoh* is the second *Sefiroh*, after *Kether* ("crown"), which blends into the Infinite *En Sof*.

The light of *Hochmoh* enters the consciousness of representative prophets and philosophers. As it filters down to the people, it determines the spirit of the age. Thus, God enters into history through prophetic experiences, which reflect His paradoxical unity of transcendence and immanence. These experiences are felt dimly by all sensitive people, though only the great men of any generation are the recipients of new ideas. Because God is above and beyond our finite grasp, we experience the shattering awareness of fear; because He lives within us most powerfully when we turn wholeheartedly to Him, we experience the exhilaration of joy; because neither His distance nor His nearness is static and unvarying, we feel the pangs and ecstasy of love. This harmonious blend of the feelings of fear, joy, and love is the mark of an authentic religious encounter.[20]

The disintegration of this symphony of feelings leads: (1) to the arid service of God through the mechanical observance of ritual; or (2) to the self-delusion of metaphysical arrogance, in the case of philosophers, or superstition, in the case of the populace; or (3) to reveling in mythological fantasies. The first is a reflection of the phase of fear, when we become aware of His distance; the second of the joyous ecstasy of the encounter eventuating in the pride of possession; the third of the playful fantasies of love. Each of these developments is a partial unfolding of one phase of faith. In the early rabbinic period, these one-sided theologies were represented in the cultivation of mystical intuition (*tsipiyat halev*), in the study of metaphysic and cosmology (*maasai bereshit*), and in the traditions of angelology (*maasai merkabah*).[21]

Krochmal did not find it difficult to identify the stigmata of Jewish religion in his own day by means of this categorization. His response was twofold—a reorientation in the field of religion and a critical reexamination in terms of philosophic discourse. In the sphere of religion, he believed, we need to elevate ourselves to that unitary ecstatic experience in which all contradictions merge. Thereby the Absolute is encountered in direct immediacy.

Living among the Hasidim of southern Poland, Krochmal appreciated the regenerative thrust of the movement at its highest levels, when it sought the attainment of *devekut*, or unity with the Divine, and endeavored to see the whole of life from the standpoint of those inspired moments.[22] On the other hand, he was also aware of the decline of the movement, especially on the popular level, where piety degenerated into superstitious belief in the theurgic powers of the "saints." The Hasidim of Poland resisted the incursion of general culture and secular learning, isolating their minds hermetically from any foreign influence.

In speculative philosophy, Krochmal continued, we need to take account of the marks of a unifying Intelligence within nature, which builds organic wholes superimposed upon other wholes. Modern science cannot but reinforce our sense of wonder at the intricate wisdom that is inherent in all living things and in the relations that obtain between them. The wonders of nature are raised to a higher pitch in the case of human societies. In the study of history, we recognize a restless endeavor to grasp the mystery of existence. This search has assumed various forms in the past, in the pagan world and in Judaism. Out of the failures of the many and diverse efforts, we may learn to distinguish the lines along which new efforts can now be made. Lastly, Krochmal contended that within Judaism the Absolute is already contained in *nuce* through "the images of the beginning of thought." Krochmal did not claim that Jewish dogmas contained the whole truth, but he maintained that the religious development of mankind was prefigured in the genesis and growth of the Jewish religion. The task of philosophy is to identify the course of the Absolute Idea within Jewish history, to discover the partial truths scattered in the various religions of mankind, and to chart the pathways of advance to God and His Kingdom for our contemporaries.

Let us analyze some of the components of Krochmal's philosophy of history. First, we note the assumption that Judaism is the Absolute Religion. We have seen that Hegel made a similar claim for Christianity in general and Protestantism in particular. For Hegel, Christianity was the Absolute Religion, firstly because in the incarnation it fuses man and God into one being, and secondly, because in history it has made itself the heir of the totality of all religious cultures. Hirsch and Formstecher had countered that the unity of man with God leads to pantheism and the blurring of the lines between ethics and naturalism. They stressed polarity rather than totality. All the non-Jewish religions belonged in the category of paganism, the worship of nature, and Judaism stood in absolute contrast to all the pagan faiths, those that celebrate life and those that seek to escape from it. Christianity is the mediating faith; hence its great task, to convert the totality of mankind. But Judaism celebrates the possession of the Absolute. Hence, it stands at the goal toward which the other faiths are moving.

Krochmal took a different tack. The Absolute Religion cannot be based on the unity of man and God, since this is impossible, even in terms of "the images of the beginning of thought." To know that we do not know God is the only knowledge we can have of Him. Here Krochmal took his stand on the *via negativa* of Maimonides. This knowledge does not exclude moments of inspiration, which Maimonides described in terms of the eleven degrees of prophecy. The prophet acknowledges that his insights are limited. He "walks humbly" with the Lord.

So the Absolute Religion is the one that affirms the unity of the goal of religion—that is, of the One God and His all-embracing Kingdom. Of God, we cannot affirm aught that is more ultimate than unity. In Kabbalah, *Hochmoh* is represented as a mathematical point, marking the genesis of finitude from the naught. But the sheer unity of God is an empty concept, to be filled with meaning through the advance of reason and the growth of the diverse cultures of mankind.

Krochmal did not clarify the sense in which the Absolute Spirit is contained within Judaism. It is not clear whether he intended to affirm his personal faith and that of historical Judaism, or whether he had in mind a more subtle affirmation—namely, the thesis that the quest of the Absolute, in the totality of His manifestations, is the heart of Judaism.[23] For all that is divine in origin belongs to the fullness of His being. Like all other cultural groups, the Jewish people can articulate in their lives only one or another aspect of the Absolute Spirit. Their fortunes as a people will reflect the emergence, growth, and decline of that aspect. In actuality, the Jews can no more articulate the Absolute Spirit in its totality than any other people. But because of their dedication to the Absolute Spirit in its unity, they will not remain dormant when the vital force of their idea has been exhausted. On the contrary, they will be moved to seek yet another phase of the Absolute and thereby to acquire a new lease on life. To put it differently, the Jews cannot for any length of time be persuaded that they have completed their role in history. To cling to the absolute Spirit is to undertake an endless journey, as long as time itself and as wide in its scope as all of humanity. Clinging to an eternal ideal, the people becomes eternal. Krochmal, however, did not exclude the possibility of temporary degeneration and torpor or even a kind of hibernation that might last for centuries.

In this interpretation, Krochmal affirmed that the Jewish religion fosters a yearning for the divine, a yearning so infinite in its outreach as to assure the survival of the Jewish people. At the same time his line of reasoning did not necessarily imply the arrogance of exclusiveness, of the belief that only the Jewish people possessed the Absolute in its fullness. In theory at least, all peoples and cultures are urged by their own great men and by the Jewish people as a whole to share in the endless quest, and all who undertake this journey are required to learn from one another.[24]

A second component of Krochmal's philosophy of history was that he did not stigmatize other faiths as false or evil but he regarded them as partial embodiments of the Absolute Spirit. Their fallacy consists in their illusion that they embrace the Absolute in its totality. "Know that every faith aims at the Absolute," at least in its genesis. But other faiths have succumbed to the delusion of being complete in themselves.

> But, we the community of those who from the beginning maintained the principle of unity, in its genuine purity believe and know that all material things are ephemeral and unreal, and even the spirit that is revealed to us in all its concreteness, as it shines through the qualities of mankind as a whole, is true and valid only insofar as it subsists in Him.[25]

Is there, then, no real difference between pagan faiths and Judaism, but a difference rather between the philosophers, who aim at the Absolute, whatever the ritual they employ, and the common people, whose mind does not extend beyond the practices that they perform by rote? In medieval philosophy, this kind of elitist universalism was not infrequent. Bahya Ibn Pakuda phrased it tersely: "Only the prophet of the generation, or the true philosopher, really serves the Cause of causes, because of their wisdom, but all others serve something else."[26] Krochmal did not concur in this judgment, since he believed that the Absolute is expressed in the culture of a people or the spirit of an age. All Jews share in the feeling of God's nearness and His love for them, a feeling that they articulate in every facet of their life; hence, they share in "the service of God," even when they lack "the knowledge of God." There is an implicit, or shall we say, unconscious knowledge of God implanted in the heart of the Jew and inherent in his soul.[27] This is not a racial quality but a direct consequence of centuries of training. The distinction between the holy and the profane, which underlies so many of Jewish practices, implies grades of nearness to the Divine Purpose; therefore, it leads to an awareness of the Ultimate. So, too, the distinction between the clean and the unclean suggests, after an analysis of the roots of the Hebrew terms (*tahor* and *tomai*), that the clean is that which is transparent to Divine Unity and the unclean is that which blocks the line of vision, preventing man's spirit from reaching out to the infinite.

Third, Krochmal's philosophy of history operated with the concept of religious nationalism. It is nations that make history, but every nation is constituted by "a national spirit," or "a national soul," and that collective spirit or soul is a revelation of Divine Truth, a partial revelation, to be sure, which will ultimately be included in the spiritual treasure of mankind. "Because one principle and root underlies all the national souls, they will be ultimately compatible and unified."[28] It is the unique spiritual élan of every nation that impels it to emerge as a creative force on the stage of history. The decline of a nation sets in when its leaders become enamored of power, or pleasure, or pride, or when they succumb to the lure of alien ideas. As the aging nation moves to the outer limbo of the universal history or departs completely from its annals, the idea it incarnated continues to be part of the human heritage as a whole. "In the case of a great nation with many achievements, the traces of its spirituality are preserved for the human race and its all-embracing Spirit."[29]

The concept of religion as being the soul of a national culture was particularly characteristic of romantic nationalism of the nineteenth century. The Russians found a special affinity for their national soul in the special form Greek Orthodoxy assumed in their land. The Germans, as we have seen, saw in Lutheranism the articulation of their special genius. Under the universal mantle of Catholicism, it is possible to discover characteristic nuances that reflect the particular qualities of diverse nationalities. The romantic emphasis on the religious mystique of the national character could be carried to the point of nullifying the validity of the universal principles of ethics and culture. If every nationality carries within itself the nucleus of its own moral universe, how can its actions be judged by the norms of other people or of humanity as a whole? We have seen this dilemma in the case of Herder, who in his first work glorified the unique genius of every nationality and in his later work elaborated the ideal of humanity as the goal and measuring rod of national greatness. In the latter part of the nineteenth century, German historicism scorned the moral limitations of humanity, or universal religion, and prepared the way for a nihilistic nationalism, which recognized no deity other than the single-minded thrust of national power and greatness.[30]

These developments, however, were still beyond the horizon in Krochmal's generation.[31] Seeing the hand of Providence in the steady growth of the culture of humanity as a whole, he could not foresee the emergence of self-deifying forms of nationalism. To him, every national élan was divine in origin and humanistic in purpose. In this sense, he conceived of the goal of Jewish life as being "to teach the human race the absolute faith contained in the Torah." Every people plays a similar role in the concourse of nations, but while the teaching of others is limited to partial truths, the task of Israel is to maintain relentlessly the unending quests of the Absolute. And this task was assigned to the Jews "by the Grace of the Supreme Being, through inspiration from beyond the realm of Understanding (*Binah*)."[32]

Fourth, Krochmal, in his philosophy, provided a conceptual bridge from the traditional notion of a national religion to the modern idea of a religious nationality. The national base of the Jewish religion was unquestioned from ancient and medieval times down to Krochmal's time. In the Roman empire, the Jewish religion was a legally recognized faith (*religio licita*), and Jews were permitted to live in accordance with "the customs of their fathers." But from time to time, severe curbs were imposed on the conversion of Gentiles to Judaism. Such converts, especially if they were prominent, could be condemned to death as "atheists." Throughout the medieval period, Jews were scorned as an anathematized race; yet baptism removed the "curse" and integrated the converts into the general population, except when large masses were suddenly propelled into the Christian community. So in Spain, the insistence on "purity of blood" (*limpieza*) was used as a means of combatting the former Jews who had become new Christians. In the debates of the emancipation period, the liberals, both Jewish and Gentile, regarded the ethnic base of the Jewish religion as a dessicated relic of the past. The vitality of Judaism lay in its religious heritage; in all other matters, Jews would become integral members of the European nations. Jewish nationhood belonged to the distant past, also possibly to the eschatological future, but it had no relevance to the living present.

In Krochmal's view, the vitality of the national body is dependent on the religious ideal; in turn, the Jewish religion is articulated in all the diverse aspects of the national culture. The Jewish people are involved in the historical process, articulating the particular drives of their own national soul and reacting to the influences of other nations. The ultimate goal of Jewish life is indeed transhistorical, but in its actual life at any time, only a partial aspect of the Absolute can be expressed. Thus Jewish people, in the determination of their own identity, should not compare themselves to the nations of antiquity, the ancient Egyptians, the ancient Babylonians, Persians, and Greeks. The latter perished because their national spirit represented only a phase of the Absolute Spirit. At the same time, the Jews should aim at a national rebirth, like the modern Germans, Italians, and Poles, for they belong to the future. To achieve this rebirth, they need but to reexamine critically their own history, to note wherein they failed, and to awaken their spirit to the call of the hour. To paraphrase an ancient saying, a Krochmalist would declare, "nothing that belongs to the Absolute Spirit I deem alien to me."

Krochmal shared with the Reformers in western Europe the vision of a new "science of Judaism." Only through the study of their past, in an objective and scientific way, can Jews come to know themselves and to prepare for regeneration. But while the Reformers sought to purify the faith from its national encrustations, Krochmal projected the ideal of a national renaissance as a consequence of a renewed faith. A new age is beginning, for nations as well as for the universal religion, and in this new age the Jews should aim to take their place as a reborn nationality, which is also peculiarly the custodian of the seeds of the universal faith.

Hegel had written of universal history as the succession of nation-states, with the Absolute Spirit revealing itself anew in every state and culture, but in only one state at a time. "This people is the dominant people in world history for this epoch—and it is only once that it can make its hour strike."[33] Krochmal envisaged the possibility of several nations representing simultaneously diverse phases of the Absolute Spirit, and the Jewish people as the cultural contemporaries of all great cultural nations, reminding them and itself that the Absolute is not yet here.

Like the Reformers, Krochmal assumed that the origins of Christianity and its development through the ages formed part of the new science of Judaism. Jews cannot know themselves truly if they fail to understand the daughter-religion of Judaism and the reasons for its triumphant career. Referring to the books of the new Testament, Krochmal wrote: ". . . it is the duty of the great and wise men in our midst to study and comprehend them and their roots, in order that we might attain through such research a recognition of our own essence and true being—namely, the general soul of Israel."[34]

Fifth, Krochmal saw the Jewish history as a series of bell-shaped curves. Each curve represents the triad of growth, maturity, and decline. Whereas other nations rose but once from obscurity and then sank back into it, the Jewish people, as we have seen, were endowed with the Phoenix-like capacity to rise again from the ashes. In the biblical period, we see the phase of growth in the time from Abraham to Moses; then, the phase of maturity in the generations extending from Moses to King David and King Solomon; then, the phase of decline, culminating in the burning of Jerusalem and the Holy Temple by the Babylonians. It is interesting that Krochmal employed a cultural-political yardstick of growth, not an abstractly spiritual one. He regarded classical prophecy as falling within the period of decline, since it is the total life of the people that counts, not merely the works of great men.

In the second bell-shaped curve he saw the phase of growth as lasting from the consolidation of the returnees in Jerusalem, under the leadership of Ezra and Nehemiah, to the beginning of the Hellenistic Age, the phase of maturity from Alexander to Pompei, the phase of decline from Pompei to the end of the great Revolt in the year 70 C.E.

In both these periods, the phases of growth and vigor culminated in a division and polarization of the people. Especially in the Second Commonwealth, this polarization was evident in the pietistic extremism of the Pharisees, which alienated the common people. Krochmal recognized the unhealthy consequences of Pharisaic piety, and he did not feel called upon to extol their virtues and defend them against the critique of Christians.[35]

In the third period the phase of growth began with Rabbi Judah the Patriarch, who edited the Mishnah and ended with the completion of the Babylonian Talmud; the second phase of maturity began with the Gaonic period and attained its climax in the Golden Age of Spain, culminating in the careers of Maimonides and Nachmanides; thereafter, the phase of decline continued until the middle of the seventeenth century.

Krochmal did not finish his monumental work. Doubtless, he believed that from the middle of the seventeenth century, a new age of rebirth had begun to manifest itself in the settlements of Jewish people in England and in America, in the emergence of the emancipated Jew in the west, and in the development of the new science of Judaism. Like Hegel, he believed that the philosopher of history cannot chart the future course of the Spirit but only interpret events after they had happened.

Krochmal set out to meet the challenge of the Hegelian philosophy of history, and he became the prophet of Jewish national rebirth.

V. *On the Crossroad Between Liberalism and Nationalism*

From the time of the Napoleonic era the western world was pulled in opposite directions by the forces of nationalism and liberalism. Rarely did these ideals appear in their pure forms, since most people felt the impact of both ideologies. Yet for the purpose of understanding the debates in which Jewish and Christian thinkers were engaged, we have to recognize that liberalism and nationalism constitute a basic polarity. The liberal ranks the freedom of the individual as the highest ideal. He assumes the basic equality of all human beings, and their rationality. He judges all existing institutions in terms of their contribution to the freedom of human beings and their equal opportunity. He regards the constitutional state, not the historical nationality, as the central focus of loyalty and tolerates all other subcultures and ethnic associations with some impatience, as vestigial remnants of the past. He is the enemy of superstition, of exclusiveness, of ethnic zealotries, of all who would reawaken narrow loyalties, mass emotions, and the enmities of the past.

The liberals emerged during the French Revolution as the critics of Christian traditionalism and the protagonists of Jewish emancipation. In every country they argued for the abolition of all restrictive laws that prevented the integration of the Jews with the general population, They combated the myths of Christian conservatives and the malice of antisemites. Against all who pointed to the "alienism of the Jew," either in the cultural or in the economic aspects of social life, they maintained that such differentia were inconsequential and transitory; basically, Jews were in no way different from the rest of the population. They asserted that once the light of freedom is allowed to permeate the alleys of the ghetto, all the stigmata of medieval separatism will disappear and the Jew will become indistinguishable from the rest of society.

The liberals defended the rights of the Jew as a human being, but they questioned the scope and the limits of a separate Jewish community. If they were single-minded and zealous in the pursuit of the liberal ideal, they were likely to be hostile to every manifestation of Jewish separateness, at times even to the continued existence of Jewish communal life. This extremist position would appear particularly in times of social crisis, when antisemitic demagogues, driven by compulsive hatred, threatened to mobilize popular passions primarily against the Jews and secondarily against the liberal institutions of society. To consistent liberals it seemed reasonable to reduce the visibility of Jewish corporate institutions to the vanishing point, in order to take the wind out of the sails of the hate peddlers. Disdainful of parochial sentiments, they were unlikely to assign high priorities to the secular institutions and ritual practices that set the Jew apart and made him an ideal target for popular frustrations.

Thus, faithful Jews were compelled at times to debate against liberals, who were admittedly their sole ideological allies in the fight for a free society. Even the Reformers, who best represented the liberal temper within Judaism, had to contend against some Christian liberals, in order to make room for the Jewish community. Liberalism in religion tended to transform both Judaism and Christianity and to enlarge their common ground. Yet, at times, the old antagonism between the two faiths reappeared even among the antitraditionalists in the shape of arguments concerning the implications of a free and open society. If the forced "ghettoization" of Jewry must not be allowed, what degree of voluntary separatism is compatible with a democratic society? Should the melting pot work to the point where no lumps are left in the soup?

European nationalism challenged Jewry in two ways. It placed in question the position of the Jew within the "nation-state," and it impelled increasing numbers of Jewish people to identify themselves as a nation.

Nationalism bases the political state on the natural community that is united by bonds of kinship, language, heroic sagas and history. So long as the nationalist ideal avoids the mystique of national feeling or the myth of a peculiar biological heritage, Jews can be included within the structure of the emergent nation-state. This type of nationalism prevailed in the republics of America, England, and France. In Germany, however, nationalism was powerfully charged from the beginning with a Teutonic mystique, which was as anti-Jewish as it was anti-western. To be sure, in Germany, there was also a liberal version of nationalism, whose leaders sought in 1848 to unite Germany on the basis of liberal principles. And in France a large proportion of the people hankered for the prerevolutionary days and *la belle France*, as the Dreyfus case demonstrated. Yet romantic nationalism was far more pervasive in Germany than in France. The Russian situation was similar to that of Germany, only more so, with pan-Slavic contempt for the "rotten" west and the exclusiveness of their version of Orthodoxy combining to harden the xenophobic policy of the czars.

In this chapter we shall deal with the following controversies as instances of the uneasy position of the Jew in nineteenth-century Germany, which was torn between the opposing pulls of liberalism and nationalism: the Bruno Bauer dispute; the Treitschke-Graetz affair; and the stir caused by the philosopher, Edouard von Hartmann.

Bruno Bauer (1809–1882) was already renowned as a Bible critic and as a Left-Hegelian when he shocked the liberal world with a book that opposed the granting of civil rights to Jews. His blast astonished the liberals as a thunderbolt from the blue sky, since the rightness of Jewish emancipation was by then axiomatic to all men of culture. In retrospect we note that the cantankerous critic foreshadowed an anti-Jewish mood that would lead to dire consequences in later generations.

Bauer interpreted the teachings of his master, Hegel, in an atheistic sense. In his view Hegel did not really believe the basic dogmas of Christianity, but he only pretended to esteem the Christian faith as the Absolute Religion, which combined the Infinite Spirit with the mind of a human being. Bauer maintained that in the nineteenth century the dogma of the incarnation really meant that God had died and that mankind became the new God. True, many Christians do not yet realize the implications of their faith, but, with the progressive growth of the spirit of the age, they will gradually become aware of this truth. So Bauer was called "the Messiah of atheism," or the "theologian of anti-theology." In his massive studies of the Gospels, he pointed out that we really know very little of Jesus himself, since the basic documents reflect contending theologies among early Christians.

This ultraliberal approach led Bauer to stigmatize Judaism on two counts: as an empty faith, left behind by the advancing spirit of the age; and as the source of all that is narrow and backward within Christianity. Paradoxically, Judaism was attacked for resisting Christianity in ancient times and for being the foundation of Christianity as a living faith in our day.

Bauer's argument runs as follows: The great state of the future must be based on the deification of humanity. But the Jew has set himself apart from humanity. The state of the future should represent the noblest attainments of human freedom. But in Judaism "only God is free," and man is compelled to obey a heteronomous law. To be sure, biblical religion was an inevitable stage in the unfolding of Spirit, but then, with the advent of Jesus, in whose consciousness God and his own self were united, Spirit had advanced to a new and higher phase. In the Christian community God is one with a portion of mankind, the portion marked off by the dogmas and rites of the Church. These limitations are the consequence of Judaic zealotry, which the Church inherited from the Synagogue. The Church owes its dynamic freedom to Hellenism and its dark burden of narrow fanaticism to Judaism, which retained its Oriental character. The Jews went through the Hellenistic period unaffected and unchanged. They repudiated Philo, the Hellenizing Jewish philosopher, and spurned the philosophical genius and the syncretistic culture of Hellenism; they rejected Jesus, in whose name a new era was opened, for the advancing spirit of mankind. While Spirit unfolded stage by stage through the various states of history, the Jews turned themselves into a "nonhistorical" community. They enveloped their life within the cocoon of lifeless legal threads, which was as chimerical as it was inhospitable. Jewish law was designed to surround the chosen people with invisible but stubborn ghetto walls, isolating them from any contact with Gentiles. The driving force of Jewish law was not historical reality, but an inner, lifeless dialectic, or pilpul.

Furthermore, and here Bauer echoed Spinoza and Mendelssohn, the Law, not universal ideals and principles, is the essence of Judaism, and this law was designed to govern a self-segregating nationality. While the Law is formally religious in origin and intent, it sanctifies the petrified customs of an ancient nation. Hence, the Jews are doubly alien to the projected ideal state—through their faith and through their nationality. When the "fruit" of Christianity emerged out of the "flower" of Judaism, the flower should have been blown away by the wind. Instead, the Jews refused to heed the call of history and continued to drag out their miserable existence as a drifting "ahistorical" enclave within the states of Europe, living amidst the peoples of Europe but disdaining to become part of them. Therefore, Bauer asserted, the typical occupation of the Jewish community is usury, an anti-social occupation that enables Jewry to feed on society without being part of it. To be integrated into the new state, the Jews would have to give up all that separates them from the general community—their religious identity, their Law, their nationality, and their social distinctiveness.

The leading Jewish thinkers of Germany published replies to Bauer. Particularly significant were the replies of the Reformers—Hirsch, Geiger, and Formstecher—who could not totally condemn the arguments of the extremist liberal.[1] Did not Bauer's strictures against Jewish Law echo their own sentiments, at least in part? As liberals themselves, they aimed to abolish those ordinances that interposed an "iron wall" between modern Jews and their neighbors.[2] Some sought to excise every vestige of ethnicism from the Jewish religion. They considered the essential ingredient of the Jewish religion to be ethical monotheism, in all its infinite grandeur, not the legalistic armor of medieval Judaism and certainly not the passions of fanaticism. As they saw it, Jesus was a Jew, faithful to the inner genius of Judaism. What the Jews rejected was the religion *about* Jesus, not the religion *of* Jesus. The ruthless, crusading spirit of Christianity, was, according to Jewish scholars, largely the consequence of

Hellenistic mysticism and Roman imperialism. Unlike the exclusionist Church with its motto, "no salvation outside the Church," the Synagogue did not maintain that it alone was in possession of salvation. On the contrary, at the beginning of the second century the sages declared, "the righteous among the nations have a share in the world to come."[3] Furthermore, the Reformers asserted, usury was imposed on the Jews by the medieval potentates, who excluded them from every other occupation and employed them as a "sponge" with which to soak up cash from the populace in order thereby to siphon the funds into their own coffers—for the property of the Jews was usually confiscated by the princes.

To be sure, the Reformers conceded that the Jewish heritage contained desiccated remnants of ancient laws and customs, which should be consigned to the slag heap of history. But, they maintained, the essence of Judaism is the dynamic spirit of ethical monotheism, which develops in accord with its own genius. The Reform movement, which was then beginning to crystallize, is not an aritificial contrivance, but the latter-day manifestation of Jewish genius for self-renewal through criticism. The Reform spirit of self-criticism and innovation was eloquently championed by the Hebrew prophets in the biblical period; it was represented in later years by the Pharisees, then by the Hillelites, and still later by the medieval philosophers. There is indeed a "trans-historical" aspect to Judaism—namely, its living core of essential truths. But in the life of the people the diverse processes of history are continually at work.

This in brief was the response of Jewish liberals to the critique of Bauer. But this response did not halt the line of reasoning that he represented. Its component themes have continued to be voiced down to our day by extremist liberals, or radicals. The ideal society should not be marred by any self-enclosed enclaves. As an ancient people the Jews have already had their say in history, and their continued persistence is a scandal. Paradoxical as it may sound to the radicals, Jesus was not the Son of God, but the Jews nevertheless lost their right to exist when they refused to accept him as their Messiah, since the new messianic community became the nucleus of a universal society. The Jews had set themselves against the massive trend of history. Kant's identification of the Son of Man with humanity set the pattern for the liberal historians. In this view the Jews refused to heed Jesus' humanistic message, not because they rejected the new myths on rational grounds, but because they cherished their own status as a narcissistic "Chosen People." The Jewish religion sheltered an "international nation"—hence, the Jew qua Jew was an alien in every European nation, and what is more, an "Oriental," a pejorative status at a time when Europeans were contemptuous of all Asians and Africans. The new states of Europe, Bauer and his followers contended, must be "post-Christian" as well as "post-Jewish," and both goals are really one at their source, for Christianity is only a continuation of Judaism.[4]

Of historic import was the reaction of the young Karl Marx to the Bauer controversy. Raised as a Christian of Jewish descent, Marx scorned Jewry, both as an empirical community and as a symbol of the capitalistic age. Agreeing with Hegel that the Universal Spirit is articulated in every aspect of the life of a state, he stood Hegelianism on its head with the claim that the economic foundations of the state determine its conceptual and cultural character, rather than the other way around. Against Hegel's maxim "the rational is the real," he countered the thesis "the real forces of production account for its rational super-structure." So, paralleling Hegel's totalitarianism, in which the Absolute Spirit is incarnated in a tight, hierarchical state, he set up a totalitarian concept of the state, rising in equally tight formation from the economy up to the sheerest abstractions of political and cultural ideology.

In respect of Judaism, Karl Marx contributed two propositions—first, that the Jew was the bearer of the capitalistic bacillus, feeding on and transforming the body of European nations; second, that the Jewish religion should be interpreted in the light of this economic function, as the product of the commercial spirit. The Sabbath-Jew in the synagogue should be seen in the light of the week-day peddler, haggling in the marketplace, not the other way around.[5]

Both of these motifs were associated with the historical "fallout" from the Jewish-Christian argument, on the level of popular theology. The second stereotype harmonized with the Gospel accounts of Jesus driving the money-changers from the Temple and the high priests bribing Judas with thirty pieces of silver to betray his master. In a deeper sense, this image tied in with a persistent trend in the interpretation of the nature of Pharisaic piety. The Pharisees, it was said, interpreted the judgment of heaven in terms of an impersonal commercial transaction—so much tangible reward for the performance of so many external acts of piety. This "carnal" piety accounts, in the belief of many Christians, for the Jewish distortion of the messianic vision of their own prophets. Instead of looking for a "spiritual" Messiah who would save them from sin, they expected the Messiah to bring them mundane triumphs of prosperity and peace. Here we enter the central theme of the rejection of Jesus, as seen in the perspective of Christian traditionalists, both Catholic and Protestant. The Lutheran scholars with their endless variations on the theme of faith versus works, were particularly diligent in filling in the details of this mercenary image of Jewish piety.

Sheneur Zalman Shazar, former President of Israel, maintained that Karl Marx shared the axiom current in his circle, that the end of Jewry was near. Marx simply offered an explanation of this imminent demise—namely, capitalism is digging its own grave. He identified the Jews with capitalism because he was familiar with a dozen or so wealthy Jewish banking families. Shazar found traditional Jewish motifs in Marx—his messianism, his passion for social justice, his eagerness to prove his faith scientifically. However, Marx himself clearly identified these ideas with his general European heritage. We note that Marx was also acquainted with the straitened circumstances of the poverty-stricken Jews in Poland. His readiness to utilize the popular stereotype of the Jew in his socialistic propaganda stands in glaring contrast to his lifelong determination to penetrate through the stereotypes and cliches of an oppressive society. The explanation, if any, may lie in his preoccupation with the philosophy of history. If the driving force of history is economics, how account for the survival of a people that bases its existence solely on faith in the One God? In answer, he asserted that, not the monotheistic idea, but the socio-economic function of Jewry kept it from disappearing off the stages of history. This world-historical role, Marx believed, was drawing to a close.[6]

Marx's identification of the Jew with the driving force of capitalism sounded a responsive chord in the bourgeois and aristocratic as well as in the proletarian circles of Europe. These classes were being pulverized by the advancing juggernaut of capitalism, which made obsolete the landed estates, impoverished the farmers, reduced the craftsmen to the status of faceless factory workers, and choked the cities with a seething mass of troubled humanity—uprooted, bewildered, and unemployed. In Germany the Industrial Revolution was frequently associated with the influence of the hated enemy, England and the West generally. Also, economic liberalism was generally described as "manchesterism," with the Jews as its agents on the European continent. The conservative social classes felt that they were threatened economically as well as culturally and religiously. It was easy and comforting for them to see these varied threats as the attack of one enemy, the commercial spirit, personified by the Jew in one way and by England in another.

Max Weber devoted a famous essay to the relationship between Protestantism and capitalism. He maintained that Protestant individualism and the so-called Protestant Ethic were largely responsible for the growth of industry and commerce in the lands of northern Europe and America. He did take note of the affinity of the Jewish spirit to that of Protestantism, but he refused to credit the Jews with any creative contribution to the progress of Europe. Since they were classed as aliens in pre-industrial Europe, their enterprise and inventiveness belonged to a separate category, that of "pariah-capitalism."

Weber defined a "pariah people" as:

A distinctive hereditary social group, lacking autonomous political organization and characterized by prohibitions against commensality and intermarriage, originally founded upon magical, tabooistic and ritual injunctions. Two additional traits of a pariah people are political and social disprivilege and a far-reaching distinctiveness in economic functioning.[7]

From the vantage point of a contemporary observer, the Jews of premodern times in Christian Europe might be classed indeed as a pariah people, though with some reservations, since Christians were not prohibited from dining with Jews or from marrying them if they converted. Furthermore, Christian hostility of Jews, even in the age of fanatical theology, was actually a blend of admiration and contempt, since the Promise of God and His love for "Israel after the flesh" were described in the New Testament as "irrevocable" (Romans 11:29). Nor was the economic role assigned to Jews comparable to the menial tasks reserved for the "untouchables" in India. In caste-conscious, medieval Europe, merchants and money-lenders ranked far below the well born aristocrats, but by the same token, they were worlds above the vast majority of the people, the oppressed and ignorant peasantry.

When Weber proceeded to interpret the role of Jewish economic enterprise in terms of the Jewish self-image as a pariah, he lost touch with reality altogether. The believing Jew regarded himself as a member of a metaphysical *elite*, whose task it was to "improve the world through the Kingdom of the Almighty"—that is, prepare the way for the universal "Kingdom of God." Weber spoke of "the unparalleled desire for vengeance manifested by Yahweh," and of "the hope for revenge, which suffused practically all the exilic and post-exilic sacred scriptures."[8] It is true that many scholars have found this hope for revenge in biblical and apocalyptic literature, though they do not always agree on the extent to which it is present. As to standard literature of the late Middle Ages, however, there can be no question that the dominant motif of Jewish piety was *Kiddush hashem*, the Sanctification of the Name—that is, to win admiration and reverence among Gentiles for the sacred heritage of Israel. This motif was far more powerful and even, in legalistic terms, far more applicable than any scattered and occasional remarks reflecting fear of or hatred for the heathen world.

Instead of an ethic of resentment and vindictiveness, Judaism called for a "reordering" of this world. Jewish piety was activistic and oriented toward this world. Indeed, it might be described by the very term that Weber employed to characterize Puritanism—namely, "this-worldly asceticism." The Jew denied himself the pleasures and pastimes of the well to do in order to save money and build up capital for large enterprises. The purpose was to become a patriarchal communal leader, a supporter of Torah institutions and charity organizations, and a representative of his people in their dealing with the Gentile authorities.

Weber questioned the productivity of "Jewish capital," contrasting it with Puritan enterprise. "How does one explain the fact that no pious Jew succeeded in establishing an industry employing pious Jewish workers of the ghetto (as so many pious Puritan entrepreneurs had done with devout Christian workers and artisans)?" The answer is that Jewish men of wealth did so, in many cases, in eastern Europe and modern America. However, the investment of capital in factories required a degree of security that Jews did not possess before the nineteenth century.[9] Weber compounded his error when he blamed the supposed "double morality" of Jews, in dealing with Jews and non-Jews, for the relative sterility of Jewish finance capitalism.[10] In general the frugal habits of Jewish people and their abstinence from intoxicating drinks contributed decisively to their success in business.

While Weber towered high above the antisemites, he helped to generate the myth that Jewish capitalism was unproductive and essentially different from non-Jewish industrial capitalism. This myth became one of the building blocks of the fantasy-laden *Weltanschauung* of the Nazis, making it possible for them to attack Jewish capitalism, while pretending to safeguard the masters of German industry.[11]

It was left to Werner Sombart (1863–1941) to assemble a mosaic of distorted data and crass assumptions that seemed to document the thesis that capitalism was indeed a "Jewish invention."

Sombart's book *The Jews and Modern Capitalism* verged on the abyss of mythology, even while it pretended to be scientific. He saw the Jews of various cultures and historical eras as constituting one community of invariant qualities, a "race," if you will. Then he exaggerated enormously the share of Jewish and Marrano capital in sixteenth-century Dutch trade, and he formed his inferences regarding all Jews at all times on the basis of that claim. He attributed the special capacities of Jews both to race and to the Jewish religion, which promotes a "rationalistic style of life." Even the rules of periodic sexual abstinence were employed by Sombart to "explain" the unique skills of Jews as moneylenders.[12]

The extent of Sombart's exaggeration can be inferred from his conclusion, "Puritanism *is* Judaism."[13] "In both will be found the preponderance of religious interests, the idea of divine rewards and punishments, asceticism *within* the world, the close relationship between religion and business, the arithmetical conception of sin, and above all, the rationalization of life."[14]

But the Jews were identified with the Puritans only when both groups were condemned by the German author. Otherwise, the Puritans were praised for their inventiveness in industry, while "Jewish capital" was, to Sombart, unproductive.

Sombart cited biased medieval judgments on Jewish business as if they were of unquestioned objectivity. "The Jews were more successful because of their dishonest dealing."[15] Disregarding individual variations, Sombart found that the Jews as a group are "committed to the supremacy of gain over all other aims." "Money is the be-all and end-all."[16]

At times Sombart appeared to praise the Jew, yet, somehow, he turned every virtue into a vice. He discovered four "Jewish characteristics"—intellectuality, teleology, energy, and mobility. One might esteem intellectuality as a noble and socially useful quality. But no: "All intellectuality is in the long run shallowness; it never allows probing to the very roots of a matter, nor of reaching down to the depths of the soul, or of the universe."[17] Similarly, purposiveness, dynamism, and quickness of mobility were interpreted as antisocial attitudes.

Sombart credited Jews with "an extraordinary knowledge of men." But then he claimed "seldom do they see the whole of man, and thus they often make the mistake of ascribing actions to him which are an abomination to his inmost soul . . . Hence, their lack of sympathy for every status where the nexus is a personal one. The Jew's whole being is opposed to all that is usually understood by chivalry, to all sentimentality, knight-errantry, feudalism, patriarchalism. . . . Politically, he is an individualist . . ."[18]

We perceive here echoes of Fichte's *Vernunft* (discussed in Chapter III) and of the romantic tendency to sentimentalize the Middle Ages in particular and an "organic" society generally. At another point Sombart echoed the judgment of Renan concerning the Semite—"the special Jewish intellectuality is of a kind associated with sandy or stormy deserts."[19] He pointed to the persistent hatred of Jews as proof of the unalterability of their characteristics.[20] While he opposed the rabid antisemitism of the prophet of Aryan supremacy, Stewart H. Chamberlain, he skirted on the edge of the mythological canyon. Renan specifically distinguished between the ancient Semitic Nomads and the modern Jews, while Sombart spoke of "the Jew's inherent 'Nomadism' or 'Saharism,'" as a quality of contemporary Jews.[21]

We have cited enough to show that Sombart gave the appearance of scholarly respectability to the notion that Jews incorporated the spirit of capitalism, in all its moral ambivalence.[22] Yet Sombart was regarded by many Jews as a non-antisemite, especially after he published an essay in 1912, urging the establishment of a Jewish state as the only way of alleviating Jewish suffering in eastern Europe. As to the Jews of Germany, he urged that they voluntarily refrain from taking up important positions, in order not to influence German culture unduly.

As Ismar Schorsch puts it: "In Sombart, the Zionists did not see an antisemite, but a Christian scholar who had identified himself with Zionism."[23] The Zionists were particularly pleased with Sombart's praise of the character of nationalistic Jews, who had given up any pretense of sharing in "the German way of thinking" (*Gesinnung*). Simon Dubnow, the exponent of "Jewish autonomy" in the Diaspora, agreed with this judgment concerning Sombart's views.[24]

Such an exaggerated thesis is, of course, on a par with the contrary assertion that Communism, particularly the Bolshevik Revolution in Russia, was a Jewish achievement. In both cases a highly selective approach, singling out Jewish individuals from among the known and unknown actors in a historic event, lends the veneer of plausibility to the desired conclusion.

The grain of truth in both propositions is the fact that Jewish individuals are likely to provide dynamic leadership, disproportionately to their numbers, to any enterprise that emerges on the margin of the fixed structures of society. Because they have been accepted only grudgingly and minimally within the "establishment," be it economic, social, or cultural, they have traditionally turned their energies to the fields that were left unplowed by the native population. Kept by Gentile pride and hate from entering the safe and proved positions of power, they became the pioneers of new fields of enterprise. Being inured to hardships, they were stimulated to work even harder by the obstacles that were placed in their path. They were not demoralized by the buckets of contempt that were poured on their heads, because they were trained by generations of martyrdom to look inward for dignity and worth. They were not restrained from innovations by the torpor that parlayzes a demoralized population and keeps an oppressed class from questioning the axioms that are employed to rationalize their misery. The high intellectual content of their tradition sharpened the keen edge of their minds and built up their self-respect, while their resilient faith buoyed up their spirits and trained them to shun the manifold corruptions of urban life. Compelled by the exigencies of history to base their safety on the ethical conscience of their fellowmen, they tended in politics to be liberal rather than revolutionary. Instinctively, they sought to build society on humanist foundations rather than on force. In Germany and the western countries, they were generally enrolled in the ranks of the liberal parties.

The great Jewish historian Heinrich Graetz (1817–1891) moved uncertainly between the two poles of liberalism and nationalism. In his early writings he set out to oppose the evolving philosophy of the Reformers. While he rejected the central dogmas of the Orthodox, especially in regard to the literal inspiration of the Written and Oral Laws, he resented bitterly the efforts of the Reformers to eliminate some rituals and folk elements from modern Judaism. The ideologists of classical Reform, such as Geiger and Holdheim, asserted that the nationalistic components of Judaism belonged to its obsolete, outer shell, while its ideal content, so-called ethical monotheism, constituted the enduring, vital kernel.

As the Reformers saw it, Jewish history moved in a continuously ascending curve, from folk culture to an ever purer faith, shedding its outworn garments as it went along. In the biblical period the monotheistic faith was still wrapped in a cocoon of folk myths and distorted by the political struggles of a small nation. The destruction of the First Temple liberated the Jewish faith from the oppressive entanglements of the Davidic monarchy. In the Second

Commonwealth, Judaism became more and more clearly a religious community, with Jerusalem as its spiritual center. When Philo spoke of Jerusalem as the "metropolis" of the Jews, he used the term in a nonpolitical sense. Dispersed for centuries in the Roman and Persian Empires, with only two or three generations of political independence, the Jews had learned to identify their true being with their faith and their laws. To be sure, during the Talmudic period, after a series of disasters, nationalistic and political elements were absorbed into the Jewish faith, more or less unconsciously, since religion in the ancient world could not be totally severed from its social-cultural context.

At times such elements of folk culture were deliberately favored in order to shield the people from the corrosive acids of syncretism. The isolationist mood is clearly apparent in the two Talmuds, which were completed in 350 C.E. and 500 C.E., respectively.

Yet, the Reformers pointed out, the prophetic ethos of Judaism was not totally crushed. It reappeared in the upsurge of Jewish philosophy during the Golden Ages of the medieval world. With the emergence of the free society in the modern world, the Reformers believed, the time had come for the unhampered efflorescence of the Jewish faith. Judaism had come into its own at last; it need no longer drag its empty shell. The light that appeared at Sinai, that was nurtured by the prophets and protected from the follies of the masses and the ambition of the kings, that was sheltered from the winds of idolatry through the Talmuds—this light could now appear in the fullness of its glory and banish darkness from the face of the earth. If such rhetoric appears overblown and naive today, it was fully in keeping with the hopeful spirit of the nineteenth century.

The Reformers identified with the rationalistic and universal currents in Judaism, repudiating its ethnic, romantic, and mystical trends. They looked to the emergence of a universal religion as the culmination of the Jewish "mission" to mankind. They maintained that Christianity could not fulfill the role of a universal faith because its monotheistic and rationalistic components were inevitably overlaid with the residue of a mythology centering on the supernatural character of a historical personality. The Jewish faith is, in its vital essence, more akin to the modern mind than is Christianity, since the mythical elements in Judaism are superficial, extraneous, and desiccated. In its Reform version, Judaism is not "the Law" but the Covenant as interpreted by the prophets—that is, it is the total commitment to the building of the Kingdom of God on earth. It is the destiny of Judaism to liberate itself completely from all obsolete practices and, in concert with liberal Christians and humanists, to usher in the messianic Era of the future, when both Judaism and Christianity will be "fulfilled" in the realization of the prophetic vision.

In contrast to this idea of the unilinear movement of the Jewish history toward a universal faith, the historian Heinrich Graetz put the perfect age in the reigns of King David and King Solomon, adopting a national-political criterion of greatness rather than a religious-spiritual one. For Judaism, as he saw it, was not a body of abstractions but a vital organism in which a living people, rooted in its natural soil, was indissolubly united with a cosmic Idea. The triangular base of Judaism consisted of Torah, Land, and People.

> Torah is the soul, and the holy land is the body of this peculiar political organism . . . Torah, the people of Israel and the Holy Land are mysteriously interrelated by invisible and unbreakable bonds. Judaism, without the solid base of political life may be compared to a hollow, half-uprooted tree, which continues to shoot forth some leaves, but it is no longer capable of producing branches and limbs.[25]

For Graetz it followed that Judaism was most alive and harmonious in those brief periods when it controlled the levers of power in an independent state. It declined somewhat in the Second Commonwealth, after demonstrating its unique capacity for rebirth. In the third period, following the destruction of Jerusalem in 70 C.E. and continuing into his own time, Judaism had fallen into a state of hibernation.

In each of these three periods there were three stages of development—growth, maturity, and decline with the reign of King David constituting the apex of the first period; that of John Hyrkanos, the second; and that of Maimonides, the third period. Moses Mendelssohn opened a new age of "scientific" awareness, making possible a new synthesis of Torah, people, and state.

On the surface Graetz' interpretation of Jewish history appears to be self-contradictory. If political power is of the essence of Judaism, how does Maimonides represent the apex of the third period? How is Mendelssohn's epoch the beginning of a renaissance? Graetz' periodization would make sense if he had openly avowed his Zionist vision and called for a renewal of Jewish life in its ancestral homeland.[26] There the triad of Torah, people, and land would be reconstituted and the curve of Jewish history would ascend to its starting point. In fact, Graetz' diary reveals his Zionist convictions at an early state in his life and more decisively in his correspondence with Moses Hess.[27] At the same time he consistently resisted and suppressed his "Palestinocentrism," since a Zionist orientation appeared in his day to be an impossible dream. Accordingly, he wavered between a folkist and a spiritual interpretation of Jewish history. In spite of his lifelong Zionist convictions and the logic of his historical analysis from a Zionist viewpoint, he allowed his friend and sponsor, Zechariah Frankel, to reject in his behalf the implication that Judaism is inherently related to any geographic locality.[28]

As a matter of fact, the three ideals that Jewish tradition regards as supremely holy, interdependent, and virtually one are God, Israel, and Torah.[29] Graetz' substitution of "land" for "God" in the traditional formulation was a bold secularistic step, prompted by the Hegelian notion that God reveals Himself in the emergence and decline of great states. The medieval Jewish community was a quasi-state, a self-enclosed enclave within the various estates, guilds, and corporations of feudal Europe. With the rise of the modern democratic state, Hegelian logic would call for the choice between a return to Zion and a wholehearted identification with the nation-state as the field of operation for the Jewish élan. The Reformers embraced the latter alternative. The notion of a self-governing Jewish community would not have been out of phase in a cosmopolitan federation of states, such as that which Kant envisioned for Europe. But Hegel and his followers rejected such a notion as abstract and chimerical. Following the Franco-Prussian War, such an international union was unthinkable.

Graetz was bitterly disappointed with the trend of political sentiment in Germany. He could no more accept the alternative of an inner identification with the modern states of Europe than he could acknowledge the Zionist logic of his argument. He was deeply disgusted with the sorry state of German liberalism and the intense antisemitism imbedded in the folk and literary tradition of the German nation.[30] For a long time he looked to France as the homeland of freedom, and in the last two decades of his life he pinned his hope on the English-speaking world. "While the Latin race is more imbued with the spirit of Hellenism, the Anglo-Saxon race is permeated by the biblical-Jewish spirit, being oriented more to the quest of truth than of beauty."[31]

Actually, Graetz was more deeply affected by classical German philosophy than he realized. In his essay "Construction of Jewish History" he described Jewish genius as being that of an "ear-man," sensitive to poetry and the inner life, in contrast to the "eye-man," sensitive to forms and esthetics, a posture German Romantics loved to assume, especially after Fichte. In describing pagan mythology as the worship of nature, he forgot that the pagans worshiped tribal gods as well as nature gods. He followed Herder and Hegel in interpreting the Jewish idea of God as being purely transcendental and the essence of Jewish piety as being awareness of the sublime. He followed Schelling in postulating a polar opposition between "nature faith" and "spirit faith." He echoed Kant in the claim that Judaism is "not a religion at all," since it is concerned with the socio-political life of a community, not with the relation of the individual to God. He followed Hegel in regarding history as the reflection of the dynamism of an Idea, that is driven forward by the impetus of negation. In Judaism the idea is of One transcendental Deity, and its content consists in an unending "nay-saying" to all forms of idolatry.

Above all, Graetz showed his "Germanism" in his impassioned romanticism, exalting the life of the "folk," its ineffable mystique, and its comforting mythology. Living in Germany, he could not be unaware of the demonic impetus implicit in the mystique of folk and race; yet in his concern for Jewish survival, he leaned heavily on these dark and dangerous motivations. The mystique of race was, in his mind, intimately associated with a great idea of universal significance. In his anonymous exchange of letters with an English lady, he spoke of sexual continence as a racial characteristic of the

Jews and of the Jewish mission as that of bringing "light and holiness to the nations" by curbing lust and promiscuity. He wrote:

> Do not scorn the *mizvot* generally, since their necessity at present (in contrast to messianic times) is clear. The dietary laws, which are included in the Jewish ritual, do not please you. But, inquire of physiologists if the nature of food that one eats does not affect his temper and character. The consumption of blood or of the flesh of wild beasts leads surely, if it be continued generation after generation, to the intensification and bestialization of carnal lust. Who can tell if abstinence from certain foods did not contribute to the refinement of Jewish character and the restraint of demonic impulses?[32]

Perhaps Graetz was influenced by the notorious maxim of Ludwig Feuerbach: *Der Mensch ist was er isst* ("man is what he eats"). Still, in his view, the ritual observances are of secondary importance. The Jewish elite should respect them in order to maintain the unity of the Jewish community, but the essence of Judaism is its ethical imperative. He shied away from the excessive praise of George Eliot, who described Daniel Deronda as saying, "Every Jew has to raise his children, as if the Messiah would emerge from them." But in his address at the Exposition of Anglo-Jewry in 1887 he spoke of the Jewish people as "a messianic nation" who were "destined from creation to disseminate and to realize the pure idea of God and the supremacy of the moral law."[33]

These ideals are achievements of the Jewish race; in turn, they reinforce and inspire the Jews to survive as a unique people. Since the messianic vision emerged out of Jewish life, "the messianic builder of universal peace may be expected to arise out of the Jewish people."[34]

In general, Graetz moved closer to the position of the Reformers in the last two decades of his life, especially in his acceptance of the ·critical approach to the study of Scripture and in his conception of the Jewish "mission" to mankind.[35] The dominant note of all his writings was an impassioned exaltation of the Jewish role in history. He saw the Jewish people as the major guardian of morality and holiness in behalf of all mankind. Indeed, he interpreted all the ritual *mizvot* in terms of religious humanism. But while his Jewish loyalty was humanist in orientation, it did not include any feeling of kinship with the emergent nations of Europe, nor any awareness of the need for Jews to forge bonds of brotherhood with the nations among whom they lived—a circumstance that led to a fateful controversy.

Heinrich von Treitschke (1834–1896) was the acknowledged dean of nationalist historians in Germany. In 1879 he published a critique of Graetz' eleven-volume *History of the Jews* (1853–1876) which had the effect of lending the aura of respectability to the rising tide of racist antisemitism. To be sure, Treitschke did not endorse either the hate-filled canards of the antisemites or the irrational mystique of Aryan racism, but as a fervent nationalist he came very close to doing both of these. He examined Graetz' massive work, especially the eleventh volume, dealing with the modern period, and announced that to his dismay he found in it no signs of an inner identification with the German spirit. On the contrary, Treitschke found that Graetz manifested bitter contempt for the great exponents of the Germanic spirit, beginning with Martin Luther and ending with Goethe and Fichte.

Treitschke challenged the Jews of his day to follow the examples of the philosopher Moses Mendelssohn and the intrepid Jewish liberal, Gabriel Riesser, both of whom were deeply involved in the political and social problems of Germany. They were, in Treitschke's view, "Germanic personalities," though they were also loyal to their Jewish heritage. He castigated the narrow loyalties of Graetz as stigmata of "Jewish arrogance," and he professed to fear the emergence of a Jewish separatist mentality among the Jews of Germany. While praising the Jews of England, especially the *Sephardim*, Treitschke condemned the resurgence of Graetz' brand of Jewish nationalism as a breach of faith with the German people.

> But, if this racial arrogance is asserted publicly, if Jewry demands the recognition of its nationhood, then the legal basis of the Emancipation is undermined. Such a demand can only be fulfilled in one way—through emigration—the establishment of a Jewish state, outside our borders, which will seek the recognition of other states. On the soil of Germany, there is no room for a double nationality.[36]

In the course of his exposition Treitschke lapsed occasionally into the antisemitic abyss, as when he wrote:

> . . . even in the circles of the most highly educated, among people who would reject with contempt either sectarian intolerance or national arrogance, we now hear it spoken, as if by one voice—"The Jews are our misfortune."[37]

Suppose it were true that the German Jews were a separate, "indigestible" nationality. How would that circumstance be a "misfortune" for the German nation-state? Obviously, the argument was incomplete. It assumed that Jewish nationhood concealed a certain malicious and mysterious enmity toward Gentiles. Jewish persistence in their nationhood appeared to Treitschke to be unnatural, a conscious repudiation of the goal of amalgamation with the Germans—Jewish arrogance, if you will. In turn, the Gentiles, he contended, are bound to react by building up, generation by generation, a folk mythology centering around an embittered and irrational phobia of Jews. As a German nationalist, Treitschke insisted that the "good-hearted" Germans cannot be all wrong. Hence, false as their mythology might be, their instincts must be assumed to be basically sound. So he wrote:

> I intended only to show that that movement [i.e., anti-semitism], which has affected our good-hearted people is not solely the product of vulgarity, jealousy and prejudices of a religious or ethnic type. But, the rising arrogance of some German Jews has given rise to this movement, which has now reached those who would not change an iota of the Emancipation. Intelligent observers will note this steady rise of doubts and deep resentment. And if my words caused a storm of acrimonious declarations, then it is proof that the Jewish question in Germany does in fact exist, even if some deny this fact.[38]

While Treitschke acknowledged that some Jews did indeed become Germanic in spirit, he maintained that those who cherished their own national separateness were bound to arouse the demonic-mythological hatred of the people among whom they lived. For in that event their very existence functioned as an intolerable irritant, a defiance of the national instincts, and a perpetual provocation. It is because of this instinctive resentment of alien enclaves, he pointed out, that nearly all the classical writers of pagan antiquity were antisemitic.

Treitschke resented not only Graetz' irreverent references to the secular heroes of Germany but also the Jewish historian's condemnation of Christianity as "the archenemy" of Judaism. Even the secularists of western countries, he claimed, acknowledge that their national culture is thoroughly permeated by the Christian spirit. After all, the nations of the West were nurtured for centuries in the faith of Christianity and in its institutions. Their national feelings bear the seal of Christian sentiment. Especially the builders of Germanic Christendom—Meister Eckhardt, Martin Luther, and Friedrich Schleiermacher—belong to the galaxy of national heroes. In law, state and church are indeed separated, but can they be kept apart totally in sentiment? Should not Jews be expected to empathize with Christianity if Christians are expected to regard Judaism with reverence and love? If some Jews cannot do so, can they truly feel at home in the western world? Goethe, who was by no means a religious dogmatist, put these words in the mouth of his hero: ". . . how can we permit him [i.e., the Jew] to take part in the noblest culture, since he denies its source and origin."[39]

Graetz' reply to Treitschke was acrimonious and insulting. The Jewish historian denied that he either misrepresented the great men of Germany or that he disdained the whole of Christendom. He justified the occasional traces of so-called Jewish arrogance in his writings by summoning to the witness stand the renowned British statesman, Benjamin Disraeli, an ardent defender of aristocratic racism, who described Jewry as an invincible "pure race." Erudite historian though he was, Graetz could not foresee the horrible consequences for his own people of the racist mystique. As to the unique place of Luther in the Germanic pantheon, he submitted that as a Jewish historian he was obliged to take note of the bitter ravings of Luther against the Jews in the declining years of his life, but he, Graetz, also faithfully recounted Luther's earlier admiration for Jews. He cited his own appreciation of the nobility and supreme worth of the message of Jesus in his multivolume history, a judgment for which he was roundly criticized by orthodox and nationalist Jews. He pointed out that in the English translation of his book he revised his pre-1870 estimate of the German masses as *Michels* ("simpletons"). Most emphatically he denied that Judaism, as he and his Conservative colleagues understood it, was nationalistic in the sense of aiming at a secular, self-segregating status. He even cited the testimony of the evangelical theologian Paulus Cassel, a converted Jew, who took his Christianity seriously as a universal faith, and who condemned the Teutonic zealotry of Treitschke as a revival of paganism.[40]

Graetz was in an unenviable position. He was blamed by his Jewish colleagues for the ethnic pathos and the abrasive tone of his *History of the Jews*, which provoked the ire of the likes of Treitschke. Some of the Jewish intellectuals scorned him as a "Palestinian" Jew. He was not invited to join the association of German Jewish historians because his Germanic patriotism and western orientation were questioned by his colleagues. As a matter of fact, in his diary and in his letters, he expressed the conviction that Christianity was an inveterate foe of progress and freedom. He looked to England and North America as the lands of hope, since the genius of the Hebrew Scriptures was deeply ingrained in the Anglo-Saxon countries.[41]

In a less personal sense, Treitschke's critique of Graetz had raised this basic question: Can an all-embracing and unrestrained nationalistic ideology tolerate a Jewish community in its midst? It would seem that, by its very nature, a nationalistic ideology that is not tempered by humanism must work toward the elimination of all "alien" bodies. Treitschke was the leading prophet of narrow, zealous Teutonism. To be sure, the concept of totalitarianism did not yet exist in the 1870s, nor was Treitschke totalitarian in the sense in which the word is used in the twentieth century. His nationalism was still modified by his earlier allegiance to nineteenth-century liberalism and by the moral heritage of Christianity. He began his public career as a liberal and moved steadily toward extreme nationalism. His comments on Graetz and German Jewry centered attention on the logic of intuitive or folk-nationalism. In this view it is the function of intellectuals to justify the feelings and intuitions of the "folk." Since the untutored masses have always hated the "foreigners" in their midst—the Jews, as well as the Poles, the French, and the English—

the Jew must cease to be a foreigner, in terms of folk-feeling. The nation-state demands much more than the observance of its laws—it demands an "internalization" of the national personality, an identification of oneself with the collective ego of the nation. What is the scope and depth of this demand? How is it to be measured? Can the Jew ever meet this requirement? If so, how?[42] This question preoccupied both Jews and Germans in the 1880s.

The young Hermann Cohen, destined to become the greatest philosopher of German Jewry, asserted in 1880 the rightness of Treitschke's demand and also the belief that the Jews of Germany had fulfilled it completely, except for "Palestinians," like Graetz, who lacked roots in German culture. Cohen rejected altogether the racist axioms of Graetz and Disraeli, contending that it was not blood but culture that provided the unifying bond of a great nation. Furthermore, according to Cohen, culture is not a mystical-metaphysical essence that common people sense intuitively. It is a body of ideas and ideals. Hence, he concluded, the Jews, or the vast majority of them, have become part of the German nation by embracing its culture in heart and soul.

In the course of his long and productive life Cohen moved steadily from a near-assimilationist position to one of ardent defense of historic Judaism. yet he remained steadfast in his belief that Judaism in its noblest reaches was akin to the creative essence of German culture. In 1916, a year before he died, he published an essay on Germanism and Judaism in which he demonstrated that the Jewish faith, in its prophetic essence, and the German spirit, in its purity, were virtually identical. He achieved this *tour de force* by a process of reductive reasoning—reducing Judaism to the moral-rational component of the prophetic tradition and reducing Germanism to the intuitionism of the medieval mystic, Meister Eckhart, the ethical rationalism of Kant, and the grand course of nineteenth-century idealism. This method of abstracting from the totality of historical Judaism and from the many-sidedness of German culture was thoroughly in keeping with Cohen's neo-Kantian philosophy, which regarded the fullness of experience as raw material to be transmuted by a dynamic culture consciousness. It is only in the course of this process that true being may be reached. As a man of culture each of us must trust not his instinct, but his mind, his conscience, and his cultivated sense of harmony.

Today no scholar would deny that Judaism had always included the awareness of a historic struggle for an independent and secure existence in this world and that Germanism contained the memory of two long periods, pagan and Christian, in which there were only brief moments of flirtation with the ideal of a free, secular, and liberal state. Jews could identify with the liberal movements in Germany. They could also recognize the kinship of their own biblical heritage with the Christian component of modern German culture. As Cohen put it in a conversation with the neo-Kantian philosopher Friedrich Lange: " . . . what you call Christianity, I call prophetic Judaism."[43] But a healthy, authentic confluence of the two streams of historic experience emerges only in the course of time and under the benign aegis of a tolerant, humanist society. Treitschke's zealous nationalism allowed neither for the effect of time nor for the need of a humanist atmosphere. He demanded an instant transformation of German Jewry—and in depth![44]

It is interesting to note that Hermann Cohen returned to the criticism of Graetz' History in 1917, when he himself was engaged in writing his *Religion of Reason, out of the Sources of Judaism.*[45]

At that time Cohen pointed out the inconsistencies in Graetz' philosophy of Jewish history. In his essay "Konstruction der Jüdischen Geschichte" Graetz wavered between the concept of Judaism as "the religion of spirit," set against the various "religions of nature," and the idea of Jewry as a nation, aiming at the building of its own state. In 1846 Graetz concurred with Zechariah Frankel's criticism of his views and admitted that Judaism may neither be "politicized," directed toward the founding of a state, nor may it be "localized," conceived as relevant to one country.

Actually, Cohen contended, the One God in Judaism is articulated in the concepts of social ethics, which in the pre-messianic epoch brings together the quest of individual salvation and the realm of secular politics.[46] Thus religion must permeate the domain of politics in order to educate "all citizens in the duties of loving one another," and politics ought to direct all national-political units toward the well-being of the individual and of the totality of mankind. "It is

Messianism that removes the antagonism between politics and religion, and Messianism is the climax as well as the root of monotheism."

Cohen rejected Graetz' description of the biblical period as essentially "political," since the glory of that period was attained not in the victories of King David and not in the wealth of King Solomon, but in the moral fervor of the literary prophets. Cohen's main objection was directed at Graetz' concept of "the Jewish Ideal." The supreme goal of Judaism is not, Cohen contended, the union of the transcendental God-idea and the power-state, à la Hegel's conception of the unfolding of Reason through a succession of world-historical states. In Cohen's view the "Jewish ideal" aims at the redemption of humanity through the ardor of religion and the refinement of culture.[47] The messianic idea is the heart of Judaism. It appeared in the Covenant with Abraham, perhaps even in the Covenant with Noah; it made possible the successive rebirths of the Jewish people, following the various catastrophes of their sorrow-laden history. The full impact of Jewish messianism is still to be felt.

So diffuse was Graetz' narration that Cohen found many points of agreement with the historian, who was his teacher at the Breslau Seminary. With all his romantic longing for a return to Zion, Graetz recognized "that Judaism was not a product of the Orient but its conscious opposition." Toward the end of his life Graetz conceded that "absolute monotheism forms the historical basis for continuity of Judaism."[48]

Cohen formulated the final lesson of Graetz' exposition as follows:

The task of the monotheistic God-idea is to direct the religious constitution of the State [i.e., of every state in which Jews live as free citizens] toward the goal of a Universal organization—i.e. to orient all the organs of the state, in cooperation with other states, toward the goal of redeeming and unifying mankind in accord with the idea of Messianism.[49]

The courageous defense of German Jewry undertaken by the famous historian Theodor Mommsen (1817–1903) satisfied neither the Jews for whom Graetz spoke nor the German nationalists of Treitschke's persuasion. Of Danish extraction, he resented the excesses of German chauvinism. As a liberal, Mommsen maintained that the German Reich must be conceived as a legal, not an ethnic, community. So long as any group of citizens abides by the laws of the state and fulfills its moral obligations to its fellow citizens, it has discharged the duties of its membership. It is the second, not the first, component of the synthetic unity, nation-state, that is decisive. Therefore it is ethically inadmissible to probe into the inner depths of anyone's national consciousness in order to assay the degree of his "Germanism." Such a venture into the dark realm of feelings and convictions is reminiscent of the medieval inquisition, and it is basically inhuman. The state can only legislate in regard to external actions, and it can take account of only overt violations of those laws. Intellectuals who take upon themselves the inquisitorial task of testing the depths of national loyalty open the floodgates to the tides of popular passions and prejudices that threaten to engulf all that is humane and cultured in society. This, in substance, was Mommsen's reproof of Treitschke.

Mommsen, however, addressed himself to the Jews as well. True, the state cannot demand the "internalization" of national loyalty. But a historic minority, insofar as it controls its own institutions, should consciously strive for an ever greater amalgamation with the emotional-cultural life of the dominant nationality. He allowed that the religious scruples of Jews stand in the way of their total assimilation, but he argued that there is no justification for the organization of secular activities—such as those of social action, recreation and philanthropy, along denominational lines. Secular Jews, at least, should not form separatist enclaves of their own, for such self-segregating tactics play into the hands of the romantic nationalists. Why provoke the belligerent bull with the red flag of separatism? Indeed, Mommsen concluded, Jewish secularists should consider joining the Christian faith, not as religious converts but as reverent cultural adherents, offering an earnest of their covenant with the great nation. He wrote:

> The blame for the [distance in feeling] rests indeed in part with the Jews. The word Christendom no longer signifies today precisely what it did in the past, but it is still the one word which embraces the character of the

contemporary international civilization and in which millions upon millions discover their common unity in this world of many nations. To remain outside these limits and within the nation is possible, but difficult and fraught with many dangers. But it is a notorious fact that many Jews are not restrained by reasons of conviction from going over to the Christian fold, but by other feelings, which I can comprehend but not approve.

Also, the great number of specifically Jewish societies which exist here in Berlin, for instance, appear to me to be definitely evil, insofar as they are not purely religious. I can only see in them the after-effects of the old status of a "protected Jewish community." If these after-effects are to disappear on one side, they must also disappear on the other side; on both sides, there is still much to be done.[50]

Mommsen did not take account of the wide area of ambiguity that extends between religion and nationalism, especially within Judaism. Historical memories, cultural creations, and a network of agencies of mutual aid form part of the penumbra of a historical faith. It is even possible to disavow a dogmatic faith and still accept a religious tradition. Graetz, for example, wrote at times as if Judaism were "not a religion at all," but the culture and élan of a race; yet on the whole he maintained that the Jewish "mission" consists in its monotheistic teaching and its insistence on a puritanical code of sexual ethics. Mommsen represented the philosophy of liberalism, which is as unhappy with fractional ethnic, and historical subcultures as it is with the totalitarian zeal of romantic nationalism. While Treitschke, the ardent nationalist, feared, or pretended to fear, the Jews, Mommsen, the Liberal, *feared for* the Jews. To Treitschke, the antisemites represented the inchoate feelings of the "folk," which the elite should "understand"; to Mommsen, the antisemites represented the vicious instincts of the masses, which intellectuals are obligated to condemn. At the same time, however, Mommsen thought it wise not to provoke the common people unduly.

Graetz rejected with contempt the counsel of Mommsen in his "Exchange of Letters with an English Lady over Judaism and Semitism." Speaking of the Jewish task to bring "healing for the wounds of humanity," he assured his correspondent that this goal is best fulfilled when Jews sail proudly under their own banner. He was certain that young and proud Jews will ridicule the seductive voice of that historian of antiquity who called upon the Jews of Germany—"if you wish to be accepted as equals in our society, you have to dissolve or to sink within Christendom. You don't have to believe in Jesus as the Savior. We ourselves no longer hold to this belief. But, there is a conventional Christian facade, which represents the majority. It is the duty of the minority to fall in with the conventions of the majority."[51]

Graetz pointed out that the Hebraic component of the Christian faith was the most progressive factor in the development of the modern world. The historic role of Christianity was to serve as the vehicle of biblical monotheism and the Judaic ethic. Again and again the moral fervor of the prophets generated reforming social movements, which led to fresh horizons of freedom and human dignity. The Reformation was only the clearest instance of the immense power of the Judaic heritage.

If this be so, Graetz continued, then it is best for society as a whole that Jews reinforce their own component of the heritage of the West and not surrender cravenly to the Christian facade. Furthermore, nothing is as deadly for society as a uniform faith, undisturbed by basic tensions. Hence, for the sake of mankind, the Jews must persevere and cherish their heritage. Let the nations of Europe revere and cultivate the Judeo-Christian tradition as a whole, in all its historic diversity, rather than the one faith that happens to prevail in any one country.[52]

It is sad to note that none of the three historians involved in this fateful debate took seriously the tremendous momentum of the historical process. Individuals may possess a large range of freedom and, if they so desire, they may succeed in deserting their historic community and adopting a new identity. But peoples, minorities as well as majorities, cannot transform themselves at will. A collective problem can only be solved collectively. If all the nonorthodox Jews in Germany had accepted Christianity, they would have become a Jewish-Christian community, scorned for their vulgar, mercenary action by the loyal members of both groups. Did not the Jewish *conversos* in Spain and Portugal endure for centuries as Marranos, while the principle of "pure blood" (*limpieza*) confined them within an inexorable ghetto, more dreadful and hopeless than the one in which they lived as Jews? The history of nations moves along several tracks at once. And only a totalitarian government will presume to control all of them.

Furthermore, the pathological antisemites necessarily aroused the embittered defensiveness of Jewish people. Do not we all assert ourselves precisely when we are challenged? So when Jews are attacked, they are likely to put forth the preachers of resentment as their spokesmen. Can anyone question the need of shielding Jewish people with the armor of pride when they are subjected to a barrage of dehumanizing insults? In order to keep their sanity in the face of the wild attacks of the antisemites, Jewish leaders replied, humanly enough, in kind to their detractors. German nationalists, like Treitschke, would express their "understanding" of, if not their agreement with, the antisemites. Thus the vicious cycle was kept in motion while the liberals, Germans as well as Jews, could only wring their hands and plead for the lowering of the Jewish profile, protesting that a so-called Jewish question does not exist at all. In the lands of the Diaspora, the Jew could prosper only if nationalism was not pressed to the point of becoming an all-consuming ideal, an exclusive, jealous god, brooking no rivals; then the liberals could afford to be less fearful of waking the sleeping dogs of irrational frenzy. Romantic or mystical nationalists tended to view world Jewry "through a glass darkly," as a kind of "anti-nation," a dark, satanic foil for the emergent nations of Europe. The "meta-myth," the axiom of Jewish metaphysical uniqueness, had begun to shadow the European horizons.[53]

Five years after the Treitschke-Graetz controversy, the appearance of Edouard von Hartmann's book on the Jews revived the debate on the nature of Jewish identity in Germany.[54] Hartmann achieved distinction as a philosopher at an early age with a striking book, *The Philosophy of the Unconscious*. He was a keen critic of Christianity and an ardent proponent of German nationalism. In his metaphysical speculations, the unconscious will was deemed to be all-powerful, while the intellect was described as a weak, surface phenomenon.

Hartmann blamed the antisemites for slowing down the process of Jewish assimilation by causing Jews to draw together and to reinforce their own solidarity. Yet he also believed that the hatred of the German masses would abate in the course of time and that the goal of total assimilation was possible. To be achieved, however, that goal must be clearly articulated and sustained over a period of several generations.

To Hartmann a blend of Jewish and Teutonic qualities was highly desirable. As he saw it, Jewish realism and moderation were likely to balance the tendency of Germans toward abstractness and immoderate sensuality. As to religion, he opined that both Judaism and Christianity were due to disappear. In Orthodox Judaism, however, he claimed to discover a nurturing of Jewish "tribal feeling" (*Stammesgefühl*) that might well prevent the complete integration of Jews into the German nation-state.

As a romantic nationalist, Hartmann assumed that all human groups moved inexorably toward the attainment of an ever deeper national self-consciousness. Small ethnic remnants that had not yet attained a high level of nationalistic fervor might be incorporated into neighboring national entities without any difficulties. But Jews had reached in the biblical period the acme of national pride in the concept of the chosen people. Their intense self-consciousness was nurtured and reinforced by centuries of martyrdom. Bluntly and directly, he put this question to his Jewish colleagues: Can you overcome the immense tug of tradition and consciously set yourselves the goal of amalgamation with a European nation-state? Is the Jewish concept of a chosen people compatible with integration into the German state? Is it not more likely to deflect Jewish feeling into the direction of a power-seeking "international free-masonry"?

Hartmann viewed the Jewish people from the perspective of organic nationalism. The Jews are a nation, not a religious community. Like all nations they must seek power, scattered though they be in many lands. Since they cannot obtain power through the instrumentality of a state, they must seek it covertly. Hence, he inferred, they are likely to be impelled instinctively to engage in secret, conspiratorial adventures in order to bend the powers of the world to their will.

To Hartmann, the formative drive of Judaism was not faith but the national will for survival and, therefore, also for power. And this national will is instinctive, indeed largely unconscious. "So, Judaism forms an international free-masonry . . . which receives its ideal content from religion, its recognition from an ethnic type, its international body from the *Alliance Israelite Universelle* [an organization dedicated to international Jewish philanthropy]."[55]

Conceding that the antisemites exaggerated the conspiratorial role of the *Alliance* and its quest for power, Hartmann nevertheless affirmed that the feelings of solidarity, which the *Alliance* represented, made it impossible for Jews to become part of the German nation as well as the German state. He repeated the suggestion first made by Schopenhauer—to wit, suppose a Jew were in a position to help only one of two persons, the first a German, the second a Jew from a foreign state. Which one will he help? Schopenhauer asserted that Jews generally would help the foreign Jew in preference to the native Gentile. "The Homeland of the Jew is other Jews."[56] Hartmann agreed with Schopenhauer and concluded that the complete enfranchisement of Jewish people in Germany might have been based on a false axiom.

As we noted earlier, Hartmann's nationalistic vantage point led him to see the Jews as an anomalous community, an international nation, seeking power through secret and conspiratorial devices. Also, since in his view cultural creativity derived from the depths of the national soul, the apparent literary and artistic attainments of Jewish savants and artists in European idioms could only be superficial, sterile imitations of the national culture of the host nation. Furthermore, such hollow creations are likely to be corrosive of the Germanic national genius. Thus, he wrote of "the destructive ferment of Jewish negativism."[57]

The mentality of Hartmann exemplified the antisemitic logic of the romantic nationalist, especially the ease with which he slipped into the ideological quagmire of the hate-filled demagogues—the mythology of the Jewish quest for power through conspiracy, the uncreative character of Jewish cultural works, the mystique of Jewish self-adulation as reflected in the concept of "The Chosen People." While he struggled against the antisemitic agitation for the disenfranchisement of Jews, Hartmann offered fresh ammunition for that very demand.

Actually, one could speak in the nineteenth century of a Jewish will to survive, though not of a collective will to power. Jewish survival depends on an alert public conscience, not on secret deals or conspiracies. As a matter of fact The Alliance Israelite Universelle was directed by men who were staunchly opposed to any form of Jewish nationalism and whose program consisted in the promulgation of the ideals of French liberalism. Jewish emancipation in France was an achievement of explicit, universal ideals contained in the Declaration of the Rights of Man. The cause of Jewish survival was intimately associated with the ebb and flow of European liberalism.

As to the doctrine of the Chosen People, modern Judaism interprets it in two ways, neither of which is inimical to the cause of the nation-state. Some interpret it in the traditional religious sense of *Kiddush Hashem*, the Sanctification of the Name. As children of the Covenant, Jewish people have been historically associated with the doctrine of ethical monotheism and the biblical philosophy of life. They must make greater demands on themselves because they are the bearers of rich ancestral memories and traditions. Which state does not benefit from a group of people so ethically motivated and so dedicated?

The nontraditional interpretation universalized this dogma. Jews are "chosen" as *example*, not as *exception*. All peoples are chosen by Providence to the extent to which they have been endowed with the capacity to serve God and mankind. At different times in history, different groups will be in the position of bringing an extra measure of light and vitality to mankind. The prophetic summons to Israel is paradigmatic for the forward-looking spirits in every age and among every people. The Talmud summarizes the whole Torah in this verse from Proverbs: "In all your ways, know Him, and He will direct your paths."[58]

As to the cultural creativity of the Jews in European lands, the court of last resort is the universal community. The nation, as well as the individual, faces the judgment of God and humanity. The attribution of creativity to the mystical spirit of the "folk" was a gratuitous assumption of the romantic nationalists, an assumption that suited the spirit of ethnic narcissism at a certain stage of

European development. Some Jewish writers, such as Martin Buber in the early phase of his career, also spoke in this vein.[59] Hopefully, we have now emerged from the miasma of contending ethnic egos into the broad and open horizons of universal culture.

This view was beautifully expressed in 1892 by Professor H. Steinthal, a foremost exponent of German Jewry in the last two decades of the nineteenth century. The "Chosenness" of the Jewish people belongs to the past tense, he argued—that is, it is a memory of inspired prophets and heroic martyrs. Whether or not a unique mission is reserved for Jews is a "mystery" that only Providence will reveal in due time. In the present, Steinthal asserted, we can only speak of a Jewish "vocation," and it is the same vocation that all men have—namely, to promote the love of God and the love of mankind.

Steinthal added that "we are no longer a Jewish people"—hence, the idealism inspired by Jewish historic memories is poured into the roles of Jews as citizens of a modern state. "We are Germans, because it is impossible for us not to be Germans." If told by religious romanticists that "the Germans are the people of religion," Jews feel doubly blessed, since as Jews they are also constituted as a people of religion. To be twice-blessed is to be twice committed to God by the principle of *noblesse oblige*. Germanism gives wider scope to Judaism: "chosenness" compels Jews to repudiate shoddy flag-waving. "We repudiate the kind of patriotism which contradicts humanity and demands the exclusion of all that is foreign."

The German mob may cry out: "Cease to be Jews; dissolve in the German nation." But Jews consider it the duty of the spiritual elite to resist the vulgarities of the mob. "In us, the German spirit lives more powerfully than it does in the hearts of millions of ethnic Germans." "Judaism is humanity," and humanism is the glory of German culture. So Judaism is consistent with every "humane nationalism."[60]

Looking back on Steinthal's essays from our contemporary vantage point, we may question the realism of the author and his clairvoyance, but we can hardly doubt either his sincerity or the nobility of his world view.

VI. *The Jews as Socialists Saw Them*

In the nineteenth century the socialist movement fell broadly into two ideological classes—utopian and Marxist. The former based its appeal on the idealistic aspiration for an egalitarian society, dedicated to freedom and justice; the latter aimed to arrive at the same goal by way of consciously hastening the impersonal and inevitable processes of history, namely, by promoting a materialistic philosophy of life and acknowledging the decisive significance of the "class-struggle," which is fated to bring about the inevitable breakdown of the capitalistic economy and the ultimate establishment of a classless society.

Both forms of socialism contained the germs of anti-Jewish hostility. We shall presently discuss the antisemitism of the utopian Socialists. We have already had occasion to mention the anti-Judaic animus of Karl Marx. His scorn was directed at the economic function of the Jew in Europe. Jews were instrumental in promoting the age of finance capitalism and bringing to an inglorious close the simpler order of feudalism. This aspect of Marxism was torn out of its historical context by antisemitic writers and used in popularizing the so-called distinction between Jewish finance capitalism and industrial capitalism—a distinction the Nazis employed in their effort to court the industrialists of Germany, while keeping up the pretense of being devoted to Socialism.[1]

However, nineteenth-century Marxism, in all its "purity," could be embraced by *secularist* Jewish people, without revisionist modifications. The mature philosophy of Marx and Engels, after all, was imbued with deep moral fervor, even though these revolutionary philosophers boasted that their analysis of society was strictly scientific, untainted by any idealism. Even if we grant that "in the end of the days" socialism will triumph, there is no compelling reason for selfish persons today to cast their lot with the proletariat. On the assumption that people will follow the selfish interests of their class, with intellectuals producing the ideological "fig-leaf" for their economic caste, the question arises, why, apart from idealism, should bourgeois intellectuals sacrifice their own well-being for the sake of the workers? Yet the leaders of socialism in nearly all lands were members of the middle and upper ranks of the bourgeoisie. No economic benefit could possibly accrue to those who identified themselves with "the morality of the future," abandoning in their own generation their real class interests.

The tremendous appeal of Marxism was, therefore, ethical and quasi-religious. With prophetic fervor the Marxists challenged the built-in institutional hypocrisy that made it possible for sincere and well-meaning people to imagine that their time-bound and class-oriented ideals and norms were right and true in themselves and forever. Marxism appealed to a deeper, more sophisticated sincerity that pierced the veil of conventional pieties. Like the great religions, it demanded agonizing sacrifices, but it promised the quasi-religious reward of unity with the real, the true, and the absolute. The future classless society will endure eternally; it will be free from the self-deceptions and the "contradictions" of the present; it will cure man's "alienation" from the roots of his own true being.

So it was possible for the biblically trained Jewish youth of the Pale to embrace Marxism as the "scientific" version of the ancient prophetic ideal. The messianic age is indeed the goal of history, but, according to the new dispensation, it will be achieved, not by divine fiat, but through the iron laws of history. Intellectuals today, like the prophets of old, live in anticipation of the future. In the present they endure the fate of the "Suffering Servant," but when the court of world history has rendered its final verdict, it will be seen that the socialists hastened the end and built in the wilderness the pathway of redemption. In the midst of the present "realm of necessity," they built the future "kingdom of freedom."

This idealistic-religious core of Marxism was wrapped in the hard shell of atheistic materialism. Along with the ardor of social justice, the movement nurtured cold contempt for the values and norms of a free society and fanned the flames of popular envy and bitterness. Idealistic at its core, socialism fostered hatred and struggle. This ambivalence of Marxism was carried over into the realm of personal ethics and family life. Young people were encouraged to throw off the shackles of convention and to reach out toward new horizons of freedom, but in their contempt for the ideal and the romantic they often rebelled against the tested wisdom of humanity, in respect to family life, shocking their elders and hurting themselves more often than not. In every facet of modern culture, the demonic and the divine components of socialism struggled for supremacy. When the rushing currents of socialism invaded the narrow alleys of the ghetto, all the ambiguities of the movement were soon in evidence.

The Bund which was formed in Vilna at the turn of the century, combined Marxist socialism with the concern for Jewish "continuity" (*hemshech*). Formed originally by emissaries of the Russian Social Democratic party for the purpose of imbuing Jewish workers with the ideology of socialism, the Bund came to stress with ever greater determination the Judaic elements in its program. It insisted that the "conception of Nation applied to the Jewish people," and it demanded "national rights" for Jews, not merely "civil rights." The Bolshevik party, led by Lenin, denounced this trend with mounting bitterness. The more the Bundists embraced their Jewish heritage, albeit in an altered, secularistic, and folkist version, the more vitriolic became the attacks against them by the left-socialists and Communists.

The Bund became the most powerful Jewish party in the state of Poland to exist between the two world wars, drawing into its ranks former Yeshivah students and intellectuals generally. The triumph of nationalism at the Versailles Conference made any insistence on the nonnational character of Jewry appear utterly ridiculous. The efflorescence of Yiddish literature demonstrated the reality of Jewish nationalism. Also the massive growth of antisemitism in newly formed Poland, that was struggling for its life in the shadow of the Swastika, proved the hollowness of any assimilationist philosophy. Accordingly in the years 1936–1939, the Bund scored impressive gains in municipal elections. However, the career of the Bund was cut short by the outbreak of World War I. When the Soviet forces burst into Poland and into the Baltic countries in 1939, they turned their attention first to the Bundists, incarcerating and executing their leaders.[2]

In France and Belgium the bitter denunciations of the status quo by the utopian socialists were dripping anti-Jewish venom from the very beginning. The schools of François Charles Marie Fourier, Alphonse Toussenel, Pierre-Joseph Proudhon, and Pierre Leroux insisted on identifying the Jews with the super-bankers, as if all Jews were partners of the Rothschilds. The Jews were the visible beneficiaries of the liberal order that supplanted the feudal way of life. For these social visionaries, however, liberalism was the supreme failure. With impassioned zealotry they undertook to demonstrate the rottenness of an individualistic society. In their hatred of the new order, some of them did not hesitate to utilize ancient popular prejudices. Catering to the vague and unfocused resentment of the proletariat, they employed the metaphors and stereotypes of the Christian tradition as well as the new scientific theories of race, which were popularized in the latter half of the nineteenth century.

Fourier (1772–1837) and his disciples called attention to the self-segregating character of the Jewish dietary laws, in consequence of which Jews stayed outside the national fraternity. Jews can only "exploit" the economy, not contribute to it, since they remain inwardly alien to the Gentile world.[3]

Alphonse Toussenel (1803–1885) produced a popular book in which socialist antisemitism was brought to a climax. In his *The Jews— Kings of the Epoch*, first printed in 1845, he employed the term *Jew* interchangeably with *banker* and *usurer*. By means of distortions of this type, he set out to prove that "Europe is now dominated by Israel." He mingled together ancient prejudices against the Jewish religion with contemporary grievances against real estate speculators and manipulators of the stock exchange. The result was an effective piece of propaganda that showed that religious hatred can be secularized into ethnic hostility and mingled with revolutionary fervor. Toussenel's amazing success encouraged many imitators from his day to the present. Like him, they combined two mystery-laden images—that of the medieval enigmatic "wandering Jew," at once uniquely blessed and uniquely cursed; and that of the modern mythical wire puller, causing successive crashes of the money markets of the world and their attendant miseries. The Anti-Christ of religion had become the legendary villain of the economy.[4]

In Germany the combination of racial antisemitism and socialist propaganda were probably best represented by Eugen Dühring (1833–1921). A stormy petrel in his own lifetime, he is today best remembered as the antagonist against whom Friedrich Engels wrote the book, *Herr Eugen Dühring's Revolution in Science* (1878).[5] It was also Dühring who convinced Theodor Herzl of the hopelessness of the Jewish situation in Europe.[6]

In the 1870s Dühring was a leading figure in German socialist circles. The author of many voluminous works, he described his own "socialitary system" as an authentic version of "German Socialism," designed to counteract "Jewish Social Democracy." Manifestly, he was one of the many intellectual "fathers" of the Nazi movement, which claimed to draw its socialist inspiration from Prussian discipline, contrasting the "organic" character of a military camp with the divisive quality of Marxism.[7]

Eduard Bernstein (1850–1932) started out as a disciple of Dühring's, but he later developed a "revisionist" form of socialism, directly opposed to all that Dühring represented. Bernstein, a Jew, imbued socialism with the democratic ideal and the fervor of prophetic ethics. "It [socialism] is something that *ought* to be, or a movement toward something that ought to be."[8]

In contrast, Dühring based his socialism on the principle that "force" is all that matters in society. Engels wrote his thoroughgoing refutation of Dühring in order to exorcise the ghost of racism and its attendant vices from the socialist movement.

> . . . and even his [Dühring's] hatred of the Jews, which he carried to ridiculous extremes and exhibits on every possible occasion, is a feature, which if not specifically Prussian, is yet specific to the region East of the Elbe. That same philosopher of reality who has a sovereign contempt for all prejudices and superstitions is himself so deeply imbued with personal crotchets that he calls the popular prejudice against the Jew, inherited from

the bigotry of the Middle Ages, "a natural judgment," based on "natural grounds," and rises to pyramidal heights with the assertion that socialism is the only power which can oppose population conditions with a strong Jewish admixture.[9]

Dühring was opposed to all religions, and, in keeping with his doctrine of "pure" races, he suggested the breeding of more and more perfect races for the society of the future, in which the state would be all-powerful—"the individual is subject to absolute compulsion by the state."[10]

The prestige of Engels within the German socialist movement was sufficient to overcome Dühring's "Prussianism" and his racism, at least insofar as the official leadership was concerned. But the unique appeal of antisemitic mythology to populist protest movements was demonstrated again and again in German and Austrian politics.

Karl Kautsky (1854–1938), a leading Marxist, attempted to combat the racist trends within socialism in his book, *Are the Jews a Race?*

Like Engels, Kautsky was impressed by the Jewish labor movement in America, which contributed so mightily to the organization and growth of the general labor unions. "The Jewish workers' movement in the United States is one of the most active pioneers of social progress."[11]

He recognized that Jewish people were divided along economic lines, like every other community, and that the myth of the Jew as the demonic villain in European society served to bewilder and confuse the uneducated population. He laid to rest the illusion of some socialist agitators that anti-Jewish pogroms might be helpful in training revolutionary cadres to make good use of guerilla tactics.

The times are passed when anti-Semitism might parade as a variety of socialism—"the socialism of the simple citizen of Vienna." Today, anti-Semitism is a phase of the struggle against the proletariat, and it is indeed the most cowardly and brutal of these phases; it has become "the socialist-baiting of the simple citizen of Vienna."[12]

Antisemitism, he continued, is the perennial temptation of the petite bourgeoisie, who find themselves pressed into the wretched ranks of the proletariat.

> The battle against capital as a whole seems hopeless. But the conflict with Judaism, with Jewish capital, which is so unpleasantly felt by many a non-Jewish capitalist, seems to afford better prospects of success.[13]

With mordant wit and by means of the statistical data then available, Kautsky demolished the various mystical theories of race that were propounded by Wagner, Chamberlain, and Sombart. If Jews do particularly well in the modern industrial society, he maintained, it is because they were trained in the arts of commerce for generations. "The capitalist mode of production is predominantly urban in character. . . . Therefore, that section of the population will make itself more felt within capitalism whose faculties have been best adapted to urban life, to trade, to scientific labor: this means the Jews."[14]

But while Kautsky refuted all antisemitic calumnies seriatim, he also characterized the Jewish cultural heritage as a reactionary, counterrevolutionary force. He attacked not only the Zionist movement and Jewish racists, but also the natural desire of Jews to transmit their cultural heritage to their children.[15] The very attempt to maintain a separate Jewish secular identity was, to him, counterrevolutionary.

> The Jews have become an eminently revolutionary factor, while Judaism has become a reactionary factor. It is like a weight of lead attached to Jews who eagerly seek to progress. . . . We cannot say we have completely emerged from the Middle Ages, as long as Judaism still exists among us. The sooner it disappears, the better it will be, not only for society, but also for the Jews themselves. . . .
>
> It will not mean a mere shifting from one medieval ruin to another, not a transition from Orthodox Judaism to ecclesiastical Christianity, but the creation of a new and higher type of man.[16]

So even the democratic socialists suffered from the illusion that they could design and build "a new and higher type of man," for the sake of whom old, historic communities must be encouraged to commit suicide.

The French school of St. Simon is of special interest to Jewish historians, since it fostered a positive appreciation of the Jewish heritage. While the school was officially disbanded in the mid-1830s, its intellectual impetus continued to be felt in the cultural and political life of France.

St. Simon's (1760–1825) ideas were gradually unfolded in the course of an eventful life. He based his utopia on the fact that human beings are not born equal. Some are endowed with artistic skills, others with the capacity for science and invention, still others with the gifts of commercial enterprise and business management. The ideal society is one in which the elite classes work together with the common people for the benefit of society as a whole.

What is to keep such a society from falling apart? Why should the elite work for the common good and not for themselves? After experimenting with diverse motifs such as honor, esteem, and patriotism, St. Simon finally arrived at the notion that was implicit in his system from the beginning. The ultimate cement of his "organismic" society will be a new, universal religion—complete with a doctrine, a ritual, a clergy, and a hierarchy. But this universal religion, which he called "the new Christianity," will be dedicated exclusively to humanitarian ideals. The clergy of the new faith will then organize and supervise the governing elite, "the aristocracy of talent."

> The new Christianity will have its morality, its creed and its dogma; it will have its clergy and its clergy will have its leaders. But . . . the doctrine of morality will be considered by the New Christians as the most important; creed and dogma will be envisaged by them only as accessories whose principal purpose it is to fix the attention of the faithful of all classes upon morality. . . .[17]

St. Simon had the highest regard for men of enterprise and skill. He esteemed investment bankers as the spark plugs of society. In moments of ecstasy he even appropriated the Jewish dream of the messianic era, casting himself in the role of the Messiah. He acclaimed the creative Jewish role in the creation of the western industrial world. In turn, some very talented young Jews were drawn to his utopia.[18] "The effect of the Saint-Simonian ideology upon the Jews who joined the cult is one of the most curious phenomena of Nineteenth century intellectual and social history."[19]

Perhaps men like the Pereira brothers, eminently successful bankers, saw in St. Simonism the certification of their own worth as inventive money managers. They might also have seen in the St. Simonian vision of a new humanitarian religion the hope of an honorable exit from the burdens of the Jewish faith. As socialists they could attain the Nirvana of total de-Judaization and dissolution in the "new Christianity."

As it happened, the St. Simonian school came to grief by reason of its excesses in religion. If all that is human is holy, what is profane? Thus, among the faithful St. Simonians "the body was solemnly reinstated; work was hallowed, food was hallowed; voluptuous appetites were hallowed. . . . The winter of 1832 was one long celebration in Rue Monsigny. Religion was crowned with roses; it appeared in the aroma of punch and in noisy harmonies of the orchestra. . . ."[20]

Emile Durkheim (1858–1917), the renowned sociologist, put his finger on the basic flaw in St. Simonian religion. It did not recognize a realm of ends, outside of society; hence, it could not orient and steer the ship of state.

> Thus, the new religion has no proper goal outside this earth. It is itself an earthly thing. Its domain is of this world. It declares that God is not exterior to things, but is part of them, blends with them. . . . That St. Simonian religion can be nothing other than a pantheism asserting the fundamental identity of all beings and deifying temporal reality as well as thought.[21]

Durkheim contended that a spiritual power is needed not only to promote productivity, but also to curb the appetites: ". . . needs and appetites are normal only on condition of being controlled."[22] A society will surely disintegrate if it does not recognize the supreme validity of some absolute prohibitions. Durkheim suggested the possibility that some regulatory forces will emerge in a free society out of the various self-governing professional associations. His suggestion, however, is not sufficient, since professional associations are likely in their turn to become self-serving and to offend against the well-being of society.

In his later years, Durkheim became deeply conscious not only of the one-sidedness of St. Simonian "religion," but also of the inadequacy of his own interpretation of religion as being the mythological expression and celebration of the life and power of the tribe. This sociological conception of religion accounts for the exaltation of public worship, when the individual feels stirred and uplifted by his identification with the tribe. It explains ancient myths as metaphors of a tribe's origin, greatness, and destiny. But this theory fails to explain the higher reaches of religion, when a person sets the voice of God within his soul against the thrust of the tradition and against the pressure of the living community. As Durkheim himself wrote: "In fact, the more cultivated a people, the less does the dogma which unifies it, bar free examination."[23]

In particular, the career of the Hebrew prophets opened a new phase in the evolution of religion; in the name of faith itself, they condemned the popular religion and the national ethos as narcissistic. Christianity, like Judaism, contains a prophetic nisus.

The crux of the utopian fallacy is its disregard for history. The role assigned to history in socialist thought is to "prepare the way" for the Eschaton; thereafter, it falls back into infinite emptiness, like the spent shell of a spaceship. Thus St. Simon conceived of the course of history as moving from the pre-Socratic era to the period of "conjectural systems," or theologies, and thence to the age of "positive systems," when all mystery is eliminated from the development of society. His disciple August Comte sharpened the focus of this line of reasoning when he described the course of history as moving from the Theological to the Philosophical age and thence to the era of mathematics. In any case, the end is known. St. Simon also wrote of the alternation between "organic" and "critical" ages. But the task of a stable society is to provide for the cleansing acids of criticism within the framework of an organismic order.

Here is where a genuine reverence for the actual confluence of diverse cultural streams in history might have corrected the utopian ideal. In the history of the western world there were tension and struggle between diverse religious traditions. If that struggle is kept within the bounds of civility and good sense, the contending religious viewpoints create an atmosphere wherein a common consensus obtains for what we might call relative moral absolutes, while a lively debate is maintained concerning the rest of the religious heritage. Such a situation prevailed in England after 1688, and it made possible the healthy balance between freedom and order that for the most part shielded that island people from the upheavals that troubled the nations of the Continent.

It follows that the universal religion, which an ideal socialist society requires, is one that includes within its purview a cluster of mutually challenging faiths. So it is not a "new Christianity" that we need, but the actual, awkward balance that is comprised within the Judeo-Christian tradition. There is a luminous core of common ideals, but its edges are blurred, defying definition. A plurality of viewpoints is built within the Judeo-Christian polarity, encouraging the voices of criticism. Emphasis on justice is set against the exclusive claims of an all-embracing love; the cold winds of human wisdom contend against the hot breath of divine inspiration; the same history of salvation (*Heilsgeschichte*) is seen from diverse angles of vision. The result is a restless ferment of ideas, a stirring climate of idealism without absolutism.

As there are caverns within caverns in hell, so there are depths below depths in antisemitism. It is necessary to discriminate between the entire class of French demagogues, the so-called *anti-juif* socialists, and the pathological antisemites. To the former, Jewish identity was a convenient symbol, to the latter, a magical mystery. The *anti-juif* agitators used the word Jew in various combinations, as a synonym for usurer and manipulator, in keeping with some of the meanings listed in the 1835 and 1878 editions of the *Dictionnaire de l'Academie Francaise*—"to be rich like a Jew," to charge usurious rates or exorbitant prices, *Juiverie—Il m'a fait une juiverie* ("he jewed me down"), etc. These writers smeared all the Jews with the brush of popular resentment of malicious plutocrats. When they wrote of *la juiverie, formule de Jesus* or *la juiverie catholique*, or *la juiverie jesuite* they expressed contempt for Christians, Catholics, and Jesuits, but at the same time they reinforced the momentum of popular hatred of Jews, and they helped distort and enlarge the spectral image of the Jew to mythological proportions.

According to legend, the ghosts of the dead acquire fresh life when they lap recently spilled blood. So the medieval Christian myths of the Jews as "children of Satan" were infused with fresh vigor by the socialist agitators. The "Synagogue of Satan" was as malicious as ever, only now its work was done in the mysterious anterooms of investment banks and the stock exchange.

It may well be that utopian socialists, like Toussenel, Leroux, and Chirac, were sincere in their disclaimers that by the term Jew they meant the financiers and industrialists of their day, regardless of religion and racial origin. Some socialists could justify even the rabid anti-Jewish ranting of Edouard Drumont, "because in creating antisemites they have created socialists in religious circles where any other propaganda would certainly fail."[24] Then, we may ask, why did this long line of socialist agitators employ the images of the mythical Jew? Did they not realize that they were grievously injuring a whole people?

We cannot ascribe the same motifs to all the *anti-juif* socialists, but we can hardly doubt that they operated on the principle "the end justifies the means." If Bismarck could deliberately make use of antisemitism for several years in his struggle against the liberals and socialists, why should we expect French socialists to be more scrupulous? The French masses were indifferent to recondite analyses of the economy, but they could be galvanized into action by anti-Jewish slogans, which catered to ingrained and widespread prejudices. Long before Hitler, these demagogues discovered the fact that the mob wants its Satan incarnated in flesh and blood, preferably in the shape of people who are alien and defenseless, yet in some mythical way worthy of their steel. Perhaps some of the agitators did not realize that the rhetoric of mythological antisemitism could lead to an Auschwitz. The conspicuous Jews of their day appeared to be not an oppressed class, but a strong and privileged group, well able to protect its interests. In any case, the Dreyfus Affair compelled the leading socialists to confront the danger of antisemitism and exorcise its spell on the ranks of organized labor.

Why did some socialists employ the weapon of antisemitism, while others shunned its use and combated it as a social plague? We noted that the St. Simonians fought against antisemitism, as did the Marxists generally, in spite of Marx's own ambivalence.

Professor J. L. Talmon suggests that "the line of demarcation in this was the approval or disapproval of change, indeed one may say of the modern world, and also the presence or absence of direct Jewish inspiration, which in most cases, meant the same."[25]

The import of the second factor cannot be determined, since the spirit of the Hebrew Bible is part of the culture and faith of the western world. As to Talmon's first and main point, we cannot agree. Certainly, the Nazis embraced with gusto the need of harnessing science to the needs of industry, and they gloried in the Nietzschean ethic of subordinating the welfare of the living for the higher good of the "Super Race" of the future. A nostalgia for the Middle Ages marked the mood of some utopian socialists, but theirs was not a Ghandi-like approach to the industrial revolution.

In our view the line separating the two kinds of socialism follows the psychological distinction between the rationalist and the romantic. The men of sentiment and fantasy naturally sympathized with the feelings of the masses and employed the myths and images sanctified by long usage. Their rhetoric reflected the involuted, emotional "logic" of the common people. With malicious intent or in sheer naiveté, they dusted off the ghostly images of "the Christian Unconscious," in which the Jew of history served as perpetual anti-hero. A good example of theological prejudice garbed in biological terminology is given by Proudhon, when he speaks of "the vile trait of Satan and Ahriman, which was embodied in the Semitic race."[26]

The men of reason, however, could not but stigmatize antisemitism as "the socialism of fools." As soon as historical developments proved that antisemitism functioned as the battering ram of the reactionaries, the Marxist socialists could not but condemn it in the strongest language. By the same token, when Marxism itself became a rigid Orthodoxy, repudiating the canons of empirical criticism, it was no longer immune to the virus of antisemitism. So, in the Soviet world, antisemitism could reappear, either as a consequence of governmental tactics, or as a side effect of a resurgent nationalism.

The moral ambivalence of Marxism is analyzed by Karl G. Popper in *The Open Society and Its Enemies*. He points out that the acceptance of violence as the inevitable instrument of revolution confers legitimacy on the attempts of conservatives to suppress forcibly any movement toward social progress. In fact, Engels expected that the bourgeoisie "will take the first shot."[27] Prior to the Nazi takeover in Germany, the Communists announced the slogan "Fascism is the last stronghold of the bourgeoisie," as if the triumph of Hitler were a necessary stage in the advance toward the millennium. So the rhetoric of Marxism helped to undermine the liberal effort to redress the grievances of the proletariat and the poor. In effect the German Communists were the allies of the Nazis in demolishing the Weimar Republic. The Marxist preaching of an ultimate Armageddon was at least in part a self-fulfilling prophecy.

Popper questions whether "moral futurism" (whatever *will* be *is* right) is preferable to "moral presentism" (whatever *is*, *is* right). Hegel's conservatism was an expression of the latter doctrine. Marx's radicalism was based on a presumed capacity to foresee the future. His "historicism," relating the validity of moral judgments to a particular stage in the evolution of history, was inevitably nihilistic in effect.[28]

Yet Popper acknowledges that Marxism was inspired by a prophetic passion for justice, a fact that Marx himself underrated:

A similar case is Marx's underrating of the significance of his own moral ideas; for it cannot be doubted that the secret of his religious influence was in its moral appeal, that his criticism of capitalism was effective mainly as a moral criticism. Marx showed that a social system as such can be unjust; that if the system is bad, then all the righteousness of the individuals who profit from it is a mere sham righteousness, is mere hypocrisy. For our responsibility extends to the system, to the institutions which we allow to persist."[29]

Because of its ambivalence, Marxism was split between the Democratic wing, which stressed the gradual achievement of social progress, and Communism, which condemned any effort to ameliorate the conditions of the poor. The Social Democratic parties of western Europe welded the ideals of socialism and freedom into a philosophy of social advancement that repudiated the resort to violence, while the Communists, entranced by their own vision of perfection condemned meliorism in social affairs and stigmatized any idealistic philosophy of life as a betrayal of the Cause. Both wings appealed to the authority of Karl Marx, who, toward the end of his life, believed that in England the social revolution could be achieved peacefully.[30]

The Social Democratic Party in Germany was strongly favored by Jews, individually and through their communal organizations.[31] Of sixty Jews who served in the Reichstag in the years of 1870–1930, thirty-five were Social Democrats. This Party conducted an active campaign against Adolf Stoecker's "Christian" crusade, which combined antisemitism with anti socialism.[32] The Social Democrats, dedicated to a fair and reasoned analysis of social problems, battled against the fantastic distortions of antisemitic demagogues, not so much from affection for Jews as "out of hatred for the vulgar ideology of Antisemitism, which destroys reason."

However, ultraconservatives were prone to overrate the potency of the irrational in man. Jacob Burckhardt (1818–1897), the great historian of the Renaissance, predicted in the eighties that the rising tide of antisemitism would sweep away all the gains of Jewish Emancipation, half justifying this development by the assertion that "nine-tenths of the German press is produced by Jews." Naturally, this fantastic exaggeration of the role of Jews in German life was as much a product of his cantankerous hatred of the common people as was his prediction of doom. For the Nazi revolution was by no means a direct consequence of the antisemitic agitation in the eighties. In the decade before World War I, the antisemitic movement reached its nadir. The success of the Nazis was owing to a combination of factors: the German defeat after their near victory; the Versailles Treaty; the Bolshevik revolution; the massive growth of vulgar "social Darwinism"; and the betrayal of democracy by the conservative parties and the military hierarchy, headed by Hindenburg. True to his antirational bias, Burckhardt believed that the liberals would desert the Jews in their time of need.

Liberalism, which had up to now defended the Semites, will soon be unable to resist the temptation to shake off that odium. It will not be able for long to let the Catholics and Conservatives keep and use the most popular trump card that there is . . ."[33]

A study of the impact of socialism on Jewish thought is far beyond the compass of this book. Large segments of the Jewish intelligentsia in Europe and in the new lands of settlement were deeply moved by this ideology in all its varied nuances. The terrible uncertainties of Jewish life in the overcrowded towns of the "Pale of Settlement"; the double alienation of the Jewish proletariat, because of its ethnic as well as its class status; the frequent association of antisemitism and reactionary clerical interests—all these social forces combined with the inherent messianism of the Jewish tradition to engender an impassioned socialist orientation. The broad spectrum of Jewish socialism included, after some decades: radical extremists who drifted into the Communist party; Bundists who combined socialism with the ideal of local cultural autonomy; and Socialist-Zionists, who in turn diverged into a number of different groupings. All of these groups reinterpreted Jewish history, identity and destiny in accord with their respective ideologies.

At this point we shall briefly analyze the ideologies of four men: a socialist forerunner who sought redemption for Jews in the dream of a cosmopolitan world; a utopian socialist; an ideologist who gave impetus and direction to those who combined the Zionist with the socialist ideal; and a latter-day prophet who represented the principles of religious Zionist-Socialism on the international scene.

Aaron Lieberman (1845–1880) was raised in a traditional Jewish home and even studied for the rabbinate. When he embraced the socialist ideal, he proceeded to preach the new gospel of redemption in Hebrew, addressing himself to the alumni of Orthodox Yeshivot. While in London, he founded a small, ephemeral society, which included in its platform the following sentences:

> As long as private ownership continues, economic misery shall not cease; as long as humanity is divided into nations and classes, hatred will not cease; as long as the clergy continues to sway the emotions of the people, religious hatred will continue. . . . We Jews are an integral part of humanity and cannot be liberated except through the liberation of all humanity.[34]

Lieberman's clarion call did not achieve any results, since in his day there was only a small Jewish working class. Still, it is important to note that a Talmud-trained intellectual, whose literary tongue was primarily Hebrew, could seek the salvation of his suffering people in the promise of a cosmopolitan socialism, which would be as "nationless" as it would be "classless." It was not the dialectic of "historical materialism" that enthralled him so much as the vision of a "new society based on socialism which will abolish the injustice and domination of capital, which will eradicate the parasites and the system of 'mine' and 'thine.' "[35]

Equally ahead of its time was Moses Hess's *Rome and Jerusalem*. Printed in 1862, it anticipated the ideals of modern labor Zionism, though it was virtually neglected until the turn of the century. In 1898 Theodor Herzl read this little book and noted in his diary:

> Everything that we have tried is already in his book. . . . Since Spinoza, Jewry has brought forth no greater spirit than this forgotten Moses Hess.[36]

Hess at one time was a close friend and associate of Karl Marx, but their cooperation was only sporadic and was punctuated with bitter bursts of mutual contempt.

Hess's chief point was that a new age of mutual accommodation among nations and races had dawned in the latter half of the nineteenth century. In primitive times races devoured one another; in the eighteenth century, the ideal of a cosmopolitan society was born; in his own day, the thesis of race and antithesis of humanity had begun to merge in the synthesis of harmonious coexistence of diverse ethnic entities. Rome, or Italy, had achieved independence. Was it not time for Jerusalem, capital of ancient Israel, to reemerge as the spiritual center of a new Jewish nation? Hess proposed the acquisition of land by an all-Jewish fund and the establishment of a series of socialist settlements, which would bring to fruition the seeds of social idealism that are contained in the Hebrew Bible. Isaiah's dream of Torah (or teaching), flowing out of Zion to the ends of the earth, could be realized in our day, though the new Torah will assume the shape of utopian socialism.

As a champion of the oppressed, Hess was concerned with the peculiar plight of the wretched Jewish masses in eastern Europe. Unlike other emigrants, they seemed to carry with them the seeds of antisemitism wherever they went in large numbers. Why not settle them in the "empty" land of their fathers, where they might build an exemplary socialist society? He was certain that France, the homeland of liberalism, would help in the attainment of this goal. The emancipated Jews of western Europe would furnish financial help to their poor brothers from the lands of oppression. In turn, they would take pride in the rebirth of their ancient homeland.

Furthermore, as Hess saw it, the entire civilized world would be enriched by the renaissance of the Jewish polity. For, in his view, in the whole of humanity there were only two culture-creating races—the Aryans and the Semites. Of these "two world-historical races," the Aryan genius strives to explain and to beautify life (reason and esthetics), while the Semitic genius aims at the moralization and sanctification of society. This racial struggle is more basic and more decisive than the "class struggle."[37]

Hess's blend of racist mystique, socialist idealism, and Jewish redemptionism was not uncharacteristic of his day. Yet his ideas were mostly ignored. The historian Graetz wrote warm letters of encouragement to Hess and endorsed the ideal of a revival of Jewish nationality, but even Graetz did not comment on the socialist ideas of Hess. Both Graetz and Hess, who were raised in Germany, were bitterly contemptuous of their native land. In spirit they were both expatriates.[38]

However, the spiritual leaders of German Jewry, particularly Geiger and Hirsch, rejected Hess's axioms and recommendations. We need hardly review the detailed criticisms of Hess's work. His sheer naiveté was as amazing as his historic intuition.[39] He was among the first to sense the emergence of a new Jewish mood—a racist-nationalistic sense of identity, which seeks to root itself in the past without actually realizing the implications of a "return" to the past. Hess, living apart from Jewish realities, indulged in sentimental nostalgia. He adored Talmudic Halachah, in the abstract, without observing its precepts; he blended Spinoza's pantheism and Hasidic pietism, on the naive assumption that such a mishmash was "authentic" Judaism.

Entranced by his vision of the Jewish future, Hess was alienated from the contemporary Jewish community, scorning the rationalistic world view of the Reformers and the master builders of the "Science of Judaism." A lifelong "outsider" and a Communist visionary, he dreamed of Zion reborn or of a perfect socialist society. With all the inconsistencies of his world view, Hess articulated the feelings of disillusioned Jewish refugees from socialism who recoiled in dejection and despair from the crusade to "liberate" the world from the twin evils of nationalistic zealotry and social injustice. The fervent "returnees" were few and far between in western Europe. But, as Samuel Hirsch pointed out, Hess's message was really addressed to the Jews in the Pale of Settlement, who did not experience the cultural efflorescence of German Jewry. It took a generation or longer before the Russian Jews were ready for the program that Hess proposed.

It is interesting that Moses Hess, whose knowledge of Judaic sources was very skimpy, wanted to form an organization for the dissemination and popularization of Talmudic material, while Graetz, a preeminent Judaic scholar, cautioned against this counsel, as follows:

> The Talmud contains many good things; but to set it up as a source of inspiration—for this, it is not fit, It formed an important transitional period. It was the container for the soul of Judaism. But, today, to set it up as a banner is like the establishment of the papal dogma of infallibility. The Talmud is a part of Judaism, not the whole of it. The national doctrine of the Talmud is too exclusive for our world view, which is after all inclined to cosmopolitanism . . .[40]

While Hess blended the Zionist ideal with utopian socialism, Borochov welded the Zionist program with Marxist socialism. His major point was that Jewish nationalism was "progressive," since it was largely brought about by the struggle of the proletarian masses to acquire a "strategic base" for the "class struggle." There are different forms of nationalism, each version reflecting the class consciousness of its promoters. The nationalist ideologies of the big capitalists, the petty bourgeoisie, and the landowners are all indeed reactionary, but there is also a kind of nationalism that derives its strength from the anger of the working people; for instance, the ethnic awareness of imported laborers in the big industrial states.

The ruling classes of free as well as of oppressed nations take advantage of this fundamental contradiction between national and class consciousness, and are often inclined to carry on a hypocritical nationalistic propaganda in order to obscure the class consciousness of those whom they oppress. . . . The ruling classes are not national, but nationalistic. . . . If, however, it does not obscure the class structure of the society it is *national*.[41]

We need hardly add that "national" is good in Borochov's terminology, while "nationalistic" is bad, for the advancement of the class struggle is the touchstone of progress. The more deeply an ethnic movement is rooted in the dire material needs of its people, the more authentic it is; the more "spiritual," the more bourgeois and hypocritical it is.

The phrase "national spirit," and all other exaggerated traditions are the best warning-signals against a confusion of the two. Nationalistic speeches are always liberally dotted with them.[42]

Borochov reflected the anguish of the Jewish workers, who flocked into the big industrial cities only to find that the Slavic workers were even more hostile to them than the Polish or Russian middle class and aristocracy. The Jewish laborers needed a strategic base in order to carry on the class struggle. The Zionist movement is therefore a "*stychic* process"—that is, a social transformation that occurs without any conscious plan and is driven by its own self-generating momentum.

"Years ago we said, 'Zionism is a *stychic* process. Our only task is to remove the obstacles which interfere with this process.'" In the last years of his life Borochov was more aware of the decisive role of national propaganda than at the time when he drew up the Platform for the *Poale Zion* movement. "*The land of spontaneously concentrated Jewish immigration will be Palestine*."[43]

In 1906, when this platform was drawn up, the vast majority of Jewish emigrants traveled to the United States, and only the tiniest trickle drifted toward Palestine. Yet Borochov and his associates disavowed any interest in the "spiritual" aspects of nationalism.

Our national consciousness is negative in that it is emancipatory in character. If we were the proletariat of a free nation, which neither oppresses nor is oppressed, we would not be interested in any problems of national life. . . . Ours is a realistic nationalism, free from any "spiritual admixture."[44]

But, though the national element was devalued in principle, it was in fact assigned priority, since "the Jewish proletariat" needed a strategic base on which to carry on its class struggle. So, the Platform continues, "Our ultimate aim, our maximum program is socialism— the socialization of the means of production. . . . Our immediate aim, our minimum program, is Zionism."[45]

Borochov hailed the "cooperative settlements" that were emerging in Palestine as stepping-stones toward "the Socialist ideal."[46] Although the sporadic outbursts of Arab terrorism were beginning to be felt even before World War I, the early Socialist-Zionists claimed that there was room in Palestine for nine million people—sufficient for the Arabs as well as the Jews. They refused to admit that the Palestinian Arabs might behave like other national groups and combat the foreign intruder with all the means at their disposal. The Arabs, they assumed, were still living in their medieval dreamworld. The dialectics of history require that a feudal society go through the stages of commercial and industrial revolutions before its workers and its bourgeoisie are readied for modern ideologies. Borochov believed that the Jewish laborers would introduce the Arab workers into the twentieth century little by little and guide the evolution of their thinking. He and his colleagues hoped that the children of the desert, unspoiled by European culture, would be glad to accept the beneficent guidance of their long estranged Semitic cousins and take their places dutifully in the international class struggle. Even the most realistic socialists could not resist the temptation to dream of utopia, where the "Land of Israel" was concerned.

The most profound response of Judaism to Marxist socialism was presented by Martin Buber. In all his varied writings he insisted that the essence of life consisted in the flashes of mutuality and concern that occur between persons. The "I-Thou" relationship bears the seal of reality. The ideal order of society, according to Buber, is the one that affords the greatest latitude for the spontaneous emergence of such relations. In Marxism the individual is lost in the mighty maelstrom of automatic, soulless processes. He is urged to sink his personal identity into the surging tide of the faceless proletariat in order to remove an obstacle or two from the relentless slide of the glaciers of the new Ice Age, which will in any case crush everything in their path.

As to the Marxist "Kingdom of freedom" following the Armageddon of the final struggle, it is fantastic to believe that a realm of boundless love and harmony will emerge out of a pitiless, brutal civil war, in which both sides will feel that their very life is at stake.

In his interpretations of Judaism, Buber had stressed the decisiveness of the deed. It is out of our actions that our attitudes are generated. Hence, the Jewish formula: "We shall do and we shall listen." (Exodus 24:7) It follows that deeds of hate and resentment cannot possibly generate the feelings of mutual trust and affection that are a *sine qua non* for an ideal society.

But even if the Proletariat should win and nationalize the means of production, would not the State then become a monstrous "Leviathan," far more formidable than the one that Hobbes envisaged? There would be no personal, direct relations between the masses at the bottom and the all-mighty figures at the top of the pyramid. Long before the Soviet system manifested its soul-crushing character, Buber pointed to the demonic potential within the radical socialist movement.

Buber, too, was a socialist, but of a uniquely utopian variety. In his book *Paths in Utopia* he defined the core of utopian socialism as the belief that even now we can begin building the ideal society of the future. The ideal must grow out of the emergent forces within present society, not through the negation of those forces. In a very real sense no genuine ideal can be fully realized. Authentic socialism, in his view, accords with the messianic way of thinking, which demands that we work daily for "the improvement of the world through the kingdom of the Almighty," even though we realize that we do not know the shape and time of the Eschaton. In Jewish terminology so-called scientific socialism is really pseudo-messianism, in two ways: one, in the claim that the Messiah has already been identified and that the way leading to his final triumph has been charted; second, in the belief that he alone is the redeemer and those who are not enrolled in his army are his enemies. In authentic messianism, on the contrary, only the immediate task is certain. Indeed, every holy action is messianic, and the outlines of the future remain fluid and protean. The utopian socialists seek to build in the present the "cells" of the living organism of the Ideal Society and that Ideal Society is defined in terms of the free and spontaneous individuals composing it rather than in terms of a perfect plan. So, in Buber's view, the utopians were the true messianists.

Of all the utopian visionaries of European socialism, Buber felt closest to Gustav Landauer, who, following the upheavals of World War I, became the head of the Bavarian socialist government and a few months later was assassinated by a band of proto-Nazis. Buber edited Landauer's manuscripts for publication.

According to Landauer, socialism is not so much a socio-economic order as it is a spiritual phenomenon. "Socialism is the attempt to lead man's common life to a bond of common spirit in freedom, that is, to religion."[47] Landauer called this version of socialism "People." Within the hearts of men and women there is a hunger for true communion with others, with their neighbors, and, ultimately, with all men. The task of socialists is not to impose an abstract pattern on society, but to awaken and nurture these communitarian longings— "to loosen the hardening of hearts so that what lies buried may rise to the surface; so that what truly lives, yet now seems dead, may emerge and grow into the light."[48]

The spirit of mutuality, Landauer contended, is the true "capital" of a socialist society, and islands of "socialist reality" can be built within the sea of ruthless capitalism. Consuming and producing cooperatives can be organized with the aim of determining the best ways of harmonizing freedom, equality, and the feeling of organic unity. The most effective islands of socialism are villages, combining the activities of production and consumption and allowing the greatest measure of freedom to its members.[49] No fixed plan, however perfect in design, should be imposed on these communes; but, in trust and love, the seeds of the future should be nurtured.

No final security measures should be taken to establish the millennium of eternity, but only a great balancing of forces, and the resolve periodically to renew the balance.[50]

To Buber the ideal commune must be small enough for all its adult members to share in the management of its enterprises. Otherwise, the sense of community is lost.

The primary aspiration of all history is a genuine community of human beings—genuine because it is *community all through*. A community that failed to base itself on the actual and communal life of big and little groups living and working together, and on their mutual relationships, would be fictitious and counterfeit.[51]

At the same time, according to Buber, the communes must not be separated from one another, nor from the rest of society. The communes express one of the great "eternal needs" of man—to be part of a greater whole; but that whole, too, must be embraced within the hierarchy of wholes that make up the nation.

Buber maintained that the *Kibbutz* movement in Israel was "an experiment that did not fail."

I have said that I see in this bold Jewish undertaking a "signal non-failure." I cannot say, a signal success. To become that, much has still to be done.[52]

The *kibbutzim* were formed in response to the peculiar set of circumstances in Palestine. The *Halutzim* (pioneers) came to build the Jewish state; they were sustained by the financial as well as the moral support of the great Jewish Diaspora; they were confronted by a hostile native population; they did not have the military protection of a government; they had to perform tasks that were beyond the capacity of individual settlers. These circumstances, however, were allied with ideas—"memories of the Russian *Artel*, impressions left over from reading the so called 'utopian' socialists, and the half-unconscious after-effects of the Bible's teaching about social justice."[53]

Buber saw the outlines of the future in the network of Israeli *kibbutzim*, which combined in many and diverse forms the ideals of individual freedom and communal living:

> So long as Russia has not undergone an essential inner change . . . we must designate one of the two poles of Socialism between which our choice lies, by the formidable name of "Moscow." The other I would make bold to call "Jerusalem."[54]

Without undertaking a detailed evaluation of either Borochovism or Buberism, we desire to dispute the name "Jerusalem" for the "kibbutzim" of Israel. If this hallowed term denotes the impetus of the Jewish tradition, it applies to many and diverse aspects of life in Israel and in the Diaspora. By no means can it be said that the Israeli communes, be they Marxist, Tolstoyan, or Biblical in inspiration, are the living embodiments of the Jewish ethos.

These communities, Buber maintains, are islands of the future, standing fast against the dark, restless tides of the contemporary world. Such islands, we presume, will eventually coalesce and the future will take over. Does not this vision of the course of world history remind us of Augustine's "City of God" being built by the Saints in the midst of the confused babel of "the City of Man"?

To the ex-Manichean theologian, history was the battleground between the two cosmic, elemental forces of good and evil. The City of Man consisted of those who were totally dominated by self-love, to the exclusion of the love of God, and the City of God consisted of those who were completely governed by the love of God, to the exclusion of self-love. In this troubled world cells of the City of God arise, representing the glory of the future within the earthly realm of Satan. Eventually, those cells will coalesce and the Eschaton, radiant and perfect in every respect, will attain its predestined triumph.

It was natural for Augustine's successors to identify the Church as a whole, at least its monastic communes, with the islands of the City of God. Doubtless, the Essenic communities near the Dead Sea and in Egypt subscribed to a similar philosophy, with opinions differing as to whether "the battle between the Children of Light and the Children of Darkness" will precede or follow the advent of the

Redeemer "with power." But, we may ask, is such a Manichean view compatible with the mainstream of Jewish thought?

This question can be answered only in the negative. Nothing was so clear to the rabbis as the conviction that good and evil are intermingled in every society. The refusal of the sages in every generation to endore monastic communities, despite the examples provided by both Christianity and Islam, is the decisive factor.[55]

To be sure, the medieval Jews contended that in a sense they formed islands of the future, since they will become the nuclei of the redeemed world when the Messiah comes. This belief, however, was not based on their perfect holiness, for they were unworthy, "exiled on account of their sins." Rather, redemption will come because of God's Grace, or on account of "the merits of our ancestors." All kinds of mythical versions of the messianic era flourished within Judaism at various times. However, few will dispute the great authority of Maimonides's Code, which cautioned that we do not really know the shape of things in the messianic era. His own vision of a magnificent abundance of all earthly goods is not peculiarly socialistic. In his letter to the Jews of Yemen, where a messianic pretender urged his followers to share all their possessions, Maimonides ridiculed the communistic principle.

Also, the Jewish vision of the holy life takes for granted the institution of private property. The holy man is not the one who gives up all his earthly goods, but rather the one who is generous and charitable toward the needy. A person must not give more than twenty percent of his possessions for charity, except in case of emergencies. The best example that we have of a holy Jewish community is the tradition concerning the passing of an open money box from house to house, with the wealthy depositing money in it and the poor taking money from it without anyone knowing who put funds in the box and who took from it.

Furthermore, self-love was not considered in Judaism to be an evil in itself. To be sure, in the ideology of Habad-Hassidism, we do find such a contrast. Kabbalah-based Hassidism, however, was but a temporary episode in the millennial history of Judaism. In the Talmud the evil desire is represented as being "very good," since it is the basic motif of civilization. Also, the *Halachah* is conceived, not as a temporary enactment, but as the reflection of a permanent cosmic reality, with God Himself meditating on the laws of "mine" and "thine."

In addition, in terms of human psychology, as we understand it today, there is indeed an "eternal need" for association and "togetherness." However, there is also an equally insistent desire for privacy and self-assertion. The synthesis of the two wills that is achieved by generous and outgoing people in our free world may, in theory at least, be far more satisfying than any synthesis that is attainable in communes. We must never imagine "that we have seen the future, and that it works."

In the latter part of the nineteenth century Jews were widely attacked as "ringleaders of revolution." With the increasing violence of revolutionary terror in czarist Russia, following the death of Czar Alexander II, the grim stereotype of the revolutionary Jew became ever more firmly fixed in the minds of the conservative classes. Even a brilliant Israeli historian attributed the supposed revolutionary impetus of Jews to their rejection of the dogma of Original Sin.

> The most distinct and the most effective "Jewish" feature of the early messianic Jewish revolutionaries was, however, I think, their inability to comprehend and consequently their unwillingness to accept the fundamental Christian dogma of original sin—the idea of the eternal and inescapable dichotomy between the knowledge of what was good and the impotence to do it, between theory and practice, the world of pure ideas and defective reality. . . . No genuine revolutionary experience is in the last analysis possible so long as that fatalistic attitude persists. [56]

In our view, Jewish people were in fact, if not in theory, keenly conscious of the depth of evil in human nature. The Fundamentalist component of the Jewish tradition did in fact include a version of the Fall of Man and a strong resistance to the belief in human perfectibility, prior to the advent of the Messiah. But the rationalistic component of Judaism reinforced the impact of the contemporary liberal trends on the minds of young Jews. Let us analyze the several components of this misbegotten specter, which was cunningly exploited by the Nazi propagandists.

Manifestly, its first component was the Jewish rejection of the presumed unity of "Throne and Altar." Feudal society was cemented by the Christian faith, and a rebellion against the dominant church was assumed to lead inevitably to a revolution against the reigning monarch. So, the liberal principle of the separation of Church and State was, to the conservative classes, a socially disintegrating factor. Since Jews in all western countries were the most obvious beneficiaries of the triumph of liberalism, it seemed plausible to identify the Jews with the French Revolution and the aftershocks of that tremendous social upheaval. As a matter of fact, Jewish intellectuals and businessmen embraced enthusiastically the twin causes of liberalism and humanism. They hailed the revolutionary events of 1789 as "footsteps of the messiah," heralding a new age of freedom and international fraternity.[56]

The affinity between Jewish self-consciousness and liberalism was derived not only from the objective circumstances of the Jewish status as a minority, but also from the ideal self-image of enlightened Jews. For them, liberalism was liberation, the dawn of a new world. They had moved out of the isolation of a spiritual ghetto into a new homeland of humanist ideals. They interpreted their own traditions in rationalistic terms, in keeping with the Maimonidean current in the stream of Jewish thought. They saw it as their mission to aid in the dissipation of ethnic pride and religious bigotry and to usher in the age of reason and social justice. They prided themselves on the fact that Judaism was nondogmatic and nonexclusivistic, requiring neither "the sacrifice of the intellect," nor the zealotry of the "true believer."

Christian leaders were far more likely than Jews to be dubious about the value and truth of liberalism, let alone socialism. As late as 1864 Pius IX, in a papal encyclical, *The Syllabus of Errors*, enumerated and condemned eighty opinions, grouped under ten headings. In this list "Modern Liberalism" as well as "Moderate Rationalism" and "Latitudenarianism" or tolerance of diverse religions, were anathematized.[58]

While Jewish leaders exulted in the irresistible advance of the liberal movement, the established churches of Europe, Protestant as well as Catholic, were generally either hesitant or hostile. Only liberal churchmen could welcome Jews as cofighters for a more human social order. Here, then, is the first component of the stereotype of the Jew as revolutionary.

Another facet of this stereotype derived from the conservative counterattack against the liberal doctrine of equality and rationality. Those who no longer felt comfortable quoting God in behalf of a hierarchical society sought to justify their position by reference to nature or the national tradition. The liberal doctrine of equality was contrary to nature, they asserted. It was an expression of the resentment of the naturally inferior classes. The notion of humanity itself became problematic in the decades when "social Darwinism" appeared to be the last word of science. Perhaps mankind is only an assemblage of diverse biological species or races. The Jew, who imposed the biblical concept of humanity upon the Aryan nations, provided the outstanding example of "the morality of slaves" triumphing over the interests and instincts of nature's own aristocrats.

The nihilistic scorn of liberalism is best known in the form that Nietzsche gave it in his famous essay, *The Genealogy of Morals.*

Human history would be a dull and stupid thing without the intelligence furnished by its impotents. Let us begin with the most striking example. Whatever else has been done to damage the powerful and the great of this earth seems trivial compared with what the Jews have done, that priestly people who succeeded in avenging themselves on their enemies and oppressors by radically inverting their values, that is, by an act of the most spiritual vengeance. This was a strategy entirely appropriate to a priestly people, in whom vindictiveness had gone most deeply underground. It was the Jew, who with frightening consistency, dared to invert the aristocratic value-equations, good/noble, powerful/beautiful, happy/favored of the gods, and maintain with the furious hatred of the underprivileged and impotent; that "only the poor, the powerless, are good; only the suffering, sick and ugly, truly blessed. But you noble and mighty ones of the earth will be, to all eternity, the evil, the cruel, the avaricious, the godless, and thus the cursed and damned!" . . . We know who has fallen heir to this Jewish inversion of values. . . . In reference to the grand and unspeakably disastrous initiative which the Jews have launched by this most radical of all declarations of war, I repeat . . . that it was the Jews who started the slave revolt in morals . . ."[59]

In the strange logic of mythology, be it modern or ancient, the principle of contradiction is overcome. Nihilists and Fundamentalist Christians can join forces in a common attack against the Jew, who is seen by them at once as the source of Christianity and its implacable enemy, and whose sole inspiration is vengeance. Is the God of the Old Testament not "the God of vengeance"? The Talmud interprets the fact that vengeance appears between two Names of God to mean that God mollifies His vengeance by His justice and compassion (Psalms 94:1; Berochot 33a). But the propagandists could always count on exploiting the popular image of an impotent Shylock, nursing the embers of hate. It was easy enough to build up an image of "the Jewish revolutionary" on the basis of this imagery, culled partly from Christian Fundamentalism and partly from anti-Christian, Aryan nihilism.

Actually, the theory of Jewish collective "resentment," or hatred of non-Jews, is entirely mythical—not because Jewish people were more saintly than others, but because of the distinctive bent of biblical and talmudic piety. As Martin Buber put it, the Jew was constantly in "dialogue with God." If he was exalted, it was God's reward; if he was defeated in war, hounded by enemies, driven to the ends of the earth, it was God's doing. "Our enemy is judgment" (Deuteronomy 32:3). In the book of Lamentations the enemy remains anonymous. He merely carries out the verdict of the Lord, Who demands more from Israel, his "first born," and punishes His people severely for their sins.

In the Talmudic apocalypse of the Final Judgment, all nations are given a second chance—the opportunity to observe the Commandment of *sukkah* (the festival of thanksgiving).[60] The account of the destruction of Jerusalem by the Romans, which was very popular among Jews during the Middle Ages, portrays Titus, the Roman general, as a generous man.[61] It was God who ordered the destruction of His city, the burning of His temple, and the dispersal of His people among the nations. Whether Jews were scattered in punishment for their sins, or for the purpose of gathering converts from among the nations, was in dispute.[62] However, there was no question that the author of Israel's troubles was the Lord Himself. Judah Halevi articulated the basic conviction of pre-modern Jewry, when he maintained that the history of Israel was unique, precisely because it was directed in keeping with ethical principles by the Lord Himself, as it were.[63]

Another factor in the making of the revolutionary stereotype of the Jew was the actual participation of Jewish people in the various revolutionary movements against the czarist government in Russia. Imprisoned in the Pale of Settlement, the impoverished Jewish masses were the target of endless, punitive legislation and organized attacks by the illiterate peasantry. The cause of liberalism in Russia seemed hopeless to many young people, whatever their nationality. Terroristic attacks against the entrenched authorities appeared to be the only effective means of breaking the stranglehold of an uncompromising autocracy.

Thus, there were few Jewish revolutionaries in western Europe.[64] Karl Marx was baptized at the age of two. Ferdinand LaSalle, the leader of socialism in Germany, stood for a trade-union type of socialism. Eduard Bernstein, head of the Social Democratic Party, was no more radical than Franklin D. Roosevelt and the New Deal. Leon Blum (1875–1950), head of the Socialists in France, was also primarily a democrat and a humanitarian. Samuel Gompers, the pioneering organizer of the American Federation of Labor, dedicated his life "to make unionism respectable as a bulwark against radicalism and irresponsible strikes."[65] In general, the "Jewish" unions in America pioneered in working out methods of arbitration and redress of grievances.

However, in Russia idealistic reformers had no other recourse than acts of terror. And Jews, as the most oppressed minority, were well represented in the reforming and revolutionary movements since the early sixties. The historian Dubnow thus describes the revolutionaries of a century ago:

> Naturally enough a portion of Jewish youth was also drawn into the revolutionary movement of the seventies, a movement which, in spite of the theoretic "materialism" of its adepts, was of an essentially idealistic tendency. In joining the ranks of the revolutionaries, the young Jews were less actuated by resentment against the continued, though somewhat mitigated, rightlessness of their own people than by discontent with the

general political reaction in Russia, that discontent which found expression in the movement of "Populism," of "Going to the people" . . .[66]

The wave of pogroms in 1880 caused many Jewish revolutionaries to reassess their role.

The Jewish student youth suffered their greatest disappointment when they realized that the socialist minded Russian students sympathized with the crusade against the Jewish masses, and worse yet, exhibited their antisemitic feelings toward their Jewish fellow-revolutionaries.[67]

The czarist propagandists sought to discredit the entire revolutionary movement by depicting it as the work of Jewish conspirators. The Czarist Minister Witte asked Theodor Herzl why Jews, comprising only three percent of the population, supplied fifty percent of the revolutionaries.[68]

This was, of course a gross exaggeration. The tendency to assign Jewish ancestry to hated revolutionaries is itself an expression of the reactionary mentality.

In the summer of 1903, when forty-three delegates of the Russian Socialist Party met to establish basic lines of policy, a split occurred, and the party was divided between Bolsheviks and Mensheviks. The Mensheviks represented the more moderate, democratic orientation. They favored "economism"—that is, the steady improvement of the lot of the workers.[69]

It is worthy to note that the leading Jewish Social Democrats were *Mensheviki*. They were led by Martov, Dan-Hurwitz, and Leon Trotsky, while the Bolshevik group, headed by Lenin, contained only a few Jews, not even one writer or propagandist of national stature.[70]

Stalin is said to have remarked, following that split, that a pogrom within the Party might prove helpful, since it would eliminate the *Mensheviks*. Leon Trotsky sided with Julius Martov, prior to the Bolshevik Revolution; later, Trotsky joined the Bolsheviks, while Martov, a close friend of Lenin, was allowed to emigrate from the U.S.S.R. in 1920 at the request of the German Socialists.[71]

VII. *The Zionist Response to Racist Nihilism*

Vitalism may be described as the philosophy that takes the felt pulsation of life to be the substancè of reality. It differs from philosophies of spirit, in all their variations, and from materialism. Vitalistic philosophies achieved widespread popularity in the western world, particularly in Germany and France, beginning with the latter decades of the nineteenth century. Their influence kept pace with the progressive weakening of the intellectual and moral traditions of the past century and with the growing awareness of the invincible irrationality of human nature.

As we shall see, most vitalistic philosophies posed a direct challenge to the Jewish people. By tearing down the rationalistic creed of moral standards and sentiments, these philosophies weakened the foundations of the liberal society that emancipated Jewry was joining. If the brute battle for survival is the real source of all valuations, then the rhetoric of the "Rights of Man," of justice and compassion, sounds hollow and meaningless. In place of universal reason and a humanist conscience, the vitalistic movement esteemed the power of instincts and the guidance of intuitions. These dark and formless forces were easily manipulated to serve the tastes of the populace. As it happened, the vitalists reinvigorated the rising mass movements of nationalism and racial arrogance that threatened to expel and annihilate the Jews as unwanted aliens. At the same time, the vitalistic approach was utilized by Jewish thinkers in their efforts to revive the flagging loyalties of their people to their religious heritage and peculiar destiny.

Arthur Schopenhauer (1788–1860) was a neglected and isolated thinker in the early decades of the nineteenth century, when Hegel and Feuerbach dominated the intellectual scene. The popularity of his works, however, grew apace in the latter half of the century, especially after the publication of Charles Darwin's *The Origin of Species* in 1859. As the categories of biology began to enthrall the European mind, Schopenhauer came to be acclaimed as a seer, not so much in the academic world as in the wide, nontechnical circles of the intelligentsia. His conception of will as the basic reality seemed to be fully in accord with the Darwinian perspective. To some, he was more than a philosopher, a veritable prophet of a new cult of art and music, and an elitist critic of popular culture.

Schopenhauer presented a direct challenge to the Jewish people as a whole. He sought his inspiration in the Hindu Vedas and Buddhist philosophy and assailed Judaism as a perverted faith, the fountainhead of an unreal optimism, which was alien to the genius of the Aryan race. This charge coincided with the rising interest of anthropologists in the ancient culture of the Indo-Europeans, who, it was believed, shared at one time a common language, Sanskrit, the sacred tongue of India. The racial consciousness of the Europeans, stirred by the worldwide dominance of western imperialism, was sympathetic to the endeavor to uncover and revitalize the pre-Judaic and pre-Christian religion of the Aryan. In this view the Christian culture of the West was imposed by guile and force upon the ancestors of the Teutons; it is a culture that does not really correspond to the biological rhythm of the Europeans. To be sure, the Germans and other Europeans transformed the Christian faith after the pattern of their intuitive insights, but Christianity was, after all, a creation of the Jewish spirit. Insofar as it is Jewish, it is foreign to the psyche of the Indo-Europeans. To become "authentic" and "creative," the Germanic nations should seek their inspiration in the works of the ancient Aryans.

While this way of thinking was not fully articulated by Schopenhauer, it was initiated by him. "It is to be regretted generally as a great misfortune that the people whose former culture was to serve mainly as the basis of our own were not, say the Indians or the Greeks, or even the Romans, but just these Jews."[1]

According to him, the Jewish psyche was life affirming and optimistic because Jews lacked the depth of insight with which to penetrate the veil of appearance. The shallow outlook of the Hebrew Bible is clearly echoed in the verse of Genesis, "And the Lord saw that all which He had done was very good." Modern rationalistic Christianity is, in Schopenhauer's view, nothing but a distilled version of Judaism.[2] The external trappings of religion are only metaphors and allegories. So Schopenhauer condemned the so-called Judeo-Christian foundation of western culture as a bitter illusion, "a dull, insipid, optimistic, Protestant-rationalistic, or really Jewish view of the world."[3]

The only grand insight in the Hebrew Scriptures, Schopenhauer contended, is the doctrine of the Fall. The sin of Adam and Eve was indulgence in sex, and their expulsion from the garden of Eden is the tragic fate of all who yield to the seduction of the will to live, of which the sexual act is the climactic expression. "Our own consciousness teaches us that in this act is expressed the most decided *affirmation of the will to live*, pure and without further addition."[4]

The New Testament is, in Schopenhauer's view, far closer to the truth in that it favors celibacy and asceticism. "Voluntary and complete chastity is the first step in asceticism of the denial of the Will to Live. It thereby denies the affirmation of the will which goes beyond the individual life. . . ."[5] The early Christians recognized the wisdom of overcoming that tyrannical "will to live," which keeps humanity in thrall, and the medieval mystics, particularly Meister Eckhart, deepened that awareness. The mysticism of the Middle Ages is like strong, concentrated alcohol in comparison with the weak wine of the New Testament.

Yet, Schopenhauer continued, the Gospels contain enough of the truth of pessimism to carry conviction with the peoples of Europe. "The Power by which Christianity was able to overcome first Judaism, and then the paganism of Greece and Rome, is to be found solely in its pessimism, in the confession that our condition is both sorrowful and sinful, whereas Judaism and paganism were optimistic."[6] It follows that an authentic revival of Christianity would "purify" it from classical and Jewish elements and bring it closer to the Hindu mentality. "Therefore, atheistic Buddhism is much more closely akin to Christianity than are optimistic Judaism, and its variety, Islam."[7] Schopenhauer contrasted his own philosophy with that of the Jewish philosopher Spinoza. The latter represented the Old Testament affirmation "Behold, it is good," whereas he saw in the crucified Savior the metaphor of man's tragic existence.[8]

In any case, Jewish influence is evil. The unerring instinct of the masses is antisemitic because it recognizes the baleful consequence of Jewish this-worldliness. In one of his essays, Schopehauer remarked: "Among all peoples and at all times, the Jews were a despised nation; in part, this may be due to the fact that they do not hold a belief in immortality."[9] Even though he was referring here to the Hellenistic and early Roman period—when, according to some scholars, the belief in the immortality of the soul was entertained only by fringe elements in the Jewish community—he maintained that the character of individuals and peoples does not change. "The difference of character is innate and ineradicable. The wicked man is born with his wickedness as much as the serpent is with its poison-fangs and glands, nor can the former change its nature a whit more than the latter."[10] For this reason he questioned the liberal thesis that emancipated Jews would take on the national characteristics of the people among whom they lived. "The Fatherland of the Jews are other Jews; this patriotism, *sine patria*, works more inspiringly than any other."[11]

It was not the pessimism of Schopenhauer that won him an enthusiastic audience, but his emphasis on the unconscious and irrational springs of human conduct. His writings provided an armory of weapons in the fight against the classical philosophy of life. It is interesting to note that Schopenhauer considered himself to be a disciple of Kant. Although he rejected the humanism and rationality of the Kantian ethic, he made use of the Kantian distinction between the realm of phenomena, structured·by the *a priori* categories of space and time, and the noumenal realm, which transcends our consciousness. Schopenhauer refuted Kant's notion of the categorical imperative as a noumenal reality, a reflection of the *Ding an sich*. Instead, he asserted that the blind will to live is the noumenal reality, assuming in each person an individualized form that is incarnated in his physical body. This will to live structures the outer world for us, in terms of ideas that seem to us to be manageable. In this way we are set to strive and labor, to suffer with only moments of relief, to procreate in fits of passion, and thereby to perpetuate the human agony.

Illusions aplenty are scattered across the paths of life, so that we are seduced and beguiled to serve the blind master within us as willing slaves. However, there are holes in the veil of illusion through which reality might be glimpsed and its evil impulses overcome. These are the windows opened by art. In the contemplation of beauty, we appreciate without greed or passion—hence, in a will-less way. The artist reflects eternal ideas, which are free from the frantic lusts of the will; therefore, they liberate us and transport us to the world of truth.

The ethic that emerges from Schopenhauer's analysis is as corrosive and demonic as his assault against intellectuality. At first reading, his is a gentle philosophy, since he based moral life on the sentiment of compassion. He condemned every form of egotism, even the determination to utilize all one's talents for the service of mankind. Out of compassion, he developed the theme of justice as a consequence of the demand not to hurt anyone. He also deduced from it the virtue of engaging in positive deeds of loving kindness. However, on closer examination, we see that compassion is for him a reflection of the fundamental unreality of human individuality. It is a dim, unconscious realization of the unity of all living things. Thus, the aura of human dignity is denied—the dignity of the one who is compassionate as well as the dignity of the object of compassion. It is the metaphysical will in all living things that alone is real. All individualities are denied in the flash of intuition, which is pity; it follows that to end the victim's agony through a quick death is more logical and merciful than to enable him to drag out a miserable existence. This would apply to most people, not only to those who are sick and incurable, for in Schopenhauer's judgment, the wretched misery of human life far outweighs its few and rare moments of pleasure.

Suffering is not peculiarly human. Consequently, the sentiment of compassion is directed toward all living things.

Boundless compassion for all living beings is the surest and most certain guarantee of pure moral conduct, and needs no casuistry. . . . In former times the English plays used to finish with a petition for the King. The old Indian dramas close with these words: "May all living beings be delivered from pain." Tastes differ; but in my opinion there is no more beautiful prayer than this.[12]

The Indian virtue of *ahimsa*—hurting no living beings—seemed nobler to Schopenhauer than the biblical ethic that focuses on the supreme sanctity of human life. In Judaism we are enjoined to take account of "the pain of all living creatures" (*tsaar baalai hayim*); but this obligation is not in the same class as duties to human beings. "Whoso sheddeth man's blood, by man shall his blood be shed; for in the image of God made He man" (Genesis 9:6). The Mishnah enlarges on this theme: "The Holy One, blessed be He, puts the seal of Adam, the first man, upon every human being, but so that not one person resembles another; therefore, a person is obligated to say, 'for my sake the world was created. . . .'"[13] Here the infinite significance of the human individual is asserted—a theme that is basic to the Judeo-Christian tradition. The love of man is related to the unity of spirit, not the unity of life. "And thou shall love thy neighbor as thyself. I am the Lord."

Kant recognized the centrality of this principle in the maxim that all human beings must be treated as ends, not as means for the pleasure of others. It is precisely this special dignity of man, however, that is rejected in Hindu speculation. Schopenhauer, following the lead of the Vedas, advocated the unity of all living things rather than the holiness of human life. He would urge the depersonalization of the ego in order to better intuit the transcendental will and to deny and overcome personal self-hood. By directing compassion to all "living beings," the unique aura of mankind is denied. Since it is impossible to be compassionate, in the fullest sense, toward all living beings, we may find, as in India, that cows and other animals may be treated with greater generosity than human beings. People may embrace vegetarianism and at the same time preach the mass annihilation of human beings, as did Schopenhauer's disciples Richard Wagner and Adolf Hitler.

Reverence for humanity is intimately associated with reverence for

rationality. If the guidance of reason is despised and brute instincts
are extolled, then the nimbus of glory is removed from the brow of
man and soon enough he is reduced to the level of the beast. Nihilism
and animalism go hand in hand. In the light of the later development
of German nihilism, the following paragraph, rejecting man's
uniqueness, is particularly significant.

> Those persons must indeed be totally blind, or else completely
> chloroformed by the *foetor Judaicus* (Jewish stench), who do not discern
> that the truly essential and fundamental part in man and beast is identically
> the same thing. That which distinguishes the one from the other does not
> lie in the primary and original principle, in the inner nature, in the kernel of
> the two phenomena (this kernel being in both alike the Will of the
> individual); it is found in what is secondary, in the intellect, in the degree of
> perceptive capacity. It is true that the latter is incomparably higher in man,
> by reason of his added faculty of abstract knowledge, called Reason;
> nevertheless, this superiority is traceable solely to a greater cerebral
> development, in other words, to the corporeal difference, which is
> quantitative, not qualitative, of a single part, the brain.[14]

This passage, with its anti-Jewish animus, anticipates the attitudes
of social Darwinism that became widespread in the latter decades of
the nineteenth century. Though Schopenhauer did not use the
symbols of Aryan mythology of the following generations, Poliakov
rightly concluded, "no author did more to popularize the Manichean
distinction between Aryanism and Semitism in Germany."[15]

Richard Wagner (1813–1883) considered himself to be a prophet
of the future German renaissance. An ardent disciple of
Schopenhauer's, he consecrated himself to the mission of articulating
in music the genius of the Teutonic race. "My life experiences have
brought me to the very point where nothing but Schopenhauer's
philosophy could have wholly satisfied me . . . it was the only one to
answer my deep suffering feelings of the essence of the world."[16]
Wagner aimed to create a Teutonic mythology that could take the
place of the Judeo-Christian foundation of western thought—". . .
friend Schopenhauer has simply helped by his enormous power to
drive away the last Judaic heresy."

Schopenhauer had assigned a unique metaphysical role to music. Wagner sought to create a "totalitarian work of art" that would center on the kind of music that reflected the inner soul of the race. The publication of Gobineau's *Essai sur l'inégalite des races humaines* (4 volumes, 1853–1855) on the racial factor as the source of civilization prepared the ground for Wagner's own mystique. Gobineau was eager to vindicate the role of the European, especially the French aristocracy, which was largely massacred in the French Revolution. In his view, the peasantry and the bourgeois were of a lower racial stock, while the aristocrats were descended from the conquering Germanic tribes in the fifth century. The latter were the unconscious bearers of genuine culture, storing their potential treasure in their genes for centuries, until the time was ripe for the efflorescence of medieval art in the thirteenth century. Only "pure" and noble "Aryan" races are capable of creating authentic cultures. All ancient cultures, he reasoned, must have come into being through the infusion of pure and Aryan blood. When the pure race mingles with a lesser breed, the former loses its vigor while the latter is in no way improved.

Such fantasies could be believed only by those who were desperately seeking for a "scientific" justification of ethnic pride and passion. Germany's racists embraced and even radicalized Gobineau's theory, treating it as proof of Teutonic racial superiority. The new mythology suited their purpose perfectly. It was mystical and intuitive, anti-intellectual and amoral, since on any rational and ethical basis the differences among the races in Europe were not as significant as individual differences. And if intelligence and conscience could be believed, the Jews of our day might serve as living proof of the fact that non-Aryans can be talented in all the realms of culture and science. So the true measure of greatness had to be located in the dark underworld of instinct and intuition. Accordingly, Wagner's magisterial musical genius was harnessed to the task of creating an elaborate mythology that would reverberate with the raw passions of the ancient Germanic hordes that shattered the Roman empire.

In this cultural crusade Wagner directed his assault chiefly at Judaism and the Jewish people. Judaism, as the source of

Christianity, was the ultimate fountainhead of western culture, which is alien to the genius of the Teutons. The Judeo-Christian edifice can be toppled most easily by undermining its foundation. If all that is "non-Aryan" is by definition corrupt the ground is cleared for the revival of the ancient Teutonic gods, reflecting the wild primitive energy of the barbarian forest dwellers. The old gods did not really die; they lie dormant in the unspoiled instincts of the masses, who know intuitively that only what is Aryan in origin is good. Only by appealing to "the voice of blood" could Wagner "prove" that the apparent attainments of Jews are hollow, meaningless, and even destructive. The new prophets of racial mysticism were compelled by their own circular logic to denigrate the apparently gifted Jews in order to magnify and sanctify the mystical grandeur of the Teutons. To be sure, non-Germanic peoples, particularly the French, and Christianity, especially Catholicism, were also the targets of Teutonic fury, along with the Jews and Judaism. However, the Jews were the most defenseless.

In the article "Judaism in Music," which Wagner published anonymously (in 1850), he set out to remove from the Germanic musical stage the two most popular composers who were ethnically Jewish—Felix Mendelssohn and Meyerbeer. He pointed out that the common masses in Germany were antisemitic. "It is necessary to explain the unconscious feeling of aversion toward the Jewish being [*Wesen*] on the part of the Volk." The good-hearted German peasants cannot be wrong, and mass instincts are better guides to the heart of reality than any sensible or rational considerations. Once the Jewish race has been stigmatized as satanic, it is easy to discredit Christian culture. So he wrote in his essay, "Religion and Art": "For us, it is sufficient to derive the ruin of the Christian religion from its drawing upon· Judaism for the elaboration of its dogmas." Buddhism, the faith of the Aryans, is closer to the instincts of the Teutons. Therefore, vegetarianism is in order. In an essay he wrote in 1881, "Herodom and Christendom," he reasserted his mystical racism and his faddist vegetarianism, arguing as follows:

In the prehistoric world, the Aryans lived in a golden age, pure and sinless, subsisting on vegetables. Then, "original sin" infested the noble race—people began to eat the flesh of animals. In turn, their blood was corrupted. Christ, an Aryan, appeared and taught symbolically the virtues of a return to vegetarianism. The Christian Church, however, being a Jewish creation, prevented the meaning of Christ's message from being understood. The Jew, being "the devil incarnate of human decadence," utilized the Catholic Church to bring about the mingling of races. In consequence, the natural instincts of the Aryans were suppressed, and, in the course of many centuries, there took place "a vitiation of our blood, not only by a departure from the natural food of man, but, above all, by the degeneration brought about by the mixing of the hero-blood of the noblest races with that of one-time cannibals, now trained to be the skilled business leaders of society."

Meat eaters are cannibals to Wagner, and the greatest sin against the future is so-called race mixing. But his *Weltanschauung*, in all its infantile phantasmagoria, was not a cry of despair. He held out the hope that a new Germanic Redeemer would arise, a Parsifal resurrected, who would restore the "purity" of Aryan blood and usher in a new golden age of vegetarian sinlessness.

From our vantage point today, it is apparent that Hitler was the dream of Wagner, just as he was the nightmare of the world.[17]

Friedrich Nietzsche (1844–1900) was for a long time an ardent admirer of Wagner. In his first book, *The Birth of Tragedy* (Die Geburt der Tragedie aus dem Geiste der Musik, 1872), Nietzsche referred to Wagner as the superb Master Artist, who is leading Germany toward a new Periclean age. Later, especially after the presentation of *Parsifal*, Nietzsche denounced Wagner as a cultural reactionary. Wagner's fantastic chauvinism was always an abomination to Nietzsche, who hated the smug and arrogant preachers of *Deutschtum*. "An antisemite," he wrote, "surely does not become more respectable because he lies on principle."[18] However, Nietzsche's powerful influence contributed significantly to the spread of nihilism in Germany and elsewhere. He wielded his pen like a crowbar, demolishing the Judeo-Christian structure of values and opening the floodgates to the passion and fury of the mob. While his own philosophy of life contained a heroic and even a saintly core, his work was rarely seen as a unit, and the shattered fragments of his brilliant thought helped pulverize the classical and balanced culture of Germany.

An early disciple of Schopenhauer's in setting will far above reason, Nietzsche turned around the main drift of his master's argument. Will is indeed the substance of reality, but this numinous will is not blind and impersonal; rather it is the will to power of individuals. In Schopenhauer's view, salvation consists in the transcendence of will by means of asceticism, pity and art. For Nietzsche, goodness consists in a massive embodiment of that will. Good is that which is done by "good" men; that is, the wielders of power. The denial of this will is a mark of degeneracy. Hence, all restraints on the raw exercise of power are hypocritical and debilitating. Mankind will enter a new age of freedom and vigor when the moral principles of equality and justice are consigned to the dust heap of history. The human race will achieve new heights of excellence through a return to the natural processes of "struggle for survival" and "the survival of the fittest." In personal life each individual should aim at "self-overcoming" in order to reach a higher level of culture. In general mankind should not labor under the moral burdens of the past nor be restrained by tender consciences in the present, but it should follow the lure of the promise of the future. And that promise is infinite in scope, from man to superman and on to divinity. Says Zarathustra: "If there were gods, how could I bear not to be a god? Consequently, there are no gods."

In contrast to Schopenhauer, Nietzsche admired the Jews of the biblical era, setting the grand and natural spirit of the Old Testament above the "degenerated" character of the New Testament. Yet, even as early as the exilic period, Deutero-Isaiah taught that God is on the side of the weak and the humble, those who suffer and wait for deliverance. So the Hebrew Scriptures prepared the ground for the Buddhist spirit of self-denial in the New Testament.

In the "Antichrist," Nietzsche scorned the categorical imperative of Kant as "dangerous to life."[19] "A nation would go to pieces if it confounds *its* duty with general duty." Similarly, the ethical teaching of gentleness, love, and forgiveness is "decadent" because the weak are aided to live on. A right action proves itself "by the amount of pleasure that goes with it."[20]

The teaching of Jesus was essentially identical with that of Judaism. Nietzsche professed to be amazed ". . . that today the Christian can cherish antisemitism without realizing that it [Christianity] is no more than *the final consequence of Judaism*."[21] The Jews rejected Jesus not because of his teaching, but because he rebelled against the priestly hierarchy. The Jews felt instinctively that their religious hierarchy was indispensable: ". . . it represented their last possibility for survival; it was the final *residuum* of their independent political existence; an attack upon it was an attack upon the most profound national instinct, the most powerful national will to live, that has ever appeared on earth."[22]

Nietzsche reserved his bitterest enmity for Paul, whom he regarded as the founder of Gentile Christianity. Paul's meekness and love actually concealed his hatred and envy of the proud and powerful Romans and of the raw, untutored barbarians. "In Paul is incarnated the very opposite of 'the bearer of glad tidings'; he represents the genius of hatred, the vision of hatred, the relentless logic of hatred."[23]

Although Nietzsche spurned the malicious myths of racial and religious antisemitism, he mightily reinforced the charge that the Jews were ultimately guilty of generating the Christian faith and imposing it through Paul and the other Apostles on the peoples of Europe. Since Christianity was to Nietzsche the religion of decadence, the Jews are to blame in the final analysis for weakening the Indo-Europeans.

> Psychologically, the Jews are a people gifted with the strongest vitality, so much so that when they found themselves facing impossible conditions of life, they chose voluntarily, and with a profound talent for self-preservation, the side of all those instincts that make for *decadence*, not as if mastered by them, but as if detecting in them a power by which the world could be defied. The Jews are the very opposite of *decadents* . . . they have managed to put themselves at the head of all *decadent* movements."[24]

The decadence in question is, as we have seen, the biblical ethic of equality, justice, and mercy. In Nietzsche's "newspeak," the democratic ideal and the socialist vision are the modern forms of

Jewish and Christian decadence. A natural society is hierarchical, with the strong lording it over the weak. The ethic of warriors and aristocrats was replaced in the Christian world by "the morality of slaves," which restrains and tames the invincible power of the Aryan races. In the medieval world the "slave ethic" of Judaism and Christianity utilized the myths of religion; in the modern world this ethic employs the slogans of democracy and socialism in order to subject the strong to the rule of the weak.

> Whatever else has been done to damage the powerful and great of this earth seems trivial compared with what the Jews have done, that priestly people who succeeded in avenging themselves on their enemies and oppressors by radically inverting all their values, that is, by an act of the most spiritual vengeance. This was a strategy entirely appropriate to a priestly people in whom vindictiveness has gone most deeply underground. It was the Jew who, with frightening consistency dared to invert the aristocratic value equations, good = noble, powerful = beautiful, happy = favored of the gods, and maintain, with the furious hatred of the underprivileged and impotent, that "only the poor, the powerless are good; only the suffering, sick and ugly, truly blessed."[25]

Nietzsche even injected a conspiratorial note in the Jewish sponsorship of Christianity.

> Has not Israel, precisely by the detour of this "redeemer" [Christ], this seeming antagonist and destroyer of Israel, reached the final goal of its sublime vindictiveness? Was it not a necessary feature of a truly brilliant politics of vengeance, a farsighted, subterranean, slowly and carefully planned vengeance, that Israel had to deny its true instrument publicly and nail him to the cross like a mortal enemy, so that "the whole world" (meaning all the enemies of Israel) might naively swallow the bait?[26]

Nietzsche's lance was tilted not only against the Judeo-Christian ethic and its modern developments, democracy and socialism, but also against the heritage of Socrates, the embodiment of rational discourse.[27] Germany, he urged, should find its own path to creativity by resurrecting and taking part in the worship of animal exuberance, as the ancient Greeks did in the orgiastic exercises of Dionysus. All art, he contended, is a blend of the Apollonian perfection of form and the Dionysian upsurge of restless vitality. Music is the expression of the noumenal will, especially the music of Wagner, which has broken through the artificial barriers and forms of an earlier age. It is through the resurgence of music that Germans will discover their soul. "For amidst our degenerate culture music is the only pure and purifying flame, towards which and away from which all things move in a Heraclitean double motion. All that is now called culture, education, civilization, will one day have to appear before the incorruptible judge, Dionysus."[28]

Nietzsche himself summarized the import of his incandescent epigrams in the announcement by the pagan prophet Zarathustra— "God is dead." The historic source of western civilization is now dried up, and the new thrust toward a new culture must come from a total self-surrender to the worship of unspoiled animal energy. The barbaric god, Dionysus, must emerge from limbo to take the place of God, and Apollo, the weaver of beautiful dreams, must create a new set of myths whereby the volcanic energy of the neobarbarians will be channeled toward the creation of a new culture.

Thus Nietzsche brought to a dead end the magnificent effort of German philosophers to substitute an unfolding, infinite spirit for the providence of God. For Kant, the spirit of humanity, in its critical purity, was divine. Christ, as the Son of Man, was the symbol of humanity. And the categorical imperative was the chief clue to transcendental reality. Fichte interpreted the whole of existence in terms of an unvarying moral order, but in his nationalistic addresses, he assigned to the Germans a central role in the intuitive apprehension of this order. Schelling established esthetics as the chief organon of metaphysics. Hegel maintained that history was the self-unfolding of absolute reason. Schopenhauer returned to the Schellingian concept of beauty and art, but to him it is the denial of the will that art reflects. Nietzsche consummated this line of development by his analysis of esthetics as the blend of Apollonist illusion of eternal forms and Dionysian delight in sheer vitality. The will to power is now the substance of reality, and a thunderous Wagnerian art is the only way to apprehend it. The new prophet is the incarnation of bold defiance, the ruthless destroyer of democratic values.

Nietzsche's philosophy reverberated with the rich overtones of a futuristic idealism. The historical consequence of Nietzscheism was felt through the blend of his "transvalued" values with the emergent ideology of Aryan nationalism which Nietzsche himself abhorred. His plea for a new European elite was vulgarized into a chauvinistic call on the Germans to repeat the ancient barbarian annihilation of Latin culture and to bring about a similar destruction of the civilization of the West. His self-styled disciples argued that out of the ashes of our contemporary culture, a new order will emerge. The new Europe will represent the principle of hierarchy, and the weak will be trained to echo the sentiments of the strong. The new "caste system" will employ biological principles for the breeding of "supermen," without regard to the "hypocritical" principles of Judeo-Christian morality. The new Messiah will have to undo the achievement of the Jews; that is, exorcise their persistent influence within Christianity and European culture in order to prepare the way for the new aristocratic morality. Israel and its God must give way to the new barbarians and their unfettered lusts.

Nietzsche's impassioned rejection of the biblical ethic was elevated into the prophecy of a new Germanic upsurge that would create its own culture and morality.[29] We noted that while Nietzsche himself was a bitter critic of "Teutonism," his antibiblicism and his futuristic vision of "the blonde beast" were congenial to the fantasies of the prophets of German world domination, the preachers of *Deutschland uber alles*. Among these priests of nationalistic idolatry Paul de Lagarde (1827–1891) occupies a special position, by virtue of his vast learning, his nationalistic nihilism, his philosophic vitalism, and his quest for a new, exclusively Germanic religion. In the publisher's foreword to the 1934 edition of Lagarde's *Deutsche Schriften* the author is hailed as the one "who most effectively prepared the way for the thoughts which form the foundation for the National-Socialist Third Reich of the Germans, the greatest herald of the folk-German ideas."[30]

Lagarde was a well-known Orientalist who specialized in Septuagint studies. He wrote with the authority of a historian of religion as well as with the passion of a chauvinistic demagogue. His call for a Germanic religion was predicated on the conviction that Catholicism was thoroughly un-German and that even Protestantism was tainted.

> If I am not mistaken, the forms which religion previously assumed are now used up. Now, only a new religion is possible which recognizes and loves God in people, naturally not in natural man, but in the one who was "reborn."
>
> Our task is not to "create" a national religion—religions are never formed, only revealed—but to do everything that prepares the way for a national religion and prepare the nation to accept it.[31]

Such a religion can be neither Christianity nor Liberalism, since its task is

> . . . to generate yearning for the homeland among the expatriated, the assurance of eternal life in the midst of time, the indestructible community (*Gemeinschaft*) of the children of God surrounded by vanity and hatred; marked by intimate life with the Almighty Creator and Redeemer, led by the majesty of the king and power of the ruler, staunchly opposed to all that does not derive from the divine race.
>
> Not humane should we be, but the children of God, not liberal but free, not Conservative but German, not believing but pious, not Christian but evangelical: manifesting the Divine that lives bodily in each one of us, and all of us united in a self-enclosed circle. . . .[32]

While the new Germanic religion rejects the Christian religion as an unnecessary ballast, it must treat Judaism as "undesirable, because it is alien, experienced as something un-German and anti-German."[33] As a Bible critic, Lagarde filled his writings with scornful comments on biblical personalities. Like the Gnostics of the second century, he was ready to make room for Christ as a cosmic symbol that could be woven into the texture of an emergent German religion, but he rejected any historical association with the Jewish faith and people. A de-Judaized, de-historicized Protestantism might in the course of time become "Germanized." The nation, as he saw it, was allergic to any ideal that did not grow out of its own vital powers. He condemned liberalism as a force that corrodes the national "personality" by its preoccupation with universal ideals and the freedom of the individual. He called it "the Grey International. . . . Without exception, every living religion is exclusive."[34] A Germanic religion must bind the community into a living whole and erect an all-inclusive wall against the outside world. "What does the call for an ethical order and the demand to love all people have to do with the German nation?"[35]

The Jews of Germany were emancipated by the spirit of Liberalism, but according to Lagarde, they were placed in an untenable position, since they were encouraged to live as an alien body thrust into the living organism of the nation. In his view the German Jews must endeavor to be "born again" through a kind of baptism in the national Holy Spirit, whereby they would cease to have any contact with non-German Jews and forswear any remembrance of their history or any sense of a separate destiny.[36] The native Germans, in turn, must by their ardor help the Jewish iceberg to melt. Otherwise, the Jews would remain "parasites" feeding on the national organism. Thus, Lagarde concluded, "only anti-liberals are truly friends of Jews, as only anti-liberals are truly friends of Germany."[37]

Lagarde's anti-liberalism included a program of pitiless subjugation and virtual enslavement of the non-Germanic ethnic groups living in central Europe. The Slavic nationalities, he argued, were destined by nature and by the God of German blood to be the helots óf the Teutons. By the same divine mandate, Germany is called upon to extend its borders to the Black Sea and to push the Russians beyond the Urals into the tundras of Siberia. This preeminent representative of German academia argued frankly in behalf of a deliberate, ruthless, "Assyrian" policy of mass resettlement and cruel repression designed to assure German supremacy. Thus, in the heart of Europe, in "the land of poets and philosophers," a cold and calculated program of genocide was proposed, not by a demagogue, but by a philosophical historian, an arbiter of German *Kultur*.

Not the Jews, be it noted, but the Russians, were slated for annihilation. Russia was to Lagarde the central target of hate, not the other historical enemies—Catholicism, Judaism, and North

America.[38] Russia was the enemy inescapably because it cut athwart German *Lebensraum* and compelled the surplus population of Germany to emigrate. As to the Slavic millions marked for annihilation, Lagarde asked when did Assyrians worry about other peoples?

Lagarde could describe the Slavs of Europe as "the burden of history" and assert that "the sooner they perish the better it will be for us and for them" and yet figure as an "idealist" in Germany, because he extolled the Germanic spiritual potential. Thus a new nationalistic ethic and a new nationalistic faith were proposed in the latter decades of the nineteenth century as the political-cultural program of the German Conservatives.

In World War I the "Germanic" writings of Lagarde were assigned to German officers as recommended reading. To liberals, Christians, and Jews, his views were so horrendous that they needed no refutation.[39] Yet, Lagarde demonstrated the immense destructive power of the Nietzschean logic of vitalism.

However, there was no immediate Jewish response to the challenge of Nietzsche. His penetrating aphorisms possessed a peculiar appeal to successive waves of young collegians, Jewish as well as Christian. Their natural, if transitory, spasms of youthful rebelliousness against the moral-political establishment was articulated incisively and metaphysically grounded by the bold, future-oriented philosophy of Nietzsche. We are familiar with some of the intellectual rationalizations of the so-called counterculture in our generation, which pretended to "liberate" society in the name of unrepressed life-affirming instincts. The rhetoric may differ, but the mood is the same. Jewish youths in Europe were as deeply affected by such movements of rebellion as were their Christian contemporaries, perhaps more so because of the marginal status of the Jew in European society and his critical posture toward conventional verities. By the turn of the century there were many thousands of university-educated young Jews who were caught up in the whirlpool of diverse intellectual movements. They were not personally committed to the so-called slave morality of the Bible. The socialists and anarchists among them articulated their revolutionary ideologies without reference to their Jewish background. Indeed, one of the attractions of the new ideologies was their seeming indifference to the Jewishness of their followers. The Jewish liberals were so confident that the western world was moving toward their vision of a free and open society that they tended to ignore the voices of reaction.

Max Nordau who in the mid-1890s joined Theodor Herzl in founding the World Zionist Organization, was an exception. In a brilliant book he condemned Wagner, Nietzsche, and Lagarde as "degenerates." Writing as a psychiatrist and social scientist, he described Wagner as a psychopath in love with death. In all Wagner's writings love is punished by death and salvation is achieved by way of self-immolation. "With a slight modification of Terence's *homo sum*, he might have said of himself, 'I am a degenerate, and nothing degenerate is foreign to me.'"[40]

As to Nietzsche, Nordau described him as an egomaniac whose insane ravings were simply the symptoms of an incurable illness. The only theme that Nietzsche expounded consistently is that of extreme individualism. But, Nordau insisted, people attain humanity only through their feelings of solidarity with other people, initially their kinfolk and ultimately the whole of mankind.[41] A healthy person, Nordau asserted, continues steadily to expand his ego by enlarging the range of his sympathies. Similarly, a healthy society is one that revolves around two poles—the sanctity of the individual and the claims of mankind. All historical and political groupings must be justified by reference to these two absolute values. The ideal society would consist of a chain of communities small enough for direct interaction of personalties.[42] The national romanticism of the Germans, from Fichte to Treitschke, to Lagarde, was condemned by Nordau as a collective version of sickly egotism. "The so-called state egotism is . . . in effect a private egoism, that of several individuals, and even if it benefited . . . all the citizens of the state, it would still be private egoism of many individuals who are violating justice and tolerating such violation."[43]

Nordau's conversion to Zionism was completely consistent with his liberal humanism. He hoped that a rejuvenated people of Israel would add greatly to the vitality of the liberal ideals in the western world by taking the wind out of the antisemitic sails. While he did not abide by the precepts of the Jewish faith, he identified his own life's work with the prophetic condemnation of all that is degenerate. He defined degeneracy in moral-rational terms, rather than in the biological terminology of Nietzsche. He rejected traditional Jewish beliefs that are associated with "supernaturalism," but he affirmed the moral and folk elements of Jewish tradition. The secret of Israel's endurance is not its possession of "eternal truths," but its striving toward a high, transhistorical goal; namely, the "kingdom of heaven."

> Our messianic ideal is high and remote like a star. It is eternal like a star. For the believer it is a living hope. For him who understands but does not believe, it is a proud symbol whose strength is its unattainability. And that, it seems to me, is the secret of the life and tenacity of the Jewish people.[44]

Among the Jews of eastern Europe the Zionist movement was made possible by a massive tide of secularism that undermined popular belief in the coming of the Messiah. Large numbers of the "enlightened" could not rest content any longer with the assurance of divine redemption from "exile" at a time known only to the Almighty. Disenchanted with Orthodoxy and frustrated by the failure of liberalism in the Russian world, they sought to become masters of their own destiny. But how could this goal be achieved? In the mid-nineteenth century, when Czar Alexander II opened the windows of his vast empire to western liberalism, the hopes of Jewish people rose high. Then, within one generation, the tide was reversed. Slowly the storm clouds gathered and burst with thunderous fury in the beginning of the 1880s. The liberal victories in the West, for all their fragility, were totally beyond the horizon in eastern Europe. If emancipation was an idle dream, was "auto-emancipation" possible? Can the Jews of the world acquire, by united action, a state of their own? Since antisemitism has become a worldwide phenomenon, can the cure of Jewish homelessness be achieved on an international basis? It was an affirmative and impassioned answer to these questions that Herzl and Nordau proclaimed at the first World Zionist Congress in 1897.

The Zionist movement in eastern Europe involved a Nietzschean "transvaluation of values." The pattern of ideas and sentiments that sustained the Jewish spirit in the Diaspora was no longer tenable in view of the decline of faith in supernatural redemption. It was inevitable therefore that young revolutionaries would lend a sympathetic ear to the challenge of Nietzsche. Could it not be that the Jewish people have become "petrified" by virtue of their submission to "the dead letters" of their Law? Have they lost contact with the instinctive forces of life? Is it not time now to reexamine ruthlessly their heritage in the light of the will to live, if not "the will to power"? Is it not time to stand Judaism on its head, as it were, to revere force rather than compassion, to extol the brute virtues that bring success in the struggle for survival rather than to continue as a people of bourgeois decencies and biblical ideals?

These sentiments were best articulated in the voluminous works of M. J. Berdichevsky (Ben Gurion) (1865–1922), who applied the Nietzschean philosophy to the Jewish situation. Berdichevsky could not bring himself to extol the sheer ruthlessness of a "blonde beast" or to declare that one must transcend the moral categories of good and evil. He argued, however, that Jews must put an end to their revered, bookish tradition and reconstitute themselves as an earth-bound, "*natural*" people, fighting by whatever means lie at hand for their place in the sun. Through their excessive intellectualism and their infatuation with spiritual values, he maintained, Jews had lost the raw vitality of a natural people. If the Zionist renaissance is to succeed, Berdichevsky argued, Jews must reevaluate their entire tradition and break radically and decisively with their past.

Jews must reinterpret their history, for instance, setting Joshua with his sword above Moses with his hands uplifted in prayer. In fact, the golden age of Israel's past was not the rise of literary prophecy in the eighth century before the Christian era, but the heroic generations of Joshua and the Judges that captured the Holy Land and slaughtered its inhabitants. King David and King Solomon could still qualify as heroes, in Berdichevsky's estimate but, he pointed out, Jeroboam II was a mighty conqueror and hence a great hero, in spite of the biblical condemnation of his regime. The prophets, and later the Pharisaic sages, were, from the nationalistic viewpoint, near-renegades, since their moralism and pacifism weakened the hands of the great heroes and the armies of Judah and Israel. Men like

Alexander Yannai, who could eat and drink while he watched with delight the torment and crucifixion of his enemies, were the real heroes of Jewish history. So were all the Maccabean rulers, including in particular that moral monster, Herod the Great. Judged by the Nietzschean yardstick, the sages and the saints, who created the Mishnah and Talmud, were contemptible. They foisted their slavish mentality on their numerous disciples and in the course of time succeeded in turning their people into a nation of weaklings who esteemed only the "inner" glories of piety and wisdom. To regain their stature as a great nation, Berdichevsky insisted, Jews must repudiate the rabbinic definition of heroism—"Who is the hero of heroes? He who turns an enemy into a friend." Jews would also have to reject Jeremiah's definition of that which is truly laudable—" . . . to understand and know Me, that I, the Lord, work righteousness and loving kindness in the world." (Jeremiah 9:23).

For two thousand years, Berdichevsky pointed out, Jews have devoted themselves totally to the biblical ideals, and what have they achieved? It is now time to set the demands of "life" for the individual and the nation above the ideals of the "book."

Berdichevsky advocated this transvaluation with a divided heart. For he himself was a child of the book, a sensitive poet, and even a mystic. He read the signs of the times, however, and he anticipated the upsurge of a tidal wave of brutality, in the lands of central Europe. Through his writings, the Nietzschean moral revolution and the esthetics of Schopenhauer were brought to the consciousness of Zionist youth. Several generations of rebellious youths, or as we now term them, "militants" and "activists," were inspired by his rhetoric and that of similarly minded writers.[45]

A'had Ha'am (1856–1927), founder of "cultural Zionism," was, like Berdichevsky, convinced of the need for a total, spiritual revolution. If the Jews are ever to succeed in becoming a modern nation, they must undertake to transform their faith and their way of life. They will have to abandon the old institutions and attitudes, which were indeed appropriate to the circumstances of a medieval ghetto. In order to reverse the current of Jewish history from dispersal to concentration and from progressive assimilation to a national renaissannce, Jewish leaders must acquire a new mentality, a fresh scale of values, and a vigorous self-image. No longer can they be content to wait patiently for the Messiah, but, taking control of their own destiny, they must set out to build a Jewish homeland and to rebuild the Jewish communities of the Diaspora, on the basis of a revived, "spiritual" nationalism.

However, the spiritual revolution that A'had Ha'am advocated was the exact opposite of Berdichevsky's transvaluation. Instead of repudiating our moral heritage, A'had Ha'am argued, we have to recapture it and structure our life in keeping with its precepts. A genuine revolution of the spirit brings a people back to its authentic self. So, by giving up the outer forms and the religious minutiae of our tradition, we shall be deepening our sensitivity to the "national ethic," which is the dynamic core of our tradition. Once we see the entire sweep of our history as the work of the Jewish people themselves, not as the result of a divine fiat, we can assay the worth of every practice by reference to the "Torah of the heart" that is alive in the people as a whole. Not the rigid specifications of the Torah and its innumerable commentaries, but the inner ethic of Judaism must be our guide. And this Torah of the heart will take on new forms as the Jewish people proceed to rebuild themselves as a living, secular nation.

A'had Ha'am projected a philosophy of Jewish revival that was compounded of three elements: the vitalism current in his day, the contemporary streams of romantic nationalism, and a peculiarly Judaic ethic that retained the mystical resonance of religion. These elements may seem to be disparate, even contradictory. But they fitted together beautifully because of certain continuities in the Jewish tradition that lent the aura of plausibility and timeliness to the A'had Ha'amist synthesis. Even today the ideology of cultural Zionism continues to hold an unfailing fascination for secularists who are deeply grounded in the Jewish tradition.

The vitalistic element in A'had Ha'am's philosophy was the chief source of his appeal to the youthful enthusiasts of several generations. In his later years his thought became more rationalistic and pragmatic, especially as he was drawn into the orbit of English liberalism, but he never repudiated the vitalistic axioms, which provided firm anchorage for his endeavors to transmute the character of Jewish life.[46] In essence he asserted that the dynamic impetus of Jewish history was not religion but a collective, unconscious "national ego" that impelled all Jews to subordinate their individual interests to the supreme concern of survival. The will to live of the national ego is unconditional and categorical, like the metaphysical will of Schopenhauer, but it rises into the consciousness of the great sons of the nation in the form of ideas, ideals, and sentiments. Thus, the blind will of the nation is articulated through the varied branches of national culture and culminates in an ethic that reverberates with the cosmic overtones of religion.

In A'had Ha'am's view, the Jewish religion was generated by the National Ego out of its peculiar unconscious depths, its historic experiences, and its aspirations for the future. It was developed and expanded by prophets and priests in response to the changing circumstances of history. At all times the living conscience of the people continues to transform the material content of religion in keeping with the dictates of its national ethic. In this way the religion of the people and its popular culture reflect the creative genius of the national ego. Religious leaders, however, may well forget that rituals and beliefs are only temporary reflections of the national will. Then the beliefs become hardened into infallible dogmas and the rituals are desiccated into an unchangeable regimen of conduct. The living faith is then petrified, and the national ego is stultified.

The Reformers in western Europe aimed to revive the Jewish faith by repudiating the archaic elements of the tradition and infusing the fresh philosophical ideals of their time into the historical patterns of Judaism. To A'had Ha'am such a conscious manipulation of religious doctrines and rites was absurd. Religion draws its vitality from the depths of our unconscious selves, where ancestral memories and personal passions are fused indissolubly. Cut off from its irrational roots, it quickly turns into an empty charade. Thus, it can only be "reformed" through the unconscious process of inner growth.[47] Indeed, and here A'had Ha'am agreed with the Reformers, religion does develop, but only through the unconscious prompting of the unfolding national spirit. Such a development can be traced throughout the biblical period, when the prophets projected the national ideal to nobler heights and the priests practiced "the art of the possible."

In the Talmudic period Judaism continued to develop, as the national ethic achieved one breakthrough after another—such as the "reinterpretation" of the primitive lex talionis, the abolition of the ordeal of the suspected woman, the seventh-year moratorium on debts, and the transformation into a dead letter of the law regarding a rebellious son. In the realm of religious philosophy, the process of religious development was also largely unconscious, since the Jewish philosophers could not but assume that the "truths" of philosophy were indeed contained in the Torah.

So A'had Ha'am disassociated himself from any attempt to reform the Jewish religion so long as the national basis of Jewish life had not been firmly established. Authentic development can only derive from the rebirth of Jewish life on its ancestral soil. In the Diaspora the Jewish religion can only exist in its ancient, naive form, untroubled by the intellectual currents of modernity. Pending its renewal in the land of Israel, the Jewish faith must be kept in suspended animation, as it were. To A'had Ha'am, as to the Jewish intellectuals of Russia generally, a nonabsolutist, nonliteral faith was inconceivable. Unlike the Jews of western Europe who lived in relative freedom for generations, the Jews of Russia were repressed down to the outbreak of the Russian Revolution. Hence, a liberal version of Judaism did not develop in eastern Europe. Those who broke away from the dogmatic structure of Orthodoxy were at best nonreligious, at worst antireligious.

Yet, while A'had Ha'am shared the opinion of his compatriots regarding the untenability of a middle position between fundamentalism and secularism, he maintained that the national-spiritual dimension of Judaism can be disentangled from Orthodoxy and cultivated independently. This spiritual dimension is basically ethical and literary, but it includes even some religious rites, such as the Sabbath and the holidays. The "vessels" of ritual belong to the sacred heritage of a people, as well as the "wine" of ideas. "More than the Jews kept the Sabbath, the Sabbath kept the Jews." Far more than the external symbols of Judaism, however, its inner dynamism is the authentic expression of the "national soul," and this subterranean power is as elusive as the mystery of life. It cannot be formulated in so many concepts and categories, for it inheres in the depths of the national psyche. The rituals of Orthodoxy cannot regenerate it, and the "reforms" of the modernists cannot charm it into life. It can only be revived by a fresh effort to plant the nation in its ancient homeland. The vital energy of a nation grows out of its life. In its own homeland a new "national vision" will emerge out of the soil, as it were, and infuse the ancient faith with its fresh vitality, transforming it outwardly as well as inwardly. The growth of a nation's soul is as mysterious as it is irresistible.

> It follows from all the above that, according to my opinion, the development of the "written letter" depends upon the development of ethical apprehension in our hearts. And this latter quality depends upon the general vitality of the people. Therefore, when our national life was cut short by our great catastrophe and subsequent flurry of disasters, our heart was squeezed into the "four ells of the written letter," and it no longer had cause to develop. Since it was not impelled by fresh power, it lost the capacity for autonomous judgment, and this is what I call, "petrifaction"—not the lack of reformers who modify the faith as they please. Therefore, I see the cure of this sickness, as to all our ethical ailments, not in a movement of criticism and external improvements, but . . . in the infusion of a new stream of life into the heart of the people. . . .
>
> And this new, wonder-working stream is "the love of Zion" movement . . . since it will revive the Jewish heart and prepare it to develop generally, it will of its own accord bring about in the course of time renewed vitality and development in all directions, including the matters of faith. . . .[48]

Here, then, is a vitalistic remedy for the ills of the Jewish religion—let the Jewish people be reinvigorated as a living nation, and its spirituality will then take on fresh life. Judaism had become petrified, having been reduced to "the recognition of man's absolute nothingness and his eternal submission to the written letter." The Torah of the heart will come to life through "the love of Zion" movement, which induces "a living heart-felt yearning for the unity of the nation, its revival and its free development, according to its own nature, on the basis of general, human principles."[49]

The love of Zion movement was, to A'had Ha'am, an unconscious outgrowth of the national will. It emerged spontaneously out of the hearts of the people—hence its indomitable vitality. Thus, he wrote:

> This will to live, which impels our people to believe in the possibility of its national existence in exile, drives it also to seek and find in every epoch the ways that are most appropriate to its self-preservation and its development, in accord with contemporary circumstances. It is the same Will, which stands guard ceaselessly, "preparing the remedy before the wound," so that a new "wall" be prepared to confront the "enemy," before the old wall had been breached . . .[50]

A'had Ha'am was dubious from time to time regarding the future viability of religion generally and the Jewish religion in particular. At times he allied himself with the French positivists, who regarded all metaphysical speculation, let alone religious faith, as obsolete and archaic. At other times he sided with the English empiricists, who interpreted the social and personal functions of religion in pragmatic terms.

> It is possible to be truly religious without faith—that is, to have religious feeling, without religious beliefs. We encounter such persons everywhere, and they form the enduring foundation of religions. After all, religion derives from feeling, not from thoughts; so, opinions can be completely reversed, while feeling remains."[51]

The doctrines of religion constitute a "popular metaphysics," which is likely to disappear, according to A'had Ha'am, but the "feelings" of religion serve as a powerful ally for the national ethic, which is the real lifeblood of a national culture.

> The true relation between religion and ethics is, therefore, the opposite of what is generally assumed. While religion lends vigor to the ethical will, the content of ethics emerges through other causes and develops of its own accord. Religion endows the abstract ethical ideal with life, by conjuring up the image of a Supreme Being who represents this ideal in its purity. But, ethical feeling in its turn continually refines the qualities of the Divine, in accord with its stage of development. . . .[52]

It follows that whether or not religion is reborn in the national homeland, the national ethic will surely come to life with the rebirth of the people—and this ethical renaissance is all that truly matters. While Lagarde sought to evolve a Germanic religion out of an impassioned and exclusive devotion to all things Germanic, A'had Ha'am similarly aimed to evolve a national ethic and culture out of the national rebirth of Jewry within the land of Israel. But A'had Ha'am aimed at a return to the prophetic ethic of the Hebrew Scriptures, while Lagarde sought to go back to the tribal ethic of the Teutonic barbarians. In theory both thinkers were "national pantheists," idealizing the creations of their respective peoples. But, in content, their teachings were at opposite poles. The German savant called on his people to become Assyrians. A'had Ha'am urged his people to become once again "sons of the prophets."

At times, A'had Ha'am's vitalism turned romantic, almost mystical, for he assumed that a Jew cannot but feel that he is "different" from all Gentiles in respect to the ultimate values of life. "But, every true Jew feels in general the existence of a fundamental distinction that sets his Ethic apart from the doctrine which prevails in the outside world."[53] The old sense of theological uniqueness was here turned into a "feeling" of secular separatism.

In a caustic critique of Claude G. Montefiore's commentary on the Synoptic Gospels, A'had Ha'am condemned Montefiore as an alienated intellectual who had lost the capacity to feel "Jewishly," to know in his heart that he is different from all other nations. A "true Jew," according to A'had Ha'am's way of thinking, may find it difficult to formulate this "difference" in so many words, but he cannot but "feel" it, instinctively, as it were— ". . . for there is not one view that is obligatory for all Jews, but there is one way of feeling that is common to all true Jews." This feeling is so deep as to transcend all the usual distinctions among nations.

A'had Ha'am's axiom of an instinctively Jewish feeling is understandable, given the vitalistic elements in his philosophy. As we have seen, he assumed that a nation is a quasi-biological organism, endowed with a will to live and a national ethic. Living organisms are usually allergic to one another. The national ethic, as the product of the national ego, reinvigorates the vital potency of the nation. If every nation, as he thought, develops a national ethic of its own, then "the Jewish people that has always dwelt alone, separated from all other peoples in its evolution and in the wondrous course of its life from ancient times to the present must surely possess a unique Ethic. . . ."[54]

So A'had Ha'am dreamed of creating a new, secularist Torah with a set of precepts encompassing the whole of Jewish life, even as did the Torah of Moses. "We have to know in authentic detail what the obligations are which the true national Ethic, apart from any foreign admixtures, imposes upon us in our relationship to ourselves and to others. . . ." If every nation creates its own language, how much more is the attitude to every aspect of life stamped by the national seal?

A'had Ha'am maintained that some western Jews, even Zionists, have already lost sight of their Jewishness. By way of illustration, he cited two plays, one by Theodore Herzl, the other by Max Nordau. Both dramas centered around heroes who rediscovered their "honor" by embracing the Zionish philosophy. But the heroes then defended their honor against insolent antisemites by challenging the latter to a duel. A'had Ha'am asserted that true Jews would not feel called on to risk their lives by resorting to this medieval ordeal, which is so contrary to "the moral feeling which lives in our hearts."

We may grant that those who were raised in a traditional Jewish milieu and educated in the sacred literature of the Bible and the Talmud would not feel disposed to defend their honor in a duel. The real question is whether or not the Jewish attitude toward this bloody ordeal is innate or acquired. If the latter is true, then young Jews educated in a Germanic university and taunted by envious, antisemitic colleagues may well react by challenging their opponents to a duel. It is a fact, however, that dueling was itself a controversial issue within the realm of western culture at the turn of the century, and many Gentiles, as well as Jews, were then rejecting the practice.

A'had Ha'am labored all his life in order to explicate the implications of the national ethic. He did not take the easy road of basing Jewish ethics on the feelings of compassion, as did Samuel David Luzzato, nor did he return to the classical exposition of Saadia, which identified goodness with the harmonious development of all one's faculties, or content himself with the synthesis of Maimonides, which combined the Aristotelian "golden mean" with the Platonic quest of *imitatio dei*. He was compelled by a dynamic, open-ended quest, akin to the infinite outreach of the so-called Faustian soul. Only such an affinity for infinite horizons could validate his faith in Israel's immortality.

As A'had Ha'am saw it, the peculiar genius of Judaism was expressed in its total condemnation of idolatry. No material representation of the Deity was permitted, for whatever is limited and concrete cannot possibly reflect the Divine Being. Said A'had Ha'am, ". . . if that Gentile who came to Hillel and asked to learn the whole Torah while standing on one foot had come to me, I would have said to him, 'Thou shalt not make for thyself any graven image . . . that is the whole Torah. The rest is commentary, go and learn.' "[55] In other words, the essence of spirituality is the refusal to confine adoration to that which is concrete and therefore only partial and transitory. We must be ready to overcome the bounds of our subjective experience and the limitations of our particular society. The Jewish ideal can only be the One, who transcends all representations. The God of Israel is the reflection of the national ideal of ethical perfection.

In answer to the question of the Gentile in the above quotation, Hillel, as is well-known, cited the Golden Rule in its negative form. In the Gospels, however, Jesus summed up the essence of Judaism in a positive version of the Golden Rule— ". . . Do unto others, as you would have them do unto you." In this contrast between the two versions, A'had Ha'am saw the essential distinction between the Jewish ethos and that of the Christian world. The negative formulation is objective and absolute in character, while a positive formulation lends itself to subjective distortions, indeed to a "reverse egotism" since a person may presume that what is good for him must be good for others also. For the same reason, Judaism stresses the objective phase of righteousness rather than the subjective feelings of love and compassion.[56]

A'had Ha'am believed that a careful study of Jewish ethics would reveal the distinctive genius of the Jewish "national spirit," but, at the same time he insisted that the formulations of the past cannot suffice for the guidance of contemporary Jews. The past provides us with certain guidelines. We learn to say "no" to any ideal or ideology that would preempt all our loyalties. We stand ready to let our hearts and minds carry us to ever greater visions of the ideal. The "national ideal" was born in the past, but its fulfillment consists in a vision of the universal society.

This orientation toward the future brings A'had Ha'am to a partial appreciation of the Nietzschean philosophy. The dynamism, openness, and even the elitism of Nietzsche are in keeping with the inner impetus of the Jewish spirit. However, the character of the superman is, in Jewish ethics, the exact opposite of the primitive conqueror, the blonde beast. The "superior person" is the saint—the prophet of Holy Scriptures, impelled by an infinite passion for moral perfection; the sage of the Talmudic period, translating ideals into laws; the philosopher-saint of the Middle Ages, seeking "perfection" in all the realms of spiritual life; the *Zaddik* of the Hasidic societies. In an ideal sense the superior person of the future is reflected in the image of the Messiah, who represents the fullness of ethical perfection. If Nietzsche called for a new outburst of Dionysian energy, A'had Ha'am appealed for a resurgence of prophetic ardor. The prophet struggles against the boundaries of human nature in an impassioned dialogue with God; then he comes down to uplift the people to his own high level. The superior person aims to create a "superior people" that will be dedicated to the moral uplift of humanity.

> If then we should agree that the goal of all our efforts is the Superior Person, we have to agree also that an integral part of this goal is the Superior People—that there should exist in the world a people that is more suited by character and training for ethical development, all of whose customs and practices will be governed by an ethical Torah, exalted far beyond ordinary standards. In this way, that people will provide "fertile soil" for the growth of such Superior Persons.[57]

A'had Ha'am did not universalize the ideal of the "chosen people," as he might well have done. Should not a contemporary idealist teach that every superior person ought to transform his own nation into a superior people? He still believed that only the Jews were endowed with a "moral genius" and that they alone constituted a superior people. In this respect he remained a child of the tradition. Did not the Jewish faith impose greater obligations on its own people than on others? We recall that Israelites were bidden to observe 613 *mizvot*, while Gentiles could acquire "a share in the World to Come" through the observance of the Noachian laws.

Thus, A'had Ha'am spurned the compromises of the westernized Jews who reinterpreted the doctrine of the chosen people in the sense of fulfilling a distinctive role by demonstrating to all men the implications of "ethical monotheism." He argued that so long as Jews lack a homeland of their own, they cannot attain their fullest development and cannot possibly convey any meaningful contributions to the non-Jewish world. If reborn in Zion, he asserted, Jews will regain their spiritual health and hopefully once again become a superior people. All mankind will be uplifted through their achievements.[58] "A living idea, a great national ideal, cannot be created in exile, when the forces of the nation, having been uprooted from their natural soil, lie dormant in the depths of consciousness, without any possibility of unfolding freely."[59]

The Nietzschean spirit is reflected in A'had Ha'am's search for a "new ideal," but, in his case, the ideal had to be peculiarly Jewish. Nietzschean also is his condemnation of western Jews as being "slaves" in a free society, since they refuse to acknowledge the national will to live, which throbs within their unconscious selves; they pretend to justify their communal existence by their adherence to religious truths, which are in fact shared by religious humanists generally. He also stigmatized the Orthodox in words made popular by Christian Bible critics.

> The national pride of the faithful Jew is the pride of a slave who is favored by his master for his loyalty and obedience to the master's whim. The pride of the free thinking nationalist is the pride of a free man, who recognizes his own inherent powers, contemplates with satisfaction the achievements of the National Ego in the past, and trusts it also for the future.[60]

All these references to "inner enslavement" were the shibboleths of an age that had discovered the reality of the "unconscious" and then identified it with the national will to live. Half a century later, in a totally different realm of discourse, C. G. Jung was to come close to embracing the mystique of racism with his theory of the "racial unconscious."

The concept of the national soul is central to the thought of A'had Ha'am. He stands, therefore, in the tradition of romantic nationalism as it was developed in the writings of Fichte and Lagarde, Danilevsky and Dostoevsky, and generally in the movements of Teutonism and pan-Slavism. At the same time, he was drawn to the English empirical philosophers, who disdained such mystical axioms. Nor was this dilemma peculiar to A'had Ha'am. His creative period coincided with the tremendous impact of the Darwinian discoveries and Spencer's application of the evolutionary philosophy to the development of society. The English and French sociologists elaborated the concept of a social organism, impelled by a quasi-soul of its own, which works in the secret depth of the unconscious. Yet Spencer, Tarde, and Durkheim claimed that the category of a biological organism was most closely suited to primitive societies and those that have become petrified, not to the civilized societies of the European world. Even in the case of primitive societies, the biological analogue applies not literally but only vestigially. Herbert Spencer, particularly, in keeping with the English tradition, insisted that individual freedom is the final flower of evolution.

A'had Ha'am was tugged in opposite directions by the liberal defenders of individual freedom and the Romantic conservative school of nationalism. He insisted, at least in the beginning of his career, on the freedom of the Jewish individual to arrive at his own convictions regarding any philosophical or religious issues. "I can pass any verdict I please over the beliefs and opinions which I inherited from my fathers, without any fear that I might break the bonds between myself and my people." At the same time, though, he maintained that an authentic Jew will be kept by his innate feelings from embracing any notions that are alien to the ethical core of Judaism. And this ethical core includes a reverent acceptance of "the God of Israel" as the vital force of history.

> He who does not really feel committed to the God of Israel, sensing in his inner soul no affinity with that "Superior World" in which our fathers

invested their hearts and minds and from which they in turn drew their moral power, may indeed be a fine person, but he cannot be a national Jew, not even "if he dwells in the Land of Israel and converses in the holy language."[61]

A'had Ha'am and his circle of intellectuals conversed in Russian and scorned the Yiddish vernacular as unworthy of the national spirit. In his judgment there was but one national language for Jews—Hebrew—and but one national impetus—the aspiration to settle in the land of Israel and to mold every aspect of life in that country in keeping with an "absolutist ethic."

One may ask, is not ethics by its very nature applicable everywhere and to all people? If so, is not the attempt of modern religious Jews to join with their Christian neighbors in the creation of a free and great society precisely the expression of the prophetic ethic of Judaism? Manifestly, A'had Ha'am's nationalistic vitalism triumphed over his presumably transcendent ethic. The life of the nation must be put ahead of its ideals. For the sake of its vitality, a revived Zion must become its living center. The national will, emerging out of a healthy, authentic body, will generate its secular ideal in the future, even as in the past it created the Jewish religion.

Conservative and Reform Jews today interpret their faith in a nondogmatic way, as an outreach to God, through all man's self-transcending faculties—through the quests of understanding, goodness, beauty, and holiness. Accordingly, the Jewish community includes agnostics, who treasure the ideals and the awesome impact of the historic tradition, within the bounds of the faith-community, without affirming any theistic beliefs. Furthermore, a reverent appreciation of the sacred tradition and the resolve to share in its vigorous continuity can be, in the non-Orthodox view, gradational, allowing for the vague affiliations of skeptics and secularists. The impetus of self-criticism is, in the view of liberal Jews, an inherent component of the living tradition itself. Because of its nondogmatic bias and its emphasis on "the things of God," rather than on the attributes of God's nature, modern Judaism is particularly hospitable to those secularists who share its institutional life and its destiny without accepting all its presuppositions.

As to A'had Ha'am's claim that the core of the sacred tradition is national-ethical, rather than religious, we have to recognize, as we noted earlier, the ambiguity of the tradition itself and the diversity of conditions between East and West. In the western world the Jews lived in relatively small numbers, and they progressively became part of the greater society, generation after generation, under the auspices of the liberal philosophy. In the "open societies" of western Europe and America, they were welcomed as individuals rather than as a closed ethnic corporation. The principles of liberalism, however, were opposed by the momentum of religious and political authoritarianism that was not completely overcome even in France, let alone in Imperial Germany. Accordingly, every romantic reaction in the lands of Europe served to put the status of Jewry under a question mark. In the normal course of history we may expect periodic reversions to ethnic romanticism and more rarely, perhaps, outbursts of racial mysticism. "But, the world does move," as Galileo put it. The Jewish hope is based on the progressive triumph of humanism.

The Russian Jews were molded in the nineteenth century by a totally different set of events. Living in massed enclaves of their own and using their own language, they were self-evidently a vigorous and self-assertive national entity. In addition, the liberal philosophy was represented in Russia by only a tiny segment of the population—the so-called "intelligentsia," which was itself divided between the westernizers and the Slavophils. Therefore, it was natural for Russian Jews to reinterpret the whole of Jewish history and tradition in terms of romantic nationalism. So ambivalent and many-sided is the Jewish tradition that some plausibility will attach to both the purely religious and the purely national explanations of Jewish identity and history, though both are partial and incomplete.

The concept of a national will to live, dwelling in the hidden recesses of the unconscious and projecting various ideas into public life, is certainly a myth. With equal certainty, however, we can affirm that people will battle more zealously for the myths that minister to their pride than for the beliefs that appeal to their intelligence. In an age of nationalistic rivalries it is difficult to resist the pressure to clothe one's true being in the panoply of pleasing myths and radiant fantasies.

Traditional ideas and sentiments possess a massive and enduring momentum, but the productions of recent generations can well alter the character of a tradition forged by millennia of devotion, providing the new experiences mesh with the web of ancient myths. Traditionally, the "root" of Judaism is faith in the One God, whose will is revealed in the Bible and the Talmud. However, two generations of unceasing struggle, centering around the building of Israel, might well shift the popular focus of Jewish consciousness from the God of Israel to the "Land of Israel," especially since the myth of being set apart from the nations of the world can easily be transferred from the religious to the ethnic-political domain. The majestic course of Jewish history, which consisted in overcoming the "natural" idols of "blood and soil" by ethical and religious values, would then end in a tragic reversion to the primitive pagan ethos of the prebiblical world. Indeed, a group of Israeli writers, admittedly small but significant, called themselves "Canaanites" to demonstrate their rejection of the prophetic heritage and their eagerness to revert to the natural values of the prebiblical world.

The synthesis of Jewish nationalism and religion is the living tradition of the Jewish people as it is constantly continued and renewed by reflection and criticism. The tradition is, of course, protean, assuming new and widely differing shapes in diverse times and places. Yet the momentum of the living tradition is everywhere immense, and the varied experiences of Jewish people in all parts of the world have many elements in common. Except for a few marginal enclaves, Jews were always in communication with one another. In the last two thousand years, Diaspora Jewry suffered some defections and enjoyed some accretions, but it remained a recognizable, worldwide association of communities. In the seventeenth century, long before the emergence of modern means of communications, the entire Diaspora was stirred by the pseudo-messianic movement of Sabbatai Zevi, which revived the powerful mythology embedded in Jewish consciousness.

The living tradition consists of both body and soul—the actual, organized communities and their ideals, sentiments, and aspirations. We may not agree with the vitalistic myth of A'had Ha'am, but we need to recognize the intimate relationship among all the components of Jewish faith and experience. By reaffirming the spiritual-ethical character of the Jewish tradition, A'had Ha'am helped prevent the disintegration and polarization of modern Jewry between nonspiritual nationalists and nonhistorical religionists.

His definition of a national ethic was, perhaps, too narrowly conceived and far too dogmatic. Jewish ethics comprises a spectrum between the "vision" of a transworldly perfection and the concept of a way of living, described in a code of laws.[62] If we define the ethical dimension both as a body of good maxims and as a quest for the good life, then its openness is manifested. It includes the imaginative and esthetic faculties, the poetry of faith, and the collective effort for self-evaluation and self-understanding. The tradition includes strong tensions between opposite ideals, and it contains also the prophet's pathos of self-questioning and the saint's quest of self-overcoming. The special distinction of the biblical religion was in no small part brought about by its many-sidedness. It included the components of wisdom as well as those of prophecy and priesthood. Wisdom is inescapably international and humanistic.

A'had Ha'am remained a humanist in spite of his vitalism and his ethnic romanticism. He recognized the immensity of the Palestinian Arab problem long before his contemporaries began to concern themselves with its challenge. He dared to affirm that he would reject the Zionist program if it could be achieved only by inflicting the agonies of exile and humiliation on another people.

At the same time he maintained that Jewish people are endowed with a special instinct, or historic intuition, whereby they feel the uniqueness of their own moral heritage. He championed the basic premise of modern romantic nationalism—namely, the contention that the authentic sons of every nation sense an instinctive repugnance to all that is "alien" to the national soul. He viewed the realm of ideas and values not as the self-determining domain of man's quest for perfection and truth, but as the fruits and products of an organic body.

It seemed natural for him to assert that a whole people can be "allergic" to the arts and values of a strange culture. This "folkist" notion, deriving from German romanticism, was combined in A'had Ha'am's mind with the traditional belief in the uniqueness of the chosen people. In his version, the Jewish people were chosen not in a theological but in a biological way. It was not the religious doctrines of Jewry that counted, but its inherent ethical intuition. Yet he regarded the sympathetic understanding of Christianity manifested by western Jewish scholars as the symptom of the diseased moral fiber of denationalized Jews. The dragon's teeth of nationalistic self-worship are strangely mixed in his thought with the prophetic passion for social justice and the pietistic quest of moral perfection.

On the whole, A'had Ha'am's lasting influence was in the direction of prophetic humanism. While he did not outgrow the sad limitations of the nationalistic ideology with its naive, narcissistic myths, he helped direct the Jewish renaissance into the ethical-rational bedrock of the Bible, the Talmud and the grand course of the Maimonidean philosophy.

VIII. *If God Be the* Élan Vital

At the turn of the century, the trend of biological nationalism in Europe was definitely in the direction of Fascism. The nation should be organized into a self-enclosed, tight, and disciplined body, like an army, and in its relations with other nations it should not acknowledge any ethical obligations or scruples. The Italian philosopher Pareto had formulated the essential principles of such a state. Generally, Jewish thinkers shunned the romantic version of nationalism, sensing the likelihood of its ultimate degeneration into a nihilistic, xenophobic mentality.

Yet, the most famous biology-minded thinker at the turn of the century was the French Jew, Henri Bergson (1859–1941). His best-known work, *Creative Evolution*, projected the concept of the *élan vital*. "Life-energy" is the dynamic substance of things, and it articulates itself in the creation of ever more complex forms. In the course of millions of years its pulsations had resulted in the emergence of new forms of life, each new form being the result of a new thrust of this "life-force," which, though simple in itself, was spatially structured into an infinity of parts. With painstaking logic, Bergson demonstrated that the appearance of so complex an organ as the eye, depending for its efficiency on the interaction of numerous inner and outer factors, could not possibly have arisen through the chance variations postulated by Darwin. The *élan vital* is manifestly a nonmechanistic intelligence that is ceaselessly at work, impelling the great chain of living beings toward ever more perfect forms. In this way the data of evolution may be read, not as so many arguments against religion, but, on the contrary, as proofs of the continuing creativity of the Supreme Being. All this Bergson demonstrated through an analysis of the data of the biologists.

Nor is the role of man, in his view, reduced to that of the animal, for in man the inner creative force reveals itself in a novel way. While instincts guide the lives of animals, man has been endowed with an intellect, which enables him to overcome all obstacles. And it is possible for the intellect itself to recognize that it had been designed for practical purposes only. However, we can develop an intuition, whereby the ongoing rush of "pure duration" may actually be sensed. In a roundabout way Bergson brought back the doctrine of man's distinction from all other creatures, by virtue of his capacity to reflect "the image of God."

> Life appears in its entirety as an immense wave, which starting from a center, spreads outward, and which on almost the whole of its circumference is stopped; at one single point, the impulsion has passed freely. . . . Everywhere but in man, consciousness has had to come to a stand; in man alone it has kept on its way. . . ."[1]

Yet it is man's intuition that captures the reality of the creative force, not man's intellect, which is merely instrumental. The intellect was designed to serve the same purpose as instinct does in the case of animals; namely, to help man overcome the obstacles to his survival. We distort the role of the intellect when we focus its glare on the inner substance of reality. The intellect was not designed to comprehend the power that generated it, the life-force, which subsists, not in the space-time of phenomena, but in pure duration. Only in the intuition of unspatialized time, in all its abundant richness, do we glimpse the *élan vital*, the vibrant life of the universe.

Bergson's philosophy is both vitalistic and spiritualistic. The life-force, which strains to transcend the existing forms of life aims to attain the realm of spirit. Its upward thrust of creative energy is directed toward ever higher levels of freedom. If matter and mechanism are at one end of the pole of existence, spirit and freedom are at the other pole. Within the heart of man, this polar tension may be sensed, as the philosopher in his quest for reality alternates between the ecstasy of intuitive insight and the soberness of mechanical analysis, when consciousness cools into quantitative and utilitarian calculations.

Bergson himself described his philosophy as a resurgence of dualism. Spirit, mind, and life, he insisted, cannot be reduced to a materialistic mechanism. However, the world revealed to our senses is not mere appearance or illusion. Bergson followed Kant in the axiom that the "categories of space" and spatialized time structure all our experience, but to Bergson, real time is not an arithmetical series of discrete, measureable moments. Rather, it is more like the organic process of growth. Real time is the upward thrust of life. The fundamental polarity in our existence is that between pure, dead space and living time, or "real duration"; the surge of life is directed toward the overcoming of death through the creation of more perfect beings, endowed with greater ranges of freedom.

As Bergson's thought developed, it became more monistic. How can the *élan vital* thrust more and more of life into the stillness of space without sharing in the same dimension of existence as matter? Thus, he moved toward an idealistic conception of the genesis of matter. The flux of existence is comprehensible in terms of the polarity between life and spirit on the one hand, and death and matter, on the other hand. The wave of life rises again and again out of the depths; new forms of life may result from this succession of efforts, and every living creature is a compromise between the pull of freedom and the dead weight of intractable matter. In a sense all the species of the plant and animal kingdoms are proof of the limited success of the *élan vital*. Like Sisyphus, it does not ever succeed in overcoming completely the dead weight of matter, but unlike Sisyphus, it does not fail altogether. We are reminded of the Kabbalistic notion that the Lord had created many worlds, which He discovered to be unworthy, prior to His creation of mankind. The pulsation of effort is at the heart of the universe. As the Jewish Prayerbook puts it, "the Lord in His goodness renews the works of creation every day."

> Life is a movement, materiality is the inverse movement, and each of these two movements is simple, the matter which forms a world being an undivided flux, and undivided also the life which runs through it, cutting out in it living beings all along its track.[2]

In the two poles of the flux of being, life is the active dynamic factor. Even if we cannot forecast the future course of creation, we can sense its direction and congruity with man's spirit. In man the genesis of the power of memory is an intimation of immortality, since the past is preserved within a living, growing perspective.

> Between brute matter and the mind most capable of reflection there are all possible intensities of memory, or what comes to the same thing, all the degrees of freedom.[3]

The world view of Bergson throbs with the assurance that man, qua spiritual being, is sustained by the forward thrusts of the life-force, "Underneath are the everlasting arms." (Deuteronomy 33, 27) Consequently, man's hope is sustained by a cosmic purpose. We can feel this assurance, hope, and promise in this eloquent passage:

> The animal takes its stand on the plant, man bestrides animality, and the whole of humanity, in space and in time, is one immense army galloping beside and before and behind each of us in an overwhelming charge, able to beat down every resistance and clear the most formidable obstacles, perhaps even death.[4]

Bergson did not set out to interpret the meaning of religion until the last decade of his life. In his first books he provided the building blocks of a spiritual philosophy. As he put it in 1912:

> The considerations explained in my *Time and Free Will* tend to illuminate the fact of liberty; those of *Matter and Memory* point clearly, I hope, to the reality of spirit; those of *Creative Evolution* present creation as a fact; from all this there clearly emerges the idea of a free and creative God, at once generator of life and of matter, and whose effort at creation is continued side by side with life, by the evolution of species and by the constitution of human personalities. From all this, there emerges in consequence the refutation of monism and of pantheism.... For the investigation of religion, it is necessary to touch on problems of an entirely different kind, moral problems.[5]

Indeed, it was as a philosopher of religion that Bergson was both condemned and hailed. "I shall never forget the emotion with which *Creative Evolution* transported me. I felt God on every page," wrote Joseph Lotte. The French Catholics in particular thought they had found a secure anchorage in his thought. "Bergson's book *Matter and Memory*, using the results of science to affirm liberty, was a direct factor in the conversion of Jacques Maritain, as it was also of Joseph Lotte."[6] In his autobiography, Etienne Gilson described the impact of "Bergsonism" on Catholic intellectuals. They found in his works a reinterpretation of the meaning of faith as an intuition of reality and a conception of freedom as the action of undivided, inwardly unified personality. "Although we are free whenever we are willing to get back into ourselves, it seldom happens that we are willing."[7] In Bergson's world view, "spirit," or the special domain that man shares with the Creator, is a supreme reality. Even the belief in immortality is reinstated as a distinct possibility:

> If we admit that with man consciousness has finally left the tunnel; that everywhere else consciousness has remained imprisoned; that every other species corresponds to the arrest of something which in man succeeded in overcoming resistance and in expanding almost freely, thus displaying itself in true personalities capable of remembering all and willing all and controlling their past and their future, we shall have no repugnance in admitting that in man, though perhaps in man alone, consciousness pursues its path beyond this earthly life.[8]

Yet Bergson's books were invariably placed on the Papal Index. He seemed to be a valiant champion of religion as long as he was engaged in the demolition of materialism, but his conception of a restless, creative, cosmic energy was anathema to traditionalists and to believers in a personal god. Like Nietzsche, he was oriented toward revelations yet to come, not toward the treasuring of the dogmas of the past. Like John Stuart Mill, he projected the concept of a God Who is essentially movement, rich in numberless potentialities, but unpredictable, limited in power but progressive. God Himself is not static perfection but a flux and a becoming. Bergson's expressed attitudes toward Judaism were totally negative. He reacted to the attacks of the Anti-Dreyfusards in the 1890s with the firm determination to be totally French. Though he was descended from a distinguished family of Hasidic Jews in Poland, he acknowledged hardly any Jewish influence or even concern. As philosophic mentors he claimed Plotinus, Maine de Biran, and Ravaisson, none of whom was Jewish.[9] In an interview with the journalist Herman Bernstein in 1912, regarding the Zionist program, he stated:

> To us, French people, this question seems paradoxical. We are so completely assimilated. If there were a new Zion, I do not think many Jews would go there.... I believe the Jewish question will be solved when the Jewish people will have attained equal rights in the countries where they have been persecuted. And the sooner that is attained the better for the Jews of course, and also for the countries in which they live.[10]

Bergson's negation of Zionism went hand in hand with his derogation of the Jewish religion as being merely a stage in the evolution of man's spirit, a stage that has long since been superseded. The Jewish faith was circumscribed by the narrow barriers of tribalism, which were made high and forbidding by a long history of persecution. Like Kant, he stigmatized Judaism as an ethnic faith, devoid of any pretensions to universality and humanism. Like Hegel, he read the unfolding history of European culture as the evolution of the spirit of mankind; accordingly, he focused attention on massive "world-historical" movements, assigning to Judaism the significance of only a transitory stage. As his thought inclined more and more to mysticism, he came to see the Christian mystics as the legitimate successors of the Hebrew prophets. Thus, in 1937 he wrote:

> My reflections have led me closer and closer to Catholicism, in which I see the complete fulfillment of Judaism. I would have become a convert, had I not seen in preparation for years a formidable wave of Antisemitism, which is to break upon the world. I wanted to remain among those who tomorrow will be persecuted. But I hope that a Catholic priest will consent, if the Cardinal Archbishop of Paris authorizes it, to come to say prayers at my funeral.[11]

As it happened, Bergson reaffirmed his Jewishness when the Nazi tide engulfed his native land. He returned all his awards and medals to the French government, when, under Marshal Pétain, it accepted a collaborationist role with Hitler. He stood in line to register as a Jew and wore the six-pointed star with pride until the day of his death.

Actually, his Jewish consciousness had not deserted him even when he flirted with Catholicism "as a complete fulfillment of Judaism." As an evolutionist, he could well esteem any branch of the Christian faith, even the whole of Christianity, as a "fulfillment" of Judaism, without concluding that it is the only or the exclusive fulfillment. Certainly, the world-historical importance of biblical Judaism is best reflected in its generation of two global daughter-faiths, Christianity and Islam. It does not follow, however, that the mother-faith must perish in order for the daughters to flourish. Franz Rosenzweig, following an honored tradition, could acknowledge the divine character of the Christian and Moslem faiths and at the same time devote himself with even greater zeal to the ancient faith, precisely because it is so deeply rooted in its own memories, so self-sufficient and self-assured, yet also challenging, creative, and fertile.

The "hope of Israel," as envisioned by Maimonides, encompassed the vision of the ultimate triumph of "the Torah of truth," which might, however, take different forms among diverse historic groups. The inner core of faith, the "Seven Principles of Noah" and the biblical ethic, would be incorporated within the various cultures of mankind. In this way each monotheistic faith is even now a fulfillment of the prophetic hope, provided it remains open to the dynamics of growth, the illumination of new ideas, and the purgation of criticism in the light of the living word of God. Above all, an authentic version of Hebraic monotheism must not tolerate the illusion among its followers that it alone is the repository of truth or that it possesses the whole truth in its fullness.

If Catholicism did appear to Bergson at times to be "the complete fulfillment of Judaism," in the sense of being an exclusive and final faith, it is because of a double error—he did not recognize the continuity of the prophetic genius within Judaism and he envisioned an ideal Catholicism, liberated from all dogmas and open to the seeds of truth wherever they are found. In such a transformed Catholicism all dogmas would be metaphors; humanism would become the substance of faith; and all intellectuals and artists would constitute the priesthood. If this was Bergson's hope, he had the support of a long line of French thinkers, from St. Simon to Joseph de Maistre, to Lamennais, to Auguste Comte. But, we must remember that the "modernists" in Catholicism were rebuked and expelled.

Among French Jews Bergson's attitude was possibly anticipated by Joseph Salvador (1796–1873), who was widely regarded as a philosophical interpreter of Judaism. Salvador considered the Mosaic legislation of social justice to be the essence of Judaism and he forecast the eventual emergence of a common Judeo-Christian faith as the fulfillment of the messianic ideal. Both Jews and Christians would attain the new "ecumenical" faith, not through conversion, but through convergence, with the impetus of the French Revolution impelling both ancient traditions in the direction of building God's Kingdom on earth, here and now. Judaism would incorporate the Christian impulse toward fraternity, and Christianity would embrace the Judaic ardor for social progress and the open horizons of man's quest of truth. The modern ideals of nationalism and socialism would be redeemed from their pagan and materialist encrustations, making possible the triumph of messianism. In Salvadore's symbolism, Paris represented this ideal future, synthesizing the contributions of Rome, ancient paganism and the Catholic hierarchy, and Jerusalem, the ethical content of Judaism.

Salvadore asked to be buried in a Protestant ceremony in order possibly to symbolize his ecumenical vision.[12]

Before turning to Bergson's analysis of mysticism and Hebrew prophecy, it is interesting to note that while Bergson himself was consistently internationalistic and liberal, the complex of Bergsonian ideas was generally favored by the antiliberals, the defenders of violent radicalism, the champions of an "organic" state, and the precursors of Fascism. In France philosophy and religion were dominated by the social issues that were raised by the convulsions of the French Revolution. Liberals and radicals were drawn to philosophies of rationalism and materialism, while nationalists, religionists, and conservatives sought refuge in a romantic and mystical world view which urged the individual to see the meaning of life either in the regimen of the Church or in the mystical unity and destiny of the nation.

The two aspects of Bergson's thought, his "spiritualism" and his "vitalism," appeared to provide justification for both the religionists and the nationalists. Leading the reaction against the materialists and the positivists, Bergson reinstated in philosophy the reality of Spirit, as being more than a product of material forces. Spirit is an independent domain, related to matter indirectly and contingently, as is a coat hanging on a nail—the character of the coat cannot be inferred from the shape of the nail. So the character of Spirit is related to but not deducible from the forces of matter. Ethical and esthetic values belong to an independent realm of spiritual life; thus, they provide a powerful boost for the individual's quest of meaning and value. Indeed, man's inner life takes place in real duration, not in mathematical time. The domain of quality in all its variations is only flattened and debased when it is quantified and spatialized. Man must look inward for freedom and meaning: "Outside us, mutual externality without succession; within us, succession without mutual externality."[13]

In the final analysis we recognize within us two different selves, one of which is, as it were, the external projection or the material representation of the other. We reach our inner soul by means of deep introspection, by an inner journey of the spirit, whereby the concrete events of external experience are viewed as fluid aspects of the stream of life, constantly *becoming*: states not amenable to weight and measure, flowing into and permeating one another. In our subjective meditation there is still a dynamic restless flux, a flow of diverse qualities and intensities, but this experience of ceaseless change in real duration is quite different from the succession and juxtaposition of separate states in a static, homogeneous space. Usually, our self simply mirrors the outer world. The moments in which we enter fully into our inner life are exceedingly rare, and that is why we are rarely free. Most of the time we live outside ourselves, hardly perceiving our own true nature, but only our ghost—a colorless shadow that pure duration projects into homogeneous space. Thus, our life unfolds in space rather than in time; we live for the external world rather than for ourselves; we speak rather than think; we "are acted upon rather than act ourselves."[14]

This world-view is sympathetic to religion, but it is also compatible with an atheistic romanticism that exalts art as the supreme gateway to reality. It is in his own deepest self that man can find the vibrant stream of life, which is perpetually straining against the rigid barriers of the material universe. Poetry, music, and visual symbols penetrate the veil of illusion that is woven by the intellect, which was designed by nature for strictly utilitarian ends.

Bergson's vitalism seemed to reinforce the anti-intellectualism of the champions of national power and grandeur, who appealed either to national instincts or to a racial "soul." For them man's intellect is only a limited, one-dimensional instrument that is incapable of comprehending the meaning of life itself. The rationalists and the cosmopolitans are, as they see it, condemned to skate endlessly on the frozen surface of reality. It is only in folk-intuition that the authentic values of life can be apprehended. So the proponents of the glory of "direct action," or of national power, or of racial pride, could seek some support in the Bergsonian philosophy.

An instructive example of this aspect of vitalism is provided by Georges Sorel, the prophet of "revolutionary socialism," who considered himself a disciple of Bergson's. Sorel saw the essence of life in the struggle for existence of historic groups. Nations are formed by "myths," which draw their strength from the inner depths of a people's life. The logical absurdity of a myth is of no account. What matters is the power of the myth to mold a group into an effective fighting unit. When this view is superimposed on the Marxist philosophy of the class-struggle and of the eventual dominance of the proletariat, the result is a determination to inject the myths of war into the life of the state, permitting no mutual accommodation and no social peace of any kind until the final ruin of bourgeois society is achieved.

> . . . But I believe it would be possible to develop still further the application of Bergson's ideas to the general strike. Movement, in Bergson's philosophy, is looked upon as an undivided whole; which leads us precisely to the catastrophic conception of Socialism.[15]

In other words, the final battle between the proletariat and its enemies should be anticipated in the preparatory period—that is at every stage of the struggle.

Sorel was contemptuous of the role of intelligence in the structuring of society and in the solution of social problems. Reason is incapable of grasping the vital forces that impel the masses of mankind. People are moved to action by myths, not by truths— myths that reflect their collective needs and desires. Genuine leaders are those whose intuition generates the myths that appeal to the people.

> The myth must be judged as a means of acting on the present; any attempt to discuss how far it can be taken literally as future history is devoid of sense. *It is the myth in its entirety, which is alone important.*[16] . . . Use must be made of a body of images which *by intuition* alone . . . is capable of evoking . . . the war undertaken by socialism.[17]

Acts of violence correspond in social life to the pulsations of the *élan vital* in nature. Their initial destructiveness is more than made up for by the surge of creative energy they infuse into human affairs.

> In the total ruin of institutions and of morals there remains something which is powerful, new and intact, and it is that which constitutes, properly speaking, the soul of the revolutionary proletariat. Nor will this be swept away in the general decadence of moral values, if the workers have enough energy to bar the road to middle-class corrupters, answering their advances with the plainest brutality.[18]

Sorel's infatuation with the creative potential of violence inspired the thinking of Mussolini, who substituted the myths of nationalism for those of the class-struggle. The Fascists, like the revolutionary socialists, were contemptuous of the liberals for their concern with the rights of the individual, their high regard for the values of freedom, their appeal to reason, and their respect for the democratic process. The parties at both extremes of the political spectrum scorned objectivity and truth, substituting their collective myths for the social reality and demonstrating the "truth" of their myths by brutish force. Bergsonism seemed to offer them philosophical support. Does it not exalt intuition and instinct over intellect and morality? Does it not extol the creative energy of nature over the reasoned abstractions of philosophers? Is not ruthless violence nature's own way of clearing the stage for the appearance of new creations?

The publication of *Two Sources of Morality and Religion* confounded Bergson's erstwhile "disciples." Condemning the totalitarians of the "right" and the "left," Bergson represented democracy as the highest achievement of mankind. In primitive society group-consciousness is sovereign and the individual is of worth only insofar as he serves the well-being of the tribe. In democracy the individual emerges as an end in himself. The democratic order is "furthest removed from nature, from the condition of a 'closed society.'" In it man is his own "lawmaker"; furthermore, the essence of democracy is more than individual freedom, even more than respect for the freedom of others—it is an outreach in love; therefore, a creative upsurge of the *élan vital*.

> . . . The third term (fraternity) dispels the oft-noted contradiction between the two others (liberty and equality), and the essential thing is fraternity; a fact which would make it possible to say that democracy is evangelical in essence and that its motive power is love.[19]

To Bergson, "the closed society" of Fascism or Communism was a regression to primitivism. He accepted Émile Durkheim's (1858–1917) description of religion as the expression of the tribe's collective consciousness, but he argued in behalf of the higher religion that now and then shatters the barriers of primitivism. We recall that Durkheim interpreted religion as being an intuitive awareness of the supreme reality of the group—its past, its sancta, and its will to live. God is the symbol of tribal unity; to commune with Him, is to rise above oneself and feel the indomitable strength of the tribe reinforcing one's own powers.[20]

"If religion has given birth to all that is essential in society, it is because the idea of society is the soul of religion."[21] Individualistic religion is, to Durkheim, an epiphenomenon, a conscious creation lacking in mythical potency. To be effective, religion need not commend itself to man's understanding. Its domain is the realm of "collective consciousness," which is deeper and more potent by far than the rationalistic cogitations of the individual.

> The cult is not simply a system of signs by which the faith is outwardly translated; it is a collection of the means by which it is created and recreated periodically.[22] . . . We are not able to appreciate the value of the radical individualism which would make religion something purely individual; it misunderstands the fundamental condition of the religious life. . . . A philosophy may well be elaborated in the silence of the interior imagination, but not so a faith. For before all else, a faith is warmth, life, enthusiasm, the exaltation of the whole mental life, the raising of the individual above himself.[23]

In the modern era of fevered nationalism, Durkheim's theory of religion as intuitive group-awareness could be used to justify the transfer of whole-hearted faith and blind devotion from the universal religions of the past to one's "folk," or nation, or race. While many versions of modern nationalism were allied with one or another religion, Durkheim suggested in effect that instinctive tribalism was really the living core of religion, stripped of its obsolete vestments. Durkheim did not rule out an eventual union of nations and the consequent emergence of an international faith: ". . . There is no national life, which is not dominated by a collective life of an international nature."[24] The heart of religion is, however, the collective consciousness of the existing society.

Bergson embraced Durkheim's theory, but he limited its application to one phase of religion, that of a closed society. He explained the origin of this type of religion in terms of "creative evolution." Since man was endowed by nature with a roving intellect, instead of invariant instincts, he needed to be protected from the solvent effects of his all-questioning mind. An ant or a termite obeys the will of its collectivity, without ever rebelling. Man, too, is a social being, but his mind encompasses numerous possibilities and open horizons. What is to keep him in line with the tribe in which he is born? As a child of nature, man alone can contemplate the certainty of his own death. What is to keep him from yielding to despair? Thus, in Bergson's view, religion is founded on a natural endowment, which is designed to counter freedom and despair. This endowment inclines man to regard the will of the group as sacred and to feel the comforting presence of a beneficent deity sustaining him in his struggle for existence. To this extent, religion is eminently functional, even if it is not true, in a logical or in an ontological sense.

However, this type of piety is only the lower phase of religion, an estimate in which Durkheim concurred, especially in his criticism of St. Simon's "new Christianity." Against the ethic and faith of a closed society, there is the living faith of great men and women, in whom the *élan vital* reaches a new level of creativity. Such individuals become channels of the divine flow of creative love. They reach out to *all* men, transcending the boundaries of the tribe or the nation; they represent a dimension of spirituality that is unconfined by customs, rites, and dogmas that divide mankind, and they impel their contemporaries to advance toward the vision of the perfect, the all-embracing society. However, the creative love that is the source of their strength is not totally successful; like the *élan vital* in nature, it is ultimately structured into laws, which govern the static society, until such time as there occurs a fresh outburst of prophetic power.

Static religion, operating with myths and symbols that counterbalance the solvent effects of the intellect, remains a social necessity, just as a self-enclosed society, geared for the exigencies of war, is inevitable as long as universal peace has not been attained. Even in the modern world, regressions to primitivism are possible. The "leader" principle appears in revolutionary times as a symbol of natural or static religion:

> Within honest and gentle men there rushes up from the depths a ferocious personality, that of the leader, who is a failure. . . . And here we have a characteristic trait of that "political animal," . . . ferocity is one of the dominant traits." . . . Such a *Führer* is bound to bring about incredible wholesale slaughter, preceded by ghastly tortures.[25]

Conversely, social progress is made possible by the incursion of the creative energy of love, which is the manifestation of the *élan vital* in the human consciousness.

> The mystic love of humanity is a very different thing. It is not the extension of an instinct, it does not originate in an idea. It is neither of the senses nor

of the mind. It is of both implicitly, and is effectively much more. For such a love lies at the very root of feeling and reason, as of all other things. Coinciding with God's love for His handiwork, a love which has been the source of everything, it would yield up to anyone, who knew how to question it, the secret of creation.[26]

This upwelling of fresh creative energy was manifested historically in the long line of biblical prophets, who burst asunder the bonds of dogma, of social custom, and the ethic of the closed society and revealed the infinite horizons of the love of God and the love of man.

We find this impetus in the prophets; they longed passionately for justice, demanded it in the name of the God of Israel; and Christianity, which succeeded Judaism, owed largely to the Jewish prophets its active mysticism, capable of marching on to the conquest of the world.[27]

Bergson extolled mysticism as the means of attaining unity with the *élan vital*. In keeping with the tradition of Hebraic prophecy, however, he considered the mystical experience to be not an end in itself, but a means of infusing fresh ardor and idealistic energy into the structure of society. The *élan vital* is not to be conceived after the analogy of a boundless sea of being, into which man sinks, yielding his personality and uniqueness. Being the flow of creative energy, the *élan vital* is manifested in the deposit of creative love, directed toward the creation of the perfect society of the future.

Mystics bear witness "that God needs us, just as we need God. Why should He need us unless it be to love us? . . . Creation will appear to him [the philosopher] as God undertaking to create creators, that He may have, beside Himself, beings worthy of His love."[28]

The prophetic experience, Bergson maintains, was carried on in Christianity, by the "active mystics," those who derived their inspiration from the Hebraic passion for the building of a holy community, not those who aimed to attain personal salvation or to sink into Nirvana. While mysticism itself is very rare, there is "in the innermost being of most men, the whisper of an echo" of the mystic's experience. Perhaps in time, through the progress of science itself, the joy of the mystic's vision will become the common heritage of all men.

Joy indeed would be that simplicity of life diffused throughout the world by an ever-spreading mystic intuition. . . . Theirs [mankind's] the responsibility, then, for deciding if they want merely to live, or intend to make just that extra effort required for fulfilling even on their refractory planet, the essential function of the universe, which is a machine for the making of gods.[29]

Is Bergsonism compatible with a dogmatic religion? If we consider *Two Sources* as Bergson's final word on the subject, we must arrive at a negative conclusion. The essence of his philosophy, more particularly his empirical method, compels a tentative, open outlook, ever ready for the emergence of the novel and the unpredictable. The *élan vital* is spontaneous, creative—bursting with new possibilities. It issues in the hot lava of religious energy, shattering all the molds of the intellect, of static religion, and of history. The Hebrew prophets best represent it, because of what they repudiated as well as what they affirmed, for they rebuked the ritualistic piety of the people along with their sins. The prophets represented "the protestant principle," as Tillich put it, the forward thrust of creative piety that liquefies the traditional "deposit of faith," even as it becomes in the course of time an integral part of the religious heritage of the people.

It is certain that any religion that considers itself complete, in possession of final truth, and which interprets mystical piety in ethically neutral terms, is totally incompatible with the Bergsonian philosophy.

Jacques Maritain (1882–1973) was perhaps the foremost Catholic theologian who sought to fit a modified Bergsonism within a modified Thomism.[30] He distinguished between "Bergsonism of fact" and "Bergsonism of intention." The latter, he affirmed, would have led the philosopher straight into the arms of "the angelic doctor." Maritain deplored Bergson's dethronement of the majesty of "metaphysical reason" and his reliance on the uncertain guidance of intuition. "To what cause," he asked, "are we to ascribe this nihilism which most certainly runs against the intentions of the philosopher himself?"[31] Maritain's critique is really directed at the entire sweep of modern philosophy from Descartes to Kant to Bergson. In his first major work he pleaded with Bergson to recognize that man needs "salvation," rather than "instruction."

> There are secrets which He alone can reveal. You yourself are one of these secrets. You would know your end and the means to attain it, if you knew these secrets. But you will only know them if it pleases God to reveal them Himself. . . . Or are you indeed masters in Israel only to be ignorant of these things?[32]

Bergson presented a fresh appreciation of the long line of Hebrew prophets and of the masters of "active mysticism," insofar as these saintly heroes expanded man's ethical and spiritual horizons. Revelation in his view does not consist of a body of facts, beliefs, or answers to metaphysical questions. For him, revelation is an accession of new, uplifting social energy, so that Maritain's appeal is totally beside the point. From Bergson's standpoint it matters little whether the hot lava of religious feeling is crystallized in one or another dogma or ritual, provided the dynamic fire is kept alive and allowed to burst into flame again and again.

"From our standpoint, which shows us the divinity of all men, it matters little whether or no Christ be called a man. It does not even matter that He be called Christ."[33] We recall a similar effort by David Friedländer to bring about a convergence of modern Judaism with an undogmatic Christianity, a "Christianity without Christ."

The basic issue is whether or not the "holy fire" of mystical inspiration is directed in love toward the building of the messianic era, or whether it is confined within walls—either the barriers of ethnicism or of dogmatism. A faith that is open and humanist is to that degree "true" and charged with divine, transcendent power.

Is the Bergsonian philosophy compatible with Judaism?

As to the repudiation of mechanism or materialism, Bergson demonstated by careful analysis and empirical observation the insufficiency of materialism for the understanding of the phenomena of life, especially of the human spirit. He has therefore repeated the titanic feat of Kant in calling attention to the spiritual dimension of existence. Theists may think they need to go beyond him in establishing the foundations of their faith, but they cannot but find him a most helpful companion, at least for part of the way.

However, in projecting the nonmechanistic cosmic force, Bergson wavers between the concepts of life and spirit. In tracing the course of creative evolution, Bergson arrives at the notion of a blind, cosmic life-force, which is unconcerned with individuals, purposeless and ruthless, trying, like Sisyphus, to overcome the dead inertia of matter, failing and trying once more. However, in some of his writings—in *Time and Free Will, Matter and Memory*, and most particularly in *Two Sources*,—the *élan vital* is conceived after the analogy of the human spirit. The cosmos is then represented as the necessary background and preparation for the emergence of heroic saints, "a machine for the making of gods."

God is, in that view, seen as the Ultimate Spirit, being at the opposite pole of matter and mechanism. In the words of Kant, "We can, however, think an Understanding, which being not like ours discursive, proceeds from the synthetic-universal (the intuition of the whole as such) to the particular—i.e. from the whole to the parts."[34]

Such an intelligence is, of course, also a power; in nature it is manifested in the evolution of living forms, and in human life it is revealed in the progressive refinement of man's ethical conscience and in the esthetic organon. The two Wholes of Life and Spirit constitute two infinite chains of being, ranging in nature from the amoeba to mankind, and in human history from primitive tribalism to prophetic humanism. Two different world views are possible, depending on our decision as to which is the more fundamental theophany—that of Divine Power in nature, or that of His Word in the human spirit.

The tension between the representation of God as Life or as Spirit reflects the dichotomy between Judaism and ancient paganism. The premonotheistic pagans celebrated the rhythms of life in their cults. There were the vegetation gods, dying and coming back to life; the rain gods; fertility rites; initiatory rites; the myths of creation and of the kings as incarnations of deities. The gods that were worshiped were not the primeval deities, symbolizing heaven and earth, chaos and time, but the second and third generation gods, with whom men and women could easily identify; thus, anthropomorphism, crude or artistic, the worship of idols, and the notion that gods appear on earth in the shape of human beings. None of the gods represented an ethical absolute, though some were generally disposed to favor one or another ethical ideal.

In Judaism, God was conceived after the analogy of the human spirit, as the Absolute Spirit. He is Thought and Justice and Love and Sublimity, in their pure and absolute states, as well as the "living God," the source of all reality and power. Therefore, idolatry is the archetypal sin, since it reduces Him to the level of "the work of His hands." While all creation attests to His power, some events are particularly hierophanous, since they reveal strikingly either His power or His majesty. It is in the hearts and minds of human beings, however, that He is best revealed. God is not subject to the rhythms of life. The ancient agricultural festivals were given fresh meaning in the Torah, in order to demonstrate God's concern for mankind. The spring festival was interpreted as the celebration of the Exodus, the fruit harvest as the remembrance of the revelation at Sinai, the harvest festival in the fall as the celebration of Providence in providing for the children of Israel in the wilderness. The rhythms of sacred history were substituted for those of nature.

Most interesting is the reinterpretation of the New Year. In Babylonia it was dedicated to the commemoration of the creation of the physical universe. In the rabbinic tradition it marked the creation of Adam and Eve, the "enthronement" of God by the Hebrew people and reconsecration of the noblest goal of history, the unification of all mankind through the bonds of mutual love and of the love of God. In the Ten Commandments, God is presented not as the Creator of heaven and earth, but as the source of freedom in all the twisted paths of history. In the Thirteen Words, He is described in relational terms: compassionate, full of steadfast love and truth, forgiving but also just. In sum, He is the ultimate source of all values—of justice and love, of the quest of truth and righteousness in society. However, the fullness of His power will be demonstrated only in the *Eschaton* (the Final Day). In the present, His holiness is experienced in the feelings and actions of righteousness.

Is Bergson's idea of the *élan vital* compatible with this conception of the Supreme Being in Judaism? Neither his concept of a self-renewing life-force, nor that of God as Love is at all an adequate reflection of the Jewish idea. His perception of God as Love reflects some passages in the New Testament, but it does not take account of God as Justice or Wisdom. Even in the New Testament the mystical potency of love and identification with the Savior are not separated from the Hebraic context of ideas; at least, not in the Synoptic Gospels. Just as the Old Testament does not lack the conviction that love is one of the attributes of God, the Synoptic Gospels do not affirm that God is fully understood as love. The fullness of God's Being as Spirit is assumed in both Testaments.

Can the *élan vital* be interpreted as Spirit, revealed in intelligence, justice, and freedom, as well as in love? Does the life-force in nature acquire the dimensions of Spirit in the case of humanity? As we have seen, Bergson wavered between the idealization of life and of spirit. If the pulsations of life are the heart of reality, the mystical experience may be the means through which mankind is thrust forward on the path of evolution. However, if Spirit be the highest manifestation of the *élan vital*, then all the forms of man's self-transcendence are, equally, marks of his continuous advance.

Certainly, the thrust of Bergson's argument is that life cannot be comprehended by the categories of mechanism, because in life an undivided whole governs a multiplicity of parts. He has also showed that in the course of evolution, ever more complex wholes come into being, which allow for a steadily increasing range of freedom. It would follow, that, in the human spirit, a new and higher phase of the life-force is manifested, permitting continuity of development along the diverse expressions of human culture—the quest of truth, goodness, beauty, sublimity, and holiness; the quest of inwardness, on the one hand, and of organic communal unity, on the other hand. Freedom is the one invariant quality of human life, even when all members of society accept the good of the whole as their personal ethic. These wholes are graded, but they are also mutually contradictory. The "I-Thou" relation between two individuals may well conflict with the holistic thinking of a nationalist or a socialist. Paradoxical as it may seem, the love of humanity in all its impeccable idealism, might be used on occasion to crush the free, spontaneous spirit. Did not both Stalin and Hitler massacre millions in the name of an ideology of love for the human race?

Our point is that objective reasoning, in the investigation of truth and in the determination of justice, is itself the highest expression of the creative spirit of God. If the thrust of God is toward wholeness, then any partial ideal, no matter how noble, becomes idolatrous as soon as it is worshiped in and by itself, apart from the infinitely complex web of the human spirit. Thus, in addition to love, there are the vast realms of imagination, which are so essential to the tasks of self-understanding and self-criticism; there are the depths and the heights of erotic life, which account for the cruelest actions of men and for their most sublime emotions; and there are the manifold lessons of history, which demonstrates the many ways in which men perverted their own noblest perceptions. The human spirit is inclusiveness, in its very essence, not only extensively, in seeking to embrace all of mankind, but also intensively, in asserting the unity of all the diverse disciplines whereby man transcends his own subjectivity.

In this view God is the spirit-force, Who comes at us from all directions of the human spirit. As mind is to the senses, Spirit is to the totality of human experience. The *élan vital* manifested in the evolution of ever higher creatures is but the lowest example of the holistic impetus. As Bergson put it, spirit is like an inverted cone, with its sharp apex thrust into the physical universe. The expanding, ever-widening spheres culminate in God. We feel His reality not only in the rare moments of mystical ecstasy, but whenever our awareness of consecration to His tasks attains overwhelming power. Holiness is not an experience that stands apart from the other directions of spiritual life, but is their synthesis and their summation. To all of us the call is addressed—"Holy shall ye be, for I, the Lord, am holy."

It is the many-sidedness of God's labors within the society of mankind that the Jewish tradition celebrates. He is manifested in all spheres of creation.

While the Torah describes God as the Creator of the entire cosmos in six days, the sages speak of Him as "renewing in His goodness every day, the works of creation." Philo, the Jewish philosopher of the first century, interpreted the story of creation as a metaphor of God's relationship to the universe and to mankind. He interpreted God's "resting" on the Sabbath in the sense of the spiritual activity of contemplation, which involves no change in the physical universe. Man was designed to be "a partner in the work of creation," helping in the establishment of "the Kingdom of God." The righteous are those who help in the advancement of this goal; the wicked are those who resist His ongoing activity.

The Hebrew prophets did not assume the continuous creation of new forms of life, but they did project the vision of a future age, in which the beasts of prey will become gentle and friendly. They spoke of "a new heaven and a new earth." Above all, God's creative continuity is manifested in His labors within the history of mankind. In contrast to the Apocalyptic writers, the prophets did not describe the *Eschaton* in detail, but they spoke of the Divine thrust and its general direction. The course of history is not predictable, since God works through all the facets of the human spirit; and man's spirit functions only in freedom—hence, it is perpetually liable to sin and regression.

In the future a religious view of life must take account of the dynamism of the evolutionary process, in nature as in human history. Of the several trends within Judaism it was speculative Kabbalah that was most hospitable to the notion of a dynamic process of redemption, operating within the substratum of existence. It was, therefore, possible for Abraham Isaac Kuk to combine the insights of Bergson with those of the Kabbalah in his philosophy of Zionism as a latter-day messianic movement and in his conception of the mystical unity of mankind. Like Bergson, Kuk believed that the mystical experiences of saints bring down to earth quanta of divine, creative power, which, because of the inner, organic unity of the human race, are then manifested in the scientific and technical advances of their contemporaries. The saints are so totally seized by the love of God and the love of mankind that they become living channels for the infusion of fresh creative energy in the substance of the universe. In turn, this infusion is articulated in those social and technical achievements that are the necessary building blocks of the messianic kingdom of God.[35]

Bergson described the Hebrew prophets as archetypal examples of those heroic saints in whom the Divine forward thrust was manifested. He then affirmed that the labor of the prophets was continued by the Christian mystics. What is it that distinguished the biblical prophets from the Shamans, the Greek ecstatics, and the Cananite "prophetizers"? Insofar as Hindu mystics are concerned, Bergson's distinction is clear. The Hindu mystics aimed at "detachment," an attitude of indifference and apathy toward this world and its concerns. At least some Christian mystics were activists, bent on transforming the world by the love of God. Actually, there were several components in the message of the great literary prophets.

They spoke of divine justice as well as divine love. Justice assumes a rational order, which implies restraints and also, on occasion, punishment. Thus, the prophets warned of "the wrath of God," mindful though they were of God's grace and His love.

As a matter of sober observation, the two Divine qualities do operate in human history, sometimes alternately, sometimes even simultaneously.

If memory is, in Bergson's view, the clearest imprint of the eternal, we must realize that to forget is not the same as to atone, to regret, and to forgive. In social life there is scarcely an evil deed without evil consequences. In our conception of God, His love is all the more meaningful precisely because it supplements the rule of His justice and the fiat of His will, mitigating and softening the natural order and the objective structure of a just society. Otherwise, Divine love would be so detached from the ethical life as to be totally meaningless.

The prophets assumed that the Torah of Moses, the archetypal prophet, was the concrete expression of a prior and supreme revelation. Every fresh expression of the Word must be similarly structured in laws. In the same manner as an individual translates vacuous ideals into specific resolves for the governance of his conduct, so a people must articulate its ideals in terms of collective undertakings, laws of conduct, and institutions of charity. Hence, the prophets were not satisfied with the Augustinian formula, "love God and do what you will." Nor were they disposed to separate politics from the teaching of faith and morals. That which belongs to Caesar must be judged in the light of the revealed ideals and norms of faith. Thus, the structuring of society through learning and legislation is the natural consequence of the prophetic movement. Ezra and his associates brought the prophetic movement to its climax by establishing their "faithful covenant," requiring among other things that the Torah and the prophets be regularly studied by all the people. In this way Ezra prepared the way for the eventual emergence of the Pharisaic movement.

To be sure, insofar as the Pharisees sought to regulate every aspect of personal and social life, they represented only one phase of the prophetic movement. At times their straitened piety provided a good illustration of the peril of fragmentation and one-sided exaggeration in spiritual life. The prophets emphasized the supreme importance of inwardness and spontaneity. Jeremiah projected the vision of a "new covenant," to be written on the tablets of the heart. This is a call for the progressive refinement of the capacity to listen to "the still, small voice" in our souls. We must strain to achieve it by the pitiless process of self-scrutiny, but we dare not delude ourselves into thinking that we have already achieved it.

The Talmudic sages were keenly conscious of "the plagues of Pharisaism," and, in their liturgy, they sought to guard against it. If in their *Halachah* they cemented ideals into laws, in their *Aggadah* they kept alive the prophetic concern for inwardness and spontaneity. In a larger sense, *Aggadah* includes the work of Philo, who records the teachings of the Hellenistic schools. In Palestine, as in Egypt, some sages sought to prepare themselves for the mystical state of delight in "the Holy Spirit." On the whole, the sages guarded the balanced piety of the people against the extremes of both mysticism and rationalism. They hammered out patterns of piety that were charged with immense power—creative power that bends and twists the forces of history. How else can we explain the powerful spin-offs from rabbinic-pharisaic Judaism, first of the Christian church, and later, of the Moslem faith?

Another major component of the genius of Hebraic prophecy is its appeal to rationality. This aspect of the prophetic movement is generally overlooked by Jewish as well as by Christian scholars. Bergson spoke of the "attraction" exerted by the prophets and the mystics on their contemporaries.

To be sure, extreme zeal fascinates the human imagination. Ecstasy is contagious, but also ephemeral. When the fire has died down, there is left only the taste of ashes. The mystics with one accord lament "the dark night of the soul." Who is today moved by the ascetic exercises of a St. Ignatius or the fantastic effusions of St. Catherine? The appeal of the prophets was so deep and enduring because they represented the dynamic wholeness and inner harmony of spiritual life. Wholeness includes reason as well as the apprehension of a realm to which our conscience and intelligence point, but which far transcends them. "The beginning of wisdom is the fear of the Lord," (Psalms 111, 10) but "the fear of the Lord" cannot dispense with wisdom in all its forms. No faith can be authentic and wholesome, if it is "a stumbling block to the Jews, folly to the Greeks." As the rabbis expressed the essence of Jewish piety: "If there be no wisdom, there can be piety; if there be no piety, there can be no wisdom." (Ethics of the Fathers 3, 20)

The prophets argued and reasoned with their audiences. At no time did they declaim against human wisdom, not even when they pointed to its incapacity to grasp fully the "thoughts" of God. For the most part they condemned idolatry as foolish fetishism, unworthy of rational beings. Jeremiah aptly formulated the critique of paganism from the monotheistic viewpoint: "Gods that have not made heaven and earth will disappear from under the sky." (Jeremiah: 10, 11) The gods that were actually worshiped in the near-eastern world were second- and third-generation gods. The "high gods" of many primitive cultures were acknowledged in theory, but were rarely worshiped in fact. The gods that were close to the people were themselves subject to the iron rule of fate, and, in the course of time, it was believed, they would succumb to their "twilight" and their doom. In contrast, the "God of Israel" was the eternal Lord of creation.

The literary style of the Hebrew prophets is restrained and balanced, reflecting a keen esthetic intuition. In their writings the Apollonian element of order and serenity is superimposed upon the Dionysian enthusiasm of the ecstatic, to use the categories of Nietzsche. The prophetic message is articulated in the accents of lyrical poetry. It is "passion recollected in tranquillity." Heschel was certainly right in pointing out the element of divine pathos in the writing of the prophets. However, this pathos is controlled, viewed in perspective, cooled by reflection, and articulated in measured cadences.

It was the rational component of Hebraic prophecy that led to these emphases in their teaching: the total integration of religious faith with ethical action, the interpretation of worship as being not formal ritual but the inward communion of the soul, the extension of God's love to all men, and the overcoming of the boundaries of the closed society. Reason is universal in essence. Once God was acclaimed as the Father of all men, the doctrine of the chosen people had to be reinterpreted in humanistic terms. So, too, the Master of the Universe could not be concerned with ritual ceremonies in themselves, but only insofar as they promoted the ethical character and growth of the worshipers.

The prophets saw every moral issue as a divine command, demanding immediate action. The Father of Mankind cannot and will not long permit injustice and oppression. They looked forward, not to the overflow of an abundant sea of love, obliterating all distinction, but to the triumph of a moral order, "when the knowledge of God shall fill the earth as the waters cover the sea." (Isaiah: 11, 9) Their love was not diffuse, like the Hindu reverence for all life, but structured, directed, reasoned, and balanced.

From all the above, it is clear that the genius of prophecy was never silenced within Judaism. As the balanced synthesis of moral passion and critical wisdom, the spirit of prophecy was alive in the labors of the Pharisees, who sought to translate the biblical ideals into the norms of a dedicated community, imbuing it with the love of learning and the mystical assurance of the Divine Presence. In later centuries, the Kabbalists concentrated their ardor on the cultivation of the mystical mood and its ecstasies. The philosophers, on the other hand, aimed to retain and reinforce the harmonious posture of the prophets.

Halevi argued that the fantastic excesses of monkish piety were not as desirable as the balanced commingling of the feelings of fear, love, and joy in the service of God. He based his argument on the analogy of the human mind, which functions properly only when the body is untroubled and in a state of perfect equilibrium. To him, piety consisted in the feeling of belonging to the greater whole—the individual Jew to God and to the people of Israel, and Israel is "among the nations as the heart is among the organs"—thus, finally, the individual in relation to the whole of mankind.

Bergson agreed with Maimonides that it is through the agency of prophets that the divine thrust impels the human race toward perfection. Even the lowest level of prophecy, that of "the Holy Spirit," endows men with the power to achieve great deeds and the charisma that moves multitudes. However, Maimonides did not regard the gift of prophecy as a unique intuition, different in character from the ordinary categories of reason. On the contrary, he followed the Talmudic sages in the claim that the road to the peaks of prophecy leads through ethical, esthetic, and intellectual perfection. The prophet differs from the philosopher in that the latter has achieved only the perfection of the intellect, while the former is, in addition, richly endowed with the faculty of "imagination."

In the usage of Maimonides, the genius of imagination is manifested in the arts of poetry and statesmanship; that is, in the capacity to perceive perfect patterns of order. The poet is gifted with the vision of esthetic wholes, while the statesman senses the place of each individual within the structure of a well-ordered society. So Maimonides portrayed the ideal man as the prophet, who is a philosopher as well as a mystic, a poet as well as a statesman, and a visionary as well as an active leader of the community. The prophet seeks to come into the presence of God by way of blending the emotional ardor of the saint with the intellectual quest of the philosopher. Through this two-sided effort, the vision of the One may be attained. The philosopher-saint may at rare moments achieve a high level of sensitivity. In the wisdom of God, he may then be favored with the power of prophecy—that is, he becomes a messenger of God charged with the task of providing leadership to the society of which he is part.[36]

The Maimonidean concept of prophecy is not limited by ethnic barriers. The prophet is sent to all men. Jeremiah wrote of God's charge to him: "A prophet unto the nations, I made thee." (Jeremiah: 1, 5) Indeed, the rabbis spoke of Gentile prophets, appointed to direct the affairs of their compatriots. In his description of the five classes of men who set out to attain the vision of the Divine Presence,

Maimonides ranked the Talmudic scholar below the philosophers.[37] In the context of the messianic hope he described both Jesus and Mohammed as heaven-sent messengers, whose task it was to bring millions of people to accept the truths of monotheism and to live in accord with the biblical ethic.[38]

Bergson believed that the Christian mystics provided the spark that lit up the great ages of western history. This spark was latent in the souls of European people for generations before it burst forth in the glories of the Renaissance, the Reformation, and the French Revolution. As a Jew and as a democrat, Bergson could not but range himself on the side of those Frenchmen who judged the Revolution to be an illumination rather than a catastrophe. Yet he attributed its genesis to the deposits of Divine love in the hearts of the Christian mystics, to whom the Revolution and the Enlightenment would have been an abomination! If Bergson had taken pains to recognize the fullness of the prophetic phenomenon, he would not have needed to resort to such specious reasoning. He would have identified the great ages of Europe as those generations in which the outreach of love was duly guided and channeled by man's critical intelligence. As soon as this ideal synthesis was broken up, either by way of religious fanaticism or through the pride of reason, the result was an impoverishment of the intellect and the frustration of love.

This lesson is written in bold letters across the pages of history. Bergson did not take account of it, because he was driven by the anti-intellectualist impetus of his generation. Clearly, his claim that Christian mysticism was the legitimate successor of Hebraic prophecy could be sustained only in the context of a perspective that substituted a mysterious intuition for the light of man's intellect. Bergson's failure to see the continuity of the prophetic impetus within Judaism was therefore largely owing to his ambivalence toward the age of reason, which prepared the way for the French Revolution. He could not but hail it as man's greatest achievement, ushering in the era of democracy. Conversely, his philosophic investigations led him to conclude that creative greatness cannot derive from the intellect, that frail and perverse instrument that nature designed as a weapon in the battle of survival. Thus, Bergson's negation of Judaism was at least in part a consequence of his rejection of "the perennial philosophy," which is represented in Christianity by St. Thomas and in Judaism by Maimonides.

By way of justifying his contention that the Christian Church was the legitimate successor of Hebraic prophetism, Bergson pointed out that Jewry became in the post-biblical era a closed society, with the outreach of love being limited to the ethnic community.

> There is no doubt that Christianity was a profound transformation of Judaism. It has been said over and over again: a religion which was still essentially national was replaced by a religion that could be made universal.[39]

The notion that Judaism lacked the universalist dimension is patently untrue, even though it was repeated endlessly by philosophers and historians. Certainly Philo, a contemporary of Jesus and Paul, interpreted Judaism in universal terms. The Jew was to him a "cosmopolitan," a citizen of the universe. The Christian undertaking to spread "the good news" among the nations was preceded by the massive propaganda of the Hellenistic Jews. We know that large numbers of Gentile "fearers of the Lord" regularly attended the synagogues in the Diaspora. Several Maccabean rulers imposed the Jewish faith by force on the inhabitants of the Holy Land. The conversion of the royal family of the Adiabene Kingdom in the northern Syrian desert was a signal achievement of the Jewish missionary effort.

However, in the first century of our era, universalism was associated in Judaism with the political and social aspirations of the Jewish people. The two hopes for the universal acceptance of the One God and the political triumphs of Jerusalem were closely intertwined, indeed inseparable. The one vision of redemption was a lambent flame blending the fires of national vindication and the salvation of mankind under God's sovereignty. Thus, while the universalist vision permeated and uplifted Jewish piety, this ideal was so burdened in practice by the sad political status of Jewish people that its impact on the non-Jewish world was greatly restricted. Jewish preaching was hampered by the tragic decline of Jewish fortunes. The persistent messianic outbreaks in the century between the crucifixion of Jesus and the revolt of Bar Kochba resulted in a long chain of catastrophes and kept alive this association of failed political hopes with the longed-for universal *Eschaton.*

In the Christian community this association was gradually severed. The leaders of the Christian community left Jerusalem at the outbreak of the Great Revolt. While Jews continued to head the Palestinian church down to the year 135, the center of gravity of Christianity was located in the non-Jewish churches, ever since the ending of the Great Revolt. For a while Christians were called the third race, being neither Jewish nor Roman. In their own view their kingdom was "not of this world." During the second century, Christians gave up their earlier opposition to military service, and their followers became part of the Roman legions. Thereafter, their propaganda was no longer undercut by the feelings of Roman patriotism.

In the case of the Jewish people, the course of development ran in the opposite direction. In the Talmudic period and in the long, dark centuries of the medieval era, Jewish consciousness became more and more self-centered and isolationist. In view of the hostility that pursued them and drove them from one country to another, they could not react differently. Yet, in the modern period, Jewish people became the most ardent universalists. Their very marginality in European society compelled them to transcend the barriers of ethnic zealotry and to fight for a humane, universalist society. They could hardly act otherwise, since their sworn enemies in nearly all countries were the champions of ethnic assertiveness and religious dogmatism. Whether or not they wanted it, the Jews were driven by the ideological storms of the nineteenth century into the camps of the liberals and the humanists. The exigencies of Jewish history reinforced the impetus within Judaism itself toward the overcoming of ethnic isolationism.

Nor was the humanist bent of Judaism ended by the rise of the Zionist movement and the establishment of the State of Israel. The Zionist program, as formulated in Basel in 1897, was conceived within the context of international order and good will. To be sure, there were occasional outbursts of ethnic romanticism, before the emergence of Israel and since, but the major thrust of the movement as a whole was kept in line with the dominant orientation of Jewish history.

While Bergson's influence was felt indirectly in the emergence of two contemporary schools of thought—the so-called process-philosophies and the existentialist movement—the one who most directly continued his line of investigation was doubtless Teilhard de Chardin. In an amazing display of creative imagination he reviewed the emergence of life on our planet from its very beginning and outlined his vision of the goal toward which the human experience is moving. He developed the spiritualist element in the Bergsonian philosophy. It is the human spirit at its noblest that provides a clue to the direction of the dynamic elan at the heart of reality. "Man is not the center of the universe, as once we thought in our simplicity, but something much more wonderful—the arrow pointing the way to the final unification of the world in terms of life."[40] Man is "nothing else than evolution become conscious of itself."[41]

The human spirit is constituted by love as well as understanding. For de Chardin, the life-force is manifested in the broad range of human thought, not particularly in the intuition of duration. Mankind is even now being inwardly impelled to reach new heights of personality and universality. This goal is already dawning on the human horizon. It is symbolized by the omega point, the glowing center of "super-life," the synthesis of the hyper-personal and the universal.[42] Teilhard de Chardin was, like Bergson, deeply conscious of the perversion of the ideal of unity in the totalitarian philosophies of our day. To the biological categories of evolution, he added the new phase of personality, which prefigures the future course of the life-force. Hence, there can be no true universalist order that is not based on the fullest development of the individual personality.

> There is no mind without synthesis. . . . The true Ego grows in inverse proportion to "egoism." Like the Omega which attracts it, the element only becomes personal, when it universalizes itself.[43]

The dialectic of "personal-universal" corresponds to the phenomenon that is specifically human—the polarity of *divergence* and *convergence*. While animal species continued to drift apart from their original rootage in the evolutionary tree of life, the human race was able to reunify its divergent branches. Through the various encounters of war and peace, but especially through the power of consciousness, the human race succeeded in gathering unto itself the riches of all its branches. As we look ahead to the future, we recognize the incalculable benefits of this dialectical phenomenon. Divergence, in the sense of each historic community internalizing its peculiar heritage, makes possible the emergence of fresh qualities. Convergence encourages the opening of fresh horizons, in which the diverse treasures of the many nations and faiths might be seen together in one perspective.

In the light of this analysis Teilhard de Chardin might have been expected to evolve a non-dogmatic concept of the confluence of the world's faiths and cultures. His life's work and his amazing creative imagination pointed in this direction. His personal commitment as a priest, however, prevented him from following the clear line of his research, so he insisted on the exclusive truth of Christianity.

> Alone, unconditionally alone, in the world today, Christianity shows itself able to reconcile, in a single living act, the All and the Person. Alone, it can bend our hearts not only to the service of that tremendous movement of the world which bears us along, but beyond, to embrace that movement in love.[44]

It would have been more in keeping with the polarity of divergence-convergence to conclude that we face the task today of integrating the diverse faiths and cultures of mankind, within a context that rejects only that which is isolationist and self-exalting, perversely insisting on its separation from the human family.

De Chardin's vision of the work of God in history is, in itself, entirely consistent with the implicit direction of classical Jewish thought. Though this inner logic of Judaism was not expliticly stated before our own times, we may, nevertheless, regard it as an articulation in contemporary terms of the classical, or the prophetic-philosophical, way of thinking. We may formulate it as follows: God works within the course of history, leading all men to His Kingdom in the end of Days. Israel's conviction of being "chosen" is an assertion of the supreme importance of its sacred heritage of faith and history. Its divergence, in de Chardin's terminology, is for the sake of convergence. Its universalist import is that *all* historic groups should likewise view the holy aspects of their own tradition, in the light of an all-human perspective.

Judaism, in its classical expressions, has stressed that its own "separation from the nations" is intended to bring "light unto the nations," by upholding the universal goal that all nations will reach if they will pursue their own respective courses of development in the same spirit. We must be true to our own collective selves, as nations and religious groups, in such a way as to serve the universal society of the future. Thus, our divergence, necessary and valuable as it is, is thinkable only as a contribution to the overall purpose of convergence. This vision is the logical consequence of today's approach to the study of man's religions and his diverse cultures.

The vivid imagination of Oswald Spengler (1880–1936) served to illuminate the steady slide of Germany toward nihilism and Nazism. His *Decline of the West*, for all its ponderous learning, was originally conceived as an ardent call to the German people to dissociate themselves from western culture and to take up their role as the new barbarians and the new Caesars. His major work must be read along with his later books and essays, in which the implications of his grand analysis of all human experience are spelled out. Outside of Germany he was by far the most famous expounder of the so-called "Germanic Ideology," as an alternative to both democracy and Marxism. Spengler saw his role not simply as that of a scholar, summarizing the results of his research, but as that of a prophet, heralding a new age. In this capacity he was widely regarded as an intellectual precursor of the Nazi movement, though he despised Hitler and all his works. His was the tragic role of "the prophet who did not recognize his own children."

Spengler derived his inspiration from the German Romantics of the first decades of the nineteenth century and the nihilistic vitalism of Schopenhauer, Wagner, and Nietzsche. He had not read either Bergson or Sorel at the time he wrote the first volume of *The Decline*.

In his own mind his intellectual mentors were Goethe and Nietzsche. In Goethe, however, he saw chiefly the unrestrained romantic, who strives to grasp the infinite in all its dimensions. While Goethe was not interested in history, the Romantics anticipated Spengler in the application of the biological analogy to the study of history. Already Herder had conceived of every national history as undergoing periods of genesis, growth, maturity, and decline. However, Herder assumed that all national cultures belonged in one common treasury of all-human ideals, and he looked forward to the emergence of the great, all-human society as the final fruit of history. In contrast, Spengler combined the nihilism of Nietzsche with the biological categories of the Romantics. He predicted a "new barbarism," a new "Caesarism," the replacement of the liberal ethic by the rule of men who love power, modeling their conduct after that of "beasts of prey." He called on the Germans to take the lead and to plunge into this "wave of the future."

In his book *Prussianism and Socialism* the enemy was England, or, more generally, the English-speaking world, which had developed the democratic, free-enterprise world order. Prussianism was founded on "the distinction between command and obedience," whereas "the distinction between rich and poor" was basic to the democracies.[45] Thus, the great issue of the future turns on the success or failure of the Germans in wresting control of the world from the English and the Americans. Is the future world order to be a "dictatorship of money or of organization, the world as booty or as a state, wealth or authority, success or vocation?"[46]

In *The Hour of Decision* Spengler changed his target. The enemy was now Russia and "the colored races." However, neither the English, the Americans, nor the French were able to provide military leadership for the Faustian imperium. Germany alone was "the least exhausted of the white world." It still preserved a residue of its ancient barbarism. It deserved to lead because it was a "strong race, the eternal warlike in the type of the beast of prey man."[47]

As Spengler read the lessons of history, a civilization is the dead shell of a living culture; in its turn, a culture is the product of a nation's soul, deriving from roots that reach far below the range of man's intellect. Each culture generates its own ethic, its own esthetic norms and ways of life, its own intellectual image of the cosmos. We must not judge the achievements and moral principles of one culture or civilization by the standards of other cultures, for different civilizations are mutually incomprehensible. There are no universal standards whereby to determine right and wrong, the noble and the base, or even the true and the false. Space itself was felt differently in different civilizations, and only Faustian man conceives space as an infinite expansion in every direction. Each civilization undergoes the same "morphology," or stages of growth and decline. While he counted eight civilizations, he focused attention chiefly on three—the Greco-Roman or "Apollonian"; the Iranian-Hebrew-Arabian, or the "Magian"; and the western or "Faustian," beginning with the twelfth century.

Interestingly enough, he divided the culture of Christianity down the middle between the first millennium, when it was "Magian," and the second millennium, when the spirit of the western nations was born. He followed the Russian historian Nikolai Danilevsky in treating Russia as a world apart, separate and distinct from western culture. In fact, he regarded Russia as the potential leader of the colored races that threaten to challenge the hegemony of the white race. Germany, too, stands on the threshold of western culture, half in and half out. Therefore, it is up to the Germans to seize control of the western world and to provide for it a unified imperium. In the coming age society will have to be organized in military fashion, and Germany has long been the bastion of the Prussian spirit.

The true alternative to the age of liberalism is not Marxian socialism but the Prussian spirit of total submission to the all-powerful state that is headed by a native nobility and is structured along military lines. England and America are effete plutocracies. The parliamentary political system is nothing but a device to obscure the triumph of money. In the rising tide of the future, "blood" will come to the fore, and "men of race," constituting a new nobility, will take over control of the western world. Actually, every nation is governed by an elite. A military nobility forms a creative elite, generating the "master morality" of Nietzsche's vision. In the course of time, as a culture hardens into a civilization, the military elite yields to the dominance of the priestly caste, the bureaucrats after their diverse kinds.

Our times call for the rise of the military elite, for the West has already entered its wintertime. It has been overtaken by the symptoms of senescence and decay—materialism, skepticism, the loss of a sense of style, the pervasive anomie of meaninglessness, and the sickly manifestations of a "second religiosity." The new leaders will appeal to instinct and intuition, to honor, courage, and a sense of destiny. Destiny is "a word whose content one feels." It is what we feel in our "guts" that counts. This entire world view, sustained though it may be by a vast multitude of selected details, is essentially based on an intuitive grasp of the whole of human experience. "The more historically men tried to think, the more they forgot that in this domain, they ought not to think."[48]

Instead of an analytical approach to the study of history, Spengler urged a "physiognomic" approach; that is, a feeling for the inner life of a culture, a response of our deeper self to the dynamic substance of a living society. Thus, he presumed to be the visionary of a realm that was completely barred to mere intellectuals.

Spengler helped to draw the mantle of respectability over the brutalitarian ideology of the Nazis. Like them, he scorned the parliamentary system and the liberal doctrines of the rights of man as products of the decaying civilization of the English and the French. Like them, he extolled "the voice of blood" and the rule of force; he enthroned passion and pride in place of rationality and humanity; he despised the hopes for a humane society and preached a return to the brute realities of the jungle; and he flirted with racial concepts and pointed to Russia as the target of German military conquest.

In what concerns "the goal of mankind," I am a thorough and decided pessimist. For me, mankind is a zoological quantity. I see no progress, no goal, no path for humanity.[49]

To be sure, Spengler was not a racist in the Nazi sense. He employed the term race in its general connotation, acknowledging that men of race, possessing the endowments of a natural elite, were to be found among all nations. He extolled the old aristocracy of Germany, and he favored a system in which men of talent, whatever their background, would attain leadership. He regarded the Nazi movement as a caricature of his ideals.

In regard to the Jews, Spengler maintained that antisemitism was caused by the fact that the Jews constituted a fossil of the Magian soul, thrust among the Faustian nations of the West. Between the Magians and the Faustians there can be no basis for understanding and accommodation. Thus, through the centuries the Jews could not understand the people of Europe, nor could the latter understand them. However, the modern Jews of Europe and America have already divested themselves of their ancient heritage. To all intents and purposes, Jews and Christians equally have outgrown their ancient cultures. Modern Jews are completely assimilated, having acquired the Faustian soul. Insofar as some remnants of the Jewish people still cling to their Magian heritage, we must be patient with their slowness to read the signs of the time and await their total assimilation. Spengler was, therefore, an avowed and consistent opponent of the Nazi "Aryan" policy.

Yet, as we examine the impact of Spengler's philosophy, we cannot but concur in the judgment that it contributed significantly to the triumph of Nazism and to the tragedy of the Holocaust. He helped to disarm and discredit the intellectuals and the liberals. The position of Jews in the European world was based on the ideals of the Enlightenment—rationality, freedom, equality, and liberation from the seduction of myths that are generated and sustained by popular passion and pride. Whenever the norms of intelligence and conscience are downgraded, the floodgates are opened for the surge of mass-hatred and mass-zealotries. In that case, the hounds of war are unleashed sooner or later, and weaker peoples are subjected to oppression. The Jews, the minority that is physically weakest and spiritually most liable to entanglement in the satanic coils of mythology, usually become the chief target of demagogic exploitation and popular fury.

Spengler sowed the seeds of contempt for non-Teutonic peoples— the English, French, Americans, Russians, and the colored races. Thereby he helped convince the Germans of the inevitability of an

Armageddon. In reply to an American inquiry regarding the possibility of staving off another world war, Spengler asserted in a telegram:

Pacifism will remain an ideal, and war a fact, and if the white peoples are resolved to wage war no more, the colored will do so and will be the rulers of the earth.[50]

In the frenzied atmosphere of preparing for a war of annihilation, the rights of individuals and of minorities are given short shrift. Generally, in Germany antisemitism was closely associated with hostility toward the cultures and peoples of the West. Xenophobia is an instinctive phenomen, and, whenever it is aroused, the hatred of strangers will be focused on the "alien within the gate."

Spengler taught the German people to consider their immediate, pressing problems in the light of massive, millennial movements. This large view may appear to be profound, prophetic, and ennobling. Actually, the distant, global vision serves to suppress the rights of individuals, unless that vision is combined with a transcendental source of right and wrong. How can the rights of the few people of the present be allowed to stand in the way of the culmination of the hopes of numberless generations? Yet the vision is inevitably partial, colored by the inescapable veils of prejudice, and its realization is forever uncertain. The sin of *hubris* distorts the outlook of the leaders as well as of the people. Loyalty is re-oriented from the living people and its laws to the person of the *Führer*, who incorporates the vision in all its presumed splendor.

Since supermen exist only in mythology, the natural failings of the people in power are multiplied in their effects many times over. In the meantime, the rights of millions are crushed, a blank check is given for the perpetration of mass crimes, in the name of the surpassing glory of the nation's destiny. If nationalism has drenched the European continent in blood, how much more so has this brand of super-heated Caesarism that lays claim to global dimensions?

In sum, the case of Spengler is an instructive lesson on the danger of arousing the ghosts of mythology in our contemporary world. The roots of mythology go down to the depths of the unconscious, where brute instincts hold sway. The myth deifies the wishes of the tribe, magnifies its fears, and silences the stirring of conscience in regard to outsiders. From its earliest beginnings, Judaism has waged a deathless war against the seduction of myths. The tribe is not the be-all and end-all of values.

Myths reflect the rhythms of life—the growth of vegetation in the spring, its "death" in the autumn, and its resurrection in the spring. The gods of mythology come to life, do battle with one another, and ultimately they succumb to the iron rule of fate. They reflect on a majestic, dream-like scale the passions, occasional caprices, and affections of human beings. In contrast, Judaism views God in the light of the human spirit. All that in man betokens greatness of soul— understanding, generosity, the feeling of the sublime, the wonder of love—is infinitely extrapolated to form the attributes of the One God. He is not subject to the compulsions of life and death, neither "begetting" nor being "begotten." He is not swayed by momentary passions, nor is He impelled by arbitrary impulses. Only as metaphors are such qualities applied to Him.

Yet, with all His transcendence, His "image" is placed within man. He is revealed not in the evolution of the communal mind or in the unfolding of the spirit of the age, but in the quest of the individual for guidance and truth. Emphasis on the conscience of the individual is as characteristic of ethical monotheism as emphasis on the tribe is of the various mythologies of life.

In Spengler's vision there is no room for self-criticism in the light of transcendent norms of right and wrong, since our contemporary standards, belonging to the "declining" West, are already decayed, and those that will emerge in the new culture are still unborn. We are left, therefore, with a crusading, yet totally unbounded moral nihilism combined with a vague and formless futurism.

One of the most seminal insights of Spengler is the concept of second religiosity. In its final agonies of senescence, he maintained, a decaying civilization will experience a false efflorescence of religiosity. Unlike the faith that generates a new culture, the piety of a decaying civilization is a vain effort to recapture the naiveté and élan of youth.

Along with the Hegelian historians, Spengler believed that a new culture is generated by the emergence of a new faith. That faith was to him, however, a collective posture of the psyche, rather than a new idea. The new faith possesses its own symbols and standards. Apart from his idiosyncratic way of dealing with the morphology of cultures, we note the centrality of religion in his view of the birth and death of cultures. In our concern with the destiny of Judaism in the contemporary world, the distinction between genuine faith and second religiosity is basic.

A genuine faith is the confident outreach of the total personality, an overflow of creative energy that is later articulated in the diverse branches of culture. In this sense it is a projection of the lines of growth in the personalities of the faithful. It is a song of joy and love; a celebration of the wonder of life, a response to its challenging mystery; and an acclamation of gratitude for the felt resonance between the soul and the Creator. Affirmative, whole-souled faith springs out of the joy and abundance of vitality, and it provides additional thrusts for the upward growth of society.

Second religiosity, conversely, is the product of a revulsion against cynicism and skepticism. In fact it is felt inwardly as a frantic flight from the realities of life. It arises in an age of anomie, of the clash of cultures and the breakdown of religious traditions. It is a desperate effort to escape from the desolation and horror of the inner "wasteland," the moral void. Basically, it is a negation of negatives, not a true affirmation—a faith in faith; the hysterical resort of a split soul, which erects barriers of the spirit against the threatening tides of the outside world, barriers of dogma and ritual, which are accepted precisely "because they are absurd," since their absurdity is a counter-symbol of what is to many persons the all too real absurdity of life. So, in the last days of the Roman Empire second religiosity of pagans as well as of Christians flourished along with and because of the prevailing disenchantment, failure of nerve, and fairly general cynicism.

In noting the stigmata of second religiosity among his contemporaries, Spengler displayed the penetration of true genius. In our own day the sickly symptoms of a phony religiosity were all too apparent. We have seen in America of the late sixties a whole generation of young people similarly driven to desperation by the spectacle of corruption in high places, by the blind momentum of a senseless war machine, and by the apparent absence of high purpose in the universities, in industry, and even in government. Our young people found themselves burdened by a multitude of disjointed tasks—subjects to cover, professions to master, and goods to acquire. But they were not given an uplifting vision, a supreme goal, a faith adequate for the perplexities of modern life. They looked at their elders and found that like the Emperor of Andersen's fable they were "without clothes"—all their elders, those of the universities, the churches, and the professions, as well as their own parents.

Bedeviled by the horror of meaninglessness, these young people spurned the whole of society as hypocritical and attempted, like the blind Samson, to shatter the pillars of the Temple. They demonstrated in droves; they sought to burn their own universities; some sought to blow their brains with LSD; others dreamed of communes of the pure and the true, who would form islands of holiness for the resurrection that would follow the imminent catastrophe; nearly all were driven to manifest their inner wasteland by donning ugly clothes and using dirty language, repudiating by their unkempt, bedraggled appearance the norms and goals of their elders.

Following the first explosions of skepticism and cynicism, there emerged a plethora of new cults and evanescent enthusiasms. A tidal wave of mysticism inundated the sensitive and the idealistic. No longer content with the sheer negation of the "hangups" of their elders, they discovered that the freedom of "doing their own thing" was actually slavery in disguise. In desperation, some followed the purveyors of the modern version of soma, the ancient, intoxicating "drink of the gods." Others turned to the Oriental cults of transcendental meditation—and the more exotic and absurd, the better. When human beings surrender their minds, they follow willingly the leadership of "a small child." Behold the followers of the fifteen-year-old Maharaj Ji! Others rediscovered the irrational fantasies cherished by sectarians in their own faiths. Thus, we now have the aggressive bands of "youth for Jesus," "Jesus freaks," Christian enthusiasts for "speaking in tongues," and Jewish celebrants of Buberian Hasidism. Also, the vast youthful assemblages for the so-called rock concerts—are not they, too, worshipers of the occult mysteries of life?

What are we to make of these manifestations of second religiosity? Are they the telltale symptoms of the advanced senility of our civilization? Are these outbursts of irrational enthusiasm the sure signs of the approach of doom?

I believe that the explanation of these phenomena lies close at hand. There is no need to escape from reason and its norms in order to understand the confluent phenomena of cynicism and blind faith. When the existing synthesis of faith breaks down, people will hold on to the dry forms of religion for a generation or two. Their descendants, however, are certain to stigmatize the followers of sheer formalistic rites as "hypocrites." In their turn, the latter will flounder between the twin poles of cynicism and fideism, running from one extreme to the other. Man must believe in a transcendent reality, if he is to be true to his own inner being. Yet, that belief must somehow be compatible with all the experiences and forms of wisdom that a generation possesses. The quest for wholeness of personality, reconciling the counsels of reason with the dim gropings of intuition and the subrational storms of the unconscious, is likely to assert itself in the long run.

Our age has lost the solace and strength of the syntheses of the past. Too much has been happening too fast for our generation to achieve that serenity of spirit that is essential for the efflorescence of a new age of classical harmony and balance. However, we must not lose sight of our goal. We do indeed need a grand vision of harmony—majestic enough to fit the expanding horizons of modern man. Such a vision, however, is quite different from any vitalistic thrusts, or mind-blowing ecstasies, or the mystique of blood. An inspiring vision of the future can derive only from the slow assimilation of the multitude of data in the history of cultures and religions. A democratic world view will emerge out of the study of mankind in all its richness and diversity and without that racial or national *hubris* that has bedeviled the western world in the past. We cannot return to the simplicities of the eighteenth century, but we can put our vastly increased reservoirs of knowledge at the service of the ideals of an all-embracing humanity.

The future of any one faith is now intimately involved in the state of all faiths. In the battle against the seduction of exotic cults, classical religions will rise and fall together. In their influence on the complexities of militant secularism, the balanced historical faiths stand shoulder to shoulder.

What, then, are the prospects for the development of a universal fellowship of faiths, a fellowship that will bring inspiration to the evolving universal society, while cherishing and reinforcing the distinctive genius and historical character of each of its members? This inquiry leads us to the next subject—the analysis of the Jewish-Christian dialogue in the past century.

Franz Rosenzweig (1886–1929) set out to counter the three kinds of nihilism that reached their climax in the first decade of the twentieth century. First, of the cosmos as a whole. The materialistic picture of the universe as a chaotic and meaningless whirl of atoms was popularized by Haeckel. It implied that human sentiments and ideals were only so many illusions, without roots in reality, like froth on the tidal waves.

Second, the meaning of good and evil. The impact of Nietzsche's critique of traditional morality was deeply felt at that time, reinforced as it was by the mighty upsurge of Teutonism, which involved an all-out fight against the entire Judeo-Christian ethical heritage. The ethical precepts of the Bible were now scorned by many as "slave morality." The Marxists helped undermine the notion of an objective ethic by their claim that principles of morality were reflections of class interests. The Freudians contributed to the nihilistic tide by their assertion that the superego mirrored in sublimated form the primitive passions and repressed drives of the unconscious.

The rise of Germanic historicism provided the third basic component of nihilism. Every folk produces its own concepts of right and wrong, its own conscience, and virtually its own faith. As that folk attains self-consciousness, it recognizes ever more clearly that it is the center of the universe—what is good for it is good; what is burdensome to it is evil. The concept of humanity is a pale abstraction. Only nations are real. Genuine culture springs out of the life of the folk—everything else is sham and pretense. History does not move toward an all-embracing society and an all-inclusive culture, but, as in Spengler's world, cultures rise and fall, emerging in the course of centuries out of the wrath and fury of conquering barbarians. Those who bear the seeds of a future culture in their loins are totally incapable of understanding the values and thoughts of an older culture.

We, living in the post-holocaust world, know that nihilism, in all its forms, threatened the very existence of the Jewish people. Rosenzweig, as a keen philosopher, felt the sting of the nihilist challenge, to his Jewishness as well as to his humanity, even if he did not foresee its ultimate consequences. As his thought matured, he decided in July 1913 to convert to Christianity and to collaborate in the promotion of a Christian countermovement to European nihilism. To his mother he said, pointing to the New Testament in his hand, "Mother, here is everything, here is the truth. There is only one way, Jesus."[51] However, he made one reservation: "I declared that I could turn Christian only *qua* Jew—not through the intermediate stage of paganism."[52]

This reservation proved decisive, leading to his determination to live in the Jewish source of the Judeo-Christian stream of thought and action. His reconversion to Judaism occurred during a Yom Kippur service, which he attended in a small Orthodox synagogue. He came to realize that Jewish piety existed in a naive, unsophisticated, and yet invincible form. As the Christian comes to God by way of Jesus, the Jew feels the immediate presence of the divine through his awareness of being a son of Abraham, Isaac, and Jacob. No one comes to the Father save through the Son, Rosenzweig agrees. But he adds, "Except for those who don't have to go to the Father, since they are already with him. The Jewish people, chosen by their Father, look beyond the world and history to that most distant point in time, when "God will be One and His Name One. At that point, where Jesus ceases to be Lord, Israel will cease to be chosen. . . ."[53]

From that time on Rosenzweig interpreted his religious experiences within the context of Jewish experience. By way of reaction against his former assimilationist posture, he became ever more decisively isolationist. "It is our lot to remain strangers, alien to all spiritual possessions of the nations. . . ."[54] Yet, he insisted, the

Jew is different because he is ahead of others, not because he stands aside from the common, messianic enterprise.

". . . There is after all only one true people, and it is really no people. The other peoples, which are indisputably peoples, are all just setting out on the road toward peoplehood."[55] By concentrating on developing the import of his own heritage, the Jew contributes most effectively to the advancement of humanity. To be a Jew, truly and authentically, is to attest by one's life to the truth of the God of Israel, Who is the source of all ethical values. In the European world it is the lot of the Jews to be "the witnesses of God," reinforcing the Judaic component in Christianity. As Rosenzweig wrote in 1923, "European culture today is on the point of collapse and can only be saved if supra-European, suprahuman powers come to its aid."[56]

Rosenzweig's basic attack against nihilism began with a personal experience, which he then discovered to be the kernel of Jewish piety. He dared to base his philosophy on a subjective experience, because he believed that all world views were subjective. "The unity of these countless relationships, its relative conclusion, is the unity of the philosopher's point of view, personal, experienced, philosophized."[57] Yet his starting point was, after all, a response to the call of the Creator—"the bridge from maximum subjectivity to maximum objectivity is formed by theology's concept of revelation."[58] The wondrous experience of revelation creates its own certitude, for the recipient is re-created, as it were. "God said—'let there be light'—and what is the light of God?—It is the soul of man."[59] In turn, revelation as a series of divine thrusts, generating man's higher soul, is a distinct possibility in a cosmos that is continually being impelled toward higher forms of life, a universe of creative evolution, à la Bergson. The possibility of revelation was turned into a certainty, first by his personal experience and second by the record of the course of revelation in history.

Like Buber, Rosenzweig felt that he was addressed directly by God, even as the lover calls to his beloved. "Man is now become the master of philosophy, therefore, ready to hear the voice of God (which he never hears so long as he works under the 'umbrella' of a philosophic system. . . ."[60] This call was, to him, inseparable from the similar calls that came to Moses and the prophets—"*Voaidiacho, beshem*" (Exodus 33:17), "I have known thee by name" in the double sense of knowing and loving that the Hebrew root, *yodea*, conveys. Revelation is not a one-time event, but a continuous series of messages, which are mutually reinforcing, and Judaism, as a whole, not merely the Hebrew Bible, constitutes the divine flame, out of which rays of light issue to illumine and redeem the world. Judaism is like the "sun," and Christianity is like the rays of sunlight that overcome the darkness. Both are true insofar as they operate to overcome nihilism or paganism.

In this central metaphor of his world view, Rosenzweig followed Hegel in treating philosophy as an exposition of the meaning of history. Did not Judaism actually function as the fountainhead of two world-conquering faiths? To be sure, Rosenzweig did not put Islam in the same category as Christianity, for in his view Islam was unidimensional, incapable of generating a great culture. In any case, he was directly concerned with the regeneration of German and Christian culture. He wrote two programmatic essays at virtually the same time, one outlining his plan for adult Jewish education, the other detailing a program for general education that was designed to promote the cultural unity of the nation.[61]

The three sources of nihilism: the ontic, the psychological, and the historical, were in Rosenzweig's mind contradicted by one flash of intuition—God communicates with man in love; God bursts into the world with fresh acts of creation; man and God together are engaged in "redeeming" the world, building in the wilderness a pathway for the Lord.

This intuition can function only in the minds of those who recognize the absurdity of the "given" world and the emptiness of the various philosophic systems.[62] The vacuity of these systems is demonstrated in that they reduce God, the world, and man to naught. But then, man fears death and resists the "scientific" image of his personality. "New thinking" arises when man discovers himself to be in dialogue with God. Such thinking is more basic than abstract thought, in which all individuality is dissolved. The first product of divine revelation is language, not the *logos*—and language means intercommunication.

God addresses man. Thus, the Judeo-Christian ethic derives from a transrational source. If that source is ignored, mankind will drift, logically and of necessity, back into the morass of paganism. One cannot "prove" the basic principles of ethics or derive them from an enlightened self-interest. Such efforts, while laudable, cannot resist the acids of nihilistic criticism. Neither can the biblical ethic be disproved by psychological or sociological arguments. The source of ethics is in "man before God." Man responds to God's call, "Thou shalt love the Lord, thy God . . ." by means of a covenant relationship, undertaking to teach his children, to write God's word in his heart, and to realize it in the marketplace. In sum, the Jew undertakes to build the ideal community, step by step, from the ideal nation to the ideal, all-embracing society of mankind.

The precepts of Torah are not only general principles but also detailed laws, designed for the building of a community "according to God's will." However, since our minds are fashioned by the intellectual climate in which we live, the laws of Torah and Talmud cannot be regarded as eternally valid ordinances. They are the collective Jewish responses to the divine call; their content inevitably is formed out of contingent historical material. They are true to the extent that they reflect the covenantal dedication of the Jewish people, but they are human, hence time-conditioned in formulation. Accordingly, we should submit to these laws, as to our personal and collective covenant with God. However, if any one law no longer serves as an adequate channel for our religious feelings, we may disregard it. The criterion is what we come to know and feel when we observe a commandment in holy awe. "What do we know when we do? . . . In the moment of doing, we know no more than the moment itself, but we know it in all the God-human actuality of the law, in which we are called to say, 'blessed are Thou'. . . ."[63]

In contrast to Buber, Rosenzweig stressed the importance of law in Judaism. Each law articulates the fact that Jews are covenanted unto the Lord of the universe. There can be no Jewish piety without submission to the general pattern of the sacred law. We are also expected to serve God with our entire being, which includes our historic consciousness. Thus, specific ordinances may become obsolete for us, but not so the covenant as a whole.

Furthermore, Rosenzweig insisted that his approach sanctified more aspects of life than the rigid code of the Orthodox, for we are called on to respond to God's love by confronting the many challenges of our fast-moving age.

> The circle of what is to be done extends far beyond the circle of duties of the Orthodox. . . . It is just that which Orthodoxy has abandoned that ought to be formed in a Jewish way. . . . Basically, no aspect of life should be abandoned. . . . Everywhere, custom and intention should be treated with equal rank as the law itself.[64]

Thus, in his letter to his future wife, he wrote that he could not regard "eating kosher" with dead seriousness, though he abided by the dietary laws. The essence of religion for him was the remembrance of the impact of "God's lash and His gentle hands upon his life," the "wonders" that happened to him.[65]

"Every acknowledgement of belief has but this one content—him whom I have recognized as the lover in experiencing my being loved—he is. The God of my love is truly God."[66] In language that recalls Buber's central insight, he wrote, "One simply knew that the I and Thou of human discourse is without more ado also the I and Thou between God and man."[67]

Rosenzweig's response to nihilism was firstly an intuition of God's love and secondly a total identification with the life and destiny of the Jewish people, as the people of revelation. A truly religious community is bound to reinforce the Judaic component within Christianity and overcome the resurgence of paganism, which is the source of modern nihilism. These responses to the divine call were, in his view, one and inseparable.

> The rebirth of the Jew . . . is not his personal one, but the transformation of his people for freedom in the divine covenant of revelation. On that occasion the people experienced a second birth, and he in it, not he personally as an individual.[68]

Doubtless, Rosenzweig operated with the notion of the "holy seed" (Isaiah 6: 13). The Jew has been touched by the Divine hand and made uniquely, metaphysically different.

"God withdrew the Jew from this life by arching the bridge of His law high over the current of time, which henceforth and to all eternity rushes powerlessly along under its arches."[69] The eternal people must maintain itself biologically untainted, keeping "the pure spring of blood" from foreign admixtures.[70] This turning inward of Jewish devotion is necessary for the redemption of the world. A Jew does not become part of "the saving remnant" by birth only. "For though he is born a Jew, his 'Jewishness' is something which he too must first live and experience for himself, something which becomes wholly visible in looks and traits only in the aged Jew."[71]

Rosenzweig's racial mystique is as un-Jewish as it is false. Judaism did welcome proselytes in the period of the Mishnah and Talmud. Throughout the early centuries of the medieval era, slaves entered into the Jewish world through conversion and subsequent manumission. Mass conversions also took place, as in the case of the pre-Moslem Yemenite Arabs and the Khazars in southern Russia. Furthermore, there is no reason to believe that an isolationist Judaism, intent on contemplating its own navel, will result in a more Judaic kind of Christianity. There is no evidence to sustain this mystical axiom.

Rosenzweig's historic determinism retained the demonic impetus of Hegelianism. As Hegel saw "absolute religion" in Christianity, Rosenzweig saw it in the loyal remnant of "the eternal people," who stood even now at the goal of history. As Hegel saw in the course of history the unfolding of reason, making use at times of a special "cunning" (List der Vernunft), Rosenzweig recognized a certain obsessive compulsiveness in Jewish history. The virulence of antisemitism was to him proof of the Jews' metaphysical uniqueness.

This people has a unique characteristic which, when one tries to dismiss it through the front door of reason, forces an entrance through the back door of feeling. It is evident in the paroxysms of an Antisemitism that never found madder expression than in the hundred and twenty years during which everyone tried to prove that the Jews were no different from other people.[72] This existence of the Jew constantly subjects Christianity to the idea that it is not attaining the goal, the truth, that it remains ever on the way. That is the profoundest reason for the Christian hatred of the Jew, which is heir to the pagan hatred of the Jew. In the final analysis, it is only self-hate. . . .[73]

Rosenzweig's concept of Christianity as the restless midpoint between paganism and Judaism was common to many Jewish theologians. Max Brod, in a lengthy essay, presented a similar thesis.[74] This thesis is as true and as false as the opposite thesis maintained by many Christian theologians—namely, that Judaism was a temporary stage in the evolution of the human spirit, which persisted into our times as an anachronism or a "fossil." Both views can be given a measure of plausibility by a judicious selection of fragmentary data and self-serving arguments. Actually, within each great historic faith there are numberless variations in respect of rationality, depth of commitment, and intensity of religious feeling. If there is one field of human endeavor that totally resists quantification, it is that of faith.

Rosenzweig was intensely aware of the rising tide of militant paganism in Germany, which attained political form in Nazism, and which stigmatized the Jew as its archenemy. As a historian, he recognized in Hegel's political thought the struggle between the worship of power and the adulation of righteousness. In Spengler's *Decline of the West* he saw a resurgence of the pagan half of Hegelianism, totally unconstrained by Christianity.[75] As a Jew, he was powerless to resist the threatening deluge. He wondered if Christians, taking their faith seriously, could or would withstand the pagan enemy. He sensed the possibility that they might succumb to paganism, though only temporarily. For the Christian way is infinite, leading to the God of Israel.

IX. *Bible Criticism and the Changing Image of the Jew*

It was the peculiar tragedy of Jewish history that even the "scientific" students of the Bible contributed their mite to the rising tide of European antisemitism. This result was an inevitable consequence of the peculiar dialectic of religious progress. Those who advance religious thought to new horizons feel the need to cling tightly to some remnants of their dogmatic heritage. At times they are driven, by an inner compulsion or by outer pressures, to proclaim their traditionalism from the housetops. In their attitude toward Judaism Christian biblical scholars in the modern period were impelled to continue the New Testament theme of "Israel after the spirit" rightfully taking the place of the faithless and rejected "Israel after the flesh." They were, after all, fervent Christians, and the role of the medieval anti-Jewish disputants was natural to them. While Jewish historians sought to rediscover their biblical past as a newly found secular and national treasure, Christian scholars, especially in Germany, sought to justify the theological polemic of the early Christians against the Jews by means of secular and even racist arguments. As if the historic significance of Christianity consisted in its "rejection" of Judaism, rather than in its triumphant conquest of the Greco-Roman world!'

In all western countries, but particularly in Germany, Jewish scholars were compelled to counteract two insistent themes—first, that rabbinic Judaism was an inferior faith, marred by an excess of legalism and distorted by ethnic zealotry; second, that Judaism differed only slightly from the near-eastern polytheistic faiths. The

282

first thesis continued the impetus of the medieval disputations, save that now humanistic and philosophical principles, not consistency with biblical verses, constituted the standard of achievement. The second thesis reflected the growth of Indo-European pride, as against Semites in general, and Jews in particular. Both theses, taken together, were calculated to narrow the range of Jewish achievement in the past and to challenge the proud self-image of modern Jews. If Jewish achievements were problematical even in the field of religion, why should modern Jews strive so hard to maintain their own identity?

As the sense of religious identity weakened during the nineteenth century, European nations began the search for a new racial identity. The discovery of Sanskrit and the recognition of a basic affinity between the so-called "Indo-European" languages led some investigators to the hypothesis of an original "Aryan" race. Friedrich Schlegel suggested that the term Aryan was related to the German word *Ehre*, or honor.

On this pinhead of etymology, inverted pyramids of racial fantasies were erected to minister to the pride of the Germanic race. Since Germanic tribes settled in England, invaded France, Spain, and Italy, and extended into the Scandinavian peninsula, all these nations could share in the pride of being descended from the mythical original race. Yet the French were a mixture of Gauls and Franks; the English of Britons, Latins, and Anglo-Saxons; and the Lombards settled only in the Italian north. It was easiest for the Germans to accept the thesis of Fichte that they alone were an *Urvolk*, a "pure" original race.

This quest of a proud Aryan ancestry poisoned the research of many biblical scholars. The more the originality and majesty of the Hebrew Bible were downgraded, the more the mythical Aryan could be credited with the noblest achievements of the human race. The "non-Aryan" Jews, with their Bible, stood in the way of the exploding pride of the Aryans. So the attacks on the Hebrew Bible converged with attacks on the integrity and honor of the Jewish people, and both movements were impelled by the hunger for a high title of nobility that would derive from nature itself.

Leon Poliakov, concluding his investigation of the Aryan myth, wrote: "The same link exists between the elaboration of the Aryan myth at the beginning of the nineteenth century, when it arraigned the truth of the Biblical genealogies, and its murderous consequences in our own times."[1]

For example, Friedrich Delitsch delivered a lecture in 1902, in the presence of Kaiser Wilhelm II, on the subject "Babel und Bibel," and a year later, responding to critics, he reinforced his thesis in another lecture, which was also attended by the Kaiser. In these addresses the lecturer maintained that the central ideas of the Bible had been proclaimed in ancient Babylonia, where the Semitic Akkadians recast the original mighty culture of the non-Semitic Sumerians. By interpreting the Babylonian practice of associating Marduk with the names of local deities in a monotheistic vein, Delitsch sought to demonstrate that there was hardly a significant boundary between the One God of Israel and Marduk, or between the Babylonian *Shabbatu* and the biblical Sabbath.[2] In his later massive work Delitsch expanded his attack on the Hebrew Bible, garnishing his scholarly exposition with pungent racist gibes.[3]

It is difficult for us today to understand why the Jewish community resented Delitsch's lecture so deeply. This famed Orientalist felt that he was called on to defend the expenditure of large sums of money for archaeological expeditions to the lands of the Fertile Crescent. Therefore, he focused attention on the origin of the Sabbath in the Babylonian *Shabbatu* and on the first seeds of monotheism in ancient law and morality, which later flowered in the books of the Bible. Fundamentalists were, of course, shocked by any suggestion that the institutions and laws of Holy Scripture did not spring complete and at once in one blaze of revelation at Sinai. Delitsch was roundly condemned by the defenders of a literal or verbal revelation among both Protestants and Catholics. Within Judaism, however, Reform or Liberal rabbis were offended by the implied suggestion that Jews did not originate the central religious ideas of western culture— monotheism, the Sabbath, ethics, and law.

To be sure, even Delitsch allowed that the ancient heritage of the Sumerians and Akkadians was transformed, developed, and refined by the biblical authors; yet, the qualities of originality and creativity were of supreme importance in an age that became increasingly infatuated with the dark mystique of racism. Would the stature of "Semites" be lowered by several notches and that of Aryans correspondingly raised, if it could be proved that the Hebrews did not create, but only "transmitted" the great ideas of non-Semitic races? In that case, contemporary racists could cite scientific authority of their claim that Jews, or the Semites of our own day, lacked the genius for creativity and originality. They are effective as "middlemen," disseminating the authentic works of others, but they are incapable of producing anything that is authentically their own.

This ugly echo of ethnic rivalry was somewhat muted in Delitsch's first lecture, but it became more and more pronounced in his rejoinders to critics, in his second lecture, and especially in his later book, in which he virtually accused the various authors of the Bible and, by implication, the Jewish people, of the sin of plagiarism. In the first lecture he stigmatized "Israelite exclusiveness".[4] In the preface to the second lecture he bemoaned the fact that the Hebrew Scriptures still serve today "for the Christian peoples of the West, as a Book of Religion, for morality and for edification! Instead of immersing ourselves in 'thankful wonder' at the providential guidance shown by God in the case of our own people, from the earliest times of primitive Germany until today, we persist in studying the Hebrew Bible—either from ignorance, indifference, or infatuation. . . ."[5]

In his reply to critics Delitsch took note of Jensen, an Assyriologist, who challenged him to provide proof for his contention that the Babylonians anticipated the biblical teaching of monotheism—" . . . we urgently request him, therefore, as soon as possible, to publish, word for word, the passage which robs Israel of its greatest glory, in the brilliancy of which it has hitherto shone—that it alone of all nations succeeded in attaining to a pure monotheism."[6]

Delitsch argued that "Israël is now indeed robbed of this, its greatest glory" on the evidence of a tablet that indicates that Marduk assumed the names of different gods in different places—". . . is not this 'Indo Germanic monotheism, the doctrine of a unity evolving itself out of an original multiplicity?' "[7]

The "Bibel and Babel" controversy signaled the transfer of anti-Jewish animus from the theological domain to that of the biological.

As with the progress of secularism, Jewish identity and pride shifted slowly from the religious to the ethnic aspect of the biblical-talmudic heritage, the German scholars experienced a similar development. However, while Jews found their ethnic and religious inspiration in the same tradition and history, the Germans were torn between the celebration of Teutonism and the continuity of Christian culture, which derived its inspiration from Jerusalem as well as Athens. They were constantly tempted to denigrate the Old Testament and to picture the New Testament as a totally new beginning of an age that became, in the course of time, predominantly Aryan. As the mystique of racism grew, this way of thinking led to the rejection of both western culture and the Christian faith, in the hope of creating a new and pure Aryan *Kultur*.

In the United States the great Egyptologist, James H. Breasted (1865–1935), sought to prove that the ethical principles of the Bible were really originated by the ancient Egyptians.[8] ". . . I found that the Egyptians had possessed a standard of morals far superior to that of the Decalogue over a thousand years before the Decalogue was written."[9]

While the archeological issues of both Assyriology and Egyptology are interesting in themselves, unfortunately their discussion became entangled with the image and character of the Jewish people. The eagerness of antisemites to denigrate the Jewish people and the zeal of Jewish apologetes to vindicate the dignity of their sacred heritage combined to inject the bitterness of ethnic rivalry into the academic atmosphere of these disciplines. Writing in 1948, Solomon Goldman maintained that scholars like Wellhausen and Delitsch "had no little share in the composition of *Mein Kampf.*"[10]

While objectivity is the watch-word of academic research, the impact of the scholar's own religious tradition cannot be denied. Perhaps, the juxtaposition of two mutually challenging traditions, the Jewish and the Christian, can help in keeping the study of religious history on an even keel.

The famous biblical scholar, Daniel Chwolson, called on Christian researchers to recognize that the world-historical mission of Christianity was to transform the pagan world by means of the ethical and religious fervor of Judaism. Indeed, the Christian faith eliminated many social and ethical abuses in the ancient Roman Empire and set a new and hopeful tone to the emergent cultures of the European continent.

In a sense, the primal mission of Christianity is not ended, for we are born pagan, susceptible to the lures of the flesh and the *hubris* of collective arrogance. In every generation, the heathen dragon is killed, only to rise again with redoubled fury in the next epoch. The criticism of the early Christians against the Pharisaic leaders of ancient Judaism is also an ongoing struggle, but one that transpires within each religious community. To serve effectively as a vital, regenerative force within society, a living faith must be perpetually engaged in an unending, uphill struggle for inner purity of motivation, for self-renewal in devotion and love. The Pharisees of the New Testament represent the established functionaries of every religion, who must walk on the razor's edge between the danger of rigid ritualism and the inescapable need for rituals and organized institutions. The anti-Pharisaic history of the Apostolic Church is significant for all religions as an example of the perennial quest for self-renewal, but the historical perspective of both Christian and Jewish scholars is completely distorted when they fail to note that Christianity was the vehicle whereby the world-transforming genius of Judaism became effective within the European world.

Chwolson's counsel was disregarded by the historians as well as by the general public. It was left to Nietzsche, at the time when he saw himself as a resurrected Dionysus, to condemn the anomaly "that today the Christian can cherish Antisemitism without realizing that it [Christianity] is no more than the final consequence of Judaism."[11]

Many were the ways whereby the critical study of Holy Scripture was used to challenge the faith and position of modern Jewry. We shall only point to some illustrative examples:

First, the denigration of Judaism, as being *only* a religion of laws. Preeminent scholars, like Schürer, ransacked the entire treasury of quotations from previous anti-Judaic collections to demonstrate that rabbinic Judaism was nothing but a lifeless body of meaningless rituals. Consider the import of the following summation:

This hope of a future retribution was therefore the mainspring of all zeal for the law. Nay, the entire religious life of the Jewish people during the period of which we are treating just revolved round these two poles: Fulfillment of the law and hope of future glory. . . . As the motives were essentially of an external kind, so also was the result, *an incredible externalizing of the religious and moral life. . . .* The moral life of the individual is a healthy one, only when it is governed by internal motives. Its regulation by external standards is an adulteration of it in its very principle. . . . In a word, ethic and theology were swallowed up in jurisprudence. . . . All this shows that the Lord has only too much reason for rebuking His contemporaries for straining out a gnat and swallowing a camel (Matthew 23:24). . . . we cannot better characterize the entire tendency of the Judaism of that period, than by the words of the apostle, "They have a zeal for God, but not according to knowledge." (Romans 10:2).[12]

Solomon Schechter, the renowned Jewish scholar, characterized "higher criticism" as "higher antisemitism." In his critique of Schürer, he pointed out that legalism in itself is not inevitably unspiritual. The Law was not as cumbersome nor as burdensome as is generally imagined.

Nor can it be proved that legalism or nomism has ever tended to suppress the spiritual side of religion, either in respect of consciousness of sin, or of individual love and devotion. . . . Now, two things are certain: first, that Ezekiel urges the necessity of the "new heart" as well as individual responsibility more keenly than any of his predecessors; secondly, that in Ezekiel, the legalistic tendency is more evident than in Deuteronomy and Jeremiah.

The Sabbath will give a fair example. This day is described by almost every writer in the most gloomy colors, and long lists are given of the minute observances connected with it. . . . But, on the other hand, the Sabbath is celebrated by the very people who did observe it in hundreds of hymns, which would fill volumes, as a day of rest and joy . . . to which such tender names were applied as "the queen Sabbath," "the bride Sabbath," and "the holy, dear, beloved Sabbath."

The legalistic attitude may be summarily described as an attempt to live in accordance with the will of God. But, nevertheless, on the whole, this life never degenerated into religious formalism.

In addition, Schechter pointed to the Psalms and Jewish liturgy generally as evidence of the inwardness and spontaneity of rabbinic piety.[13]

Schechter could have offered the testimony of his own life as proof of the compatibility of scrupulous observance with the freshness and depth of piety. Israel Abrahams, an exponent of Liberal Judaism, stated that legalism could on occasion distort the feelings of piety, but he pointed out that every religious posture was susceptible to perversion. On the whole, the Pharisaic-Rabbinic mode of living was an eminently authentic form of faith. Abrahams, like Schechter, could offer his personal experience as proof of the exhilarating effects of the Law:

> I have lived and in a sense still live, under the Pharisaic Law myself. I have felt its limitations, I have groaned under its lack of sensibility to all that we call aesthetic. I have resented its narrowness, its nationalism, on the one hand, and its claim to the Jews' undivided allegiance on the other. . . . But I have known the Law's manifold joys, its power of hallowing life, its sturdy inculcation of right, its sobriety of discipline, its laudable attempt to associate ritual with heart service, its admission that the spirit giveth life, its refusal to accept that the letter killeth . . .
>
> Many Pharisees undoubtedly held an external view of the Law as something imposed from without, and they regarded themselves as bound to obey it because it was the Law.
>
> . . . But the external view of the Law was not the final statement of the belief of the higher Jewish mind. . . .
>
> I and many Jews with me have no resentment whatever against the general spirit of the criticism to which the Law was subjected by Jesus, against his healthy onslaught against externalism.[14]

A whole generation of Jewish scholars elaborated the arguments of Abrahams and Schechter.[15] They were most ably seconded by the British scholar, Travers Herford, and the renowned American historian of religion, George Foot Moore.

In his epochal study, *The Pharisees,* published in 1924 (an earlier study appeared in 1912), Herford refuted the widespread notion that Christianity continued the prophetic heritage, while the Pharisees abandoned it.

> Between the Prophets and the Pharisees there was no breach whatever. There was a change of method, not of principle. . . . Pharisaism is applied prophecy; and to treat it as the negation or repudiation of the work of the Prophets is to make the largest error of which the case seems to admit. The Pharisees, in relation to the Prophets, "came not to destroy, but to fulfill"; not to depart from a high ideal in order to set up a lower one, but to make a more effective approach to the higher one. . . . Unless it be contended that the practical application of the prophetic teaching to life was a matter of slight importance, it must be allowed that Pharisaism was the direct sequel and necessary completion of the work of the prophets.[16]

Herford focuses the spotlight of attention on the austere ethical core of the Pharisaic way of life. It formed an organic unity of the free conscience, which is the source of morality, and the boundless ardor of self-sacrifice, which is the heart of religion.

> It is not that there was a Jewish religion and, alongside of it, a Jewish morality, but rather that there was, in the Jewish mind, a varied activity of thought, feeling, aspiration, belief, effort of will, all rising out of a deep sense of nearness to God, and recognition of His authority, and that all this together made up what is elsewhere distinguished as religion and morality.[17]

This argument can hardly withstand the criticism that the Pharisees themselves took great care to distinguish between their religion and the requirements of morality, since their religion was binding only on the congregation of Israel, while the moral law was of universal validity. As Abrahams pointed out in Ibn Ezra's commentary, "there were three revelations of God—in nature, in man's conscience and in the Law."[18]

In general, Herford pays scant attention to the ritual laws of "pollution," "holiness," and "sacrifices," which loomed so large in the life of the Jerusalem Pharisees prior to the destruction of the Holy Temple. Nor does he take note of the apparent predicament of the Diaspora Pharisees, who, like Philo, welcomed the philosophic influence of the Hellenic world. Herford regarded Philo as a lonely, isolated figure, whose writings could be considered Jewish only by virtue of two ideas that he shared with the Jews of his day—belief in God and in the Torah.[19]

As Wolfson summarizes the basic posture of the Hellenistic Jewish tradition—"Greek religion was false; Greek philosophy was an inferior form of Judaism. That courage and forthrightness was caught by early Christianity, when it was only a struggling minority in a pagan world, and, with but one slight change in the wording, it repeated the same proclamation—Greek religion was false; Greek philosophy was an inferior form of Christianity."[20]

In the Diaspora the Law was no longer an all-embracing self-evident way of life. Its significance was instrumental and secondary. While Philo argued against those who abandoned the Law, in their belief that its indwelling spirit alone was valid, he wrote with the clear awareness of battling a formidable antagonist. As M. Friedlander put it:

> That the Jews in the Diaspora soon found the national and religious cloak which they had brought away with them from their homeland too tight, and that they commenced to tear it to tatters, is demonstrated by the desperate attempts of their noblest leaders at already an early period to patch up the threadbare garments with new pieces of cloth, and refill the old bottles with new wine.[21]

The fact that Stephen, a Hellenist (Acts 6:5), could be killed by a Jerusalem mob, while the Christian Church under James, brother of Jesus, was left unmolested, demonstrates that the antinomian trend in Christianity was most favored in the Jewish Diaspora. There Jewish dietary laws established an "iron curtain" against commensality and sociability. The feeling of Diaspora Jews that they were living in a perpetual state of ritual pollution could not but engender a sense of remoteness from God.

By far the most effective attempt to refute the traditional Christian image of Jewish piety was that of the Harvard historian, George Foot Moore. In a critical survey of the major Christian polemical writings, he took note of the fact that the two chief themes of late nineteenth century polemics—the "transcendent" character of the Jewish God and the "legalism" of rabbinic piety—were not known in the ancient, medieval, and early modern periods.

Nowhere, so far as I know, is a suggestion made that in this respect the Jewish idea of God differed from the Christian. So it is also with the "legalism" which for the last fifty years has become the very definition and the all-sufficient condemnation of Judaism. It is not a topic of the older polemic; indeed, I do not recall a place where it is even mentioned. Concretely, Jewish observances are censured or ridiculed, but "legalism" as a system of religion, not to say as the essence of Judaism, no one seems to have discovered. This is the more remarkable because this line of attack might seem to have been indicated by Paul, and because the earlier Protestant, and particularly Lutheran controversialists, were peculiarly keen on the point by reason of their conflict with the Catholic Church over works and merit.[22]

In his monumental study *Judaism in the First Centuries of the Christian Era* Moore points to the inner consistency of the Jewish faith as a revealed religion. The Law was the Will of God, articulated in all detail. Being perfect, it was unchangeable. "The rabbinical doctrine could not be better expressed than in Matt. 5:18: 'Until heaven and earth pass away, not the smallest letter, not an apex of a letter, shall pass away from the Law till it all be done.' "[23]

The attitude of Jesus and his immediate followers toward the so called ceremonial law was, as has already been observed, entirely orthodox. Not only does he declare in the most sweeping terms the perpetuity of the whole Law (Matt. 5, 18), but he enjoins obedience to it in ritual details, such as the cleansing of a leper (Matt. 8, 4, Luke 5, 14) and even approves of rabbinical extensions like the tithing of garden herbs. (Matt. 23, 23) That justice and compassion and fidelity are "weightier matters," does not mean that neglect of tithing mint, anise, and cumin is commendable. The disciples in Jerusalem had so little notion of exempting themselves from the ceremonial law that they were slow to admit that Gentile believers could be saved without assuming by circumcision the obligation to keep every article of it.[24]

Moore maintained that the casuistic development of the Law by the Pharisees was a "consequence of a clearer and more consistent notion of what is involved in the possession of a revealed religion. . . . If this is what is meant by the 'legalism' of the Scribes and Pharisees, the name cannot be denied, though another derivative of *lex*, 'loyalty,' would express their conscious attitude better."[25]

Moore also called attention to the fact that, according to Pharisaic doctrine, the children of Israel, including those who joined them, were favored by the protective shield of divine love.

> It should be remarked, further, that "a lot in the World to Come," which is the nearest approximation in rabbinical Judaism to the Pauline and Christian idea of salvation, or eternal life, is ultimately assured to every Israelite on the ground of the original election of the people by the free grace of God, prompted not by its merits, collective or individual, but solely by God's love, a love that began with the Fathers.[26]

While Moore's interpretation of rabbinic Judaism was an excellent corrective to the ingrained prejudice of previous Christian versions, it suffers from the defects of its virtues. In his eagerness to counter the bias of earlier scholars, he presented a narrow band of opinion, styling it "normative Judaism." Consequently, he failed to appreciate the *tension* within Judaism of contrary views, a tension that allowed for a variation of mood and opinion. The coexistence of opposing views within a historic community is likely to engender both an attitude of hospitality to fresh currents of thought and a mood of resolute exclusion of all that is new, with the result that in critical periods groups of uncertain and changing size will range from one extreme to the other. So, depending on the challenges of the hour, the issues of nationalism versus universalism, or inwardness of piety versus legalistic isolationism, may at certain times lead to social cleavages.

Prior to the outbreak of the Great Rebellion, the Shamaiites and Hillelites got along very well; with the increase of patriotic fervor on the eve of the rebellion, their debate turned into a bloody feud.[27] The "legalistic" trend in Judaism was certainly a potent factor at all times, but occasional protests against the excessive sway of casuistry are also recorded.[28] "The All-Merciful seeks man's heart."[29] If the accumulation of so many merits was a widespread motif, so too Rabbi Judah the Patriarch could cry out weepingly, "It is possible for a person to acquire his world in one hour."[30] If the Law was conceived to be "perfect," and "unchanging," there was also the conviction that "the words of Torah are self-generating and self-multiplying." The Book of Jubilees does indeed represent the Torah as a copy of writings on "heavenly tablets," but in the dialectic of the sages, every generation is expected to add to the sacred deposit of tradition.[31] Wisdom derives from God as well as the Law, and the application of logical analysis to the interpretation of Torah results in the vitalization of the Law and its growth. The Lord studies Torah, as it emerges fresh from the mouths of the sages.[32] Furthermore, the greater part of the burden of piety was clearly and specifically acknowledged as "the ordinances of the rabbis."[33] The community was expected to legislate for itself, in keeping with the needs of the hour. If God was transcendent, He was also deemed to be immanent in man's conscience and intelligence.

Finally, if the early Christians were divided in regard to the indispensability of "circumcision" for salvation, an opinion that conversion is effected by baptism without circumcision is also recorded in the Tannaitic tradition.[34] The sages debated whether or not the pious of the nations shared in the "world to come."[35]

Doubtless, the ongoing disputes in the biblical period among priests, prophets, sages, and psalmists generated the creative tension and electric atmosphere of Israelite religion. A similar dynamism accounts for the outbursts of creativity within rabbinic Judaism from time to time. It should also be admitted that in difficult times the anxiety of the Orthodox party to preserve the past might become the decisive factor, resulting in the crushing of the liberal temper. In that case, we note a creeping ossification of rituals, a fearful withdrawal from the intellectual arena, and, in Gilbert Murray's phrase, a "failure of nerve."

The occasional responsiveness of the Law to the socio-economic flow of events was beautifully illustrated by Louis Ginzberg.[36] Since then, many scholars have contributed to our understanding of the development and growth of opinions and institutions in the Second Commonwealth. Solomon Zeitlin and Louis Finkelstein summarized the latest researches in their monumental works.[37]

Recently, Ephraim Urbach, an Israeli scholar, offered the following assessment of Moore's classic:

Moore did not penetrate sufficiently to the essence of the problems under discussion. He did not describe the evolution of the ideas and opinions, as they gradually took shape through struggle and controversy, the dynamism and vitality of spiritual life in the Second Commonwealth, the various tensions between the several parties, sectarian groupings, and the diverse schools among the Sages themselves. The character and position of the Sages was not clarified. The very concept of a "normative Judaism" is untenable, from several vantage points. . . .[38]

We may summarize the entire discussion by calling attention to the richness and diversity of Jewish thought in the age of the Tannaim. Generally, Christian authors interpreted the character of Judaism by making use largely of apocalyptic literature. This procedure was erroneous. However, it is equally wrong to exclude Philo and Hellenistic and apocalyptic works from consideration; non-canonical books were not classed as heretical, though the sages prohibited public lectures on them. The Apocalyptic writers constituted an esoteric group, but such groups frequently enjoyed wide popular acclaim. As Louis Ginzberg put it:

The apocalyptic writings by their fixed literary forms and their obscurities were not meant for the people, but for the initiated ones. The true mirror of the religious life of the Jew we find therefore in the homely and simple sayings of the teaching of the rabbis and not in the literary productions of the Apocalyptic writers who wrote primarily for a class of men like themselves, and not for the people.[39]

Moore's remark that the search for the "essence" of religion on the part of Christian scholars was the cause of their condemnation of Jewish legalism can be abundantly illustrated. As the range of authentic Christian belief was narrowed down by modern criticism to the luminous core of a few ethical-spiritual affirmations, the momentum of Christian tradition dictated that the Jew be represented as the dark background for this illumination. If Jesus was no longer the Savior in a mythological sense, he could still be worshiped as the exemplary personality. In that case, the Jews of his day who rejected him, and by extension the Jews of all generations, would be described as the champions of moral darkness—willful opponents of all that is noble and true. In effect, the narrative plot for the life of Jesus, as construed by "modernist" and "critical" historians, transferred the Jewish-Christian argument from the dogmatic to the ethical-spiritual plane. It was not that the Jews refused to accept Jesus as the Man-God or as the Messiah that mattered, it was their obduracy and deafness to his humanistic, spiritual message. The more glorious the personality of Jesus, the blacker and baser his Jewish antagonists must have been—they barricaded themselves behind the barriers of the Law in order to keep their God-given treasure from being shared by the Gentiles.

This line of reasoning was pursued again and again by successive generations of Christian scholars, with the counterarguments of Jewish historians being scarcely heeded.

M. Güdemann, writing in the first decade of our century, noted sadly, "It is the scientific Christian theology of our day, which in many ways disseminates an ideology that calls for our defense." In their endeavor to hold on to a presumed vital core of Christianity—its religious humanism—they are impelled to depict Jews as enemies of the humanist ideal. "It is the fashion nowadays to speak of the 'essence' of a religion."[40]

Presumably the Christian essence is contained in the Hebrew Scriptures, but somehow that essence was appreciated by only a few so-called "Christians before Christ."

Julius Wellhausen wrote, "The choking effect of the Law was effected gradually. . . . Until Pharisaism, the free impulses of the prophets retained their vital power, which flowed from the prophets; the older Judaism is the preliminary of Christianity."[41] "Out of originally pagan material, the armor of monotheism was forged," Wellhausen wrote, adding that by the time of the Pharisees there resulted "a true idolatry of the Law," which "removed the soul of religion." It seemed natural to distort the ideal of lawfulness into a petrified legalistic piety and to interpret the casuistry of a law-oriented faith as "a religion of business."[42]

Güdemann demonstrated in rebuttal that "the bearer of monotheism in Israel was the people, and it did so despite all storms."[43] The words of the prophets were treasured by the people—otherwise, they would not have been preserved. Pharisaism, far from being anti-prophetic, was actually an attempt to apply the prophetic ideals to the regulation of the lives of the pious.

The Pharisees, we recognize today, took seriously the words of Torah, the injunctions of the Prophets, and the poetry of the Psalmists. But how do you apply the teachings of revelation to constantly changing life situations? Two alternatives come to mind. Either you try to get at the inner principle of a Torah-itic or prophetic injunction, or you develop hermeneutic devices whereby the letters of the sacred law yield additional teaching. Both ways are forms of "taking seriously" the divine word—the one following the *spirit*, the other following the *letter* of Scripture. They are not mutually exclusive, nor are their conclusions always different. Both procedures were followed within the Pharisaic movement—the "spiritual" one in the school of Rabbi Ishmael, the "letter-bound" one in the school of Rabbi Akiva. Both schools flourished in the first decades of the second century.[44] We may confidently assume that the two schools continued earlier trends, which may well go back to the interpreters of the Law in the time of Ezra.

M. Güdemann maintained that up to the time of Rabbi Akiva, the Haggadic preachers felt free to ignore the letters of Scripture in order to reveal its deeper meaning. The *Tannaim* of the first and second centuries agreed that "the letter killeth but the spirit giveth life" (2 Corinthians 3:6). They could not otherwise have justified the innovations they introduced into Jewish life. "We have seen that the Tannaim and Amoraim used, as it were, to play ball with the letter of the Bible for the sake of the spirit, and I may here recall the *Haggadah* above referred to, that at the breaking of the Tablets of the Covenant the letters flew into the air. What can this *Haggadah* mean, if any meaning is to be assigned to it at all, but that it is not the letter of the Bible but the spirit that is of value?" Güdemann concludes that the veneration of the letters and their "crowns" was introduced by Rabbi Akiva in order to guard the spirit of the Jewish tradition against the radicalism of Pauline hermeneutics. The letters were sanctified, "for the spirit's sake, against the spirit emphasized by Paul."[45]

Observing the profusion of Talmudic and Midrashic material as an outsider, Wellhausen saw the contribution of Jesus in his repudiation of the legalistic shell of Judaism. "The originality of Jesus consists

precisely in that he removed and emphasized most effectively the true
and the eternal elements out of the chaotic wasteland. How near and
how far he was to Judaism is shown in the contrast between Mark
12:28–34 and the Book of Esther."[46]

Mark 12:28–34 presents Jesus as instructing a young man that the
essence of Judaism consists in the love of God and the love of one's
neighbor. The questioner is duly impressed, since the answer of Jesus
fell within a well-defined tradition. Among the formulations of the
essence of Torah in rabbinic literature, we find the following:

(1) " 'Whatever is hateful unto you, do not do unto others'—This is the
substance of the whole Torah. The rest is commentary, go and learn."
(Shabbat 30a.)

(2) "Which is the small statement that contains all the essentials of Torah?
'In all thy ways, know Him, and He will direct your paths.' " (Berochot
63a.)

(3) "In the image of God, made He him—This is the great rule of Torah."
("Torat Kohanim," Kedoshim, 19)

(4) "Only two commandments were given by God to the Israelites—'I am
the Lord. . .' and 'Thou shalt have no other gods beside Me'—all the
others were spoken by Moses." (Makkot 23a.)

(5) " 'Be ye holy, for I am holy'—most of the principles are here
embraced." (Sifra, Kedoshim, 1)

(6) " 'After the Lord, your God, ye shall walk'—as He is merciful, so be ye
merciful; as He is steadfastly gracious, so shall ye be. . . ." (Shabbat
133b.)

The Book of Esther is presented as a historical episode—the first
instance of antisemitism—not as a body of teaching.

Josephus, writing in the latter decades of the first century, found
that the Law of Judaism had permeated the Mediterranean world.
With deep anger and biting scorn, Tacitus confirmed this fact. The
ancient world was used to the abundance of laws and customs in the
life of religion, and Jewish institutions, especially the Sabbath, were
more revered than the doctrine of One God. The modern Protestant
critics, especially the Lutheran historians, however, regarded the Law
with the mingled hate and contempt of a Marcionite Gnostic. Thus,
Edouard Meyer wrote:

Circumcision, hallowing of Sabbath-day, rejection of pork and similar strange practices governing food, and basic withdrawal from and contempt for non-Jews, which the latter heartily reciprocated—these are the characteristics of Judaism in the time of Antiochus, Epiphanes, of Tacitus and Juvenal, as at present.

But is it necessarily true that withdrawal from outsiders implies contempt for them, especially if the purpose of this isolation is to be a "light unto the nations"? The renowned historian went further, maintaining that legalism was the very soul of Judaism and external rituals its sole substance:

"This is in general the essence of Judaism; the noblest and the most repulsive thoughts, the sublime and the base lie close together, united inseparably, one the reverse of the other."[47] In this judgment, Meyer disregarded the facts previously detailed, which showed that the rabbis clearly distinguished between general revelation to mankind and specific laws that only Jews are obliged to respect.

Joseph Ernest Renan (1823–1892), the humanist philosopher and historian, opposed and, at times, fought against the antisemites of his day. Yet, as a historian, he set out to interpret the "Life of Jesus" as that of a noble rebel battling against a desiccated Jewish orthodoxy. He described Jesus as an exponent of "the religion of the heart," miscast among uncomprehending fanatics and ethnic zealots. Furthermore, he suggested, the Semitic mentality was incapable of appreciating the noble teachings of Jesus.

Far from condoning the myths and passions of antisemitism, Renan described with deep feeling the pathos and grandeur of ancient Jewish history.

Israel became, in fact and by eminence, the people of God, while the pagan religions around were more and more restricted—in Persia and Babylonia, to an official charlatanism; in Egypt and Syria, to a vain show. That which the Christian martyrs did in the first centuries of our era—which the victims of persecuting orthodoxy, in the very heart of Christianity, have done up to our time—the Jews did during the two centuries which preceded the Christian era. They were a living protest against superstition and

religious materialism. A wonderful activity of ideas, leading to the most
opposite results, made of them at this period a people, the most striking
and original in the world.[48]

In Renan's view, the Semitic race attained its climax in the faith
and culture of the Bible, but with the creation of monotheism, the
Semites shot their bolt, leaving the stage of history to the Aryans.
"Once this mission [monotheism] was accomplished, the Semitic race
rapidly declined and left it to the Aryan race alone to lead the march
of human destiny."[49] Needless to say, other races did not count at all.

Renan called attention to the tensions within the Jewish soul,
concluding that the good qualities of Judaism were absorbed in the
Christian heritage. Distinguishing between the landscapes of Galilee
and Judea, he wrote:

> Every nation called to high destinies, must form a complete little world,
> including within itself the opposite poles. . . . Complete absence of feeling
> for Nature, almost amounting to something dry, narrow and even
> ferocious, has stamped upon all that Jerusalem alone effected, a character
> grand indeed, but sad, arid and repulsive. . . . It is the North which made
> Christianity: Jerusalem, on the contrary, is the true home of the obstinate
> Judaism which, founded by the Pharisees and fixed by the Talmud, has
> traversed the Middle Ages and come down to us.[50]

Renan's contempt for Pharisaic learning was affected by his
disdain for the old-line Catholic. "The science of the Jewish doctor—
the *Sofer*, or scribe, was purely barbarous, utterly absurd, and
without a spark of moral life."[51]

Conversely, Renan exaggerated the modernity of Jesus. He argued
that, while Jesus might have looked on himself as the Messiah, he was
principally concerned with "the Kingdom of God in the heart."[52]
With dubious evidence, he inferred that Jesus opposed the sacrificial
system, adding, "From this moment he is no longer a Jewish
reformer; he shows himself a destroyer of Judaism itself."[53] "Pride of
blood appears to him the chief enemy he has to combat. In other
words, Jesus is no longer a Jew."[54]

Fantastic is the ingenuity of the human mind! The Pharisees who
are accused by Jesus of traversing the earth to make a single proselyte

(Matthew 23:15) are condemned by Renan for "the pride of blood," while Jesus, who warned his followers against preaching to the Gentiles, is extolled as an antiracist. In spite of his anticlericalism and liberalism, Renan coopts Jesus in the company of those who scorn the Jewish people. "That Nessus-shirt of ridicule which the Jew, son of the Pharisees, has dragged in tatters after him these eighteen centuries, was woven by Jesus with supreme skill."[55]

The denigration of the Jewish people as a consequence of the exaltation of Jesus came naturally to European liberals. As culture advances, it appears altogether right and proper for the great teachers of the age to maintain intact the historical nerve centers of ethics and religion, while reinterpreting the myths and symbols that are associated with them. Every Christian generation might be expected to reinterpret the life of Jesus in keeping with its own highest ideals; but, we may ask, why must Christian scholars continue to portray the Jews as the foil and contrast to the luminous figure of the Savior? Jews also change. Certainly the Jews of Renan's time were far more likely than not to agree with his summation of the message of Jesus' life: "The religion of humanity is thus established, not upon blood, but upon the heart."[56]

The Reform movement of Geiger, Holdheim, and Hermann Cohen agreed with Renan on the need of overcoming the stranglehold of national loyalties. They venerated the universalistic aspects of the Jewish tradition and the ethics of the prophets. They resented, not the heroic ethic of early Christianity, but its mysticism, its demonism, and its rejection of rationality.

However, the upsurge of Jewish nationalism in the twentieth century led nationalistic historians to revise the Reform view of the Jewish rejection of Jesus. Since the essence of Judaism was not religious, but ethnic, according to the nationalists, the fateful deviation of Jesus had to be seen as one that the healthy national instinct of Jews had spurned. Secular Jewish historians felt it their duty to justify the historic repudiation of Jesus by their people in modern terms. A'had Ha'am, Joseph Klausner, and Simon Dubnow, maintained that Jesus was repudiated by the sages because of his individualistic, antinationalistic teachings.

Here, then, we see exemplified the paradox of "idealization."

Christian liberals would describe Jesus as the great humanist, while Jewish liberals would see him as an ethnic enthusiast. Jewish nationalists would agree with Christian liberals that Jesus was a universalistic teacher of the religion of the heart. When the mystique of Teutonism gripped the minds of many Germans, popular mythologists such as H. S. Chamberlain hastened to depict Jesus as the great Aryan prophet.

To complete the picture, we need to recall that Renan endeavored, in his later years, to present an appreciative picture of both ancient and modern Judaism. In a famous address he pointed out that the essence of Christianity was preached by the great Hebrew prophets. "The true founders of Christianity are those great prophets. . . ."[57] The tragic separation between the two branches of the faith occurred gradually, "chiefly through the influence of Gnostic doctrines . . ."[58]

As to the present: "Every Jew is a liberal. He is so according to his inner being. On the other hand, if you examine the enemies of Judaism, you find that they are in general enemies of the modern spirit."[59] Looking to the future, Renan asserted: "In one word, the purest religion that we can apprehend, the one capable of unifying all mankind will be the realization of the religion of Isaiah, that ideally Jewish faith, which is free from all admixtures of dross."

At this point we cite a contemporary Christian view, that of F. C. Grant, which reinforces Renan's final judgment: "It is the separation of Christian ethics from their natural background in the Old Testament, their true realm of presupposition in ancient Judaism, which has done the greatest harm to their interpretation at the present time."[60]

Grant affirms as a Christian that "our own sacred book is distorted and our own religious life is deformed, in the interest of maintaining a theological principle, namely, the 'rejection' of the Jew and the divine condemnation of 'moralism' and 'legalism!' "[61] He maintains that it was precisely the loose and unprincipled syncretism of the pagans in the Roman Empire that accounts for the Jewish effort to resist the drift toward formlessness by way of raising barriers of law to protect the integrity of biblical monotheism.[62] Christianity was initially, and long continued to be, a Jewish movement.

"We may go even further and describe the theology of the New

Testament in its main outlines as a Jewish theology in transition—a theology which was basically Pharisaic."[63]

Leon Poliakov sums up the role of Renan as follows: "As a propagandist for the Aryan myth, Renan deserves to be placed side by side with Max Muller. . . . The warnings which both of them issued after 1870–71 against seeking political advantages from the confusion between languages and races . . . had little effect."

Perhaps the most renowned of all attempts to expound the essence of Christianity was the series of lectures by Adolf Harnack on this theme.[64]

A preeminent church historian and theologian, Harnack interpreted the essence of Christianity in humanistic and rationalistic terms. It consists of three essential principles:

First, the Kingdom of God as a living reality, which enters man's soul, seizing hold of it: "This Kingdom which comes to the humble and makes them new men and joyful, is the key that first unlocks the meaning and the aim of life. . . . It is a supernatural element alone that ever enables us to get at the meaning of life; for natural existence ends in death."[65]

Second, the feeling of God's Fatherhood, experienced as a reassurance that entails a commitment to live as His child: "Religion gives us only a single experience, but one which presents the world in a new light."[66]

Third, the task of a "higher righteousness"—that is, to focus on the ethical challenge of the moment: ". . . the love of one's neighbor is the only practical proof on earth of that love of God which is strong in humility."[67]

These principles are clearly not in conflict with the teachings of Judaism. As a Jewish scholar, Felix Perles, pointed out, "Indeed, Harnack's work is, without the author's desire or intention, the most brilliant justification that could possibly be desired."[68]

Harnack eliminated "the Christology, the whole doctrine of the trinity, hereditary sin, the bodily resurrection of Christ, the so called truths of salvation . . ." In consequence, "not much more than Judaism remains."[69]

In truth, Harnack demythologized the notion of a "Son of God."

"Jesus is convinced that he knows God in a way in which no one ever knew him before, and he knows that it is his vocation to communicate this knowledge of God to others by word and deed— and with it the knowledge that men are all God's children."[70] In brief, "the Gospel, as Jesus proclaimed, has to do with the Father only and not with the Son."[71] Harnack disavowed both the dogmatism that afflicted Catholic Christianity and its exclusiveness—"The Gospel nowhere says that God's mercy is limited to Jesus' mission."[72] He also appreciated the spiritual import of Jewish history—"the profoundest and maturest history that any nation ever possessed, nay, as the future was to show, the true religious history of mankind."[73]

At the same time, Harnack insisted on the centrality of Jesus in the religious progress of mankind. "Words effect nothing; it is the power of personality that stands behind them."[74] When Jewish scholars say "What do you want with your Christ?" his answer is that Jesus purified the faith from all the dross with which it was previously associated. "They [the Pharisees] spoke excellently; the words might have come out of Jesus' mouth. But what was the result of their language? That the nation and in particular their own pupils condemned the man who took the words seriously."[75]

In Harnack's view, the break with Judaism was needed in order to prevent a return to the old laws.[76] Catholicism, with its sacraments and its hierarchy, and Greek Orthodoxy were regressions. "It was to destroy this sort of religion that Jesus Christ suffered himself to be nailed to the cross. . . . Catholics subjected their souls to the despotic orders of the Roman papal King."[77]

Harnack's Protestantism was not untouched by Germanic pride, although he warned of "the risk of Protestantism becoming a sorry double of Catholicism."[78]

"From the time that the Germans endeavored to make themselves really at home in the religion handed down to them— this did not take place until the thirteenth century onwards—they were preparing the way for the Reformation. . . . So the Christianity of the Reformation may be described as German, in spite of Calvin."[79]

There was much in Harnack's theology that modern Jews could applaud. After all, he came as close to Judaism as a theologian could and still call himself a Christian. Yet, at the turn of the century, his position seemed more challenging to Jewish leaders than did that of orthodox Christians. Laboring under the weight of unrelenting pressure to give up their millennial struggle for survival, Jews were particularly tempted by a version of Christian faith that was intellectually unexceptionable. Harnack's Christian status was itself marginal. He had been condemned by the Pastoral Conference in Berlin. Still, he appeared to foreshadow "the wave of the future." How, then should Jewish scholars react to the challenge of those "enlightened" Christians, who shared their own basic principles, while insisting that Judaism was anachronistic and lifeless?

Strange as it may seem, there was no lack of *odium theologicum*, when the two faiths came so close as to preempt virtually the same humanistic position. In part this bitterness was owing to the different interpretations of the past. In large measure it was owing to the explicit demands of German nationalists for Jews to give up their historic identity and dissolve completely within the German nation.

Felix Perles acknowledged the closeness of Harnack to the theological position of Judaism. Harnack excluded from Christianity "those very elements" which Jews had stubbornly rejected. In fact, "not much more than Judaism remains."[80]

To be sure, Harnack expressed "antipathy to Judaism," underrating the Old Testament, and ignoring the evolution of Judaism in the past eighteen centuries. However, Harnack's condemnation of Jewish ethnicism and legalism was thoroughly in line with the arguments of Reform Judaism. Some of Harnack's strictures, Perles felt, were merely *pro forma*, "as if Christianity could be saved by belittling Judaism," but, essentially, Harnack had provided "the most brilliant justification of Judaism that could possibly be desired."[81]

By stripping Christianity of its mythological outer garment, Harnack provided ample justification for those Jews who wanted to baptize their children in order to save them from the impending threats of antisemitism.

From time to time liberal Jews were challenged by well-meaning German historians to draw the logical consequences of their own faith and embrace a liberal version of Christianity. In 1907 Theodor Noldeke caused a stir by challenging the right of liberal Judaism to exist, since the persistence of Jewish people as an alien element thrust within the body of the German nation was a source of anguish for all concerned. He concluded that Judaism had no longer the right to exist as a separate entity, "in the face of modern education"—in other words, the cultured world had caught up with the cultured Jew.

In reply, the famed philosopher Hermann Cohen declared: "One cannot demand public morality at the cost of private, nor love mankind at the cost of the fatherland, nor help the religion of mankind by wronging one's own religion."[82] Furthermore, "the unique God possesses no commonality with Christ, since He is Himself and Alone the Savior. No matter how the conception of Christian salvation is 'idealized,' there remains an ineradicable opposition to the Jewish idea of God."[83] Both Judaism and Christianity are historical faiths, and the modern spirit is deeply conscious of continuities in the flow of history. "*In our religion, we love our historical honor, the honor of our historical personality.*"[84] "Our religion is *our* religion. It is our right and our honor. Our love of it is love of our historical-ethical personality."[85]

In general, Jewish scholars maintained that Judaism is compatible with every form of "humane nationalism." H. Steinthal went on to claim that the Jewish doctrine of a chosen people is intended to point the way to all nations, calling on them to direct their ethnic sympathies toward the building of the universal society. Our Jewish vocation is that of all men, and German loyalty is also crowned by a humanist dimension. "There is no contradiction between being German, being Jewish and being human. . . . We are Germans because it is impossible for us not to be Germans." Our Jewishness, Steinthal continued, is no longer national, but religious. "We are no longer a Jewish folk." And the prophetic interpretation of the chosen people impels us to combat "the kind of patriotism which contradicts the claims of humanity and demands the exclusion of all that is foreign."[86]

In the western world generally, and in Germany in particular, the modern Jew was menaced by the two horns of a dilemma. If he clung to the Law, he was hoisted on the old Christian condemnation of legalism, which is incompatible with "true inwardness" and "free grace." If in keeping with the Liberal philosophy he abandoned the shell of the Law altogether in theory and partially in practice, without deserting his historical faith-community, he was taunted by the charge of vestigial ethnicism. Very few German nationalists and liberals were prepared to accept a separate Jewish communal identity as a permanent feature of their national *Kultur*. The new Bible scholars retrojected the "stubbornness" of Jewish survivalism into the first century, interpreting as "typically Jewish" every instance of resistance to the advance of the human spirit toward spiritual depth and an emergent international society. By the same token, the noble insights of the Hebrew Scriptures were described as the building blocks of Christianity. So, Gunkel referred to Psalm 103 as "a piece of New Testament in the Old Testament."[87]

Perhaps the best illustration of the use of meticulous scholarship in a polemical distortion of the Jewish-Christian dialogue is the monumental work, "Kommentar zum Neuen Testament aus Talmud und Midrash," by Hermann L. Strack and Paul Billerbeck. The authors hardly exaggerated when in their preface they spoke of their massive achievement as proof "of the vitality of German science." Nor can they be fairly accused of antisemitism, since they clearly warned against the possible misuse of their negative judgments of Talmudic ethics by the hatemongers of their day. Yet, in the feverish atmosphere of Europe between the wars a genuine Jewish-Christian dialogue was impossible, and even works of painstaking research were impregnated with the acids of contempt. For this reason, an international concourse of scholars has now undertaken to cover the same ground afresh, in keeping with the postwar ecumenical spirit.

One theme that runs through this vast commentary is that Judaism is a self-redeeming religion. "The old-Jewish religion is accordingly a religion of the most complete self-redemption."[88]

There is nothing blameworthy in this description, if the authors had merely pointed to the Jewish belief in free will and the rejection by the sages of the doctrine of "original sin," in its extreme form. Said Rabbi Akiva, "All is foreseen, but choice is allowed" (Ethics of the Fathers III, 19). Yes, it is possible for man to distinguish between good and evil, life and death, and to choose the "way" of God, that is true "life." God, in His goodness, is certain to reinforce man's determination to shun evil. "He who seeks purity will be helped from above"[89] But the authors take pains to exaggerate this notion to mean the magical self-sufficiency of the Talmud-trained Jew. He need no longer yearn for inner purity and for "the nearness of God." He did not have to walk humbly with the Lord, since he had the *mizvot* of the Torah at his disposal by means of which he could assure himself of his place in paradise. Indeed, his heavenly reward was virtually automatic, fixed, and calculable. As if the *mizvot* of Judaism were so many mechanical or rather magical devices, which every Jew could manipulate to his own advantage! The picture that emerges from this vast compendium is of a soulless worship of the letter of the Law.

As if pious Jews did not pray three times daily for the wisdom, holiness, healing, and forgiveness that come only from God! As if the infinite dimension of "the duties of the heart" of Bahya Ibn Pakuda was really alien to the souls of Jewish people!

The authors were able to arrive at so fantastic a distortion of ancient Jewish piety, because in their eagerness to dramatize the novelty of Jesus' preaching, they picked and chose some passages as truly expressive of the Jewish soul, while they rejected other passages as unrepresentative or purely "ornamental." Altogether, they juggled rabbinic lore at will, without any attempt to empathize with the people whose literature they dissected. They did not seek to "understand in love."

Referring to the many calls in rabbinic literature for the right intention of the worshipper and for the service of God "in love and fear," the authors wrote:

> But these requirements and maxims remained without any penetrating success: they have neither shattered the opinion that the literal fulfillment of God's Will, that is the Law, was all-sufficient, nor could they modify the basis for the soteriology that grew out of legal faithfulness. Those utterances are like decorations and ornaments that are put on the outside of the nomistic structure of teaching; the nomistic soteriology remained untouched by it.[90]

Commenting on the parable of the workers in the vineyard

(Matthew 20:1–16), the authors contrast it with a beautiful legend in the Talmud about an old couple who suffered severely from poverty. The aged woman was no longer able to bear the pangs of hunger, so she asked her husband who was reputed to be a saint to have some of their treasure in heaven transferred to this world. The old saint yielded to the entreaties of his wife and, sure enough, a big bar of gold came down from heaven. But very soon the pious couple bethought themselves that that bar was part of their heavenly furniture which they would be certain to miss in the world to come. They decided that eternity is more important than mortal life, and they begged God to take back the gold.[91] Manifestly, this legend was told as a parable, like the parable of Lazarus (Luke 16:19–31), in which the saints and the sinners watch each other across an impassable abyss.

While Strack-Billerbeck recognized metaphors in the New Testament, they insisted on a literal reading of Talmudic legends. Obviously, this legend teaches contentment in this world and the principle that good deeds will not go unrewarded. The authors condemned this tale severely, as follows: "This was the curse of the reward-sickness of Israel that it even stained the bliss of heaven . . ."[92]

One need not take offense at the insistence of the authors that when we find similar statements in the Talmud and the New Testament, we must conclude that Jesus was the "original" source.[93] But, when the authors contrast starkly the Jewish "justification through one's own earning" and the Christian "justification through grace," we should pause and reflect that the ardor of polemics tears asunder two aspects of living piety. There are a number of rabbinic maxims that teach that all our blessings are owing to God's free graciousness, not to our merit. However, there is room for scholarly differences of interpretation. We can speak of differences in emphasis, or of a spectrum of colors shading into one another and of different positions within this spectrum. After all, we are not dealing here with an "either-or" situation.

Did Christianity, taken as a whole, refrain from teaching the importance of good deeds in the sight of God? Did it spurn the notion that the just and good God rewards the righteous? Did not the Catholic Church weigh and measure sins and atonements with casuistic exactitude, far beyond any parallel in Talmud or Midrash? In our momentary intimations of the divine, call them what you will, we apprehend the divine *yea* as well as its *nay*. The *yea* is an assurance of being accepted, "chosen," or "covenanted"; hence also the feeling that we can seek and find His nearness. He has taken the initiative. The *nay* is the awareness of our sinfulness, our frailty, our ignorance, our nothingness in comparison with the infinite task set before us— we are "lost," only God can save us. But, there is no assurance without its corresponding negation, and no "sinfulness" without the certainty of grace.

As I have explained elsewhere, Judaism and Christianity, having grown out of the same stem, are "mutually challenging, not mutually contradictory."[94]

The major failing of Christian teachers vis-a-vis the faith of Jewish people was the tendency to view the Jews of their own time and place, as if they were identical counterparts of the people who "rejected" Jesus and caused him to be crucified. At this point we are not concerned with the theological doctrine of "deicide" and its continuance within the Catholic Church down to Vatican II, but with the psychological quirk of some modern Protestant theologians and scholars. Since Talmud and Midrash form part of the sacred literature of Judaism, even progressive Protestant scholars were prone to think that Jews remained of one mind all through the centuries, as if they were lifeless "fossils." In regard to their own faith, they realized that patristic literature did not afford an adequate description of contemporary Christianity and that even so-called "orthodox" believers keep on growing imperceptibly, despite their protestations of standing still. In regard to the Jews, they imagined that even modern Jews, of all persuasions, were driven by the "hatred" of Jesus, which they presumed to find in the New Testament.

Such beliefs were sustained by the ancient "Palestinian" formula of the twelfth benediction, which implored God not to favor the "Nazarenes." This version of the "curse of heretics" (Birkat Haminim) was rediscovered by Professor Schechter in the Cairo

Genizah.[95] No such curse, not even a distant approximation of it, is found in the liturgy of European Jews, which derived from the original "Babylonian" version. Similarly, the rabbis of Europe interpreted the folkloristic references in the Talmud to a certain Jesus, "who bewitched, seduced and misled" the people, as having reference to a person who lived a century or more before the common era.[96] In a word, with a few exceptions Orthodox Jews ignored Jesus altogether, concerning themselves only with their own duties and destiny. On the other hand, philosophers like Maimonides, who reflected on the course of world history, conceded that Christianity fulfilled a divine mission in preparing the world for the messianic era of the future, "when the Lord will be one and His Name One."[97]

Because one stereotype sufficed for all Jews of all ages and places, the various studies of the career of Jesus tended to portray the Jews as inimical to all the virtues and ideals that the Savior represented to Christians. Even theologians could not free themselves altogether from the tendency to see the Jews of their day as "Christ-killers." Thus, in 1871 the *Oberkirchenrat* of Berlin, the highest authority of the Prussian Evangelical Church, issued a statement condemning those who converted to Judaism "for their joining a community that rejected the Son of God in his lifetime and continued to hate him to this day."[98]

While the work of Strack-Billerbeck was not free of "odium theologicum," it did help to set the record straight insofar as vulgar accusations against the Talmud were concerned—accusations that cropped up periodically in the modern world. Apart from its alleged legalism, "externalism," and preoccupation with trivia, the Talmud was described at times as teaching Jews to take undue advantage of Gentiles, spurn all friendly advances of non-Jews, and generally nourish the millennial hatred, which the Romans described as "odium generis humani."

Jewish apologists were kept busy defending the Talmud, but not always convincingly, since they could not deny the accuracy of certain quotations, which appeared to sustain the charges of the antisemites, when they were cited out of context.

The rise of the Reform-Conservative body of scholars made possible a reasonable, historical approach to the evaluation of such Talmudic-Midrashic teaching. It runs as follows:

1. These ancient writings frequently reflect the bitter rivalries of their day. The Jewish-pagan civil wars, accompanying the rebellions of 65–70, 111–115, 131–135, were brutal and wide-ranging, leaving a heritage of bitterness that seeped into the academies. On the whole, it is amazing that the pure and generous spirit of the sages remained unbroken by the bloody vicissitudes in the first two centuries of our era.

2. The two Talmuds were not edited, in the modern sense of the word. They were left more or less in their present form when, due to a series of disasters, the academies were closed, around 350 C.E. in Palestine and 500 C.E. in Babylonia. So, there is some disarray in the two monumental collections; some marginal notes, even jokes and tongue-in-cheek "wisecracks" reflecting the antics of individuals, were included in the body of the work. This fact was noted by Jewish scholars in the twelfth century. At times, such insertions can be easily documented.[99]

In any case, the medieval Talmudists encountered no difficulty in sifting the wheat from the chaff. They applied the bitter condemnations of "nations" in the Talmud to ancient heathens and ranked the Christians and Moslems of their day in the category of the "pious among the nations."

3. The spirit of the Talmud is best summed up by Maimonides— "As to your question regarding the nations [of our day], know that the 'All Merciful seeks the heart,' and things depend on one's intention. Therefore, our true Sages said, 'the pious among the nations share in the World to Come,' if they understand the Creator and order their lives in keeping with ethical standards and human wisdom. . . ."[100]

Shmuel Ettinger summed up the state of the Jewish-Christian dialogue in the latter decades of the nineteenth century as follows: "It is precisely those who were loyal to the old Christian tradition, who could set aside for the Jews an enclave where they could remain a group apart, but the radical liberals could accept them fully within their own society only as individuals—a minority that is absolutely removed from its religious and historic roots."[101]

In an age of rising national fervor, liberal Jews could defend their separateness from liberal Christians in three ways: They could insist on the rightness of a pluralistic state, which does not eliminate the diverse heritages of its minority nationalities; they could maintain that the "external" signs of the Jewish faith were expressions of its religious life, containing no admixtures of ethnicism; they could endow the historic role of the Jewish people with a special and unique radiance, which exempted it from the proper fate of other ethnic minorities. In practice, all three apologetic policies were pursued with varying degrees of emphasis.

The third alternative amounts to staking out a claim for a central and unique cosmic status that no outsider is likely to grant to another people. It is actually a new version of Balaam's exclamation— "Behold, here is a people that dwells alone, and is not counted among the nations." (Numbers 23:9) Whenever the Gentiles did apply the notion of metaphysical uniqueness to the Jewish people of their day, they did so with a peculiar twist, identifying uniqueness with the demonic as well as with the divine. We need only recall the medieval taunt, "the Witnesses of God." Still, even modern Jewish thinkers could not resist the appeal of a unique cosmic status, which lifted their people above the ambiguities of history. Solomon Formstecher wrote, "Israel has suffered and endured steadfastly for the love of mankind, in order to lead it toward perfection and bliss. Thus, Israel has symbolized the living Messiah, as the prophets foresaw and foretold it."[102]

Franz Rosenzweig took up the same theme, maintaining that the Jewish people is the unfailing fountainhead of Christian zeal to convert the world. The Jew is like the sun, cherishing its own luminosity, in and for itself, while the Christian is like the life-giving rays of the sun, which traverse the infinity of space. However, the world-conquering and all-illuminating rays are powerless without the sun itself. Rosenzweig ignored the fact that Judaism did convert large numbers of people, long after the emergence of Christianity, such as the Himyarite Arabs and the Khazars. Furthermore, the Christian missionary enterprise proceeded quite triumphantly in areas that contained no Jews. But he was eager to demonstrate that the essence of Jewish life was a peculiar metaphysical "mystery," which unfolds in the course of human history.

This approach is hardly consistent with a rational or a liberal philosophy, which regards as axiomatic the equal dignity of all human beings in the sight of God. However, it accords all too well with the mythical perspective of the ancient and medieval Christians, which underlies the mystique of modern racial antisemitism. However, the threads of thought are woven, at times, in strange and unpredictable ways.

From the Jewish standpoint it is of great interest to note the operation of this notion of metaphysical uniqueness in the teaching of pro-Jewish theologians—Catholic and neoorthodox.

Jacques Maritain (1882–1973) the renowned Catholic theologian, was a valiant fighter against antisemitism. A disciple of Henri Bergson, he criticized his master's downgrading of the role of human intelligence. He was among the foremost humanists in the renaissance of modern Catholicism. In 1939, seeing the gathering storm over the heads of European Jews, he addressed himself to the interpretation of "the Jewish question." We note first his emphasis on the mystery of Jewish life.

> Thus, from the first, Israel appears to us a mystery; of the same order as the mystery of the world and the mystery of the Church. Like them, it is a mystery lying at the very core of redemption. And we must say that, if St. Paul be right, what is called the *Jewish problem* is an insoluble problem, that is, without *definitive* solution until the great reconciliation foretold by the apostle, which will resemble a resurrection from among the dead.[103]

The claim that Jewish being is an "insoluble problem" cannot but serve as an indirect endorsement of the judgment of the racial mystics who, long before Hitler, put in question the very existence of the Jewish people. Antisemitic demagogues were accustomed to refer to the "feeling" of the masses, when all other arguments failed them. The mystery of theologians coincided conveniently with the momentum of medieval hatred. Insofar as Jews are concerned, the subtle, well-meaning theologian joined the vulgar masses in shifting their perspective from the present to the period of the New Testament.

"But since the day when, because its leaders chose the world, it stumbled, it is bound to the world, prisoner and victim of that world which it loves, but of which it is not, shall not be and can never be."[104] Did the Jews "choose the world" when they disallowed the claim of Jesus to be the "man-god"? Did they then become "the prisoners of the world," because they loved it? Does not John tell us that "God so loved the world . . ."? It is useless to argue with so fantastic a thesis, which fades as soon as it is seen in the broad light of day.[105] To the Catholic theologians of the old school, the Jewish ideal, "to improve the world by means of the kingdom of the Almighty," was a source of social unrest. Liberalism, in all its aspects, was condemned in the papal "Syllabus of Errors."

The idealistic impetus of the Jew is deeply flawed, in Maritain's opinion, for it manifests "a materialistic messianism which is the dark face of its vocation to the absolute."[106]

Maritain pleaded for a new social order, "freed from the ills of capitalistic materialism as well as from the even greater ills of Fascism, Racism and Communism."[107] In that order, "far removed from the old Liberalism, there will be room for Jewry to occupy an 'ethico-juridical status.'"

Here, then, is a plea for a Christian "corporative" state, consisting of structured estates and reflecting a dogmatic, transcendental philosophy. In such a "closed society," protected from the fresh breezes of liberalism, the Jews will be granted the peculiar status that is proper for a peculiar people.

It is apparent that while Maritain himself was opposed to antisemitism, he nevertheless continued to foster the old mythological way of viewing the Jewish role in history. If the Jews are supernaturally determined to be "outsiders" and a mystery, we can feel fairly certain that they will be viewed as a hostile, indeed a malignant, power. Intellectuals may generate ideas, but they do not determine the consequences that people are likely to draw from their ideas. While Maritain intended the term "mystery" to be purely "theological," a paradoxical blend of metaphysical categories, we know from the tragic lessons of history that people are far more likly than not to view the mystery of outsiders with the down-to-earth feelings of fear, hostility, and suspicion—all the more so when the "aliens" in question are supernaturally fixed in their inscrutable ambivalence.

Yet, Maritain's basic premise is still held by leading authorities within the Catholic Church.

Augustin Cardinal Bea was Chairman of the Commission of the Second Vatican Council, which drew up the Declaration of the Relation of the Church to Non-Christian Religions, including the Schema on Judaism, which was adopted in October 1965.

This declaration rejects any antisemitic inferences that might be drawn from the event of the crucifixion. The Church "decries hatred, persecutions, manifestations of anti-semitism, directed against Jews at any time and by anyone." The Council asserted its eagerness to foster and commend mutual understanding and esteem. "This will be the fruit above all of biblical and theological studies and of brotherly dialogues."

The historical import of this official action can be appreciated only by those who have familiarized themselves with the many ways in which the Catholic tradition was used in order to keep alive a mythical image of the Jew as the minion of Satan. In his book *Jésus et Israël* Jules Isaac has amply documented this tragic trend throughout many centuries. As late as 1947, with the fires of the holocaust still casting their lurid light on the European horizon, the authors of a French manual for teachers could still write as follows:

> The punishment of the Jews who had committed the crime of deicide was not long in coming. Thirty-six years after the death of the Savior, the Roman Emperor Titus seized Jerusalem. . . . The Jews, scattered all over the world, never succeeded in re-establishing a nation. They wandered everywhere, looked on as a race accursed, an object of contempt to other peoples.[108]

We are justified in indulging the hope that such venomous teachings will no longer be tolerated by the highest authorities of the Church.

Yet the Church continues to point to the Jewish people as being a mystery—a people uniquely set apart by the Lord of history. Does not this basic axiom dehumanize the Jew, putting him, his characteristics, and his destiny under a menacing cosmic cloud, in a metaphysical quarantine, as it were?

Cardinal Bea's commentary on this declaration is not completely reassuring. To be sure, he condemned those who set themselves up as "avengers of Christ."[109] He chastized those who would condemn *all* the Jews for the crime of deicide.[110] Still, he wrote that guilt "falls upon any one who in some way *associates* himself with the 'perverse generation,' which is primarily guilty. . . ."[111] In other words, while the Church does not condemn *all* Jews, it does maintain that the metaphysical guilt is somehow continued within the Jewish community. He added, "Generally speaking, refusal to believe in the Gospel and in Jesus is a factor in this judgment, and so, in one way or another, is a free decision to ally oneself with the 'perverse generation,' with the powers opposed to God."[112] To be sure, the Cardinal spoke of "a factor," not "the determining factor." The metaphysical cloud is held up, suspended in the air, like the sword of Damocles.

The opponents of the declaration entertained no such compunctions. As Cardinal Bea quotes their leader, "In this specific sense, and taking into account the biblical mentality, Judaism after the time of Christ also shares in the responsibility for deicide, in so far as it constitutes a free and voluntary prolongation of the Judaism of former times."[113]

Can the Church, committed as it is to a dogmatic interpretation of Scripture, give up the notion that a special mystery attaches to the nature and destiny of the Jewish people? Logically, the situation is similar to that of an Orthodox Jew, who affirms that a special providence watches over his people and that its triumphs and tragedies are not comprehensible in secular terms. To be sure, in affirming their own metaphysical uniqueness, Orthodox Jews take upon themselves extra burdens and do not exempt themselves from any of the duties of humanity. No moral evil is implied in that belief. All that is noble in history is achieved by those who consider themselves chosen, or called upon, to advance the great causes of humanity. So, right or not, all religious groups feel that they are somehow chosen in this sense. But to stigmatize another people as living under a "curse" is to commit a mass crime in the name of God. Yet the question remains, can the Church affirm its own mission, as Israel after the spirit, without changing the valence of Israel's chosenness from plus to minus?

It would seem that the Church could simply declare that the role of the Jews as the medium of divine salvation has ended with the coming of Jesus. The Jews are not rejected, but they are "not included" in the newly constituted scheme of salvation, save as individuals. Thereafter, the Jewish people are included within the range of humanity in general. In other words, they can assert that the plus of Jewish chosenness has been changed to zero, not minus. After all, the Church has not rejected the ancient axiom, "outside the Church, there is no salvation." It now recognizes that many and diverse truths of faith are cherished outside the Church. These truths can be assayed and embraced by men and women of good will. It could therefore teach that following the formation of the apostolic community, the aura of a cosmic mission was taken from the Jews and they became like the rest of mankind, who seek God in their own way, finding Him and failing Him, like all men. As to the mystery of which Paul writes in his letter to the Romans, it is not difficult to harmonize his words with this conception. Paul's mystery is nothing but his teacher Gamaliel's in reverse.[114] The Jewish faith is "from God," and in "the end of days" the pious men and women of all nations will become one great society of the redeemed. Up to the advent of the Eschaton, however, the several "communities of God" should make each other "jealous," competing in deeds of love and holiness. The all-important requirement is to see Jews as human beings. Therefore, the dialogue with them can be based on the common ground that all men and women take up, especially those who share the "common patrimony" of the Old Testament.

An example of a genuine attempt to reinterpret the role of the Jew in Protestant theology was provided by the great neo-orthodox theologian, Karl Barth (1886–1968). He burst upon the theological horizon as a super-bright nova, continuing to dominate the scene for many years. He emphasized the "nay" of God as against its "yea," defying the self-assurance of a generation for which "science" and "progress" have become magic words. "The Gospel is not a truth among other truths. Rather, it is a question-mark against all truths."[115] He dared defy the Kantian trend and to assert the heteronomous phase of religion. "The recognition of the absolute heteronomy under which we stand is itself an autonomous recognition; and this is precisely *that which may be known of God*."[116]

Barth interpreted the Pharisaic order in particular and the Jewish people in general as institutions representative of the Church, which perennially and inevitably denies God, even as it is busily engaged in expounding His will. Consequently, he applied the New Testament critique of Israel to the Church as an institution that is both human and divine. "The Church needs to be continually reminded of the most serious of all symptoms. It was the Church, not the world, which crucified Christ."[117]

In Barth's view, the two Testaments are recombined as one mighty flow, and the Church is viewed as the earthly instrument of the dynamic nisus of God. The Christian vocation was not to negate Judaism, but to carry forward its essential message. While its achievements in overcoming paganism were great indeed, it would commit the primary sin of "boasting" if it rested on its laurels and did not recognize the evils of "Pharisaism" in its own sanctified establishment. He asks: "Are we free of the Satanism of the 'Grand Inquisitor,' who though he knows God, yet for the love of man refuses to know Him, and would rather put Christ to death than allow the Word of the freedom of God to run its course?"[118]

Thus, Barth repudiated the century-long dispute over the contrast between grace and works. He would have none of Schleiermacher's presumed antithesis between the "calculating," "heteronomous" piety of Judaism and the self-surrendering, "autonomous" self-giving of Christianity. He acknowledged the inner unity of Gospel and Torah.

Historically, and when it is treated as the negation of divine revelation, the New Testament seems to be no more than a clearly drawn, carefully distilled epitome of the Old Testament. What is there in primitive Christianity which has not its clear parallel in later Judaism. What does Paul know which the Baptist did not? And what did the Baptist know which Isaiah did not?"[119]

Can there be a "supreme religion," a highest pinnacle of all human work, in the relation between God and men? If such a religion were to be found anywhere, it would be in the "religion" of the prophets and psalmists of Israel, which is nowhere excelled, certainly not in the history of Christianity, and not even in the so called "religion of Jesus." But, in fact, a religion adequate to revelation and congruent to the righteousness of God, a law of righteousness, is unattainable by men, except in the miracle of the absolute "Moment." And faith is a miracle. Otherwise, it is not faith.[120]

From the vantage point of Judaism, the weakness of the Barthian position lies in its total negation of ethical principles, let alone laws of conduct. It comes perilously close to the diffuse, unfocused benevolence of Hinduism, which, because it is so all-embracing, verges on the meaningless. If all of us are "sinners," painted blood-red by the same brush, what is there to sustain the landmarks of the good life? Morality is meaningful, precisely because it projects the light of eternity into the nooks and crannies of our earthly existence. Even in the great moral dilemmas of life, we can at least debate the action to be taken. Principles and laws serve well enough in the vast majority of cases, and even in the moments of "crisis" we find ourselves arguing in terms that are meaningful to others, for we know that we share in the same illumination. If it is ethical, it is universal, dictated by the conscience that is common to us all. Kierkegaard's "category of the individual" reflects an authentic if one-sided *religious* motif, which is, however, tangential to the ethical life.

Barth dwelled on the occasional "paradoxes" of the good life, refusing to see that these dilemmas are themselves subject to the painful process of judgment by the moral-rational conscience. He wrote: "Christianity is unhappy when men boast of the glories of marriage and of family life, of Church and state, and society. . . ."[121]

For him, there was only one standard of judgment—that of the man "under grace." "*Agape* is the answer of the man who under

Grace is directed toward the unsearchable God."[122] Is "grace" so infallible? Barth himself cautioned against the corruptibility of all that is ideal. "There are no moral actions, such as love, or honesty, or purity, or courage, which have rid themselves of the *form of this world*, which are not 'erotic.' "[123] "Whenever men claim to be able to see the kingdom of God as a growing organism, or—to describe it more suitably—as a growing 'building,' what they see is not the Kingdom of God, but the Tower of Babel."[124]

On this basis, what is to keep us from sliding down the slippery road to the depths, which are "beyond good and evil"? Barth acknowledges that "apart from relative positive human behavior," man is free to follow his spirit wherever it leads. "The possibility that from time to time God may be honored in concrete human behavior which contradicts the commandments of the second Tablet must therefore be left open."[125]

As Jews, we too admit that instances may arise when, as the Talmud puts it, "great is a sin for the sake of God."[126] In Judaism, those instances too must be evaluated in the light of the ethical principles involved in the situation. Ethical principles are affirmed in the very process of judgment, whereby the seemingly unethical action is commended.

Perhaps the Jewish ethos derives not only from the Law of the Old Testament, but also from a millennial experience of persecution. We agree with Nietzsche that ours is an "ethic of slaves," which is constantly and for very good reason suspicious of the freewheeling "ethics of the nobility." It is out of the depths of suffering that God is most truly called (Psalm 130:1). Those who aspire to be "supermen," either in mundane power or in monkish penitence, are all too often liable to sink to the ethical level of the subhuman.

Rolf Hochhut, author of the famous play *The Representative*, showed deep insight when he described the satanic "Doctor" from Auschwitz as one who loved to attend the lectures of the "existentialist" theologian R. Bultmann.[127] With all due respect to that great theologian, the Satans of our time pass themselves off as individualists, guided by their private revelations.

Karl Barth himself met the ethical test of his generation. He remained a valiant fighter against Nazism, even in the darkest days of World War II. In his address to the German people after the war, he interpreted Nazi antisemitism as a rebellion against Christ.

> It is that the Germans are possessed of the real meaning of Christianity and have understood the Grace of God, in the person of the Jew, Jesus, more deeply and fundamentally than any other people. For this very reason, they, and they alone, have been capable of such thoroughgoing and logical repudiation of Jesus, his people, and his message, as they have now brought to completion in their political and military practice from Frederick the Great through Bismarck to Hitler.[128]

Karl Barth disavowed the notion of any missionary campaign to the Jews. He noted that in terms of "ideas," or expressions of the "essence of faith," there is nothing that Judaism can learn from Christianity. Faith in Christ can come only from God Himself, as it did to Paul on the way to Damascus. "The Gentile Christian community of every age and land is a guest in the house of Israel . . . How then can we try to hold missions to Israel? . . . What have we to teach him that he does not already know, that we have not rather to learn from him?"[129]

Yet even Barth could not liberate himself from the compulsion to see the Jewish people through the distorting prism of Christian dogmatics. As if the essence of Jewish life consisted in the rejection of Jesus and in the terrible retribution that followed!

> Secondly, however, there is the shattering fact that at the decisive moment the Same Israel denied its election and calling. . . . Necessarily, therefore, the Jew who is uniquely blessed offers the picture of an existence, which characterized by the rejection of its Messiah and therefore, its salvation and mission, is dreadfully empty of grace and blessing.[130]

In one sentence, then the Jew is described as being both "uniquely blessed" and "dreadfully empty of grace and blessing." If he had written, "empty of *Christian* grace and blessing," he would have been right, but tautologous. However, we have to be grateful for the distinction between the sheer lack of blessing and the actual hurt of a curse. Yet Barth is an ardent "ecumenist," looking forward eagerly to the formation of one community of faith.

> Even the modern ecumenical movement suffers more seriously from the absence of Israel than of Rome or Moscow. The Church must live with the Synagogue, not as the fools say in their hearts, as with another confession or religion, but as with the root from which it has itself sprung.[131]

This "organismic" metaphor, first used by Paul, is not auspicious, for it assumes that the existing branch is first lopped off, then the "wild olive branch" is grafted onto the stem.

It is exceedingly difficult for the Orthodox and the neo-orthodox, be they men of the greatest goodwill, to view Jewish people through dogmatic Christian binoculars, and to see them truly. Inevitably, the viewer sees a "corporate personality," extending from Abraham to Jesus and from Jesus to the holocaust, metaphysically exalted and spurned by turns, set apart from humanity by an invisible hand, at once gracious and wrathful.

The only fruitful method in the Judeo-Christian dialogue is the one based on the common ground of "religious humanism." Judaism and Christianity add their truths and metaphors to this base, but they cannot build without it. No religion can supersede the axioms of humanity without stultifying itself. The revelation of Torah at Sinai did not negate the previous revelations to Adam, to Noah, or to Abraham. Was not the evil of the Pharisaic movement, insofar as it contained a peculiar rot, precisely the paradox that its teachers gave the impression of neglecting the basic human virtues in their attempt to achieve a more perfect holiness? History has demonstrated abundantly that those who would rise above the ethical, in the name of a private truth that they seek to keep unspotted by the world, are prone to be inhuman in relation to those who stand outside their impassioned, hermetic community.

We must not regard the gray reality of the merely human as the be-all and end-all of the mystery of life. We must acknowledge our limitations, even perversions—yes, our sins. And in every generation special follies and sins appear in tandem with special insights and virtues. As our spirit advances in some directions, it is likely to wither in others. We need the "deposit of faith" from previous generations for its affirmative as well as its negative aspects, sustaining our forward movement and cautioning us to beware of blind spots. Again and again, we have to break through the shells of the conventional and the complacent. But we must never forget the humanist base on which we stand. Standing somewhere on a rung of Jacob's ladder, we are called to climb ever higher, but not by way of knocking down the rungs or closing our eyes to them.

As Jews, we must shun like poison any notion that would interpose a cosmic wall of "uniqueness" between the several branches of humanity. We can speak of the unique worth of our tradition, acknowledging the values of other faiths and cultures. But, when we speak of ourselves as "being chosen," we do so in the sense in which all dedicated, covenanted communities are chosen—i.e., called to serve a high purpose. This doctrine can serve as a useful and inspiring metaphor only if it is purged of all exceptionalist, racist, and mystical connotations.[132] We may call ourselves chosen, "set apart," "called," or what have you—providing always that we do not draw the negative inferences from this doctrine and apply them to the non-Jewish peoples, as if they were "un-chosen," "undistinguished," or "uncalled." Our affirmation of "chosenness" is our way of appreciating the peculiar gifts of our past and our destiny. In other traditions there are other ways. Christians are "redeemed" in Christ. However, as between the boundaries of the historic communities, the rules of humanism must apply. Thus, the Jew reminds the Christian of the claims of non-Christian humanity, and the Christian reminds the Jew of the claims of non-Jewish humanity. In both cases the reminder refers to a component of the community's own tradition, for within the Judeo-Christian family of religions, the life of faith consists in the perennial tension between private insight and public wisdom, between the historic rhetoric of faith and the evolving ethic of mankind.

Of all the various Jewish schools of biblical interpretation, those of Ezekiel Kaufman and Martin Buber are of special interest—the former because of his emphasis on the national character of Judaism, the latter because of his religious approach. Both systems of interpretation, for all their meticulous scholarship, may be regarded as Jewish responses to some of the trends in biblical criticism.

Ezekiel Kaufman maintained that the Jewish people emerged on the stage of history as a purely monotheistic people. In fact, they were so truly monotheistic that they became totally incapable of comprehending the ideas and sentiments of their pagan neighbors. Between the world view of monotheism and that of paganism there yawns a gulf so wide and deep that it can never be breached. So the Jews, who broke into history as monotheists, could not make sense of the myths and rites of their pagan neighbors. Since their own mythical faculties were atrophied by the monotheistic idea, they stigmatized all pagan worship as sheer, mindless fetishism, "the worship of sticks and stones." As to the idolatrous practices of which the Israelites themselves were guilty, those were only desiccated remnants of ancient customs, devoid of roots in the national culture and preserved only by marginal elements of the Jewish people.

Accordingly, Kaufman saw the monotheistic philosophy of biblical Israel as growing like a tree out of a unique seed of inspiration, affected only externally by the accidents of rainfall and sunshine, but unfolding essentially in keeping with its own special genius. There was no step-by-step evolution from primitive animism or ancestor worship to the God of Deutero-Isaiah, but, in the course of Israel's checkered history, the inner world of monotheism grew and took shape in accord with its organic laws of development. Here, then, we have a reassertion of the traditional Jewish self-image of total separation from the nations and their ways. Kaufman's thesis was supported by a tremendous array of scrupulous analysis and critical erudition. The monotheistic idea was the soul and essence of Israel's national culture. Not an act of God but the mysterious works of history generated a people that "dwelt apart," free from the trammels of mythology, molded and structured by the idea of monotheism. The same idea, in its Christian and Moslem manifestations, achieved similar, though incomplete, triumphs over the various forms of paganism in the western world.

The association of the monotheistic idea with the empirical people of Israel did not, even in biblical times, imply a diminution or limitation of the universalist dimension of Judaism. The idea enters history and unites with an empirical organization, which becomes its historical instrument. Thus, the Christian Apostolic Community became a bearer of the monotheistic idea, as did the Moslem Brotherhood, six centuries later, and the people of Israel, a millennium and a half earlier. In each case contingent historical factors created the human base for the idea, which is in itself universal and trans-historical. Those who wish to embrace the idea must join the existing fellowship of believers by a concrete act of conversion— either by circumcision and baptism, or by baptism, or by a public avowal of some sort. As to the expulsion of foreign wives and their children from the Jerusalem community at the time of Ezra and Nehemiah, Kaufman pointed out that the tragedy occurred in a critical period, after the lapse of the pre-exilic form of welcoming the stranger into the fold and prior to the emergence of rabbinic legislation concerning conversion.

The usual explanation of the failure of Judaism to win over the pagan world is that it was hampered by the barriers of national egotism in two ways—the Jews were not interested in converting Gentiles, and the Gentiles who wished to join the Judaic community of believers had to pay the price of becoming part of the Jewish nation. Kaufman rejected both theses. Yes, the Jews did feel obliged to preach to the nations, and the rite of conversion was an act of faith, not a change of national allegiance. Yet the Jewish failure to obtain mass conversions was owing to the association of the Jewish faith with the Jewish fate. The successive defeats of the Jewish people in the rebellions of 65–70, 111–117, and 131–134 seemed to prove to the inhabitants of the Roman Empire, and to the barbarian invaders, that the Jewish cause was lost and that God had indeed turned away from His people. Who would want to join a people that is so clearly "under the wrath" of God?

It would take us too far afield to analyze and criticize the central theses of Kaufman's philosophy of Jewish history. It is apparent that he retrojected a Jewish version of romantic nationalism into his interpretation of the Bible. He absolutized the distinctions between monotheism and paganism, as well as the differences between ancient Israel and its neighbors. He succeeded in exposing the biased assumptions of other Bible critics. No student of the Hebrew Scriptures can afford to ignore his massive contributions. In his affirmative views, however, he reflected the tragic world of central

Europe between the two world wars, when nations seemed to be so many wolf packs, ready to devour one another. The lamb of Israel could hardly expect to live in peace among the nations that were casting off the restraints of Christianity.

In terms of contemporary ideologies, Kaufman identified completely with Herzlian Zionism. In his view, romantic nationalism was the wave of the future. Jews cannot assimilate, because their national character has been stamped indelibly with an unyielding, eternal idea. Therefore, in the lands of the Diaspora, they will never be accepted as equal and true citizens in any nation-state. They will find security only if they establish their own state in Palestine.[133]

Martin Buber (1878–1965) set out to prove that the "I-Thou" relation is the soul and substance of the biblical faith. Taking account of the vast critical literature, he sought to uncover the underlying dynamic drive which generated the ideas and pattern of biblical religion. Unlike the rationalists, he was concerned, not with the evolution of the monotheistic idea, but with the nature and growth of that whole-souled piety that we discover in Holy Scripture, a piety which centers around the direct relation of God to the living community. The Hebrew Scriptures contain the record of a community that took seriously the I-Thou relation and its consequences. Biblical faith, especially in its last stages, was a unique exemplification of the dialogue between man and God.

In the story of Gideon we have the clearest expression of this faith in "the kingship of God."[134] Wellhausen may have been right in postdating the idea and the "institution" of theocracy, but, Buber insisted, the folk feeling of a direct relation to God as king certainly prevailed in the time of the Judges.

> In addition to "idea" and "institution" in Wellhausen's sense, there is a third possibility: namely, the real, struggling, religious-political will to fulfillment, wresting ever again from the resistance of the times a fragment of realization, however altered; a will, not just late-prophetic, but inseparable from the historical Israel. The Kingship of God is a paradox, but an historical one; it consists in the historical conflict of the subjected person against the resisting one, a conflict which, without its naive, but on that very account, most important, original form, cannot be grasped.[135]

Buber traced the origin of God's kingship in Israel to the ancient Semitic concept of the leader-god, who precedes and leads a tribe in its wandering (*Malk* or Melech; that is, king). While *Baal* is the Lord of the place, *Malk* is the lord of the people. "He [Malk] is, however, not as the French school of sociology wishes to conceive of this sort of thing, the personified spirit of the community, but he represents the power which transcends it, happens to it, which *changes* it, even historicizes it."[136]

This ancient Semitic belief underlies the vision of Moses in the wilderness of Sinai. YHVH is truly "nameless"—He cannot be conjured up. He tells Moses, "I shall be there, when I shall be there." In His Presence all other loyalties are dissipated. It is this yielding of man to the all-pervasive Eternal Thou that is the vital kernel of genuine monotheism. "The piety of the Exodus is related to that of Deutero-Isaiah as the folded-up leaf is related to the unfolded leaf." Out of the feeling that one must not concern himself with other kingships, there emerges the explicit affirmation that there are no other powers.[137] Another consequence is the resolve that every aspect of life be determined by this supreme orientation.

> The doctrine of uniqueness has its vital ground certainly not in this, that one formulated thoughts about how many gods there are and perhaps, also, sought to establish this, but in the exclusiveness which rules over the faith-relation as it rules over the true love between man and man. . . . The theism of Israel is characterized finally in this, that the faith-relation according to its nature wishes to be valid for, and to bear upon all of life. . . . The uniqueness of "monotheism" is . . . that of the Thou in the I-Thou relation, so far as this is not denied in the totality of the lived life.[138]

The kingship of the One God issues in a theocratic frame of mind, which is paradoxical in essence—God is the one source of authority, but He insists on the freedom of His people to accept or to reject His rule.[139]

> While Joshua neither names a successor nor otherwise arrives at an ordinance in order to transform the charismatic authority into a "perennial institution," he strips theocratic reality of its severe garments of power: now it is surrendered unarmed to the freedom of man.[140]

Buber interpreted the entire narrative concerning Moses as a saga, that is, neither as a string of legends nor as a chronicle of events, but as a reflection of that which the believing people experienced. "The meeting of a people with events so enormous that it cannot ascribe them to its own plans and their realization, but must perceive in them deeds performed by heavenly powers, is of the substance of history."[141]

The saga of Moses reached its apex in a series of religious experiences and in the exodus. None of the events can be fully conveyed in cold and sober terms. In the experience of the burning bush we are face to face with "that singular region where great personal religious experiences are propagated."[142] The prophet recounted his experience and his interpretation in such a way as to awaken echoes of that experience again and again—"the certainty of the presence of the God as a quality of his being, began to possess the souls of the generations."[143] This nuclear religious experience transmuted the various elements that Moses and the Israelites encountered and absorbed in their cultural environment. The institution of the Sabbath, whatever its origin, illustrates how a borrowed custom became the clearest expression of the union of a man and God, and the correlative unity of all men, free and slave, citizen, and stranger. "If we take away all the legendary traits of Moses, we must still recognize him as the spiritual force in which the Ancient Orient concentrated itself at its close and surmounted itself."[144]

As the ideal prophet, Moses represents in ways larger than life, the situation of every man who looks for and encounters the eternal Thou.[145] "The soul of the Decalogue, however, is to be found in the word, 'Thou'. . . . At all times, in any case, only those persons really grasped the Decalogue who literally felt it as having been addressed to themselves. . . ."[146]

The work of Moses went through many developments, which Buber traced. In his view the prophets were the agents through whom one breakthrough after another was achieved. "Amos had proclaimed YHVH to be the liberator of the nations, who, in contrast to Israel, do not know His name or His nature. Deutero-Isaiah proclaims Him as the future liberator of the subject nations, who do not know Him yet, as Cyrus called by Him to begin the work of liberation, does not know Him: decisive for the things to come is that the nations should know Him."[147]

They should be moved to acknowledge Him through their suffering, for He, too, suffers, loves, and redeems.

> YHVH's love for faithless Israel, a hurt and suffering love, renews itself from the prophet's love of God, a love, hurt and suffering for God's sake. . . . There is a nucleus of Israel, preserved through the generations, that does not betray the election, that belongs to God and remains His. . . . They are the small beginning of the Kingdom of God before Israel becomes a beginning of it. . . .[148]

The problem of God's justice and the suffering of the righteous is merged into the inquiry concerning Israel's destiny. The answer of God to Job is that God's justice is translogical, but it is enough for the sufferer to know that there is a *God Who answers*.[149]

It is the task of Job-Israel to pray for his "friends," and he is healed when he proceeds to pray for them. Job-Israel must demonstrate the life of dialogue with God and love for men, and in this role it attains the fullness of its personality. Of course, God's message is not conveyed in so many words, yet it is real and imperative.

> He, to whom and by whom the word is spoken, is in the full sense of the word a "person." Before the word is spoken by him in human language, it is spoken to him in another language, from which he has to translate it into human language, to him this word is spoken as between person and person. In order to speak to man, God must become a person; but, in order to speak to him, He must make him too a person. . . . Only Jeremiah, of all the Israelite prophets has dared to note this bold and devout life-conversation of the utterly inferior with the utterly superior—in such a measure is man here become a person. All Israelite relationship of faith is dialogic; here, the dialogue has reached its pure form.[150]

Israel was "elected" to work on itself in such a manner as to become a light to the nations, and the prophet, or "suffering servant," was similarly elected to represent the destiny of his people. "He is Israel as servant. When the nations look at him, they look at the truth of Israel, the truth chosen from the very beginning."[151]

To Buber, the experience of the "Thou" was not a subjective feeling, but a real event of revelation. While the content of this revelation can only be articulated in contingent terms, borrowed from the mental climate of the age, the living kernel of revelation is an assurance of the Divine Presence and a call to respond in love.

> He who draws near with a pure heart to the divine mystery, learns that he is continually with God.
>
> It is a revelation. It would be a misunderstanding of the whole situation to look on this as a pious feeling. From man's side, there is no continuity, only from God's side. The Psalmist has learned that God and he are continually with one another.[152]

As we have seen, Buber's concept of revelation does not imply that any concrete laws represent the Divine Will. Man is called on to respond to the "eternal Thou" in a spontaneous and original way and by means of sanctifying every facet of life, albeit with due regard for the sancta of the people.

It might seem that Buber's repudiation of lawfulness in favor of spontaneity put him on the Christian side in its debate with Judaism. In fact, in his early addresses on Judaism, he regarded the early Christians, along with the Essenes and the eighteenth-century Hasidim as the most authentic exemplars of the Judaic faith. These faith communities represented the unity of devotion to the eternal Thou and to the members of the community. Their total life was governed by this double-faceted relationship, which was altogether spontaneous and original, free from the fetters of an unyielding law.

However, Buber maintained that the Apostolic community soon lost its vital character. Christianity became a dogma-centered faith, allowing but marginal room for the immediate I-Thou relation. Distinguishing between two kinds of faith, "believing in" and "believing that," he pointed out that the former was a relationship of free and direct trust in the eternal Thou, whereas the latter was a declarative affirmation that this or that was the pathway of salvation. To be sure, there is no believing in that is permanent and communal, which is not also capable of being formulated in the rhetoric of believing that. To Buber, however, not the ideas but the nature of faith was all-important. Like Mendelssohn, he contrasted the undogmatic, non-mediatory faith of Judaism with the dogmatic, mediator-centered faith of Christianity. In Judaism, especially "in Hasidism, *devotio* has absorbed and overcome *gnosis*."[153] In Christianity, beginning with Paul and John, *gnosis* has prevailed over *devotio*.

Buber endeavored to reclaim Jesus not only as his "great brother" but also as a messianic personality, within the context of Isaiah's "suffering servant." Messiahship is a process, not the unique moment of the Eschaton.

> The men through whom it [the messiahship] passes, are those of whom the nameless prophet speaks when he says, in the first person, that God sharpens them to a polished arrow and then conceals them in His quiver. Their hiddenness belongs to the essence of their work of suffering. Each of them can be the fulfilling one; none of them in his self-knowledge may be anything other than a servant of the Lord. With the tearing apart of the hiddenness, not only would the work itself be suspended, but a counter-work would set in. Messianic self-disclosure is the bursting of Messiahship . . . whatever the appearance of Jesus means for the Gentile world (and its significance for the Gentile world remains for me the true seriousness of western history), seen from the standpoint of Judaism, he is the first in the series of men who, stepping out of the hiddenness of the servant of the Lord, the real "Messianic mystery," acknowledged their Messiahship in their souls and in their words. That this first one in the series was incomparably the purest, the most legitimate, the most endowed with real Messianic power—as I experienced ever again. . . .[154]

Still, Buber did not hesitate to put the "holy yehudi" in the same messianic category as Jesus. In his preface to his book *For the Sake of Heaven* he wrote, "Whatever in this book the Yehudi may have in common with Jesus of Nazareth, derives not from a tendency, but from a reality."[155] However, Buber scorned Paul for reducing the richness of Torah to the narrowness of law, and substituting *gnosis* for *devotio*.

Taking the work of Buber as a whole, we recognize that his interpretation of faith in general and of Judaism in particular was extremely one-sided. His penetrating genius was poetic rather than philosophical.

Faith can assume dialogic form, but it can be genuine and comforting, even when His Glory is felt to be everywhere and His Presence nowhere. "I know that my Redeemer liveth," Job exclaims, long before he hears the voice out of the storm (Job 19:25). The Psalmists reveal many aspects of faith that are nondialogic in character.

While the role of the prophet in generating the faith of Scripture is great, we must not minimize the aspects of faith that were expressed in the rites of the priest, or in the wisdom of the sages. If Paul erred in reducing Torah to law, did not Buber err in eliminating law and ritual and the ideal of "Torah for its own sake" from the range of pure *devotio*? For God comes at us from all directions of our spiritual life.

Indeed, the special quality of Judaism is its recognition of the fullness of the holy life. It is not "fear and trembling" only, nor is it the ecstasy of love only, nor is it the delight in His laws only, but it is these and much besides. It responds to man's craving for the nearness of God, but also to his fear of the divine judgment; to man's servility and obedience, but also to his impassioned assertiveness; to man's surrender of his mind to blind belief, but also to his intellectual boldness; to man's self-assurance, but also to his self-denial. Buber left out of his purview the laws of Torah and Talmud, the deliberations of the sages, and the bold intellectual adventures of the philosophers. His portrait of the Hasidim is an idyllic myth, a poetic metaphor, which possesses its own generic truth; but it is not the kind of truth that we seek in sober daylight. Buber is a wonderful guide to the inner sanctum of the spiritual life, providing we remember that he is not an objective reporter, but a poet and a prophet, "a sweet singer in Israel."

X. *Jewish Self-Image in the Postwar World*

At the close of World War I, it looked as if the predicament of European Jewry had been resolved. The guns were silenced, reconstruction was begun, democracy and socialism were praised by the defeated nations as well as the Allies. The war-weary peoples of Europe believed that the great and liberating ideas of the West would usher in a new and glorious era. President Wilson's arrival at Paris signalled to millions that the spirit of America had come to bind up the wounds of the Old World.

The dawn of the new age was especially welcomed by Jews, who imagined that they would now be able to articulate every aspect of their collective identity.

In Russia, the Czarist regime had come to an inglorious end. That ancient and implacable fortress of anti-Jewish hatred had been completely demolished. The entire managerial and governing class was fleeing to western countries. Antisemitism was abjured by the short-lived Kerensky government and condemned as a capital offense by the Bolsheviks.

The successor-states of the Russian and Austrian empires were pledged to respect the collective as well as the individual rights of the minorities living within their borders. The League of Nations was assigned the task of monitoring compliance with the Minorities' Treaties. The national character of the Jews living in the Old Pale of Settlement was officially recognized in the Balfour Declaration, in the Palestinian Mandate, as well as in the various Minorities' Treaties.

It seemed as if the implied limitations of the earlier emancipation in France had now been removed for the Jews of Central Europe. At that time, Clermont-Tonnere had voiced the general consensus when he declared; "to Jews as individuals, everything; to Jews as a nation, nothing." Now the Jews living in Central Europe were assured that they would be accorded both civil rights as individuals and the collective rights of protected nationalities. An international convention safeguarded their right to practice their faith, without restriction and repression.

They could choose to affirm whatever aspects of their identity they wanted to preserve, defining their collective being as they pleased. They could describe themselves in either religious, or national, or racial, or Zionist terms, or they could adopt the socio-economic terminology of Marxism. Or they could emigrate to the countries of the New World and take up a fresh identity as Americans, Canadians, Argentinians, or Australians.

We know now that this rosy picture was a cruel mirage. Before the signatures to the Versailles Treaty were fully dried, the first clouds of the coming hurricane could be seen on the horizon. Already in the halcyon days of "the self-determination of nations," the stage was being set for the horrors of the Holocaust.

In Russia, a civil war broke out, with the "White" armies of Petlura, Denikin and Kolchak fighting to overthrow the Bolshevik regime. The Czarist generals were long accustomed to regard all Jews as revolutionaries. In their view, the Bolshevik regime was Jewish-inspired, even when it was not led by Jews. Indeed, some prominent Bolsheviks were Jews, notably Trotsky, Zinoviev, and Kamenev.

To be sure, the Jewish communists constituted but a tiny fraction of the Jewish population. Still they played a disproportionately prominent role in the upper echelons of the Bolshevik regime. In one study of the makers of the October revolution, the proportion of Jews in the various executive organs of the Bolshevik government was reported to be 4 out of 8, 3 out of 30, 2 out of 7, 5 out of 10.[1] This tremendous overrepresentation of Jews in the Bolshevik regime of the early years was due largely to the cruel repression of Jews by the Czarist regime and to the virtual exclusion of the Jewish intelligentsia from gainful employment in the ranks of the government and in some sectors of the economy. Still, the vast majority of Jewish activists were Liberals or Centrists. But, when the center-parties, under the leadership of Kerensky, proved unable to control the course of events, the armed forces were drawn either to the Soviet or to the Czarist side. For Jews, the Czarist alternative was virtually closed. Former Mensheviks and Social revolutionaries as well as Kadetniks threw their lot in with the Bolsheviks.

Neither the Red Terror of the Bolshevik regime nor the White Terror of the Czarist armies was pursued with concern for the rights of individuals. The Reds aimed to crush, if not to liquidate, entire classes of the population, not merely those who were guilty of treason. The White Armies were similarly undiscriminating. They massacred the Jewish population of nearly all the towns that they captured. The common Cossacks were long accustomed to take part in government-inspired pogroms. Similarly, the Russian officers had been taught to believe that simple, pious peasants would never turn against "the little Father," their Czar, if they were not corrupted by an ethnically alien and anti-Christian people.

The infamous forgeries, "The Protocols of the Elders of Zion," which blamed all economic depressions and social revolutions on the sinister machinations of a cabal of Jewish Elders, were originally produced by the secret service of the Czars. Following the outbreak of the Bolshevik Revolution, those forgeries were updated in order to lay upon Jews the responsibility for the horrors of the Red Terror and the Civil War.[2]

When the White Armies were defeated and driven back in disarray, the wretched Russian refugees brought the "Protocols" with them to the lands of Central and Western Europe. The bizarre myth of the "Protocols" was dear to the hearts of the miserable exiles, since it exonerated them from the charge of mismanaging the affairs of their native country. Their opponent was, according to the "Protocols," not an enemy of flesh and blood, but a sinister Satanic Power, threatening ruin to the entire Christian world. They were entitled to the sympathy and high regard of the western world, since they had battled against the infidel incarnate, the anti-christ in his twentieth century manifestation.

The irrational obsessions of the Russian emigrés were transplanted into all the lands of western Europe. For a while, the "Protocols" were proclaimed as gospel truth even in the countries of the New World. The Dearborn *Independent* printed the "Protocols" in the early twenties along with commentaries and updating notations, adding the prestige of America's hero, Henry Ford, to these fantastic forgeries. Still later, in the middle thirties, the scheming charlatan, Father Coughlin, resorted to the "Protocols" in order to bolster his propaganda against President Roosevelt and the New Deal.[3] But it was in Germany that the "Protocols" were destined to prove most explosive.

Under the tutelage of Alfred Rosenberg, a Baltic German and emigré, Adolf Hitler perceived the "real" character of Communism as a Jewish "plot" to dominate the world. Rosenberg was acclaimed as the "philosopher" of the Nazi movement and the high-priest of its sacred "mysteries." It is from him that Hitler learned to view Communism as a racial phenomenon, the articulation of the "non-Aryan" mentality.[4] Slavs were designed by nature to be slaves, uncomplaining servants of the Master Race. Slavic "blood" was weakened by the admixture of a Mongolian component. The Russian nobility was long able to govern because it was largely Teutonic in origin. The Jews, as an "antirace," succeeded in stirring up the Russian peasants to rebel against their Aryan masters. Following the Bolshevik Revolution the Jews have become the real governing class of Russia, since according to this "myth," the Slavs are unable to govern themselves. It is the "manifest destiny" of the Teutons to reclaim their dominion over the Slavs in general and the Russians in particular.[5]

We return to the story of the Jews in Russia. As soon as the Bolshevik regime was consolidated, a rigid and narrow identity was foisted upon the Jews. Their identity as a religious community was steadily whittled down to the vanishing point. Since the teaching of religion to young people below the age of 18 was prohibited in Russia, the religious identity of Jews was condemned to a ruthless process of attrition. Synagogues were closed; all religious activities were regarded as suspect and counterrevolutionary. So Jews were now defined as a national community. However, even the national designation was emptied of historical content, in view of the millennial association of the Jewish nationality with the Bible and Hebraic literature, on the one hand, and with the Jews in the free world, on the other hand. Only the "national" sentiments and the Yiddish language as spoken by the Jewish proletariat could be tolerated in the Soviet world. Stalinist policy aimed to seal Soviet Jews off from the rest of world Jewry. To emphasize this isolation, the *Yevsektsia*, the Jewish section of the Communist party, proceeded to modify the Yiddish language, eliminating all Hebraisms from its orthography and rewriting Jewish history in the light of Marxist theory. And the new Yiddish, Soviet-style, together with a new literature defaming the historical Jewish faith and extolling the virtues of the proletariat, became the substance of an approved Soviet Jewish identity.

Yiddish schools were established in White Russia and the Ukraine; Yiddish newspapers, journals, and books were printed by the government presses. Even a Jewish "homeland" was proclaimed in the Siberian province of Biro Bijan. But the narrow parameters of Jewish identity in the Soviet world nullified the positive aspects of these ventures.

It appeared for a while as if, in spite of these restrictions, a cultural efflorescence of Yiddish-Jewishness was emerging in the Soviet world. Actually, Stalin put an end to all such hopes in 1948, when he caused many Jewish writers and artists to be executed and all Jewish schools to be closed. In Stalin's view, national loyalties are secondary in character; they may be utilized as instruments of propaganda for Communist doctrine. But when a national language, or its literature, is no longer needed for communist purposes, it becomes counterrevolutionary to cherish it. Jews as a leading progressive and metropolitan community were expected to lead the way to ethnic self-immolation.[6]

Stalin made use of antisemitism from time to time, in the course of his relentless struggle to eliminate all potential enemies. In his later years, the dictator became virtually paranoiac and violently antisemitic. Following the establishment of Israel, Stalin regarded all manifestations of Jewish concern and loyalty as treasonable. The appearance of Golda Meir in a Moscow synagogue, which set off a huge Jewish demonstration in her honor, became the pretext for the launching of a vast repressive campaign.

Stalin's anti-Jewish animus was further aroused by a plan to turn the Crimea into a Jewish province. He came to suspect that in a war with the United States, Jews would prove disloyal to their native land.

Paradoxically, the only aspect of Jewish loyalty that was now accorded a grudging toleration was the ritual of the synagogue. The few synagogues that were left standing in the big cities became the only Jewish spatial symbols in the entire landscape of the Soviet Union.

The years 1949–1953, culminating in the so called "Doctors' Plot" and the death of Stalin, were seared in the memory of Russian Jewry as "the Black Years." Had Stalin continued to live, he might have ordered a mass deportation of Jews to remote places in Siberia. During those years, Jewish identity was totally negative, except for the ragged remnants of synagogue life. The Jews became an un-people.

In the Khruschev era, many of the exiled Jewish leaders were rehabilitated. A crude anti-Jewish policy was no longer permitted. But Khruschev did not make a concerted effort to undo Stalin's heritage. Instead, he indulged in occasional remarks which were used by underlings to maintain the image of Jews as being not wholly trustworthy. He spoke of Jews as "cosmopolitans," or as "individualists." He criticized the Polish government for harboring "too many Abramovitzes" in high posts. Altogether, then, Jewish identity in the Khruschev era continued to be vaguely shadowy.

The Six Days' War in June, 1967, set off an explosion of Jewish pride in the Soviet Union. Faced with the choice between a narrowed, denigrated, and suspected identity in the U.S.S.R. and a radiant, vigorous identity of Israel reborn, many young Soviet Jews underwent a "conversion," as it were, and discovered their hidden selves. Many young Jews suddenly found courage to demand exit visas to Israel. Their persistence and the eagerness of the Russians to achieve some sort of detente with the West ultimately led to a relaxation of Soviet policy against emigration. By a mixture of penalization and leniency, the Russians arrived at a compromise solution, which they could tolerate. They allowed some 100,000 Jews to leave in the years 1970–1974, while continuing to discourage severely any would-be emigrants from applying for visas.

In the official Soviet view, there are two kinds of Jewish identity—that of loyal Soviet Jews, who are moving steadily toward complete assimilation within the Russian "melting pot," and that of stubborn Jewish Jews, who dream of emigrating either to Israel or to one of the western countries. Jews are faced with a bifurcation of loyalties, leading either to Russification or to self-assertion. Inevitably, those who identify completely with the former category find it extremely difficult to convince the Soviet authorities that they no longer harbor any intentions to join their kinsmen of the latter category.

This ideological dilemma is the root of the bitter frustration of Russian Jewry. Many of those who opt to remain in the Soviet world, for personal reasons, continue to cherish a deep sense of Jewish identity, and a goodly number of the emigrants are motivated not by passion for Judaism but by the mundane ambitions of personal advancement and dreams of sharing in the material prosperity of the West. Also, the Jewish organizations of America dare not abandon all restraints in their efforts to encourage the emigration of Soviet Jews to Israel, without rendering aid and comfort to those Soviet authorities who discriminate against the Jews that remain in the U.S.S.R. on the ground that they are potentially disloyal candidates for emigration. Can we assume that Russian Jews who do not choose to emigrate no longer share in Jewish identity?

At this writing, the Soviet government has narrowed the exodus of Jews to about a thousand per month.

Looking to the future, we note that the character of Jewish identity in the U.S.S.R. depends in large part on governmental policy. If the government should decide to permit the revival of religion in Russia, especially the teaching of the young, the nature of Jewish identity will be radically altered. The government might also permit a massive tide of antisemitism to overwhelm its Jews, by harping on the evils of "Zionism" and the sins of Israel. In that case, many marginal Jews might be expected to assert their ethnic identity with defiant pride. The government might also practice a policy of "benign neglect," encouraging the vestigial loyalties of Jews to fade away slowly and irreversibly. In any case, Jewish identity in Russia is only partly voluntary; the government gives and the government takes away.

In the period between the two World Wars, there lived in successor-states of the Russian and Austrian empires—the Baltic republics, Poland, Czechoslovakia, Hungary, and Rumania—approximately six million Jews. They lived in hamlets and cities, forming either the majority or the major segment of the population in the small urban centers. They were separated from their neighbors by all the marks of nationality and by centuries of history, in addition to religion. They spoke Yiddish, settled their disputes in their own courts, played and prayed in their own unique ways. They cherished their own memories of grandeur and of resentment, and dreamed of their own homeland, in keeping with biblical assurances and the Balfour Declaration.

Following World War I, the Jews in all these countries were suddenly confronted with governments that were committed to various versions of romantic nationalism. While these governments had signed the Minorities' Treaties, which the League of Nations was ordered to monitor, they did not think of themselves as states, dedicated to the welfare of all their citizens, but as *nation*-states, primarily dedicated to the aggrandizement of their own nationals.

Could one expect the Jews in all these eastern European countries to forge in the course of time firm and meaningful fraternal alliances with their neighbors? Could one expect the majority-nationals to accept the Jews more and more as an integral part of their own homeland?

The answer to the first question depended in part on the answer to the second. In France, after the Revolution, this fraternal ideal was made possible by the prevailing spirit of liberalism, which esteemed as sacrosanct the rights of the individual, not the cultural-racial character of the nation. At Versailles, however, the supreme principle was "the self-determination of nations." The newly resuscitated nations were naturally jealous of their own historic identities. They regarded the Jews in their midst as an alien element, a foreign nationality. They had to carve out economic opportunities for their own people at the expense of all the minorities, not only the Jews, who "occupied" a part of their heritage. In effect, the Poles, the Rumanians, and the Hungarians were engaged from the very beginning in a war against the Jews, as well as against the other minorities—a war in the sense given to this term by Clausewitz—namely, "War is nothing but a continuation of political intercourse with the admixture of different means."

The "different means" in this case involved quasilegal devices whereby the Jews were driven steadily from one economic position after another. The logic of romantic nationalism considered every store which a Jew was compelled to give up because of confiscatory taxation as a position won in the war for national expansion. At times, the "different means" involved the use of more "direct" methods, such as riots and pogroms. In the universities, restrictive and humiliating measures were employed in order to discourage the attendance of Jews, such as compelling Jews to sit on different benches or driving them out of laboratories. In every case, the governing principle was the same: if it is right for a nation to engage in war in order to expand its horizontal space (*Lebensraum*), why is it not right for a nation to war against an internal, alien nationality, in order to occupy vertical space, desirable economic positions? Indeed, the logic of romantic nationalism was incontrovertible, if unconstrained by humanistic principles.

In war, the first casualty is truth. All nations are impelled to believe the best of their own champions, the worst of their foes. "The Will to Believe," normally operative in the life of religion, is transferred in wartime to the realm of ethnic pride and prejudice. In the case of Jews, there was so much incendiary material, built up in the course of centuries, that no effort of imagination was needed in order to cover the aggressive instincts of unfettered chauvinism with the comforting mantle of self-righteousness.

Of course, to liberals, the entire argument is obscene. War for the acquisition of the "living space" of other people is no better than highway robbery. And when war ends in victory, the occupying power is obligated to respect the individual civil rights of the conquered population. Furthermore, in this case, the emergence of the Central European states was conditioned on their undertaking to honor the civil rights of all their citizens. However, these and similar arguments could be dismissed as "idealistic," or "humanistic," or "abstractly altruistic" by the nationalists.

Since romantic nationalism was the most potent force in virtually all the successor-states, the Jews found themselves caught in an ever-tightening vise. Only a tiny fraction could consider seriously the option of the French Revolution: to accept the identity of the nations among whom they lived, confining their distinctiveness to the realm of faith. The hostility of the surrounding nations precluded any such development; the reality of Jewish national separateness in all these countries was self-evident; there was no time for the slow processes of acculturation to take effect. Even so, it is nothing less than astonishing to learn that in the Warsaw ghetto, under the Nazis, 70% of the Jews were Polish-speaking.[7]

The six million Jews in the successor-states were not of one mind in respect of their collective self-image. One characteristic of Jewish history is that the experiences and ideas of one segment of Jewish people exert an impact of some sort upon other Jews. So the vision and reality of liberal Judaism in the countries of the West was not totally ignored by the Jews in the Eastern European countries. But in those lands the vision appeared pale and distant, an impossible dream. Some hundreds of thousands managed to emigrate to the countries of the New World, before the gates were closed to immigration. For the vast majority, the liberal promise had gone sour.

The vast majority of the Jewish population interpreted its identity in one of three ways: the Orthodox, the Zionist, the Bundist. The Orthodox asserted that the biblical and talmudic categories still applied in modern times. In the sight of God, there were two categories of humanity, Israel and "the nations." The Jews were lifted out from among all the nations and assigned a unique destiny. The God of all mankind had made a special Covenant with the Jewish people; hence, all the events of Jewish history must be interpreted in the light of that Covenant. The troubles of Jews are due to their sins. But the ultimate triumph of Jewry is certain.[8]

Until the advent of messianic redemption, Jewish leaders must endeavor to safeguard the separateness and uniqueness of Jewish people as "sons of the Covenant."

The Orthodox were willing to assume the citizenship of European nation-states, but they wanted no part of the latter's cultural-social identity. They refused to permit secular education in their *Yeshivot*. They drew a strict line between political cooperation and cultural participation. While they were willing to share the responsibilities of a new Fatherland, they insisted that all covenants with other nations were temporary—that is, valid until the coming of the Messiah. They sought to protect their pre-war communal organizations (*kehillot*) and aimed to reduce to a minimum the cultural contacts between their faithful followers and their Gentile neighbors.

The Zionists asserted that their identity was that of a secular nation, Hebrew-speaking, as in the biblical period, which was engaged in rebuilding itself by means of rebuilding its homeland in Palestine. They established a network of schools (*tarbut*), in which all subjects were taught in the Hebrew language. They organized camps for the training of agricultural pioneers, who were preparing to emigrate to Palestine (*hachsharah*). In their view, the Jewish faith, in whole or in part, interpreted literally or figuratively, was an aspect of Jewish national culture, rather than the other way around. Zionism, to the Eastern European Jews, meant the actual determination to emigrate to the National Home, sooner or later. Hence, Zionists were not interested in any kind of cultural integration with the nations of Europe. However, Zionist ideology was permeated by the spirit of liberalism from the days of Herzl and Nordau. As an international organization, officially recognized in the Balfour Declaration and in the Palestinian Mandate, the movement was imbued with faith in the brotherhood of nations and in the sanctity of international convenants. They esteemed the Minorities' Treaties of Versailles as their basic charter, in dealing with the governments of the countries in which they lived. Nations are bound to abide by international agreements. Until such time as the Jews had actually moved out of their native lands in Europe, they were entitled to national as well as individual rights. In sum, the self-image of Zionists was that of a nation on the move, eager to be helped into its new homeland and hopeful that it would not be driven out of its temporary dwelling places before its new home was ready.

The Bund did not adhere to the same self-image throughout the period of its existence (1897–1939). In the first years of its functioning as the "League of Jewish Workingmen of Lithuania, Poland and Russia," the unity of socialist workers was stressed, and the use of Yiddish was regarded only "as a propaganda medium among the masses." At the 1905 convention, however, the Bund demanded "national-cultural autonomy." Even so, the Bund at that time considered itself to be more a branch of the Russian, or international, proletariat than of the Jewish community. After the Great War, the Bundist self-image underwent a transformation whereby Jewish identity became of central importance. This development was accelerated by the horrors of the Bolshevik Revolution.[9] The Bund subscribed to the international socialist credo, but added that the Jews were a historical nationality, entitled to foster their own secular Yiddish culture. There was no room for national rivalries within the socialist fraternity. Different nations can coexist side by side in an interethnic harmony. So the Bundists saw themselves as both Jews and socialists, supplementing their socialist identity by their Jewishness and their Jewish identity by their socialism.

They regarded Zionism as an attempt to retreat from the field of battle for a new socialist society. They were determined to stay in the lands of the Diaspora and to join their fellow-workers in the building of a humanistic, pluralistic society, free from all ethnic and religious bigotries (*do-igkeit*—"here-ness"). Antisemitism was, in their view, a remnant of medieval fanaticism, which ruthless capitalists and power hungry Fascists exploited for their own ends. In a socialist world, antisemitism will disappear, like a nightmare in the broad light of day, and different nationalities will work together in friendly cooperation. For it is the aggressive impetus of capitalistic competition that turns a benign nationalism into a demonic force.

These three versions of Jewish identity could be combined and recombined by ideologists. So, there were Zionist Socialists, Orthodox Socialists, Orthodox Zionists. In Central Europe, non-Orthodox Judaism was extremely weak. Essentially these three basic orientations formed the parameters of Jewish identity: identity through God's Command, or through national rebirth in the historic homeland, or through the socialist vision of a new order.

Germany and the Holocaust

Even at this writing, thirty years after the death of Hitler, we stand aghast at the enormity of the Nazi crimes. Our first task is to recognize the unprecedented character of the Holocaust. Antisemitism was already an ancient phenomenon when Christianity appeared, adding a new dimension to this complex of hate and puzzlement. But traditional antisemitism, for all its virulence, could not have brought about a policy of planned and total annihilation. Within the European tradition, there were sufficient restraining and countervailing forces to rule out a deliberate policy of genocide. So long as either Christianity, or liberalism, or democratic socialism provided the ideological framework for national policy, a holocaust was nearly inconceivable. The genocide of the Armenians in Turkey was carried out in an undemocratic, uncultured, unchristian country. To be sure, the "limpieza" rules in sixteenth-century Spain and Portugal established racial criteria for various offices, and the Inquisition pursued with fantastic cruelty tens of thousands of persons descended from Jews or from Moors, whose orthodoxy was suspect or whose wealth was tempting. These lapses from moral integrity made it abundantly clear that Christianity would bend under pressure, to accommodate the passions of the masses and the greed of their overlords. Bend, yes; break, no. Popular outbreaks, with some connivance by the authorities, could and did take place. Traditional excuses for such spontaneous or engineered outbursts of popular fury were drawn either from ethnic folklore or from the arsenal of medieval religion. Hypocrisy is not without its usefulness in blunting the weapons of malice; it prevents an all-out assault by the depraved underworld. In any case, systematic and deliberate mass-murder was inconceivable before the "Final Solution" was inaugurated. The closest any European statesman approached to any such horrendous proposal concerning Jews was the oft-quoted private remark of Pobedonostsev, who served as "The Supreme Prosecutor of the Holy Synod" in Russia (1880–1905); "One third will die, one third will leave the country, and the last third will be completely assimilated within the Russian people." In Europe of the twentieth century, such ruthlessness was inconceivable.

Jewish historians are particularly prone to view the Holocaust as a natural and logical development of age-old antisemitism. Did not Herzl foretell that Jews would be driven out of Europe with fire and sword? Did not the Dreyfus Affair in France and the spotty successes of antisemitic parties in Germany and Austria foreshadow the grim outlines of the Jewish fate? Did not even the staid and pious Conservative party in prewar Germany approve antisemitism in its (1892) Tivoli program?

While all these facts must be taken into account, we must also recall that the antisemitic tide had been receding in all western countries, that the Dreyfus Affair had ended with the total discomfiture of the antisemites, that the percentage of Liberals and Social Democrats had climbed rapidly before, during, and after the Great War; that the antisemitism of the Conservatives was merely a propaganda ploy which was used as a bait to gain the votes of the anti-groups—the antiurban, antiprogress, antiindustrialization "mixed multitudes."

Explaining the vaguely worded antisemitic plank in the Tivoli Program of 1892, Chairman Manteufel declared:

"The Jewish question was not to be avoided unless we wanted to leave the full wind of the movement to the demagogic antisemites; with it, they would have sailed right past us."[10]

Traditional antisemitism was still traditional; that is, it was rooted in a complex of values. It charged that the Jew undermined the concept of a "Christian state," or of a national fraternity of like-minded idealists, or of an agrarian, nonmaterialistic society of status as against a bewildered crowd of money-chasing individualists. In each case, there was an appeal to a body of values. Granted that this collection of ideals was unreal, utopian, dreamy, nostalgic, reactionary, escapist—still, these ideals were incompatible with a policy of mass-murder.

The Holocaust was made possible by a radical break with the European tradition, a rupture which denied clearly and consciously the validity of both the Christian and the liberal traditions. Such a total break with humanist as well as religious idealism was long foreshadowed in Germany. Still, hardly any one imagined that the Nazis would be as bad as their words. Certainly, the Jews did not.

Khruschev tells in his memoirs that he was surprised to see long lines of Jews in 1940, following the division of Poland, queuing up in Lemberg to obtain permits to return to Nazi-occupied Poland.

So strong was the faith of Jewish people in humanity that even in 1942, when the gas chambers in Treblinka and Maidanek were working full blast, the harried and starving masses in the ghettoes refused to believe that the Nazis were actually engaged in a deliberate policy of total annihilation. The first reports by ragged survivors were disbelieved not only by foreign observers but by the ill-fated victims themselves.[11]

The Nazi Program

The Holocaust was a logical result of the Nazi program. But then we need to know how it was possible for such a vile ideology to come to power in a cultured country like Germany. Many theories have been proposed to explain this phenomenon:

First, the militaristic theory. For many Germans the Great War never ended. They continued to fight in the "free corps" and then in the *S.A.* (Sturmabteilungen) against the Versailles Treaty. Hitler began his career as a paid spy on workers' organizations. And the conservative forces secretly supported the Nazi storm-troopers, helping them to overwhelm all opposition. With the parliamentary system reduced to impotence, Hindenburg was compelled to hand the government over to Hitler.

Second, the Communist theory. Fascism is the final effort of the capitalists to hold on to power. The social class which Hitler won over to his banner consisted of white-collar workers, lower middle-class people, who fearfully saw themselves sinking into the working class, and the masses of the unemployed, the so-called "*Lumpenproletariat.*" The Ruhr industrialists financed the storm-troopers and the Nazi political machine in order to terrorize the workers and to bewilder them with slogans of phony "socialism." The "Thule" society sponsored the initial efforts of Hitler.

Third, the Liberal theory. It was the imposition of the Versailles Treaty and the subsequent attempts of France to collect "reparations" that plunged the country into an infernal inflation, and radicalized the German people. So hated was the Versailles Treaty that Hitler succeeded in mobilizing a large segment of the people to undo its provisions.

Fourth, Nazism was the final product of certain romantic trends that were peculiar to Germany. The French historian, Vermeil, traced all the identifiable components of the Nazi program to their roots in German literature and philosophy, concluding that Nazism could have arisen only in Germany.[12]

Fifth, the peculiar genius of Hitler and the clever opportunists who formed his entourage. Hitler was a master propagandist, able to wield the weapon of the "big lie" with deft skill. His was that peculiar mixture of passion and cunning, of frustration and fantasy, of anger and eloquence, that, like a match, set off a devastating prairie fire. Somehow, his hoarse voice and his impassioned style of oratory were perfectly suited at that time for the evocation of an irresistible mass appeal.

Erich Kahler sums it all up when he writes:

"All these theories are correct as far as they go, but no one of them alone is sufficient to explain the complex phenomenon of National Socialism. . . . It is not just an isolated episode in European history, but the embodiment of a civilization in its last stages of decay and dissolution."[13]

Germany was simply in the vanguard of European development, according to Kahler. Political life in Europe was actually based on the struggle of nations for power. But what other countries managed to package in idealistic slogans, the Germans under Hitler developed into a conscious principle. "The Nazi movement . . . was novel only because it worshiped power openly."[14]

The repudiation of all ideals and the worship of power is the essence of nihilism. The Germans, in Kahler's view, were ahead of other nations in developing the implications of nihilism. And they saw in the Jew the symbol of the universal values which they set out to destroy.[15]

In all these approaches, the role of the Jew was incidental. He was a convenient target for propaganda. The German people wanted *simple* answers and a *concrete* enemy, easy to attack because he is weak and close at hand, yet mythically powerful so that he is worthy of one's steel. Also, Jewish wealth could be used as bait to lure the greedy careerists. Joachim C. Fest quotes Hitler as saying, "If the Jew did not exist, we would have had to invent him. A visible enemy, not just an invisible one, is what is needed."[16]

Indeed, the mythical image of the Jew was politicized in Germany, long before Hitler. The target of hate and contempt for centuries, the Jew was ideally suited to serve as the battering ram against liberalism in Germany. Attacks against him were collective exercises in the promotion of the Aryan race-theory. Once the racial source of cultural greatness is accepted, Hitler reasoned, it will be easy to carry out the other implications of the Nazi program for the establishment of its "New Order."

We cannot here enter into an analysis of all the factors that brought Hitler to power. With the Holocaust as our focus, we ask whether it could have happened in any other part of Europe. Our judgment is that it was projected and carried out as part of the Nazi "New Order." It was not a consequence of antisemitism in general but an outgrowth of the special ideological and political factors prevailing in Germany. These included a vision of a "New Order" as part of the "German ideology" or of Teutonism, as it was developed by Wagner, Lagarde, Langbehn and Spengler. This vision drew its inspiration from the peculiar forms which "social Darwinism" assumed in Germany; it was incubated in the hothouse of nihilism, as a conscious rejection of Christianity; at the same time, it awakened associations of a return to ancient prewestern values. It thrived on the mood of opposition to all that was modern; it capitalized on the fear of Communism; it was the opening wedge to a new social order, which the new war would hopefully make possible.

These factors were peculiar to Germany. Not all the followers of Hitler agreed with every one of these anti-Jewish associations. A resurgent wave of Teutonic fury, aimed at launching a war of conquest, might have been organized by a military dictatorship, with only a tincture of antisemitism—the kind of contemptuous attitude toward Jews that prevailed in conservative and military ranks before and during the First World War. But the German people were not eager to plunge into a new war. They needed to be bewildered and stampeded by a hysterical propaganda machine. A popular movement for the renewal of the war could only be organized in the way which Hitler pioneered, or so it seemed. For this purpose, the pomp and panoply of a quasireligion had to be created, complete with "sons of the gods," seeking to reclaim their treasure, and the minions of Satan, easily identified, wearing yellow stars, waiting to be led to the slaughter.

Wagner's "Nibelungen" operas served as the Bible of the new racial superreligion, ringing all the changes in the propagation of the Aryan myth.[17]

After his successful occupation of the Rhineland, Hitler mused:

"I have built up my religion out of *Parsifal*. Divine worship in solemn form . . . without pretenses of humility. . . . One can serve God only in the garb of the hero."[18]

That a form of Nazism, without antisemitism, was possible in Germany is demonstrated by Spengler. Consider the following excerpts from the unfinished work which he wrote in 1933:[19]

1. Liberalism, Communism, Pacifism are branded as perversions, which arose "out of the absence of spiritual discipline, personal weakness, lack of training through a sacred, old tradition."[20]

2. He hails the reemergence of "the age old barbarism"[21] asserting that "man is a beast of prey."[22]

3. The establishment of the Bolshevik regime in Russia means that "Asia has recaptured Russia."[23]. The genuine Russian has the soul of a Nomad, "who wanders without a goal." He lacks a strong will, whereas the "German life-feeling is the will to conquer."[24]

4. In the case of England, its racial treasure was used up. But the Germans are still "young."[25]

5. "Equal rights is against nature".[26]

6. "The Will to own property is the Nordic 'meaning of life' (*Sinn des Lebens*). Whoever lacks this instinct does not possess 'race.'"[27]

7. The greatest issue is not Communism but the struggle "between the leading elements of the white peoples and the others . . ." "The great emerging danger is of the colored races."[28]

8. "The Prussian idea is as much against Finance-liberalism as it is

against the socialism of workers." "I have hated from the first day the dirty revolution of 1918 as a betrayal by the less-worthy part of our people . . ."[29]

9. Yet, Spengler disassociated his extremist and Darwinist conservatism from the antisemitic dogma of the Nazis.

"This barbarism is that which I call a strong race, the eternally warlike in man, the human beast of prey type." He adds in a note, "I repeat: race which one possesses, not a race to which one belongs. The first is an *ethos*, the latter is Zoology."[30]

Spengler's neobarbarism, nihilism, antiwesternism, antislavism, and Prussianism are components of the Nazi ideology, which were peculiar to Germany and not inherently antisemitic. But, without the smokescreen of antisemitism, this crusade could not have won popular support.

Neobarbarism was the utopianism of the Prussian conservatives. In German minds, the destruction of the Roman Empire by the Goths and the Vandals was recollected with pride and held up as a model for the future. As many German historians saw it, the Roman Empire was "old" and effete; the Germans were "young," bearers in their blood and seed of fresh creative energy. In history, the "young" nations, conscious of the nobility of their "blood," are destined to destroy the old, overintellectualized, overcivilized empires. The barbarians of the fifth century annihilated millions and demolished an outworn civilization, but they infused the survivors with new blood and pitiless courage, preparing the soil for the emergence of a new "culture." They were hard, cruel and murderous, but they carried out their historical mission with unflinching determination.

It is this "German Ideology" that formed the basic framework for the Nazi vision of the "New Order." And this "New Order," in the view of the Nazis, included the requirement to eliminate the Jews altogether from the "*Lebensraum*" of the Germans.

In peacetime, this "German Ideology" would be expressed in generalized and camouflaged terms, in deference to the feelings of liberal and humanist Germans. But in the grip of war-fever, the preachers of a resurgent "Prussianism" did not have to hide their preference for Sparta over Athens. The Spartan system required a perpetual war against "the enemy within." Did not the Spartans engage in the sport of periodically cutting down the number of Helots?

The Nazi movement thrived on self-deception as well as on propaganda. Their guiding star was the value of the "big lie" in propaganda but they "believed" their own lies. The Nazis described the mythical Jew as the most powerful force in the concert of nations, yet they aimed their arrows at him precisely because he was so weak and defenseless. They isolated the Jew by inventing a classification, "non-Aryan," that applied only to him; yet, they intended at the same time to use his degradation as the lever whereby all of non-Teutonic mankind was to be reduced to diverse levels of enslavement. They were taught to "think with their blood," believing whatever the racial genius projects as reflections of their own deepest self. Paradoxically, the great example for the Master race was provided by the "antirace" at the other end of the ethnic spectrum. In their view, Jewish "slave morality" and the Chosen People concept were "myths" projected by the Jewish race, in order to dominate the world. Through Christianity, the Jewish "myth" enthralled the minds of hundreds of millions. Now, the Aryans projected their "myth," as Wagner had done in his myths of Parsifal and the Nibelungen. Alfred Rosenberg set out to elaborate the details of the "Myth of the Twentieth Century," in which the Teutons are nature's own "Chosen people." This new myth can be embraced by a "leap of faith," aided by the elaborate pageantry, the fantastic displays at demonstrations and the intoxication of torch-light parades at Party meetings.

It is not the rhetoric of Nazism but its practical program that offers us a clue to the understanding of its nature. Consequently, to understand the "Final Solution," we have to see it within the perspective of the war for the establishment of the Thousand-Year Reich and its New Order. The Jewish tragedy was intended to be a curtain-raiser for the new age and its "heroic" morality.

Directly after the conquest of Poland, the Nazis proceeded to annihilate the Polish elite: the clergy, the professionals, the graduates of colleges, the teachers and the high-school graduates.[31] Soon after their initial successes in Russia, the Nazis believed that they had won the war and that they could proceed with impunity to establish their New Order, in which Slavs would be forced into slavery, denied any education beyond what was needed for them to follow the instructions of their Teutonic masters. In Hitler's vision of the new Europe, there was no room for too many Slavs—that is, many more than the Germans needed to service their "colonists." Therefore, a hundred million or more Slavs, chiefly Russians, would have to be eliminated.[32]

In this context of Teutonic aggrandizement and the helotization of the Slavic population, the Holocaust of the Jews can be seen in its true dimensions. In the case of the Slavs, the elimination of the educated elite was sufficient to render the survivors tractable, since in Nazi doctrine, Slavs were slaves "by nature." They would be employed to do hard labor, as farmers, miners and expendable workers. Some of their children might be adopted by the S.S. and sent to the Reich for ethnic reeducation.

In the case of the Jews, Nazi theory assumed that only a total program of annihilation would safeguard the permanence of the New Order. Their cleverness or cunning would raise the Jews to the higher echelons of society, in spite of their initial disenfranchisement. Jews were not designed "by nature" to serve as submissive, dumb helots. Hence, their total removal was imperative.

In sum, the theory of Teutonic blood as the source of a "noble," aristocratic ideology required at the opposite pole another people which is the source of the "wicked" ideologies: Christianity, liberalism, socialism, internationalism. And the Jew of history was "manifestly" the source of the "degenerate" ideologies. In this way, the logic of Manichean dualism was vindicated. The prevalence of popular antisemitism throughout the world could therefore be employed as a means of discrediting the ideologies which stood in the way of Nazi triumph. Early in his career, Hitler discovered that whenever he denounced Jews he was greeted with thunderous applause. The ignorant masses needed an incarnate Satan to combat, even more than a god of "wood and stone" to worship. They could hardly blame the evils of the world on the abstract concepts of economic theory. In their impassioned regression to political infantilism, to premodern and prerational modes of thought, they fell back into the comfortable mythology of the age of witch-hunts and demonism.

Still, all these explanations do not fully account for the mentality which made the Holocaust possible. In her brilliant study of the Holocaust, Lucy Davidowicz asserts that it was Hitler alone who was ultimately responsible for the so called "final solution." Traditional antisemitism had created a certain rhetoric of hate, which massaged the collective egoes of European peoples, especially that of the disaffected and the disoriented marginal elements of the population, the so called "Lumpenproletariat." But Hitler took that rhetoric seriously and with pedantic literalism undertook to put into action the verbiage that was intended to let off steam, as when uncultured people employ swear-words and even complicated formulae of foul rhetoric. So, in her view, the personal character of Hitler accounts for the difference between the previous, occasional outbursts of anti-semitic fury and the cold, deliberate calculation of the "final solution."

The personal idiosyncrasies of Hitler certainly affected the Nazi anti-Jewish policy. He did not trust the regular bureaucracy to carry out his nefarious design. Instead, he assigned this task to a picked corps of S.S. men, who were especially trained and indoctrinated for this purpose. To be sure, there was no overt opposition to the policy of extermination. Even in a totalitarian state, determined mass protests cannot be ignored. Some of Hitler's orders were withdrawn in the face of implacable opposition, such as the order to kill the sick and incurables, at the beginning of the war, and the orders to destroy Paris and to follow a "scorched earth" policy in Germany itself in the closing weeks of the war.

We need to understand two questions above all: Why did so many of Germany's conservative leaders facilitate Hitler's rise to power, though they were aware of his infernal intentions? What was it about the German people that predisposed them to carry out so brutal a policy without flinching?

To take the second question first, we take note of the answer of Joachim C. Fest. The German, in his view, is alienated from reality, disposed to wander off into comforting fantasies and to follow the logic of ideas whithersoever they may lead. Discussing Hitler's tendency to "take off, in conversation, into 'higher regions,' from which he had constantly to be 'pulled down to the solid ground of facts,'" Fest observes:

"What was German about it was only the intellectual consistency with which he constructed these mental systems. What was German also was the merciless rigor, the shrinking from no logical conclusion."[33]

We do not believe that any nation is permanently stamped with a certain invariant character. However, at any one time, the momentum of history and the chemistry inherent in the prevailing mood of the nation produce a certain consensus. In the case of Germany, Weimar represented a break with the conservative tradition, and it seemed to fail. In desperation, the people sought solace in regaining the sense of unity and in plunging into the surrealistic world of racial mysticism and grandeur. At the crucial moment, they were encouraged by the leadership of the conservative elements to feel that they were relying on the traditional guardians of their past. They could safely close their eyes and savor the sweet feelings of unity, of surrender to the incarnate spirit of the nation, of stirring pride and of the glow of a mighty destiny.

So the basic question is the first one, the policy of the Conservatives, culminating in Hindenburg's yielding the scepter to Hitler.

The leftist and liberal elements of German society were overwhelmed by force, terror and numbers, but the conservative elements in the army, in industry, and in politics pushed Hitler up the ladder of power, and they sought to get rid of him only at the eleventh hour.

Certainly, the action of von Papen and his allies, which handed Germany over to the Nazis, was not an accidental, unprecedented phenomenon in Germany. Whenever the Conservatives in the Second Reich were politically hard-pressed they embraced the radical antisemites, whom they themselves regarded as the "lunatic fringe" of their movement. It is sufficient to recall the so called Tivoli program of the Berlin Party Congress of 1892, which adopted many antisemitic slogans. As the historian Bracher put it, "they hoped to use the radicals to manipulate the petty bourgeoisie."[34] Long before the industrialists of the Ruhr undertook to finance the Nazis, the Thule Society, first organized as an upper class order dedicated to the mystique of racism and Teutonic supremacy, acted as "the godfather of the Hitler party."[35] In its fantastic rituals, "German runes and swastikas were used."[36] It served as a rallying point for the remnants of the Free Corps; it sponsored the most violent antisemitic campaigns, and it enjoyed "the benevolent approval of militaristic circles."[37] Its motto was "German, keep your blood pure!" It was the financial assistance of this society that enabled Hitler's party to launch its first newspaper and to secure the assistance of some wealthy supporters, of whom Fritz Thyssen was the best known.

The Conservatives were after all raised in a great cultural and Christian tradition. They proved to be tactically wrong. They had neither the wit nor the power to keep Hitler on a tight leash, and they paid a terrible price for their folly. But their tactical failures were evidently due to a deeper cause: their desire to be deceived with regard to both domestic and foreign policies. A large class of people cannot be fooled, unless they subconsciously want to be fooled.

Faced by the choice of either surrendering the leadership of the nation to a coalition of Liberals, Socialists and Catholic Centrists or making a pact with the devil and reverting to the program of Prussianism at home and aggressive Teutonism abroad, they preferred the latter alternative. And they knew that the latter pathway could be followed only with the aid of a modern "pied piper."

The Conservatives in Germany despaired of winning the people over to their side by sober arguments and by the normal methods of persuasion. The masses, especially the unorganized and the disorganized, the unemployed embittered workers and the dispossessed and impoverished farmers, would have to be mobilized by hate slogans. Already Bismarck had shown the way, when for a brief spell he utilized the antisemites for his political ploys, though he was not an antisemite. Other Conservatives had followed a similar road. It was possible to see Hitler simply as a clever demagogue, who mastered the art of seducing the masses. Did not Hitler write that politicians must employ the "big lie," if they are to win the acclaim of the people? And did he not prove himself to be a master-politician, by his manipulation of the masses, chiefly by reducing all issues for the masses to the fact of one's "blood?" And did not the aristocrats of all nations believe that their nobility consisted primarily in their "blood," their genetic heritage, their natural gifts? Hitler had proved that the masses could be controlled and manipulated, without such dangerous concessions as are implied in the liberal vision of equality or the socialist vision of continuous social progress.

To the aristocrats, then, antisemitism was a political weapon, to be used as the exigencies of politics required. Hitler proved that this weapon "worked." It may be assumed that had the Conservatives succeeded in controlling Hitler, as they had hoped, they would not have allowed their nation to sink to the depths of Auschwitz. They might flirt with "prejudice" as the cement of society, in keeping with Burke's counsel. They might endorse the "feelings" of the people, as being invariably right, as did Wagner and Treitschke, especially when those "feelings" of envy and hate are deflected away from their own privileged positions. They might even agree with Hitler's "voice of blood" or "song of blood," so long as this blood-thinking reinforces their own domestic and foreign policies. But, to engage in cold-blooded mass murder—there, the line would have been drawn by the demands of religion, the habits of culture, the conscience of Europe.

To be sure, neither the mass-slaughter of Russian prisoners of war nor the attacks of the "*Einsatzgruppen*" against the Jews of Eastern Europe could have been carried out without the active connivance of the German Army. But to be charitable, we note that it is one thing to hide behind the shield of "orders from the chief" in wartime, and quite another to initiate such plans and execute them directly.

We must remember that a pact with the devil appealed to the Conservatives for reasons of foreign policy as well as domestic politics. Hitler's vision of a "New Order" in the East was only a radicalization of their cherished plans, as revealed in the peace-treaty of Brest-Litovsk: namely, to convert most of Poland and the entire Ukraine into a Teutonic colony. Again, if the Conservatives had had their way, the helotization of the Slavs would have been carried out with only tentative stabs at the implementation of projects of "depopulation," for the sake of Teutonic "supremacy." But, such is the character of a pact with the devil: in the end, he wins the soul of his partner.

In this case, the soul of Hitler's aristocratic and industrial partners was corroded by the nihilistic propaganda, which asserted that there were no truths and no values—only the instincts and intuitions of the racially "noble" vs. those of the racially "base." And this racial nihilism, which burst out sporadically in other parts of Europe and America, acquired a special patriotic tinge in Germany because it awakened echoes from the past. Perhaps history does repeat itself. May it not be the destiny of Germany to undertake once again the role of the destroying and reinvigorating Barbarians? Perhaps the hour has come to give the *coup de grace* to the heritage of Athens and to the spirit of Jerusalem in order that a new culture might grow out of Teutonic blood, in particular, and out of the regenerated Aryan race in general?

From our analysis thus far, it is clear that antisemitism was, to the Nazis, firstly an article of faith in their ideology of mystical racism, which exalted the Teutons to the top of the Aryan hierarchy of peoples; secondly a weapon with which to shatter domestic resistance, and thirdly the visible part of the iceberg, the clearly announced portion of their vaguely affirmed crusade to institute a "New Order," based on race, which would turn all "non-Aryans," all Africans and Asians, virtually 95% of the human race into slaves of varying categories. Because only the Jewish part of the program was openly put forward, the other nations and races of Europe could delude themselves into thinking that they would be among the favored few. In the meantime, the future victims could join the fraternity of hate against those who at the moment were ranked as "the lesser breeds without the law."

In the other countries of Europe and America, the tides of antisemitism might rise and fall. But, it is hard to see a situation where it becomes the central plank of a movement aiming at the subjugation of the world and parading under the banner of patriotism. What was German about Nazism was not merely the tendency to be consistently "ideological," forcing the totality of experience into the preconceived molds of certain "ideas," as Fest maintains, but the peculiar German situation, in the heart of Europe; the memories of the Barbarian attacks on Rome, of the Holy Roman Empire, of the Order of Teutonic Knights setting out to conquer the Slavic peoples, of the massive expansion of science and industry in the Second Reich, of the near-victory of Germany in the First World War. Given this situation and the political polarization of Germany in the postwar world, Nazism could draw upon the peculiar versions of German nationalism in the Romantic period and German ambivalence in regard to the West as well as upon the underworld of antisemitic mythology, pressure-cooking this vicious brew with its realistic program of conquest. No parallel to this situation occurred anywhere in Europe, except perhaps in those areas of Russia which were occupied by the "White" armies during the Civil War.

It has been correctly said that France experienced a catharsis of its medieval fantasies and racial myths during the Dreyfus Affair. At that time, the alliance of the General Staff of the army with the phony "patriots" and the reactionary "Catholic Action" forces, in order to protect a traitor and to hurt a patriotic Jew, was obviously pathetic and artificial. Still, it took men of great courage and a host of young politicians, who truly believed in the great ideals of nineteenth-century liberation, to bring France to reason.

Germany was virtually caught in a civil war during the twenty-year interval between Versailles and the Second World War. The *free corps* and the Storm Troopers fought against the Communists in the early twenties, continuing their terroristic attacks without letup, down to their seizure of power. The army, the judiciary and the constabulary intervened only occasionally and fitfully. The full force of the law was never invoked against the paramilitary force of the Nazis, so that the latter were able to concentrate their full fury first against one segment of the population, then against others. In this way, the academic communities were terrorized. As Hitler put it:

"Terror at the place of employment, in the factory, in the meeting hall and on the occasion of mass-demonstrations will always be successful unless opposed by equal terror."[38] Hitler's storm troopers were drawn from the gutter and officered by nihilistic careerists. They succeeded in silencing all opposition, but whether or not they really won the German people over to their views, at any time, is open to doubt. After all, when the Nazi regime fell, the people awoke as from a nightmare and could hardly believe that they had ever participated in the worst horrors of recorded history.

Israel and the Diaspora

The Nazi Crusade for a "New Order" and the Holocaust intensified both the sense of uniqueness and the universal quality of Jewish identity.

At no time in history did Jews feel as lonely and deserted as they felt on the eve of the Second World War. The rising shadow of the Swastika over the lands of Eastern Europe reminded them that they, and they alone, were being branded with the mark of Satan. All the European peoples could be designated as Aryan, in various degrees. They alone were "Non-Aryan." To be sure, the vast majority of mankind were also "Non-Aryan," and as we have seen, the Slavs were stamped as subhuman, with the Celts only a cut above them, while the Mediterranean peoples could hardly claim to approximate the Nazi ideal of "the blonde beast." The Arabs were certainly Semitic and the Japanese basically Mongolian. When the "big lie" is consciously made into a policy, such objections are irrelevant. For practical reasons, the Jews alone were stigmatized as "Non-Aryan," partly in order to lull the non-Teutonic world into a false sense of security. In order to further emphasize the difference between Jews and other ethnic groups, the Nazis characterized the former as "antihuman," whereas the latter were "subhuman" in various degrees. In their fiendish view of human nature, they imagined that people would be content to accept a low place on the racial totem-pole, provided they could see that other groups were lower still.

This exclusion of the Jews from the entire body of European humanity drew some plausibility from the ancient official religion and the new religion of sanctified ethnocentrism:

First, we bear in mind the heritage of popular Christianity which stigmatized the Jew as the bearer of a divine curse. This dogma was reinforced by medieval folklore which associated the Jew with demons and sorcery. The fact that the most immoral, the most antispiritual, the most anti-Christian ideology in history appealed to the hateful residue of Christian sentiments did not bother anyone except the intellectuals.

Second, the rising tide of chauvinistic nationalism in the successor-states of Czarist Russia and Imperial Austria deepened the gulf between the Jews and their neighbors. The idea that "the self-determination of nations" would usher in a messianic era proved to be a terrible delusion in that part of the world, where no national ambition could be fully satisfied without hurting other nations. And the Jews were an urban minority in all these countries, surrounded by an impoverished, barely literate rural population.

The memory of pogroms against the Jews as traditional folk-activity served to lend color of legitimacy to the anti-Jewish program of the Nazis. For the law of momentum works in history as in nature. Ideas and events of the past exert their effect in the present. They would be repeated if they were not held in check by a greater force, in this case, the "modern" ideas of the liberal elite. With the breakdown of the liberal leadership, the beastly instincts of the masses reinforced by their recollection of past excesses could take over. The Nazis encountered no difficulty in mobilizing Ukrainians and Lithuanians, even some Poles, to assist them in their nefarious work.

In sum, the intent and the consequence of the Nazi anti-Jewish policy was to set Jews apart as a pariah-people and at the same time identify them with the progressive forces in society. They employed antisemitism deliberately as a battering ram against the liberal world and non-Teutonic humanity. All the principles of the French Revolution—liberty, equality, brotherhood, international amity, respect for the rights and dignity of the individual—all these ideals were "Jewish." In fighting against the Western countries, they claimed, they were really fighting against the phantom of "international Jewry." So, in Nazi eyes, the Jews came to stand for the ideals of democracy, of scientific truth, of thinking objectively rather than "with one's blood," of the fraternity of peoples and the inviolability of human rights.

As the plans of the Nazis for the conquest of the world unfolded, it became clear that their anti-Jewish animus was really directed against humanity itself. They directed their fire at a mythical enemy in order to build up a smoke-screen to deflect attention from their real plans, which were anti-Celtic, anti-Slavic, anti-colored races, anti all non-Teutonic humanity. In their arrogant mythology, the Jew represented the very ideals which western man had cherished ever since the inglorious reign of medieval feudalism and fanaticism.

Hence, the impact of the Nazi crusade on the Jews of the West was felt in two opposite directions. On the one hand, the Jewish sense of uniqueness was reinforced; on the other hand, the universal dimension of Jewish life and destiny was demonstrated on a global scale. These two aspects of self-consciousness were deeply rooted in Jewish tradition, as we have seen. They reflect the different components of the tradition, but they are not really contradictory. For the uniqueness of Jewish destiny consists principally in the fact that the Jew is the litmus-paper of civilized humanity. The champions of fanaticism and tyranny in European history invariably singled out the Jews as the special target of their poisoned barbs. In medieval times, this fanaticism was religiously inspired; in modern times, it was fueled by the massed fury of national pride; at all times, the suppressed hate, the prevailing prejudices of the gullible masses and their self-glorifying mythology could be mobilized against the Jews.

If Jewish people had not been faced at the end of World War II with a mass of refugees, concentrated in camps, and a beleagured community in Palestine, eager to absorb them and to become an independent state, the universal character of Jewish destiny might have been reinforced. For the Jews that were concentrated in the so called Pale of Settlement most clearly represented the ethnic aspect of Jewish identity. As it turned out, they were the principal victims of the Nazi annihilation program, and outside of the U.S.S.R, only Western Jewry had survived. But, the historical realities were such that the Jews of the Diaspora had to mobilize all their forces in order to carry out two tasks; to bring the refugees to their "homeland" and to restructure that "homeland" as a political state. In human terms, this two-pronged effort brooked no delay.

The Jews of the western world were burdened by a sense of guilt for not having done more to save their European brothers, and the Christians of the West were similarly shocked by the demonic depths to which a leading Christian nation, like Germany, could sink. Jews and their Christian friends brought pressure to bear upon the British, and later the American government, with the result that the Partition Plan was adopted by the United Nations in 1947 and the State of Israel was officially proclaimed on May 14, 1948.

The internal Jewish opposition to Zionism, as an ideology, was overwhelmed by the course of events. By the time Israel came into being, the ideological opposition of such groups as the American Council for Judaism was reduced to a pathetic shadow. And while prewar Zionism was vague about the meaning of a "homeland," the Biltmore program adopted in 1942 was clear about the need of a Jewish state. During the fifties, as the fledgeling state grew by leaps and bounds, the ideological debate concerning the nature of Jewish identity became more and more irrelevant.

Jacob Blaustein, the dominant figure in the "non-Zionist" American Jewish Committee, was worried over David Ben Gurion's call on American Jews to emigrate to Israel. In behalf of the Committee he negotiated an agreement with Ben Gurion, in which the latter pledged that Israel would not attempt to speak in behalf of all Jews and would not call upon Jews in the "free world" to cut their roots and become Israeli. Blaustein was concerned that such propaganda would undermine the Jewish position in America and the western world. Ben Gurion was fearful that American Jews would not support Israel on the scale that was needed, if they did not feel that their own fate was involved in the building of Israel. Also, he believed that Israel had to increase its population very rapidly in order to survive the future bouts of Arab attacks that he anticipated.[39]

As it happened, the rush of history produced a solution, independently of ideologies. The population of Israel expanded rapidly through the influx of Jews from Arab lands, and through the refugees from Europe. Only a tiny trickle of Jews from Western Europe and America emigrated to Israel and remained there, barely a fraction of the number of old and new Israeli emigrants, "Yordim" who left Israel to settle in America and Canada. While Israel and the Jewish Agency did call loudly and insistently for *Aliyah* from western countries, in spite of the Ben Gurion agreement, the response was exceedingly meager. A mass migration is not set in motion by an abstract ideal but by massive economic pressures. Israel managed to establish a standard of living that ranged midway between those of the Soviet world and America. Furthermore, cold hatred pursued the Jews in the Arab lands and in Eastern Europe, but in the West antisemitism had been associated with the policy of the archenemy and was totally discredited.

The genesis and growth of Israel did not lead to any embarrassments for the Jewish people in America, as some feared. Except for rare occasions (as in Israel's 1956 attack on Egypt, in collusion with Britain and France), the specter of "double loyalty" was banished from public view, principally because Israel "tilted" ever more decisively toward America and away from the Soviet Union. In turn, America was moved by a combination of moralistic-sentimental reasons and the cold logic of geopolitical strategy to treat Israel as its protégé. While this development was unsteady and vacillating at first, it was demonstrated clearly in the Six Day War of June, 1967, and even more clearly in the Yom Kippur War of October, 1973.

The departure of Israel from strict neutrality was not evident during the War of Independence, when the Soviet Union helped to arm Israel, through its control of Czechoslovakia, and granted it full diplomatic support. But after the Armistice, Israel drifted into the American orbit, in part because of its dire financial needs and in part because of its cultural-religious affinity with the West. In its turn, the Soviet Union launched a massive and bitter campaign against any manifestation of Jewish nationalism and Zionism. The term "Zionist," became a swear-word in the U.S.S.R. and the Russian Jews were condemned to endure a period of cruel repression that became steadily more severe. Hostility to Jews, which was formerly disallowed by Soviet dogma, was now respectable, providing it was directed at "Zionists."

It is idle to speculate about the consequences to American Jews, if Israel had "tilted" toward the Soviet Union and had become dependent upon its military and economic support, in its life and death struggle against the Arabs. Would American Jews, then, have fallen into the suspected category of their Soviet brethren? Would the Nazi identification of Jews with Communism have gained in plausibility and force? Of course, America is not a police-state and its people do not live in terror of vague suspicions. But, then in the McCarthy era, it was apparent that there were limits to American tolerance. In many a defense or electronic factory, there were two sets of workers—those who enjoyed security clearance and those who did not. Howsoever it might have been, the fact is that Israel is now firmly included within the range of American strategic defense.

The Awakening of Russian Jewry

The sudden reassertion of their Jewish identity by young Russian Jews is an arresting phenomenon. We can list the causes: the alignment of Israel in the anti-Soviet camp and the courtship of the Arabs by the Soviets, eager to obtain a foothold in the Middle East: the identification of Soviet citizens in their passports according to nationality and the official designation of Jewishness as a nationality; the infighting of nationalities within the bureaucracy for greater shares of the pie and the envy of Ukrainians and others of the higher intellectual qualifications of the Jewish people: the actual suspicion of the loyalty of young Jews, who might at a later time opt for emigration to Israel, and the possibility of using that suspicion as a pretext for discrimination; the tendency of the children of those who were tortured in labor camps to join the dissidents and to turn their back upon the Soviet system; the years of western prosperity prior to the recession in 1974; the opportunity of acquiring in Israel an unambiguous identity and of sharing in the building of a new society that would be both socialist and democratic.

All these causes can be listed, but we have no way at this writing of evaluating their respective potencies. Most importantly, we cannot tell the extent to which the Jewish population has been affected by these causes. How many would leave if they could? How many identify themselves as Russian and Soviet? How many are children of intermarried couples, thoroughly assimilated, who are bitterly disenchanted with the Soviet policies of oppression, à la Solzhenitsyn, Medvedev or Sakharov, and who make use of their tenuous Jewish linkage in order to obtain the right to leave their homeland?

Another set of questions refers to those who sincerely hunger for the reassertion of their Jewish identity. What is the role of religion in their lives? Do they seek spiritual fulfillment as Jews? Or do they want merely the "warmth" of ethnic culture and the psychic support of "pooled pride?"

Still, another set of questions refers to the possibility of a renewed growth of the Jewish religion and religio-cultural life in the Soviet Union. There is no basic reason for the Soviets to suppress religion as such. In Hungary and Poland, the Catholic faith is allowed considerable freedom. In Russia itself, the Greek Orthodox religion continues to be relatively strong. After all, the association of religion with reaction no longer holds true in most of the world. Can we join with leaders of other faiths in an effort to persuade the Soviet authorities to allow greater freedom for religion for their citizens? Would Judaism then be treated as fairly as other faiths? In respect of the last question our uncertainty is not due to the persistence of antisemitism but to the fact that many Jews themselves claim that Zionism, specifically political Zionism, is an integral portion of the Jewish religion. And the Soviet attitude to Zionism and Israel depends upon international factors, which are not likely to change very soon. Do the Soviets fear that any concession to Jewish faith and culture will result in an increased stream of would-be emigrants? Probably so.

On the other hand, does not our present policy of pressing for greater numbers of emigrants virtually condemn the vast majority of Russian Jews to the total obliteration of their identity as Jews? Furthermore, does not the persistent propaganda for emigration encourage the Soviet authorities to deny young Jews entrance to universities, research institutes and technical training centers? As they see it, higher education is an investment in young people, and it should be reserved for those who will serve the nation.

The dilemma faced by Jewish leaders in the free world is a very real one: should they press for emigration only and ignore those who will stay? Should they argue for religious and cultural freedom? Should they press for human rights in general, including the right for religious practice within Russia and the right to emigrate for those who choose to do so? If the latter two courses are chosen, it will be difficult for outsiders to monitor the pace of progress. Furthermore, the Israeli government is still wedded to the old Zionist principle, which affirms that there is no future for Jews outside the Homeland.

In any case, Russian Jewry has already demonstrated that Jewish people cannot be assimilated in one or two generations. A people that is formed by religious as well as ethnic ties and is actively involved in world affairs cannot be made to forget either its contemporary identity or its historic past. And any effort to suppress that collective consciousness is certain to boomerang.

Ambivalence of Liberalism

In their struggle for the fullness of emancipation, the Jews relied most heavily on the help of liberals and they redefined their identity in terms of individual freedom. The ideals and the temper of liberalism were ranged solidly on the side of Jewish people, as they struggled to overcome the effects of religious prejudices and ethnic zealotry. The conservative mood, apart from party platforms, resented any kind of change, and esteemed highly the worth of prejudice, as a helpful brake against the changing and disintegrating forces that operate in modern society.

In the case of Zionism, however, liberalism was ambivalent. The sympathies of liberals were with the Jews, but their ideals called for the solution of Jewish homelessness through the securing of the rights of individuals, wherever they happened to live. Already in the days of Herzl, the antisemites of Russia, Germany and France found it easier to sympathize with the cause of a Jewish homeland than the liberals, the old-time friends of Jewish people.

England was a special case, since its imperial interests coincided from time to time with its idealistic concern for the fate of Eastern European Jewry. The "Jewish homeland" was needed, it would be said, not for the solution of "the Jewish question" in England, but to provide for the stream of refugees from the East. Also, in England, the biblical tradition was strong and the Zionist ideal awakened echoes of ancient romantic visions. As J. L. Talmon put it:

"For one thing, no Jewish historian, whatever his evaluation of the various factors involved in the restoration of Jewish statehood, can ignore the fact that Zionism would never have had a chance for success if centuries of Christian teaching and worship, liturgy and legend had not conditioned the Western nations to respond almost instinctively to the words 'Zion' and 'Israel,' and thus to see in the Zionist ideal not a romantic chimera or an imperialistic design to wrest a country from its actual inhabitants, but the consummation of an eternal promise and hope."[40]

Anglo-American liberals were particularly sensitive to the charge of injuring the Palestinian Arabs, in the effort to render justice to the cause of world Jewry. After the establishment of the State of Israel, the cause of the Arab refugees clashed in the American conscience with that of the Jews in Israel.

A good illustration of this conflict is seen in the hesitant and equivocal posture of the *Christian Century Magazine* toward Zionism and Israel. While this central organ of the non-Fundamentalist Protestants was naturally sympathetic to the plight of Jewish refugees, it fought a persistent rear-guard action against the establishment of the Jewish state.

In his study, "American Protestantism and a Jewish State," Herzl Fishman concluded:

"A basic contradiction exists between the attitude of American Protestantism toward Jews as individuals and its attitude toward the Jewish people as a collective entity. Modern liberal Protestantism has consistently protested overt antisemitic acts against individual Jews and has labeled antisemitism a theological sin. But it has remained blind to the sharp contrast which exists between its theoretical objections to antisemitism and the practical injurious effects of its own subtle antisemitism on the destiny of the Jewish people as a collective body. Protestantism's liberal attitude toward Jews as individuals stands in sharp contrast to its persistently hostile attitude toward Jewish peoplehood."[41]

To be sure, Protestant liberals were joined in their critical attitude toward the Jewish State by such non-theological thinkers as Virginia Gildersleeve, Dorothy Thompson and the renowned philosopher, Ernest Wm. Hocking. On the other hand, Reinhold Niebuhr, a Christian "realist," was an ardent defender of the State of Israel.

We might perhaps discern the root of this ambivalence in the distinction between an ideological liberalism, that does not allow for the occurrence of exceptional situations, and an empirical liberalism, which recognizes the imperfection of all categorizations and takes account of the unique elements in every historical event.

So Jews were equally divided, with the ideological liberals holding on tenaciously to the concept of Jewish identity that was developed in nineteenth-century western Europe, while the empirical realists recognized that an unprecedented situation called for a new response. The empiricists had to mediate between the ideological Jewish nationalists, for whom the center of Jewish life the world over was first the vision of Zion and later the state of Israel, and the ideological liberals; the compromise consisted in offering help to the poor immigrants in Israel and elsewhere, without identifying with them. While the ideologists at both ends of the Jewish spectrum affirmed their respective beliefs, the actual policy of Jewish leadership tended to reflect the views of the empiricists, since the logic of events was on their side.

It was the liberal concept of a society of individuals banding together to form a government that Jewish leaders accepted with alacrity ever since the American and French revolutions. But, the liberal Society was never born in czarist Russia, where the majority of the Jews lived. As Jews from the Pale of Settlement moved westward toward Germany, France, England and America, they clung in the early generations to their identity, either in the form of Yiddish Socialist ethnicism, or Orthodoxy, or Hebraic Zionism. Had the tide of liberalism continued its vigorous flow, the ideals of Jewish "folkism," or of Zionism, or of "sacred ethnicism" would have remained the preoccupation of a few visionaries. But, the course of history was involuted, troubled by the "cultural lag" and by the ebb and flow of romantic nationalism. The liberation of the common man implied attention to popular prejudices. More people are moved by sentiment and passion than by logic and principles.

Within the Jewish community, the Holocaust, the subsequent long fight to bring the refugees to a safe haven, the battle to establish Israel and secure its existence, the series of crises and wars which followed— all these developments and challenges involved the cooperation of a generation of Jewish leaders in a vast effort of rescue and rehabilitation, which was totally unprecedented. It would have been strange indeed if such a tremendous undertaking had not generated feelings of fraternity and unity, so intense and pervasive as to surpass the visions and hopes of previous generations.

The liberals who approach the Jewish situation, armed with ready-made ideals of an open society, have to recognize the scars on the consciousness of today's generation of Jewish leaders, scars made by a series of cruel and unprecedented events. On the other hand, it is equally wrong for Jewish ideologists to create a theology of Jewish exceptionalism, based upon a concept of mystical "peoplehood," that they would not want to be adopted by other historic communities. The everlasting enemy of Jewish people is the champion of a "closed society," closed religiously by the ramparts of dogma and the acids of contempt for the outsider, or closed politically by reducing the state to the service of one historic nation, or closed bureaucratically by confining the privileges of citizenship to those who espouse the ideas of the ruling elite. In an open society, there will be at any one time some tension between ethnic subgroups, whose militant leaders clamor for more and more power and influence, and those who champion the national interest as a whole. It is not true, as a general rule, that what is good for any one such subgroup is good for the whole. On the other hand, the exponents of the national interest must recognize the evil consequences of the kind of patriotism that freezes minorities out of the national consensus. Such a rigid mentality would in time destroy all "creative minorities" within the nation. What is needed is a view of the national society that allows for a sympathetic understanding of the special needs of its component groups, and an implicit commitment on the part of all ethnic and historical communities to keep their respective concerns within the parameters of the national interest and the national ideal.

Basically, the Jews of America and of the free world generally remain ardently liberal. The vast majority describe their Jewish identity as being that of a religious community. They reject any tendency to secede from the general community and to form separate enclaves. Their Jewishness imposes upon them additional obligations, such as assistance to Jews who are in distress and to the state of Israel, which was set up for the purpose of rendering such assistance.

Their Jewishness is also a cluster of memories, a pattern of living and an indomitable hope, all interpreted in the light of a religious tradition. But their Jewishness does not separate them from other citizens, save in the dimension of religious faith and practice, and in the maintenance of a worldwide network of philanthropies, previously directed at diverse centers of distress and now focused on Israel.

J. L. Tamon, an Israeli historian, is somewhat unhappy with the tendency of liberals to interpret Jewish issues "in terms of tolerance or intolerance, in the context of the struggle between liberty and tyranny." While "Jewish nationalism and racist anti-semitism both attribute great significance to the Jewish phenomenon," the liberals view even the Holocaust "as an unfortunate, but only temporary, relapse into intolerance. The intentions of the liberals are good. But in one sense, their attitude is at best superficial, and at worst somewhat offensive to Judaism. The majesty attached to a unique fate is impaired and the awesome grandeur of an apocalyptic tragedy is wholly missed."[41a]

Insofar as Talmon inveighs against the tendency of ideological liberals to gloss over the specific details of the Jewish situation, we go along with him. But, he also articulates a longing, however vague, for the aura of unique "majesty" to adorn Jewish self-consciousness. Is not this passion for national "grandeur" the very sin which perverted the national visions of the Fichtes and the Dostoevskys? Talmon speaks not of a Jewish mission but of a Jewish "fate," "to serve as a testimony, as a living witness, a touchstone, a whipping block and symbol—all in one." Again, we can go with him only part of the way. In a continent inflamed by the mystique of nationalism and race, the Jew served as "the outsider," the only concrete exemplar of the preponderant mass of humanity that is "non-Aryan."

But in a situation already bedeviled by an excess of mysticism, why deepen the mystery? As rational students, we cannot speak of an eternal or a unique fate. As circumstances change, the roles of nations are apt to change as well. From its very inception, Judaism opposed the notion of fate. Nations may choose tasks or missions, but fate is imposed from without by a blind force. We can do without such "grandeur." In order to survive as a creative religious community, the Jews of America need only to do their best in generally human terms, and the Jews of Israel need to win their neighbors over for coexistence in peace.

In neither case do we encounter an overwhelming need to strike the posture of "uniqueness." In history, all groups are actually different, therefore unique, but the essential goals of all people are alike and rational. To insist on fostering "uniqueness," as a presumed basis for survival, is to court the sickly fantasy of narcissism.

Toynbee and His Challenge

The English historian, Arnold J. Toynbee, virtually shocked the entire Jewish community by the challenge that he presented in his monumental work, "A Study of History." Completed at a time when Jewish people were undergoing both the anguish of the memories of the Holocaust and the exhilaration of Israel's triumphs, Toynbee's analysis touched a raw nerve in Jews. They were offended more by his comments on the nature and destiny of modern Israel than by his assessment of Diaspora Jewry. His views were resented all the more because he wrote as one who belonged to the traditional friends of Israel. Toynbee was a humanist, a liberal Christian, a cultivated intellectual and an avowed disciple of the great Hebrew prophets, particularly Deutero-Isaiah. Jews were accustomed to attacks from demagogues, chauvinists, purveryors of "mystiques" of one kind or another. But, to be the target of criticism at the hands of a superintellectual and a champion of humanism—this was a different matter altogether.[42]

In fact, Toynbee was by no means antagonistic either to Judaism or to Jewish people. Far from being an antisemite, he described the antisemitic heritage of the Christian world as one of its two great sins, the other being the institution of Negro slavery.[43] Furthermore, as an expert in the British Foreign Office, he was a dedicated anti-Nazi, having shared in the task of awakening the British public to the menace of Hitlerism.[44] All the more, then, Jews were shocked by Toynbee's critique, especially in respect of the following areas: his reference to Jewry as "a fossil of Syriac civilization," his persistent references to "Judaic zealotry" as the heritage of the Christian world,

his denigration of Jewish nationalism in general and his critique of
Israel in particular; his view of Jewish history as culminating in tragic
failure in spite of remarkable spiritual achievements; and his gloomy
estimate of the future of Israel. Each one of these critiques
challenged the emergent self-image of Jewish intellectuals in the post-
Holocaust, post-Israel's birth, post-Vatican II world. These barbs
hurt precisely because they were partially true, though only partially
so.

The term, "fossil," emerged out of Toynbee's classification of
civilizations. In contrast to Spengler's description of cultures in terms
of their respective "souls," symbolized by their diverse conceptions of
space, Toynbee aimed to be empirical, down to earth, concerned with
hard facts. A civilization was a "field of study"; that is, a geographical
area, within which a measure of cultural unity prevailed, whether or
not it was governed by one "universal state." In fact, the
establishment of political unity was in his view a mark of regression
or the beginning of the "breakdown" of a civilization, since further
spontanous growth was likely to be inhibited by the imperial
Leviathan.

Toynbee's approach to world-history was motivated in large part
by his revulsion against the great German historians, who prepared
the way for the monstrous ideology of Nazism. The Hegelian
tradition, which idealized the power-state as the incarnation of
World-Reason, was implicit in the works of Ranke, Treitschke and
Meinecke, let alone in the proto-Nazism of Spengler's
"Prussianism."

In their so-called "world-historical" perspective, might is right, for
"world-history is the world-court"; the war-making power of a state
is the measure of its moral strength, and each historical epoch
generates its own self-contained realm of values. It follows that such
power-states cannot be judged in terms of a transnational, universal
law. This adulation of the state was reinforced by the growth of
romantic nationalism, which substituted the character of the "folk"
and "the voice of blood" for the Hegelian World-Reason. The
historical nation, as a biological entity, with all its dark mystery, was
the heart and soul of the "nation-state." It is easy to see that such a
"folkist" view made life intolerable for all ethnic minorities in

Eastern Europe and, in the case of the Jews, it helped to bring on an antisemitic tide which seemed irresistible.

Toynbee was thoroughly disenchanted with European nationalism and the Teutonic worship of "blood and iron."[45] The two World Wars were seen by him as mighty civil wars; comparable to the Peloponnesian War, in which the confederation of Hellenic cities led by Athens battled against the alliance headed by Sparta. Nationalism was a social disease, the virulence of which was proportional to the extent the nation-state included elements of different nationalities. Hence, his projection of a transnational field of study, defined by external factors of similarity of language and mores.

In the case of the ancient Near East and the emergence of the Jewish people, he chose the entity which he entitled "Syriac Civilization," encompassing Babylonia, Syria, Canaan and later Judea. Within that ancient civilization Judaism functioned as the great Reform movement, transmuting the culture of its peoples in the light of the monotheistic ideas of the prophets, from Abraham to the great unknown prophet of the Exile.

Syriac civilization has been superseded in its homeland by Islamic civilization. It no longer plays a role in world-history. Only scattered remnants of it remain; the Nestorians in the Near East, the Parsees in India and the Jews in Europe.

But, though Toynbee made heroic efforts to overcome the Germanic tradition in the philosophy of history, he retained some of its impetus. He did not free himself altogether from the spell of biological categories. A society is, after all, not an organic entity, tempting as it might be to describe it in terms of birth and abortion, maturation and senescence, fossilization and death. In his effort to overcome the fascination of German historicism, he failed to go far enough, to judge by his own lights, and continued to substitute biological metaphors for sociological realities. A "fossil" is a biological term, borrowed from the theory of evolution. It refers to a creature which remains the same and no longer responds creatively to new challenges. This characterization opens the way for the nose of the camel of "Social Darwinism," with all its destructive potentialities. It reflects the romantic distinction between "old" and "new" nations. The latter are presumably entitled by the law of historical progress to sweep the former off the stage of history. Now, Toynbee distinctly disavows this conclusion, but it seems to be implicit in his categorization.[46]

In the self-image of Jewish people, the aura of antiquity is reverently extolled, but modern Jews also think of themselves as pioneers in every cultural endeavor. The Jewish people today, in Israel and in America, are far from being encased in a cocoon of ancient rites and dogmas. Apart from isolated enclaves here and there, they are in truth "old-new," engaged in transforming themselves as well as their environment. All great, civilized communities are "old-new," and the Jewish people are possibly "more so." By Toynbee's own definition, a growing civilization is one which presents ever fresh challenges to itself and then responds to them. As outlined in this volume, Jewish people in modern times have kept abreast of every European ideological movement, reacting individually and communally to the changing winds of doctrine.

The average Jewish reader might not have resented Toynbee's characterization so much, if the latter had used a more felicitous phrase—such as, "the unchanged embodiment of ancient Hebraic culture." The term, "Syriac," appeared to many Jews as a deliberate obliteration of the Hebraic contribution to the treasure of human culture. Was not the character and destiny of the Jewish people determined largely by its deep sense of distinctiveness "from all the nations?" Why then have it coupled in one category with those ancient peoples that had no inner bonds with it and were related to it only by the external factors of geography, linguistics and chronology? Furthermore, at a time when Jews and Arabs were engaged in a mortal struggle, some readers felt that by subsuming Hebraic history under the Syrian rubric, Toynbee added insult to injury.[47]

But, the most telling objection to this phrase is the fact that it enshrines a "reductionist" view of Jewish life, that is all too prevalent. The tremendous variety and vigor of modern Jewish life is treated as if it were no more than the medieval ghetto-community; the latter is "reduced" to the ancient dispersion of the first century, and that community in turn is viewed as if it were the congregation of the returning exiles at the time of Ezra and Nehemiah. As Martin Wight points out, Toynbee at times identifies Judaism, not with the prophets, but with the pre-prophetic, so called "Yahweh-religion," emphasizing "God's jealousy and Power."

In all these judgments, Toynbee reflected the ancient Christian view of Jewish history. Though he regarded himself consciously as a post-Christian, he was deeply steeped emotionally and imaginatively in the old Christian tradition, which continued to serve him as a source of myth and imagery. So, he wrote again and again of Jerusalem that "did not know the time of her visitation." While he did not believe that Jesus was the Messiah or "the Son of God," he utilized the saga of the New Testament as a treasury of metaphors, thereby contributing to the denigration of the Jewish people.

Every historian is tempted to write as if he were a judge of nations, rendering the verdict of history. With the benefit of hindsight, does it not appear fairly certain that Jews would have been happier if they had "accepted" Jesus as their Messiah and had then proceeded to convert the world? St. Paul himself was apparently convinced that the Gentiles would not have embraced Jesus as their Savior, if the Jewish Sanhedrin had recognized him as the Messiah. Furthermore, suppose the Jews of the first century saw the "handwriting on the wall" and recognized that their interests would best be served if they turned Christian, would they have become a great people, if they silenced their doubts for the sake of worldly success? Obviously, they would have been untrue to the teaching of him who exclaimed, "what boots it for a man to win the world and lose his soul." As the Jewish people in Jesus' day and later saw it, the question at issue was one of "truth" and "falsehood," not of "survival," or "success," or "grandeur." And Toynbee himself, being a post-Christian, agreed that Jesus was not a "son of God," or the one in whom Israel's hope was indeed fulfilled.

Martin Wight pointed out that "Christianity did not 'break decisively with Judaism by recognizing and proclaiming that God is love.' "[48] The issue was "Messiahhood," not the character of God. Judaism affirmed that God is Love, but also Justice and Power. He is "our Father, our King," "Gracious and Merciful." According to an ancient Midrash, when the Lord set out to create mankind, He provided for the mingling of His two attributes of Justice and Love in the conduct of Providence; otherwise, the society of mankind would have fallen apart.[49]

Nor did Christianity emphasize only the quality of Love in its preaching: The early Christians accepted the gloomy perspective of the Apocalyptic preachers, like Ezra IV, who imagined that the vast majority of mankind would be cast into the everlasting fires of hell.[50] In contrast, the *Mishnah*, the authoritative edition of the Oral Law, declares, "the judgment of the wicked in hell is twelve months." On the other hand, in the comments of the later teachers of the Talmud, eternal hell is reinstated.

Also, as is well known, the liberal Pharisees asserted that "the pious among the nations will share in the World to Come."[52] It is not necessary for Gentiles to become Jews in order to attain salvation. All they need to do is to abide by "the seven Noachian principles," which may be described as the universal laws of religion and ethics. They need not become part of any "Israel of the spirit," though they are welcome to join "Israel of the flesh"; they could continue to practice the "ways of their fathers," providing they imbued their traditional worship and social institutions with the love of God and the love of man.[53] Naturally, rabbis like Hillel believed that their Oral Law was the best "commentary" on the Golden Rule.[54] But then, there is all the difference in the world between the appreciative claim of a religionist, who maintains, "Your practice is good, mine is better" and the strident assertion of a fanatic, "Your ways lead to hell eternal; mine alone lead to salvation."

I do not maintain that all the Pharisees were liberal and tolerant and that all the early Christians were intolerant and obsessed with the fear of damnation. There was tension within both communities. Some Jewish teachers maintained that only Jews would be "saved."[55] In Christianity, the doctrine of *praeparatio evangelica* implied that seeds of divine truth were scattered in diverse pagan cultures, but they were fully contained in the Old Testament, albeit in a concealed, metaphorical form. In Judaism, the climax is still to come, in the messianic future. All cultures and faiths are in the stage of *praeparatio*, if they incorporate and cherish the Noachian principles; all are bidden to help prepare the way. So, after describing the glory of the Messiah, Micah states, "For all the nations will walk, each in the name of its god, and we shall walk in the name of the Lord, our God."[56] (Micah 4,5)

Why, then, did men of immense erudition and overflowing good will, like Toynbee, repeat the disparaging judgments of Judaism that have become virtually traditional in the Christian world down to our own day? In the first place, it is natural for nonspecialists to ignore the great body of rabbinical literature that was in effect a continuing commentary on the Hebrew Bible. For a long time, only fragments of that literature were available to Christian scholars, and these fragments were frequently selected with guile and malice in order to prove the "depravity" of the rabbis.[57]

Consequently, modern Jews were viewed at times, as if they stepped bodily out of the pages of the Old Testament. And Israel's treatment of the Arabs is sometimes discussed against the background of the Deuteronomic injunction to annihilate the original inhabitants of Canaan.

As if there had been no growth and development from the earliest strata of Israel's tradition to the present! We recall that even masters of biblical criticism, like the radical New Testament scholar Bruno Bauer, described the Jewish people as "ahistorical," i.e., unchanged and unvaried by the ups and downs of history. Christian scholars of this type, be it noted, concurred with the Orthodox Jewish teachers who maintained a similar thesis, but one charged with inverse valence, namely, that in view of the absolute perfection of Torah there was no development and no change in Jewish teaching from Moses at Sinai to the Yeshivot of our day.

A persistent notion among Christian scholars, for which there is no Judaic parallel, is that the great prophets and saints in biblical Israel were "Christians" before Christ, whom Ezra and Nehemiah repudiated when they fashioned the basic patterns of Jewish life. A century of Jewish scholarship has uncovered the threads leading from the prophets to the Pharisees and to the rabbis of the Talmud. The rabbis regarded the prophets as interpreters of the Torah, not its opponents. On the Sabbath day, "The Law and the Prophets" were read in order to provide a dialectical basis for a fuller comprehension of the Divine Word.

In a deeper sense, the prophets at their best articulated the Divine

Word, as it is perceived in a flash of mystical experience and then recollected and formulated in accord with the "inner light" of conscience and intelligence. In contrast to the ecstatic "prophetizers," the classical prophets appealed to the minds and hearts of their hearers. They sought to overcome the barriers of ethnic arrogance and ritualistic magic in order to present the "I-Thou" relation of man and God in its fullness. Therein lies their perennial charm and youthfulness.

It is precisely in this sense that the Pharisees continued the work of the prophets. They applied the canons of logic and ethics to the inherited tradition, transforming many an ancient law, which was in their view unjust.[58] They sought to translate the ideals of the Prophets—"the knowledge of the Lord," "the love of kindness," "deeds of justice," "walking humbly with the Lord"—into a daily pattern of living for all the people.

We may add that the great philosophers of Judaism, from Philo to Hermann Cohen and Martin Buber, continued to interpret the tradition in the spirit of the prophets. They sought to uncover the inner meaning of all the laws, in the assurance that clear thinking and ethical living constitute the Primary Intention of all the Commandments.[59]

With all the caveats, it cannot be denied that Toynbee's image of the "fossil" does reflect an important aspect of Jewish life, as it is seen from the standpoint of universal history. The scattered Jewish communities of the Diaspora form a different entity than the peoples around them. Toynbee recognized that what makes the Jews different is more than a creed.

Jews are a people, as well as an ecclesia, indeed a people that is darkly shadowed in the minds of their neighbors by a protean cloud of vague myths, hostile judgments and a disturbing sense of alienation. All these differentia were formed long ago in another culture. In the *milletal* system of the Turkish empire, the Jewish situation was not as peculiar as it might appear in the western world, but even there it bore the stigmata of inferiority and rejection. We recall that Leo Pinsker sought to capture the Jewish differentia in the image of a "ghostly" nation, arousing fear, suspicion and hate. Pinsker proposed what he called "Auto-emancipation," the acquisition of a territory, where Jews could settle and form a state of their own. In this way, they would acquire the blessing of "normalcy."

Short of that total transformation, the Jewish dispersion could be regarded either as a relic of the past, or as a precursor of the future. Toynbee accepts both alternatives. He regards Diaspora Jewry as a "fossil" of an ancient civilization. At the same time, he maintains that the Jews of the Diaspora could well serve as a vanguard of diaspora-communities scattered throughout the world. He cites the phrase, "civilization is deracination."[60]

"If we are right in looking upon the universal states that have already come and gone as having been the forerunners of a future world-state, the social structure for which the Jewish diaspora provides a model will have a practical, as well as an academic interest for the living generation of mankind and our successors . . ."

"Now that the World is becoming one city, we may expect to see associations based on neighborhood come to be overshadowed by others based on spiritual affinity: that is to say, by diasporas in the broadest sense of the term in which this includes ubiquitous scattered minorities that are held together by religious and other ties of all kinds that are independent of locality."[61]

"In the Jewish model we see Man in the same chapter of his history clinging to some revelation, discovery, achievement, or way of life that he feels to be of supreme significance and value, and therefore exerting himself to preserve the separate identity of the 'Chosen People' that is the custodian of this pearl of great price. The 'Chosen People's' belief in its national mission gives it the spirit to maintain itself in diaspora after losing its national state . . ."[62]

It will be recalled that Simon Dubnow also regarded the model of the diaspora to be the "wave of the future." To Dubnow, Jews have reached long ago the highest level of national existence, that of "a spiritual nation," a level which other nationalities are likely to reach in the future. But whereas Dubnow was concerned with the maintenance of ethnic identity, Toynbee sees the great merit of the Jewish Diaspora in its potential to rise beyond ethnicity, as indeed Judaism has opened its gates before the first century to would-be converts and "spiritual converts," or "semi-converts." Toynbee calls upon the Jews to become more a "value-centered" community, than one obsessed with sheer survival. He would have Jews stress their ideals and values, their "mission," so to speak, rather that those exclusive preoccupations with ritualistic niceties and ethnic impediments which have made them a "peculiar people." Like Claude G. Montefiore, he urged that Jews include portions of the New Testament in their sacred literature, and reclaim as properly their own both Jesus and Paul—the former standing for the superiority of spirit to Law, the latter for the opening of gates wide to the Gentiles.

In these counsels, Toynbee arrived at the same position that so-called classical Reform attained at the turn of the century. He also reaffirmed the essentially liberal counsel to the Jews, given by the nineteenth century historian, Theodor Mommsen. Liberal historians do not themselves resent the external particularities which separate the Jew from his neighbors, but in the light of history they fear the resurgence of popular antisemitism and the reappearance of demagogues ready and eager to fan the flames of hate and contempt for those who appear to be "outsiders." In the eyes of the populace, it is the appearance of alienism that counts, especially when those who so flaunt their separateness are also favored by an outsized share of the national pie. These liberal scholars, like the Reform ideologists, cannot be faulted for bringing us a message that some of us may not like.

Like the Jewish Reformers, Toynbee was basically optimistic. Though he chronicled the decline and fall of many civilizations, he believed that western civilization will arise from its present troubles, and overcoming the idolatry of the nation-state, proceed to build the great society of the future.

Like the Reformers, too, he was an impassioned foe of Jewish nationalism. But his anti-Zionist message was proclaimed at the very time when the hope of Zion had become the only viable solution for the hard-pressed Jews of Central and Eastern Europe. By the time the last four volumes of his "Study" appeared, the state of Israel had come into being and the anti-Zionist argument had lost its relevance and force within the Jewish community. Toynbee's critique of Zionism came up against the morally irresistible drive for the settlement of refugees in the Jewish Homeland and the need of guarding against a second Holocaust, this time in the Holy Land itself.

Toynbee's attitude toward the newly born state of Israel was motivated by a deep, subrational factor as well as by a number of meticulously reasoned considerations. It is not generally known that, as a young man working in the British Foreign Office, he had a hand in the issuance of the Balfour Declaration. During World War I, he concentrated on plans for the Near East. He argued in behalf of the breakup of the Turkish Empire into four successor-states; Turkey proper, Arabia, centered on Damascus, a national home for the Armenians, a national home for the Jews. He even asked Dr. Weizmann to read the part of his book dealing with the Jewish national home.[63] One of his articles in 1917 has been cited by a Zionist historian as "a major contribution to shaping and propagating the pro-Zionist policy in the War Cabinet."[64] At that time, the British were eager to secure the help of Russian and American Jewries for their cause and to forestall the plans of Germany to preempt the sympathies of the Zionists.

In his pro-Zionist argument, the young Toynbee acknowledged the validity of the claim of self-determination on the part of indigenous populations, but he claimed that the people of some areas in the Turkish Empire, particularly Palestine, were not yet ripe for freedom.

"There are some units, however, so raw in their growth or so deeply sunk in decay as to lack the attribute of sovereignty altogether—units which through want of population, wealth, spiritual energy, or all three together are unable to keep the spark of vitality aglow. Such dead units are the worst danger that threatens the peace of the world . . ."

There is no question but that the young Toynbee and his colleagues in the Foreign Office regarded the Arabs in Palestine as forming such a "dead unit":

"The people west of the Jordan are not Arabs, but only Arabic-speaking. The bulk of the population are *fellahin*; that is to say, agricultural workers owning land as a village community or working land for the Syrian *effendi* . . .

"These are Arabs in name who have nothing Arabic about them but their language—most of the peasants in Syria are such . . ."[65]

It is perhaps the early involvement of Toynbee in the undertaking of Great Britain to "facilitate" the building of a "Jewish homeland" in Palestine that accounts for the passion with which he later condemned that enterprise. In keeping with the tide of anticolonialism and anti-imperialism, Toynbee changed his position on all issues involving European predominance.[66] In his "Study," he inveighed against the *hubris* of western powers and bent over backward to render full recognition to non-Judaic religions and non-western cultures. He harped on the moral failure of all the religions deriving from Judaism—their exclusiveness, their intolerance, their inability to recognize that more than one pathway may lead to God. In contrast, he extolled the Hindu religions, which in his view, permitted and even favored the proliferation of divergent rites and creeds. So enamored did he become of the Hindu faiths that he virtually ignored the terrible "communal" battles between Hindus and Buddhists, which resulted in the elimination of Buddhism from the land in which it was born. There is today no dearth of religious fanaticism and intolerance on the Indian continent. And the effects of the Hindu religion on the liberation of the common man are certainly not comparable with those in the Judeo-Christian religious sphere. Consider the vile customs affecting widows, the aged and the untouchables, which still prevailed in India, at the time when the British assumed control. Certainly there is a strong, if subtle, connection between the ethical ardor of the Judeo-Christian tradition and its imputation of "jealousy" to the God of the universe, a "jealousy" which was then misdirected by dogmatists and fanatics. In the biblical view, God, who has taken the children of Israel out of the land of bondage, is also "jealous" of His people degenerating and regressing to lower, more primitive ways of living. For if God be the source of all ethical and spiritual ideals, then any unfaithfulness to Him must result in the decline and decay of the ideals He champions.

From our perspective today, it is certainly possible to separate ethical sinfulness from ritualistic transgressions. But, it took western mankind a long time to reach this stage. In history, the demonic and the divine are closely intertwined. So, the relative "tolerance" *vis a vis* different gods in India was associated with a horrible caste-system, the burning of widows and the degradation of the individual. By the same token, the social dynamism of western Europe which generated the efflorescence of the Renaissance, the religious democracy of the Reformation, the liberalism of the English, American and French Revolutions, was the product of inner tensions within the Judeo-Christian tradition.

At this point, we take note of Toynbee's persistent description of the perversion of intolerance, or so called "zealotry," as being Judaic in origin. He writes of "Judaic intolerance in the ethos of Christianity" or of "Judaically fanatical ferocity,"[67] But, except for passages in his volume of "Reconsideration," he does not point out that the Christian belief that "God is love" is also derived from the same root.[68]

In sum, Toynbee's extreme anti-Zionist, anti-colonialist, antiwestern *hubris* in religion and culture, are all inwardly related.[69] They reflect the passion of a penitent who bends over backward to beat his chest and say "mea culpa." But, one may question whether the ardor of penitence, good as it is for one's soul, is the right prescription for the channeling of the "pooled pride" of nations.

A good example of the issue before us is the allure of the notion of the chosen people. Toynbee regards the biblical notion of a people, set apart from the rest of mankind, as the source of the self-aggrandizement of Christian nations in the modern world. Ultimately, this narcissistic belief of the ancient Israelites took root in the minds of anti-Christian Germans, emerging as the Nazi madness of our own generation. Because he took this long view of the migration of an idea, he felt that his critics missed the point when they pointed to the usual "idealistic" interpretations of the chosen people concept in Judaism and Christianity: that "Israel of the Flesh" or "Israel of the Spirit" was chosen to serve and bless mankind, rather than to dominate and oppress it, or that "the concept of Israel's choice is one of humility, not of arrogance," or that Israel's destiny turned out to be one of suffering and dispersion, not of joy and triumph.

In a long note on this subject, he wrote, "I find this apologia unconvincing. I agree that the role of the 'Chosen People' has been 'everlastingly reclaimed' by the Jews, but I do not know of any evidence that it was 'reluctantly assumed' in the first instance. The Jews are not the only people who have been willing to offer up costly sacrifices on the altar of their collective self-centeredness. But self-centeredness remains the sin that it is, however high the price one may be willing to pay for the psychological satisfaction that one obtains from committing it."[70]

Toynbee expressed his agreement with my comment that the chosen people concept is bi-polar in character; collective self-centeredness in tension with collective self-dedication to the service of God and mankind. The former pole is known all too well, but the second is equally real in biblical and Jewish history. In the intertwining of the demonic and divine forces within this concept, the potentialities for great good and absymal evil were certainly to be found. Nazism is an example of the demonic component of this notion, blended with the fury of a distraught and defeated people, which was maddened by the delusions and myths of racial mysticism and demoralized by the nihilistic theories of "social Darwinism."

But we may ask, would not Nazism have emerged in any case, even if all references to the chosen people in Scriptures had been deleted? This is of course an unanswerable, iffy question. However, in all the writings about Hitler, we have yet to find a fascination for biblical themes. To be sure, the romantic nationalists, Fichte, Dostoevski, Mazzini, Mickiewicz, did employ biblical imagery. And they did prepare the way for Hitler and his hordes.

On the other hand, it is impossible to remove ideas and beliefs from the records of history. We can reinterpret historical notions, stressing their idealistic components and calling attention to the dangers implicit in their demonic side. Can we question the powerful motivation for good of the chosen people idea, if it be regarded as an *example*, rather than as an *exception*? On this view, all peoples may at any one time be so situated as to be capable of rendering great blessings to mankind. And, as Kant reminded us, "'Can' implies 'Ought.'" It is the collective duty of a talented or privileged people at any one time to render its service to other nations and "to become a blessing." Did not America after World War II act as a truly chosen people, in inaugurating the Marshall Plan and in offering aid to many impoverished and stricken nations? Is not the creation of the "Peace Corps" a similar expression of American generosity and its religious fervor? Sometimes, such a role is inescapable for a great people, in which case we can speak of its being "chosen" both by Providence and by its own voluntary commitment. Should we not encourage this concept of "chosenness" as an ideal for other nations as well—say, the oil-rich kingdoms and sheikdoms?

We agree with Toynbee that a demonic factor easily insinuates itself into a people's belief in its unique role. Therefore, whenever the notion arises, it should be subjected to merciless criticism, along prophetic lines. But we also maintain that the biblical notion contains a noble, divine aspect, for which there is a crying need in every generation, and more particularly in our rapidly shrinking world, which is divided between the prosperous and the poverty-stricken.

In Toynbee's criticism of Zionism and Israel, ethical and pragmatic elements were commingled. He was appalled by the flood of Palestinian refugees that resulted from the Arab-Israel civil war which followed the British evacuation in May 1948. In his judgment, a large number were expelled from Arab areas, while many refugees simply panicked. The net result of that catastrophe was the transfer of the status of refugees from hundreds of thousands Jews of Europe to hundreds of thousands of Palestinian Arabs.

In his indignation, Toynbee went so far as to compare the fall of the Israelis from Grace to that of the Germans sinking into the moral abyss of Nazism. It was an unfortunate remark, which had only a modicum of justification in the context of his teaching that suffering ennobles and sanctifies. This biblical doctrine, Toynbee applied to the Jews of our day and expected them to behave like saints at the time when their very life was at stake. But the survivors of the Holocaust were driven by the fury of despair; they feared a repetition of their agony at the hands of the Arabs and they took no chances.

In his "Reconsiderations," Toynbee reasserted his condemnation of Zionism in general.

"On reconsideration, I do not find that I have changed my view of

Zionism. I think that in the Zionist movement, Western Jews have assimilated Gentile Western civilization in the most unfortunate possible form."[71]

There is no doubt that the lot of the Arab refugees was tragic. But the blame was widely distributed. The United Nations did not undertake to carry out the Partition Plan which it voted. The neighboring Arab nations promptly invaded Palestine, threatening to complete the work of Hitler. In the conflict between an irresistible force and an immoveable wall, great heat will be generated, and very little light. Some Israeli writers agree that the conflict was tragic, in the dramatic sense—that is, it was a collision between two equally justified rights, not merely a conflict between right and wrong. The tragedy unfolded step by step, and none of the participants foresaw the end. Originally, the Zionist leaders were convinced that they would be heartily welcomed by the Arab people. They believed themselves to be bearing the gifts of westernization and prosperity to a long lost cousin-nation. The early rebellions of the Arabs in 1921 and 1929 were not taken seriously—they were the work of demagogues. And once Hitler came to power in Germany, the Jews had no choice. The "national homeland" was no longer a dreamlike vision; it was now the only practical possibility for large scale Jewish immigration.

As for the Arabs, their successive defeats in 1949, 1956, 1967, and 1973 generated an incredible psychosis, the full measure of which is still unknown. Accustomed to think in long-range terms, Toynbee foresaw a progressive aggravation of the bitter mood of the Arabs. In private conversations and letters, he expressed the fear of an emerging Arab mass psychosis, directed against Israel in the first place and indirectly against all Jews. The madness of European antisemitism, with all its monstrous myths, he feared, would be duplicated in the Arab world, which was certain to grow in wealth, in population and in power. The hurt of an inferiority complex, rubbed raw by successive defeats, inflamed by whipped-up ethnic pride and sanctified by religious fantasies can result in a deadly brew. The longer the Arabs delayed taking their revenge against Israel, the more tragic would be the final struggle. And more than the life of Israel might be at stake, since in our shrinking globe an Arab-Israel war could easily set off a global Armageddon. While these fears seemed unduly pessimistic in the sixties, they appear more realistic in the seventies.

Toynbee was not alone in recognizing the terrible potential of a deepening Arab mass psychosis. J. L. Talmon wrote after the Six Day War:

> The anti-Israel obsession gave rise to a kind of systematic Manichean metaphysic, the focus of an entire philosophy of history, with the Jew as the devil incarnate from the days of patriarch Abraham himself till his assumption of the role of the lynchpin of an American-Imperialist-Zionist world-plot against the Arab world, the Socialist Commonwealth and all colonial peoples.
>
> By an unspeakably tragic irony the Zionism of Jewish exiles marching to the tune of 'If I forget thee, O Jerusalem,' not only created an Arab Zionism, propelled by a similar sense of exile and dream of a return to that very Jerusalem, but imparted the mad obsession with a world-wide Jewish conspiracy to the Islamic world, which however contemptuous of and unfriendly to Jews had in the past not known that essentially Christian neurotic preoccupation with Jewish deicide and the Protocols of Zion, from the dire results of which the Jews sought refuge in Palestine.[72]

Since those lines were written, the Yom Kippur War has been waged and the Arab oil-offensive launched, along with an intensified boycott of firms dealing with Israel. While the situation is at this writing more fluid and more promising, the fears of Toynbee and Talmon are still with us. Jerusalem is associated with the hope of moral perfection and ultimate peace in the minds of both Jews and Christians. But unless the course of events since the end of World War II is reversed, it is hard to believe that it has ceased to be the burning fuse of another catastrophe, of possibly global dimensions.

In sum, Toynbee's challenge to the self-image of Jewish people was deeply felt, but for the most part, bitterly resented. He projected the universal perspective, with which Jewish intellectuals have identified since the days of Moses Mendelssohn; he wrote as a liberal historian, subjecting all great events to the scrutiny of reason; he followed the empirical tradition of Anglo-American philosophy, testing every thesis, as he went along; he accepted the biblical world-view, though he tried to liberate himself from the parochial limitations of his time and place. For all these reasons Jewish intellectuals could not but feel ambivalent toward him. Just at the time when they had rediscovered their nationalism and had taken immense pride in the courageous saga of Israel's birth and growth, he, speaking for a cherished aspect of their own mentality, challenged their newly won self-image and their vision of the future of Jewry.

Jewish Nationalists and the Liberals

Do Jewish intellectuals feel now that their alliance with liberalism belongs to the past? There is no question but that some short-sighted nationalists whose sole concern is the promotion of Israel are inclined to discard the liberal orientation. They are more comfortable with the conservatives, who favor the Cold War, a return to a policy of strategic confrontation with the Soviet Union, an imperialist, hard-line posture toward the oil-countries, including the threat of their occupation, and a general reliance on force rather than on the building of an international order of law and justice. We have referred to the anger aroused by the editorial policy of the "Christian Century." The publication of the Peace Plan by the Quakers in 1972 antagonized the Zionists quite as much as the comments of Toynbee. On the other hand, conservatives, by virtue of their regard for the uniqueness of every historic community, their allergy to general principles, their indifference to anticolonialist and antiimperialist pleas, might be expected to react sympathetically to the cause of Israel and to the romantic-metaphysical ties of Diaspora Jews with Israel.

Such views, however, are not likely to prevail in the Jewish community. In the judgment of this writer, liberalism is part of the enduring self-image of Jewish people. It derives from both the dominant trend in Jewish philosophy and the invariant direction of Jewish life in the Diaspora.

The historical stream of Jewish thought consists of three confluent currents: the mystical, the folkist-romantic and the rationalistic-liberal. The mystical current has recently aroused a great deal of interest, especially as a subject of study and wonderment. The article on Kabbalah in the recently published *Encyclopedia Judaica* is more extensive by far than the one in the *Jewish Encyclopedia*, which was printed at the beginning of this century. The antics of the Hasidim, of the anti-Zionist variety (Satmar) and the pro-Zionist faction (Liubavich) have drawn the interest of the media. But apart from temporary fads and academic fashions, there is no reason to expect a mass-return to mysticism. While in his early years, Buber was virtually a mystic, in his later life, he moved toward an inter-personalistic philosophy. The vogue of Buber among intellectuals today does not result in any conversion to mysticism or Hasidism.

The folkist-romantic current, associated in the Middle Ages with the name of Halevi and greatly favored in the modern era by the preachers of Zionism, is not likely to achieve dominance. For this philosophy is so close to the world-view of the romantic precursors of Nazism as to scandalize those who take the trouble to study the history of ideas. A mystique of "the holy seed" has indeed been part of the total complex of Jewish thought. But it is a residue of ancient myths that Jews today cannot but disavow decisively. In the nineteenth century, racial mysticism was so innocent an idea that even a rationalist like Geiger could embrace it and make use of it in his endeavor to promote Jewish loyalty. An Eastern European philosopher like A'had Ha'am could similarly proclaim his belief that Jews are by nature "different" from all other nations in their perception of ethical issues. Today the massive horror of mystical-metaphysical racism is plain for all to see. No one who is at all aware of the momentum of ideas is likely to reclaim the poison of this mystique and reinfuse it into the body of Jewish thought.

By default then, if for no other reason, the dominant current of Jewish thought is the one of liberalism or rationalism. Associated in the Middle Ages with the name of Maimonides, it has stimulated waves of enlightenment, whenever circumstances permitted. In Israel, too, there is good reason to feel that the present gap between the self-enclosed Orthodox and the insular secularists will be bridged, once the political tensions are eased. As soon as Israelis can turn their energies from the harsh realities of war to the arts of peace, they will begin to fill the gap which now divides the intellectuals from the religionists with a neo-Maimonidean synthesis, more or less along the lines of the American liberal movements of Reform and Conservatism.

Insofar as Jewish experience in the past two centuries is concerned, there is no doubt whatever that the cause of Jewish freedom and dignity is one with that of liberalism. Recent studies of the politics of American Jews demonstrate that this association is well understood by the great majority of our people. Indeed it is as deeply rooted in the major works of Jewish thought as it is a reflection of contemporary realities.

However, the kind of liberalism which Jews are likely to embrace is one that is nonideological and nonrigid. It is the liberalism of the Anglo-American world, which is empirical and down-to-earth. It includes a reverence for the domain of religious faith, which articulates in one way or another man's awareness of the transcendental character of his inner being. By the same token, it includes a deep respect for the diversities of collective experience which are enshrined in the hearts of different historical communities. It steers clear of both extremes—the obliteration of all traces of irrationality deriving from history and the glorification of such cultural residues as manifestations of the national soul. In sum, as liberalism balances the sanctity of the individual by the discipline of the state, so too it aims to bring into an unforced balance the individualities of sub-groups and their parochial concerns with the national personality and its overall needs, all within the framework of universal ideals.

Such a balanced liberalism is dynamic, by its very nature, responding to the ebb and flow of innumerable factors. Jews are likely to be very sensitive to the changing moods of society, and with good reason. They can be easily hurt, if the swing of the national mood becomes extremist and irreversible. As J. L. Talmon put it:

> The tragic parodox of the Jews in modern times has been the fact that their existence and success have been dependent upon the triumph of the idea of oneness as represented by liberal democracy and socialism, while the very phenomenon of Jewry is an unparalleled demonstration of the enormous power of the element of uniqueness.[73]

Where "oneness" or national homogeneity is taken to be the essence of liberalism, the Jewish situation becomes indeed paradoxical. And it is not much help to tone down the more conspicuous features of Jewish distinctiveness. But genuine liberalism is freedom, as well as fraternity and equality. Its essence is not "oneness" or "fraternity," but rather a high regard for the individual; hence, also a decent respect for collective individualities. It does not aim at the homogenization of society, but at the maximization of freedom so that each of its components may attain its fullest realization. In a free society, there are likely to be any number of lumps in the soup. A Jewish community, open to all influences and not distorted either by a rigid fanaticism or by an insular nationalism, is not likely to be a misfit in a liberal society.

A Concept of Jewish Identity

What is the concept of Jewish identity that emerges from this study? We have seen that thoughtful Jews have reinterpreted their identity in response to the various ideological challenges of the modern world. The great ideological trends of the past two centuries are still part of our intellectual climate. We may expect that climate to be even more restless and dynamic in the future than it was in the past. How then shall we stake out the basic dimensions of Jewish identity?

Three geometric images of Jewish identity have come down to us from the past. One, the Herzlian view, which foresaw the concentration of those who wished to preserve their ethnic heritage in Israel and the assimilation of the rest. Two, the A'had Ha'amist view of the Jewish people as forming a circle, with Israel in the center and the various lands of the Diaspora on the periphery. Three, the view of Ravidowicz, suggesting that Israel and American Jewry form the two centers of an ellipse, with the rest of the Diaspora deriving inspiration from both.

Of the three images, that of an ellipse comes closest to the reality of the present day. It is also the least dogmatic of the three. The Herzlian view has long become obsolete, for most Jews repudiate assimilation as a possibility, let alone a goal. The A'had Ha'amist view is altogether too simplistic.

The components of Jewish life are so many, so dynamic and so diverse that "centrality" in one respect may be offset by "peripherality" in another. Certainly, in political terms, Israel is not the "center" or focus of Jewish loyalties, nor does it claim to be. In the future, an Arab-Israeli type of personality, self-confident and proud of living in two cultures, may well emerge. Religiously, the lines of division in Judaism are not geographical, but ideological. To modern Jews, the "holiness" of the land of Israel is not literal, but metaphorical, reflecting the association of the land with historical memories and with the current pulsations of Jewish life. For a long time to come, Israel is likely to be the focus of concern and anxiety, as well as of compassion and pride for Jews the world over. So long as Israel is the finger of Jewry, caught in the door, to use Bialick's metaphor, it will be the chief worry of world Jewry.

Furthermore, it is dangerous, from a public relations standpoint, as well as frustrating from the vantage point of inner Jewish loyalties, to impose an abstract geometric pattern on a living, dynamic society, that is likely to face new and unpredictable challenges.

Instead of a fixed and frozen geometric image, we need a sociological category that permits and even encourages diversity and dynamic interaction with the several non-Jewish cultures of the Diaspora. Our self-image should allow for pluralism and growth.

Clearly, the one inference that we can draw with fair certainty from the above points and counterpoints is that no monolithic mold can possibly encompass the whole of the Jewish community. *We suggest the concept of a Jewish family of communities.* The great variety of responses to modern ideologies indicates that there is no specific and unvarying essence which is exclusively Jewish, other than descent from Jews and identification with the historic Jewish people. The Jewish religion is one of the unifying bonds, but theologically Judaism encompasses the entire spectrum from the naturalism of a Mordecai M. Kaplan, the "polydoxy" of Alvin Reines and the "paganism" of Rubinstein to the rock-ribbed ultra-Orthodoxy of the Hassidim, who are themselves divided into rival groups. The distance between the diverse theological positions within Judaism is fully as great as that which obtains within the Protestant world, and greater if we do not apply the Protestant label to the Unitarians-Universalists. To be sure, there are no clear demarcation lines between the several groupings, and the ideological gulfs are often bridged by sociological beams and ties. But, this is precisely what we mean by a family of communities.

The concept of a family suggests that Jewishness is both a matter of birth and of personal choice. One is born into a family, or he joins it by choice. While the unity of families is weakened as they expand, the family of Jewish communities is sustained by the momentum of a common history and by a conscious acceptance of the same faith. The Talmud describes the global fellowship of the Jewish people as a family of which God is the Father and the Congregation of Israel (Kenesset Yisroel) is the Mother.[74] The latter term refers to the biological-historical matrix of the Jewish people, the former to a personal relationship with the One God that a Jew is expected to acquire. It is pertinent to add that those who acknowledge only one parent are also members of the family.

Indeed, it has been the historic role of the Jewish people to explore the implications of a communal identity in which biological descent is sublimated into spiritual commitment. Identities fall into three categories—that of choice, as when a person chooses a profession or a religious fellowship or a political party; that of status, as when people are born into historical communities; that of covenant, in which personal choice and public status are blended together. Love is a matter of choice; marriage of covenant, children of birth. Jewish identity has always been of the covenantal variety. So, the prophet Hosea speaks of the betrothal of Israel to God, in all eternity, "through righteousness and justice, through steadfast love and compassion" (Hosea, 2,21).

Variously as this Covenant has been interpreted, it is essentially three-dimensional, containing a personal code of conduct, a cluster of communal obligations and a dedication to the service of God and mankind. In ancient and medieval times, the covenantal obligations were articulated in a rigid and monolithic set of precepts and beliefs. Today, the range of pluralism is vastly increased. And rightly so. In a living faith-community extending into many parts of the world, diverse challenges are bound to lead to a diversity of responses. Indeed, Jewish people since the days of Jeremiah have learned to combine a deep attachment to Judaism with a fervent devotion to the countries in which they lived. (Jeremiah 29,7)

Families grow out as they grow up. Through marriage, people come to belong to at least two families. So, Jewish people have learned to become part of the nations among whom they lived, without giving up the covenantal bonds which relate them to God and to the global fellowship of Israel. As members of a spiritual family, Jews need not fear that their heritage will be diluted and adulterated through the alliances they forge with members of other families. For a spiritual heritage is not impoverished but enriched by the influence of other cultures. An American Jew will become more deeply Jewish, the more he absorbs the creative genius of the American nation, and vice versa.

A branch of the Jewish family is even now becoming a fresh and vigorous entity, the Israeli nation that is at once "new" and "old." If and when peace finally dawns in that part of the world, the Arabs in Israel will become part of that nation. At the same time, the divergence in character and outlook between the Israeli and the Jews of the Diaspora will become as obvious as the bonds of sentiment and mutual concern that will continue to bind them together. There is no telling today where the geopolitical currents of history will drag the state of Israel in the decades that lie ahead: toward a continued close association with America, toward neutral ground, toward the Soviet orbit, or toward new configurations that are still beyond the horizon. A state follows the logic of national interest, whithersoever it leads. In the flux of history, communities with common memories may undergo new realignments of their own free will. The major portions of the Jewish people are like trains set on different tracks, moving off into the unknown horizon, with only a few people here and there jumping the tracks to join a different train. Consequently, we may indeed employ the slogan, "we are one," newly coined by the Jewish philanthropic agencies, providing we understand that we are also many and diverse. We are one, not as a creedal community and not as a political-cultural nation, but as a family of religious and national communities, a family of adults who are mature enough to go their separate ways and loyal enough to their common tradition to feel that they form "one fellowship." Hopefully, the various members of this family will continue to cherish not merely their common past but also their shared dedication to the building of the messianic kingdom, "when all nations will form one fellowship to serve God with a perfect heart."

Does this concept of Jewish identity imply an assimilationist or a nationalistic version of the future? In my view it implies the freedom for individuals to choose either direction and the likelihood that in several ways they will choose both. Mature adults sever the "silver cord" which keeps them enchained to the past and prevents them from submitting with hearts entire to new loves and fresh alliances with persons of other families. At the same time, healthy-minded adults find that they love their parents and families even more, when they fall in love and conclude a covenant with their loved ones. Some members of the Jewish family will choose to return to their ancestral home and throw in their lot with those who build the new Israeli nation. By the same token, many Israelis are even now moving in large numbers to America and Canada. But regardless of where they choose to live, they will belong to the Jewish family to the extent that they accept the one God as their Father and the Congregation of Israel as their Mother.

In both Israel and the lands of the Diaspora, Jews will choose to identify themselves in varying degrees with diverse aspects of the "sacred tradition." The entire spectrum of the Jewish religion, from an individualistic atheism or a nationalistic pantheism to the extremes of Orthodoxy, may now be encountered in both Israel and the Diaspora. To be sure, the proportions differ, the nuances of observance and the forms of organization are peculiar to the special circumstances of Israel and to the cultural climates of the various Diaspora lands. We may expect a continuous interaction among the several branches of the Jewish family, particularly in view of the explosion of the travel industry in recent years. At the same time, each community is likely to reflect the impact of its own peculiar cultural environment.

So, it appears likely that we shall be returning to the original conception of the Jewish people—a family of tribes, "the twelve tribes of Israel," all affirming loyalty to the One God. Each community will seek to achieve its own best synthesis of the common Jewish tradition and the prevailing culture. And the terms of that synthesis will be likely to reflect in each case the full panoply of possibilities.

In our perspective of the Jewish family of communities, dynamic change and development are to be expected. Our people will be constantly challenged to discriminate between that which is essential to Judaism and that which is merely accidental. The process of assimilation may assume benign as well as malignant forms. If people acquire from the general culture of their country its best elements and blend them with their historical tradition, they assimilate well. If they choose unwisely from among the elements of their own tradition and from the prevailing culture, preserving the dross and neglecting the pure metal in both cultures, they assimilate badly. In either case, they will be assimilating, in some respects and preserving their heritage in other respects, for every living organism is constantly engaged in assimilating some element from the environment and rejecting others.

The problem that each Jewish community faces is to assimilate wisely the diverse influences that impinge upon it, and to grow in understanding, refinement and sympathy. In other words, the criteria of growth in each case are intrinsic to the life of that community, which includes the impetus from the past, the concerns of the present and the universal society of the future. And all the branches of the family share the same tradition, the same history, the same concerns, and the same hopes.

APPENDIX *Some letters from Arnold J. Toynbee to Jacob B. Agus:*

(From Union Theological Seminary, New York)

November 4, 1955

Dear Rabbi Agus:

I was very much touched by your most kind letter of November 1st and by the line you take in your article in the Fall issue of "Judaism".

So far, I have only had time to read the article very rapidly, but I greatly appreciate the generosity with which you point out the things in which you agree, as well as those in which you disagree, with my presentation of Judaism.

This kind of constructive criticism is, of course, not only a help but also a call to go on thinking. My mind is, I hope, still an open one, and as a matter of fact I am proposing to produce a series of studies in which I shall be reconsidering questions in my book which are obviously debatable either because of new knowledge or because of the discussion that has been aroused by what I have written.

I can see that Judaism will be one of these issues, and when I come to this, your article will be one of the things that I shall have at my elbow.

Meanwhile, may we keep in touch? I should be particularly interested, as you proceed, to learn something of your projected examination of the application of the various philosophies of history as they apply to the Jewish situation.

Thank you again.

Yours sincerely,

(signed) Arnold Toynbee

(*From Washington and Lee University, Lexington, Virginia*)

April 1, 1958

Dear Dr. Agus:

I have been reading your reprint from *Judaism*, 1956—"Towards a Philosophy of Jewish History"—with very great interest and profit. Have you yet published the larger book that is announced in the last instalment? And, if so, would you very kindly tell me who the publisher is?

You have illuminated for me two questions that had been puzzling me for a long time; (i) Why the world adopted Jewish monotheism, not by conversion to Judaism, but by inventing "heretical" deviations from Judaism, Christianity and Islam; (ii) Why the Israelites, after the revelation to them, or discovery by them, of God, have continued to be a national community and have not become a universal one, like the Christian Church or the Islamic Umma—in spite of the fact that Jewish monotheism has proved to be something that the whole world wants. You have shown that these two questions are facets of the same question, and that the answers to them are interdependent.

I am now working on a volume of second thoughts about a number of things in my book "A Study of History". In this connexion, may I venture to ask your opinion on some points?

What do you think is the source of the missionary impulse to convert the whole human race? You point out that, in the Jewish community, this impulse was partly inhibited by the counter-pull of ethnic loyalty. How was it that the Jewish founders of Christianity exceptionally broke out of this? Might it be because they were Galileans whose Jewish ethnic loyalty was recent and perhaps shaky? And why didn't Islam remain just "the religion of Abraham for the children of Ishmael"? The Arabs do not seem to have opposed the conversion of their conquered non-Arab subjects, though this eventually undermined the Arabs' political hegemony. Buddhism, again, seems to have broken, straight away, out of the confines of caste, and it also broke out of the limits of the Hindu World as soon as it could. You have shown that the Jews' retention of ethnic loyalty was something that was to be expected, rather than something peculiar, and this makes the out-and-out missionary religions and philosophies seem exceptional and in need of explanation.

On a quite different point: How, if at all, does the re-establishment of a Jewish state in the Land of Israel affect the Jewish expectation of the Messiah? I can see that this perhaps might not be affected at all, as the

Messiah is to bring with him the conversion of the Gentiles to the original Jewish monotheism besides bringing the restoration of Israel in Palestine. At the same time, the return to Palestine is now an accomplished historical fact for Israelis, while for Jews remaining in the diaspora it is no longer an unattainable aspiration but one that they can now satisfy if they want to. Will this change in the situation produce a change in Jewish religious outlook and feeling?

One last question: Is there any precedent for the problem of a dual political commitment—a loyalty to his adopted country and an attachment to the State of Israel—with which a member of the Jewish diaspora now has to cope? The problem did not arise for the Babylonian diaspora over the Jewish state of Zerubbabel, Nehemiah, and Ezra, because Jerusalem and the diaspora were both inside the Persian Empire. It did not arise for the diaspora in the Greek World in the time of the Hasmonaean and Herodian state, because this state (if I am right) did not seem to contemporary Jews to be a fulfilment of Jewish religious expectations and therefore did not have much hold on their affections.

The present problem would, of course, be eased if we could get an agreed settlement between Israel and the Arabs. But I fear this could only be reached through a compromise that would require large concessions from both sides, for which neither side is yet in the mood—though I don't think time is really on anyone's side except the Russians' and the atomic bomb's.

Please forgive me for troubling you with these questions. I venture to do so because your monograph has set my mind working.

Yours sincerely,

Arnold J. Toynbee

(*From The Royal Institute of International Affairs, London*)

11 November 1959

Dear Rabbi Agus,

Would you have time to look at a chapter on post-Exilic Judaism that I have written for publication in a forthcoming volume of "reconsiderations"?

I am writing now because this chapter will soon be in type.

Of course I have not been able to deal fully with so vast a subject. I have concentrated on two things. (i) I have tried to look at post-Exilic Judaism, not through Christian spectacles, but for its own sake, as something whose value lies entirely in itself. (ii) I have touched on the tension between Judaism as a universal religion and the Jewish people's urge to maintain itself as a distinct ethnic community.

If I were able to have your comments to take account of before sending this chapter to press, I should publish it with much greater confidence. This is my excuse for bothering you with this request.

With very best wishes,
Yours very sincerely,

Arnold Toynbee

(From The Royal Institute of International Affairs, London)

8 December 1959

Dear Rabbi Agus,

It is indeed kind of you to have read and commented on my chapters, and to have made time to do this so quickly when you have very many calls on you.

Besides making, throughout, the two verbal changes that you suggest, I am revising, particularly, the concluding section of my Chapter XV in the light of your comments under your heading 'C'.

These revisions of my text do not, however, do full justice to your comments. To be appreciated properly, these ought to be read in full in the form in which you have put them.

Would you allow me, besides making my revisions of my own text in the light of them, to print them, as they stand, under your name in this volume of "reconsiderations"?

If you felt able to let me do this, it would put the issues in the dialogue form which is, I feel sure, the most enlightening way of presenting any subject.

This is why I venture to make this request.

In any case, thank you again, most heartily.

Yours sincerely,

Arnold Toynbee

(From The Royal Institute of International Affairs, London)

19 September 1960

Dear Rabbi Agus,

I have read the chapters* that you sent me with the very greatest interest, and have now mailed them back to you, registered (the four folders in one packet). I did not mark typing errors, because I did not want to take my mind off the substance.

I have no suggestions, at all, to make for any alterations. Indeed, I have not the knowledge that one would need for this.

The general conclusion, as I see it, is one that you have expressed before, in another context (I have quoted that passage in my own "reconsiderations"). In spite of the segregation, and the will to keep segregated, on both sides, there has been, during the last 160 years, at any rate, the closest interplay, in the intellectual field, between Jews and gentiles.

I remember that, in a correspondence that I had with Dr. Weizmann (I had asked him for comments on what I had written about Zionism in my draft for my vols i–iii), I was startled to find him declaring his belief in the reality of racial characteristics. I had not realized that the founders of Zionism had seen, and said, that their pre-suppositions were the same as those of the anti-Semites.

What is depressing about this piece of history, as you record it, is that the interplay between the two communities seems to have stimulated, on both sides, the most unfortunate thing in the modern [world,] de-spiritualized ideology: the insistence on physical race as being the fundamental principle of unity and division among human beings.

How are we to reverse this current? And how are we to get over the racialist reservations that persist, among both gentiles and Jews, even in countries in which 'emancipation' has, in law, been complete?

I know personally both Jews and gentiles of my own generation who have truly become unconscious of any barrier between them because, on both sides, they have become complete religious agnostics. But, even if this were acceptable as a satisfactory solution from the spiritual point of view, it would be a solution only for a small sophisticated minority. The majority are more likely to keep the traditional prejudice and fanaticism, simply shifting this on

---

*The reference is to chapters of Agus, *The Meaning of Jewish History,* 2 volumes, Abelard Schuman, New York, 1963.

to a racial basis from the former religious one, and so making it something even worse than it used to be.

You bring out the strength of the emotional resistance, up to date, among Jews, to giving up the ethnic part of the traditional basis of the Jewish community and making the religious part, exclusively, the basis for a continuance of the Jewish community in the modern world. This is the only happy solution that I can see; but history indicates that it is a psychologically difficult one.

This *is*, I suppose, the solution that has actually been adopted by non-Jewish immigrants into the United States. Greek, German, Scottish, Italian and other once 'hyphenated' Americans have dropped their ethnic distinctiveness after several generations but have kept their religious distinctiveness as Orthodox Christians, Lutherans, Presbyterians, Roman Catholics and so on. This seems to be compatible with ethnic assimilation. Can Judaism find its place in the modern world on these lines?

As you know, I believe that Judaism as a religion, and also the "diaspora" or "millet" structure of society, have great futures in the new world society into which we are moving.

Thank you, again, for letting me see these chapters in typescript.

> Yours very sincerely,
> Dictated by Dr. Toynbee and
> despatched in his absence.
> Norah Williams
> Secretary to Dr. Arnold Toynbee

(*From The Royal Institute of International Affairs, London*)

July 7, 1963

Dear Dr. Agus,

I have now read the galleys, concentrating on the beginning and the end, as you have suggested. I think you have fully succeeded in doing what, in you. letter to me of June 10, you describe as being your aim. You have managed to look at Jewish history *both* from the inside *and* with an outside observer's initial objectives. This is difficult and rare. When an insider does succeed in being objective, of couse he carries much more weight than an outsider can carry, so I look forward to this book having an important influence on the thinking of both Jews and non-Jews.

You bring out the fact that the tension inside each Jewish soul and inside the Jewish community has the same cause as the tension between Jews and non-Jews. The tension between the religious and the ethnic pole of the Jewish consciousness is at the root of it all.

As you know, I believe, like many other people, that, in the Atomic Age, mankind is going to have to choose between destroying itself and growing together into something like a single family. If this is correct, what is the future of ethnic loyalties? They may not have to be eliminated, but they may well have to be subordinated to an overriding loyalty to the human race.

I agree with you that the two nodes of the World Jewish Community are going to be the Diaspora in the United States, and Israel. I believe the American Diaspora is going to be, by far, the more important of the two. If so, its sorting-out of its relations with non-Jews is going to be decisive for the Jewish future. Here, like you, I am optimistic. I believe that the American atmosphere and American traditions and ideals are particularly favorable for the working-out of a new and better relation between the Diaspora and its non-Jewish neighbors and fellow citizens.

Well, congratulations on the book. It must be a great satisfaction for you to have completed it.

It was a great pleasure for my wife and me to see you and Mrs. Agus again last month.

Yours very sincerely,

Arnold Toynbee

(*From The Royal Institute of International Affairs, London*)

3 July, 1967

Dear Dr. Agus,

Your letter of June 27, like so many of your previous letters, has given me happiness and encouragement.

I am enclosing a copy of a letter that I have just written to Professor Talmon of the Hebrew University of Jerusalem as a follow-up to a remarkable paper of his which he sent to Sir Isaiah Berlin of All Souls' College, Oxford, and which Berlin passed on to my son Philip.

Now is the moment when all men of good-will shall unite in all-out comprehensive effort to get a genuine peace in the Middle-East.

We have no time to lose.

Yours very sincerely,

Arnold Toynbee

I hope you will like my review.* I wrote it with zest, and my praise is sincere.

(*From London*)

3rd July, 1967

Dear Professor Talmon,

I have just been staying with my son Philip, and I have read your paper 'For Total Peace in the Middle East' which Isaiah Berlin passed on to him. I believe, like you, that this is the moment for everyone of good will and good sense to make an all-out effort to get total, genuine, and lasting peace there. I believe there is a real opportunity for this, if we seize it now. I am just back from the United States, and, three weeks ago, I stuck my neck out by writing, for the United Press International, an article, saying this, and making some concrete proposals for bringing it about. The United Press tell me that my article has been reproduced pretty widely in the U.S. press, so a copy of it may come into your hands some time, but, as there is no time to lose, I am writing to you now direct.

I feel a responsibility for doing anything I can to help towards getting a permanent peace now. I have a number of reasons: (i) I am British, so I have a share of responsibility for my country's past actions; (ii) as a young man during the First World War, I was working as a 'temporary Foreign Office clerk' on Middle Eastern affairs, particularly on British war-time commitments in the Middle East, so I know the history of these from the inside; (iii) I am known as a Western spokesman for the Arab cause, and it is therefore just possible that what I say in public now might have some influence in the Arab World, though it is perhaps more likely that the Arabs might write me off with the verdict that I am no friend of theirs after all.

*Professor Toynbee's review of three books by Dr. Agus—*The Meaning of Jewish History, The Vision and the Way* (Frederick Ungar Publishing Co.), and *Dialogue and Tradition*—was published in the quarterly journal *Judaism*, Summer, 1967.

Anyway, I believe that the truest act of friendship that any friend of either the Arabs or the Israelis can do for them at this moment is to try to help them to see that the facts make genuine peace a prime interest for both parties; (iv) being now an old man, with grandchildren, I feel what Johnson and Kosygin seem to have felt when they met. One's grandchildren symbolise for me, in a concrete way, all the future generations of the human race—70 million unborn generations who might be deprived, by our generation, of their right to life if we, in our time, were to stumble into an atomic third world war; (v) thinking also in terms of the present, I want to see something done now which, besides saving the world from an enormous catastrophe, will reduce present human suffering in the Middle East to a minimum. I should have been as much horrified at genocide of Jews in the Middle East as I was horrified at it in Europe. I also think it very wrong to use the Palestinian Arab refugees as political pawns, instead of treating them as suffering human beings whose alleviation ought to have priority over any political considerations. In discussing the Arab states' policy about this with my Arab friends, I have always pointed out to them that West Germany's post-war policy towards refugees from Eastern Germany and from east of the Oder-Neisse line has not only been humane, but has paid dividends to Western Germany, economically and therefore also politically.

Now about the facts that each side has to face and about practical possibilities for a settlement.

In your paper, you, yourself, have put your finger on the fact that Israel has to face. A series of more and more sensational victories in successive wars does not, in itself, give Israel the vital thing that she wants and needs; that is, real peace with her Arab neighbours. So long as Israel has no mutually agreed permanent frontiers, but only a military front, always smouldering and periodically flaring up into full-blown hostilities, Israel has to stay constantly on the alert and cannot concentrate her energies on her own internal development, which is, and always has been, her real objective. She has demonstrated now conclusively that, in war, she can always conquer more Arab territory without any foreign military aid; but, the more of this that she occupies, the more she will become militarily over-extended, and the larger the proportion of her limited and precious man-power she will have to keep unprofitably mobilised. The Arab World has the same passive military advantage as Russia and China have: there is virtually no end to it. So Israel's overriding interest is in genuine peace; even the greatest military victories will be fruitless unless they can be converted into that.

The Arabs have to face the fact that Israel has come to stay; that a three-times repeated experience has shown that they cannot defeat her; that the

Soviet Union is not going to go to war with the United States for the Arabs' sake; and that, in the unlikely event of the Arabs becoming, one day, able to destroy Israel, the United States would not let this happen.

I need not dwell on your psychological analysis of the present-day Arab state of mind. It is masterly; you have shown a power of sympathetic understanding by which you have entered into it imaginatively. This is very important and very encouraging, because Israel, as the present victor, holds the initiative. The party that has suffered injustice and has been humiliated is the one that is the more sensitive and that therefore needs the more delicate handling. The Palestinian Arabs have suffered injustice. To put it simply, they have been made to pay for the genocide of Jews in Europe which was committed by Germans, not by Arabs. The Arabs as a whole have been humiliated, because, in the establishment, first of the Jewish National Home and then of the state of Israel, the Arabs have, as you point out, never been consulted. It has all been done over their heads. They have been treated as 'natives', with no more than sub-human rights. For a people with a great, but no longer actual, historic past, this is infuriating. The present Arab and present Chinese states of mind have the same explanation.

So I would plead with Israel to make the first move towards achieving the total genuine and lasting peace which is the supreme common interest of Israel, the Palestinian Arab refugees, and the Arab states. For Israel publicly to make the first move would be magnanimous as well as far-sighted. I suggest that Israel should now propose that the two sides should make the following simultaneous declaration: 'The Arab states and the Palestinian Arab refugees pledge themselves to recognise, bona fide, the existence of Israel with the intention of making a permanent peace with her, and they also guarantee to negotiate permanent frontiers with Israel on approximately the 1948 armistice lines. Israel pledges herself to accept these agreed frontiers bona fide, with the intention, on her side, of making permanent peace, and she also undertakes to take the initiative in bringing about a satisfactory permanent settlement of the problem of the refugees'.

If both sides would give these reciprocal pledges in a formal agreement of the kind that used to be called 'preliminaries of peace', this would open the way for a negotiated treaty about details, and then things that have so far been impossible would become possible, e.g.:

(i) In the conversion of the 1948 armistice lines into permanent frontiers, there could be minor rectifications, so long as these offset each other fairly on balance.

(ii) There could be a mutual opening up of communications that are vital for both parties. Israel could be assured of a right of way not only through the straits of Tiran but through the Suez Canal too. Egypt could be assured of a right of way, across Israel, to Lebanon, Syria, Jordan, and Saudi Arabia, thus removing the 'Polish corridor' irritant of Israel's having split the Arab World in two by extending from the Mediterranean coast to the Gulf of Aqaba. Syria and Jordan could be given a free port at Haifa, with a right of way to it, and Jordan could be given a second one at Jaffa.

(iii) The Palestinian Arab refugees could (a) be given monetary compensation for the loss of their property situated in Israel; (b) be given an extra indemnity for having been forced, as innocent victims of the conflict between Israel and Arab states, to spend twenty years as refugees; (c) be given the option of either returning to their former homes on condition of becoming loyal citizens of Israel (as the Galilaean Arabs have been during the present crisis) or else being settled on good land outside Israel; (d) a fund could be raised for the refugees' resettlement, whether inside Israel or outside it. I am sure the majority will opt for resettlement *outside* Israel; but for Israel to offer the choice of returning home (on condition of their becoming bona fide loyal Israeli citizens) is psychologically very important for producing a change of heart among the refugees. If Israel appealed to the world to help her raise a fund for these four purposes, money would pour in.

(iv) Water for irrigation: in the London *Times* a few days ago, there was an important letter from Edmund de Rothschild about this, followed up next day by a long and constructive article by a desalination expert. They make the point that, even though desalination has not yet been made possible at an economic price, it would pay the world to subsidise it for the use of Israel and Jordan. This would (a) make it no longer necessary to pay a pittance to the refugees; (b) in combination with the Jordan water, it would supply abundant water for *both* Israel *and* Jordan, and would therefore make it unnecessary for them to contend with each other over their respective shares of Jordan water.

The future of the Old City of Jerusalem is a question of special urgency and danger. It is of crucial importance that Israel should not take unilateral action for annexing it. This would not be valid in international law; it could not be accepted by the United Nations; it would make genuine peace between Israel and the Arabs impossible; and it would arouse the whole Muslim World, and probably a large part of the Christian World too, not only against Israel, but against the Jews in general. It might seriously prejudice the diaspora's position in many countries.

Moreover, possession of the Temple area (the Muslim's Haram ash-Sharif) would be an embarrassment for Israel. She would have either to refrain from rebuilding the Temple or else she would have to demolish the

Dome of the Rock and the Al Aksa Mosque, which would really be unthinkable. Of course, Israelis and all other Jews must have free access to the Wailing Wall. I like the Pope's proposal for an international trusteeship for the holy places of *all* religions in Palestine. But any change of sovereignty here would be most provocative unless it were freely negotiated in exchange for some equivalent quid pro quo. For instance, Jordan might conceivably say to Israel: 'Cede to us the fields, now in Israel, that belong to villages on the Jordan side of the frontier, and then we will cede to you the southwest corner of the Old City of Jerusalem, up to the western face of the Wailing Wall.' A bargain on these lines would be all right, but unilateral action by Israel would be disastrous.

Well, I am writing this to you, and am sending copies to Isaiah Berlin and to a friend of mine in Baltimore, Maryland, Rabbi Agus.

I am now an old man, and most of my treasure is therefore in future generations. This is why I care so much, and why I am writing this letter to you.

Please make any use of my letter that you think useful. I am not marking it "confidential".

Yours sincerely,

Arnold Toynbee

Professor J. L. Talmon,
Department of Modern History,
Hebrew University of Jerusalem,
Israel.

(*From The Royal Institute of International Affairs, London*)

2nd June, 1969

Dear Dr. Agus,

I was very glad to have your letter of May 22nd, 1969, enclosing a copy of your recent article in the Journal of Ecumenical Studies.*

I feel despondent about the situation in the Middle East. After Israel's

*Journal Ecumenical Studies, 1969. Vol. 6, no. 1. *Israel and the Jewish-Christian Dialogue.*

lightning military victory in the Six Days' War, I had hoped that she would make some very generous offer to the Arabs—above all, to the Palestinian Arab refugees—that would win the Arab's hearts. But I fear that this opportunity has now been lost. I see no possible military solution for the conflict. Even if Israel could compel her Arab neighbours to sign the equivalent of the 'Versailles Diktat', this would be as worthless a guarantee as that was. As I see it, the only objective that would be of any value to Israel would be to gain the Arabs' willing acquiescence in Israel's presence on what was formerly Arab territory. This would, of course, be difficult to achieve, but I see no other hope than this of genuine and permanent security for Israel

Veronica and I had hoped to have a chance of seeing you and Mrs. Agus in April, but a coronary thrombosis prevented me from travelling. I am making a very good recovery, though slow, and my doctor expects me to get back to normal life.

With all good wishes to you both,

Yours very sincerely,

Arnold Toyrbee

(*From The Royal Institute of International Affairs, London*)

10 December, 1970

Dear Rabbi Agus,

I was very glad indeed to have your letter of December 1, 1970.

Peace in the Middle East is urgently needed for humanity's sake, to spare human beings on both sides of the line from further suffering, and also because the confrontation in the Middle East between the Soviet Union and the United States is, as I see it, the most likely situation in the World today to produce an atomic World War.

As I said in my article, I believe the key to peace lies in giving something to hope for and to live for to the Palestinian Arabs (all of them: those who are citizens of Israel; those in the Gaza Strip and on the Left Bank who at present are under Israeli occupation; and those in Transjordan, for whom King

Hussein's regime, kept in power by an American-armed Bedouin professional army, is not so different from a foreign military occupation).

Egypt, Hussein, and now, unexpectedly and happily, Syria too are evidently willing to make a sincere peace on the territorial basis of the 1949 armistice lines. As you say, the question is whether the Palestinian Arabs will agree to this basis, which at present the Palestinian guerrillas reject.

Naturally this is more difficult for the Palestinians than it is for the non-Palestinian Arabs, for what is now Israel is the Palestinian Arabs' own home country, and to renounce one's right to the possession of one's own homeland is difficult for any people. We cannot be sure that the Palestinians will bring themselves to make this renunciation, but it is certain that the guerrillas will remain intransigent if the Palestinians are not given hope. On the other hand, I guess that, if the Palestinians are given something to live for, Al Fatah will fall into line with Egypt, Jordan and Syria.

My own view is that the whole of Jordan, within its pre-1967 frontiers, together with the Gaza Strip, with a right of way across intervening Israeli territory, ought to be made into a Palestinian state, and that King Hussein ought to agree to becoming a constitutional monarch, transferring his present autocratic powers to a ministry elected by the Palestinian majority of the population of his Kingdom. If Hussein and the Palestinians would both consent to this settlement, the World would, I am sure, then be eager, for the sake of World peace, as well as for conscience' sake, to give aid for the development of this Palestinian state on the scale of the aid that Israel has received from the world-wide Jewish community and from the U.S. Government.

I do believe that, if this prospect were opened up for the Palestinian Arabs, there is a strong likelihood that they would turn their energies from guerrilla warfare (which leads nowhere) to economic and social development. The Palestinians are capable of making a success of a country of their own, if they are given the chance. Next to the Lebanese, they are the best educated of the Arab peoples, and, like the Lebanese, they have a great deal of natural ability.

This, to my mind, is the solution for which we all ought to work.

With all good wishes to you and Mrs. Agus from Veronica and me.

Yours very sincerely,

Arnold Toynbee

(From The Royal Institute of International Affairs, London)

31 December, 1970

Dear Dr. Agus,

Your letter of 22 December, 1970, arrived at the same moment as the news that the Government of Israel had agreed to resume the Jarring Talks.

Both Israel and Egypt seem to be pessimistic. This may be a more promising state of mind than excessive expectations of success.

Both countries are now so heavily armed that a resumption of hostilities would be catastrophic, and there would be a greater danger than before that the U.S. and the U.S.S.R. might become militarily involved in spite of their determination not to be.

I wish we were going to see you and Miriam here in March. Now that I cannot travel as I used to, I look forward to seeing my friends, who are still mobile, passing through London.

I much look forward to *Dialogue and Tradition*.

Best wishes to you and Miriam for the New Year from Veronica and me. Besides our personal good will and affection for each other, we have the same great wish for the Middle East and for the World: a peace that will be not just formal but will be heart-felt. This would be the first step towards reconciliation.

Yours very sincerely,

Arnold Toynbee

(From The Royal Institute of International Affairs, London)

22 March 1971

Dear Dr. Agus,

Dialogue and Tradition has just arrived. So far, I have read only Part II, but I do not want to wait to thank you till I have read the rest.

You are, as usual, large-minded, and you have the gifts of seeing all round a question and of being able to appreciate, and profit by, other people's points of view.

About the situation in the Middle East, I become more and more pessimistic. Mr. Rogers' offer to Israel on behalf of the United States, and Mr. Eban's rejection of it, are two momentous acts. There was, it seems to me, a possibility of a secure peace for both sides on Mr. Rogers' lines, and the Russians had done their part by prevailing on Egypt and Jordan to accept peace and co-existence with Israel on these terms. I fear that this chance of peace has now been lost, and the prospect is now once again alarming, in spite of the manifest wish of both the U.S. and the U.S.S.R. to resist being drawn into a confrontation with each other.

With my best wishes,
Yours very sincerely,

Arnold Toynbee

(*From The Royal Institute of International Affairs, London*)

25 October, 1971

Dear Dr. Agus,

My wife and I were so glad to have your letter of 1 October, 1971. It is very good news that, in the United States, the dialogue between Jews and Christians is going forward. I should have liked to be able to listen in at your Institute for the Catholic Clergy in Maryland. If the Jews and Christians continue the dialogue, I believe it will spread to the followers of other religions

The Soviet Government is very reluctant to allow freedom for the expression of opinions and beliefs. Unfortunately they inherit a tradition of repression that dates at least as far back as the fourteenth century of the common era. However, today, as in the nineteenth century, there are individual Russians who have the courage to protest publicly against oppression—for instance, the General who is now imprisoned as 'insane' for having taken up the cause of the Crimean Tatars.

I fear that an appeal to the Soviet Government to relax its oppressiveness would be likely to have a 'counter-productive' effect. If such an appeal were to be made, it would be important, I think, to make it on behalf of political, intellectual, and religious freedom in general, and not on the particular issue of allowing Jews from the Soviet Union to migrate to Israel. As I see it, this would be a boomerang, considering that the Arabs who have been dispossessed from their homes and property in what is now Israel are shot if they try to return. There is a parallel to this in the Soviet Union in the treatment there of the deported Crimean Tatars, but Jewish Soviet citizens are, I should guess, better off than the Arab citizens of Israel, or than Jordanian Arabs now under Israel military occupation, or than the Catholics in Northern Ireland.

According to statistics published by the Soviet Government, the number of Soviet Jews holding desireable posts is higher than the ratio of Jews in the Soviet Union's population. Of course these figures are suspect, because they have been published for the purpose of rebutting the charge that Jewish Soviet citizens have been singled out for specially harsh treatment. All the same, the figures are credible, because they correspond to the figures in countries in which there is no motive for rebutting charges of anti-Semitism. I have the impression that, in Jewish families everywhere, by comparison with non-Jewish families, the parents are, on the average, more ambitious for their children and the children are more responsive to their parents, with the result that Jews (like Scots) get a better education than non-Jews and therefore get more desirable jobs in adult life.

I am still as pessimistic as ever about the situation in the Middle East. It is most unfortunate that this has become entangled in the Russo-American competition for World power. Both superpowers now seem to wish for a detente, but I doubt whether either side will be willing to give up the cold war to a degree that will make detente possible.

Veronica and I send our best wishes to you and Miriam. Whether we count the new year from the equinox (which seems more reasonable) or from the solstice, I long for it to bring peace, though my hopes are not so strong as my wishes.

Yours very sincerely,

Arnold Toynbee

Notes

I. *A New Kind of Christian-Jewish Disputation*

1. Letter of Moses Mendelssohn to an unknown recipient, dated 1770, in M. Samuels, ed., *Jerusalem*, vol. 1, London, 1838.
2. Letter of Moses Mendelssohn to Lavater dated January 15, 1771. Quoted in A. Altmann, *Moses Mendelssohn*, University of Alabama Press, 1973, p. 261.
3. Quoted in A. Altmann, *Moses Mendelssohn*, p. 262.
4. See the most recent study, Lester G. Crocker, *Jean-Jacques Rousseau*, vol. 2, New York: Macmillan Co., 1973, p. 151.
5. Mendelssohn, *Jerusalem*, vol. 1, p. 130.
6. The sources are listed in: Emil Schürer, *A History of the Jewish People*, rev. ed., New York: Scribners, 1891, vol. 2, p. 831; G. F. Moore, *Judaism*, Cambridge, 1946, vol. 1, p. 325; H. A. Wolfson, *Philo*, Cambridge, 1947, vol. 2, p. 369.
7. Maimonides, *Guide of the Perplexed*, III, 32.
8. Maimonides, *Guide of the Perplexed*, III, 28.
9. My translation.
10. *Hilchot Melochim* VIII, par. 11.
11. Quoted in Spinoza, *A Theologico-Political Treatise*, Elwes translation, New York: Dover, 1951, ch. 5, p. 79.
12. *Hilchot Melochim* X, 14 ed. Constantinople.
13. *Guide of the Perplexed*, II, 16. Pine's translation, Chicago, 1963, p. 294.
14. *Hilchot Akum* IX, 4.
15. Joseph Albo, *The Book of Principles*, translated I. Husik, Philadelphia: Jewish Publication Society,* 1929. In III, 25, Albo argues that an irrational, or an unjust faith cannot be divine. He was compelled to fortify the resolution of his coreligionists to persevere in their faith by pointing to the irrationalities and unethical conduct of the fanatical Inquisitors of his day.
16. Mendelssohn, *Jerusalem*, p. 213.
17. Mendelssohn, *Jerusalem*, p. 101.

*hereafter abbreviated as J.P.S.

18. The historian Simon Dubnow regarded the quest of autonomy as a characteristic of Jewish history. "In this way the people build for themselves in every place something like a kingdom in miniature." Quoted by Koppel S. Pinson, in *Nationalism and History*, Philadelphia: J.P.S., 1958, p. 49.

    On the *herem* as the means of law-enforcement, see Salo W. Baron, *The Jewish Community*, Philadelphia: J.P.S., 1942, pp. 228–36.

19. Mendelssohn, *Jerusalem*, p. 104.

20. Mendelssohn, *Jerusalem*, p. 106.

21. Maimonides, *Guide of the Perplexed*, III, 28.

22. The ultimate goals of life were summarized by Maimonides in *Guide of the Perplexed*, Part 3, chapters 51, 52–54. In chapter 51, he described the goal of ecstasy. In the last three chapters, he described the creative acts of the philosopher who has attained the highest knowledge.

23. This description of the course of messianic redemption was presented by Maimonides in the last chapter of his Code, *Hilchot Melochim 11, 10*. In his "Letter to the Jews of Yemen," however, published in *Iggeret Teman*, Philadelphia: J.P.S., 1950, he spoke of the overwhelming effect of the miracles that the Messiah will perform (p. 101). Nachmanides, in his commentary on Isaiah 53, described the Messiah as a more exalted being than the patriarchs, Moses, and the highest angels; he will convert all the nations and through his merit the sins of Israel will be forgiven. This commentary is printed in Chavel's *Kithvai Rabenu Moshe ben Nachman*, vol. 1, Jerusalem, 1963.

24. Mendelssohn, *Jerusalem*, pp. 200, 203.

25. The phrase "fenced us round with impregnable ramparts and walls of iron that we might not mingle at all with any of the other nations" occurs in *The Letter of Aristeas*, verse 139, ed. R. H. Charles, Oxford, 1913.

26. In the first edition of the *Responsa of Moses Isserles* (No. 124), reference is made to the neglect and virtual disappearance of this prohibition in some Bohemian and other provinces. In later editions, this remark was eliminated. *Ozar Yisroel*, vol. 5, New York, 1952, p. 135.

27. It is interesting to note that Spinoza, too, insisted that Jesus did not intend to abolish the law. "Christ, as I have said, was sent into the world not to preserve the state nor to lay down laws, but solely to teach the universal moral law, so we can easily understand that He wished in no wise to do away with the Law of Moses, inasmuch as He introduced no new laws of His own." *A Theologico-Political Treatise*, ch. 5, p. 70.

28. Spinoza, *A Theologico-Political Treatise*, ch. V, p. 68.

    But with regard to the ceremonial observances which were ordained in the Old Testament for the Hebrews only, it is evident that they formed no part of the Divine Law, and had nothing to do with blessedness and virtue, but had reference only to the election of the Hebrews, that is (as I have shown in chapter 3) to their temporal bodily happiness and the tranquillity of their Kingdom, and that therefore they were valid only while that Kingdom lasted.

29. Spinoza had argued similarly, in regard to political sovereignty, that man *qua* man cannot barter away the freedom of his mind: "No one can ever so utterly transfer to another his power and consequently his rights, as to cease to be a man." *A Theologico-Political Treatise*, ch. 17.

30. In his last work, *To Lessing's Friends*, Mendelssohn had written that Spinoza could be interpreted in a theistic way. "Besides, I knew that there was purified Spinozism, and [that this] purified Spinozism was quite compatible with Judaism in particular; that irrespective of his speculative doctrine, Spinoza could have remained an Orthodox Jew had he not contested authentic Judaism in other writings of his, and had he not thereby withdrawn from the law." Mendelssohn, *Gesammelte Schriften*, vol. 3, p. 5; A. Altmann, *Moses Mendelssohn*, p. 753.

31. Nathan Rotenstreich, *Jewish Philosophy in Modern Times* (New York: Holt, Rinehart and Winston, 1968), p. 29.

32. In his own lifetime, Maimonides's eschatology was interpreted in this way. He composed his essay "On the Resurrection of the Dead" to counter such views. Yet, his disciples could still insist that this dogma was "a necessary belief," not a "true belief" (*Guide* III, 32); that is, it is necessary in order to maintain the cohesion of the Jewish community.

33. Introduction to *Code, Yad Hahazakah*.

34. That Rabbi Isaac Luria (the "holy Ari") was the recipient of authoritative revelations, the Mithnagdim (opponents) as well as the Hasidim (pietists) agreed. The Gaon Elijah of Vilna (1720–1797) disputed the accuracy of some printed versions of Lurianic Kabbalah. Rav Sheneur Zalman of Liadi (1747–1812) maintained that "the Holy Ari" attained greater revelations than Moses. *Iggeret Hakodesh*, par. 19, in Vilna edition 1928, p. 254.

35. The Hasidim were not alone in believing that their leaders, the Zaddikim, were guided by the Holy Spirit (*Ruah hakodesh*). Similar experiences were attributed to the leader of the Mithnagdim, the Gaon Elijah of Vilna, by his disciples. See introduction of Rabbi Hayim of Volozhin, (1749–1821) to Elijah's commentary on *Safra dizeniuta*, in "Shiveat Hameorot," (Vilna, 1913).

36. R. Mahler, in volume one of his *Dorot Ahronim* (Merhavia, Israel, 1952), assembled the relevant documents of the debates in France and Holland. The Orthodox *Parnassim* were, of course, opposed to any diminution of their power over the communal life of Jews. Some documents are discussed in Baruch Mevorach's *Napoleon Utekufata*, Jerusalem: Mossad Bialick, 1968.

37. G. E. Lessing, *The Evolution of the Human Race*, first published in German as, *Die Erziehung d. Menschengeschlechts*, 1780, par. 69.

38. Mendelssohn, *Jerusalem*, p. 356.

39. G. E. Lessing, *Theological Writings*, transl. H. Chadwick, ch. 1, p. 219.
40. *Ibid.*, ch. 3, p. 26.
41. Spinoza, *Gesammelte Schriften* III, p. 5.
42. A. Altmann, *Moses Mendelssohn*, pp. 698–759. Mendelssohn, *Morgenstunden* 1786, and *To Lessing's Friends.*
43. A. Altmann, *Moses Mendelssohn*, p. 200. B. Mevorach, Zion 30 (1965) pp. 158–70.
44. Christian Wilhelm Dohm, *Über die bürgerliche Verbesserung der Juden*, part 2, Berlin, 1783, p. 72, where the critiques and responses regarding Dohm's proposal are printed.

    Comte de Mirabeau, *Sur Mendelssohn et sur la reforme politique des Juifs*, second ed., Leipzig, 1853, p. 105.
45. Quoted in *Kayserling, Moses Mendelssohn—Sein Leben und seine Werke*, Appendix 57, Leipzig 1863.
46. On Hasidic messianism, see the chapter on Hasidism in this author's *The Evolution of Jewish Thought*, Abelard-Schuman, 1959; Arno Press, 1973. On the messianic philosophy of the Gaon Elijah of Vilna, see the voluminous work of Menahem M. Kasher, *Hatekufah Hagedolah* Jerusalem, 1969. On the interpretation of the Napoleonic Wars by the Zaddiks of Poland, see Martin Buber's novel, *For the Sake of Heaven*, Philadelphia: J.P.S., 1946.
47. J. B. Agus, *Evolution*, pp. 348–354.
48. See the discussion of this passage in I. Heinemann, *Taamai Hamizvot Besifrut Yisroel*, vol. II, Jerusalem, 1956, pp. 16, 38.
49. The brochure of N. Z. H. Weisel, *Divrai Shalom Ve-emet*, 1782. Ezekiel Kaufman, *Gole Venaichar*, Tel Aviv, 1930, vol. II, p. 31; Mendelssohn, *Gesam. Schriften*, vol. VIII, p. 301; vol. III, p. 105.
50. Perez Smolenskin, *Maamorim*, Jerusalem, 1925, 4 vols., chiefly the essays *Am Olam* and *Et Lotaat.*
51. Raphael Mahler, *Divrai Yemai Yisroel-Dorot Ahronim*, Tel Aviv, 1956, vol. I, pp. 121–251.
52. In other books and articles, I described this belief as the "meta-myth," an essential component of mythological antisemitism. See also: *The Meaning of Jewish History*, vol. 2, ch. XVI; *Guideposts in Modern Judaism*, pp. 171–203; Arthur A. Cohen, *The Natural and the Supernatural Jew*, New York: Pantheon, 1962.
53. A. Cohen, *The Natural*, pp. 28, 29.
54. A. Altmann, *Moses Mendelssohn*, p. 502.
55. A. Altmann, *Moses Mendelssohn*, p. 509.
56. H. J. Schoeps, *The Jewish-Christian Argument* New York: Holt, Rinehart and Winston, 1963.
57. H. J. Schoeps, *The Jewish-Christian Argument*, p. 129.
58. Eugen Rosenstock-Huessy, ed., *Judaism Despite Christianity*, University of Alabama Press, 1969, "Prologue-Epilogue," p. 75.

59. *Judaism Despite Christianity*, p. 70.
60. *Judaism Despite Christianity*, pp. 125 and 126.
61. *Judaism Despite Christianity*, p. 113.
62. *Judaism Despite Christianity*, p. 113.
63. *Judaism Despite Christianity*, p. 136.
64. Maimonides, *Guide of the Perplexed* III, 51.
65. Maimonides, *Guide of the Perplexed* III, 54.
66. Doubtless he was affected by the reactionary course of Catholicism culminating in 1864 in the acceptance at Vatican I of the *Syllabus of Errors*, which condemned every manifestation of liberalism.
67. Jakob Wassermann, *Mein Weg als Deutscher und Jude*, Berlin, 1921, p. 122.
68. *Judaism Despite Christianity*, p. 135.
69. Published in "Die Folke," 1819. See "Saul Ascher—First Theories of Progressive Judaism" by Ellen Littman, in Leo Baeck Institute *Yearbook V*, 1960, pp. 107–21.
70. F. Schleiermacher, *The Evolution of a Nationalist*, Austin and London: University of Texas Press, 1966.

II. *In the Light of Philosophical Rationalism*

1. Arthur M. Wilson, *Diderot* (Oxford University Press, 1972), p. 236, writes, "The necessities of polemics therefore gave the views of the *philosophes*, rather fortuitously, an anti-Jewish cast. This was a field in which the playful Voltaire loved to caper. Diderot and his colleagues, because of this dialectical necessity, were unfair to the Jew."
2. Arthur Hertzberg, in his excellent work *The French Enlightenment and the Jews*, sets out to prove that Voltaire was a pathological antisemite and that his animus derived from his rationalistic disdain for all separatist groups. Along with Graetz we concur with the first part of his thesis, but not with the second. Voltaire was obsessed by a certain personal anti-Jewish animus. But we should stretch the facts unduly if we were to attribute to him tendencies toward the homogenization of society, which became manifest much later in European history. The impact of his thought was toward a free and open society. The decisive consideration is the fact that the rationalists of the Revolutionary generation, who considered themselves to be disciples of Voltaire and Diderot, championed the emancipation of the Jews. Voltaire's peculiar anti-Jewishness was so well known and deplored by his colleagues that Rousseau, in a sarcastic tone, chided him for it. (*Pleiade*, vol. 3, p. 799).
    (See Arthur Hertzberg, *The French Enlightenment and the Jews*, [Philadelphia: J.P.S., 1968], p. 280).

3. Voltaire, *The Philosophy of History*, paperback reprint of 1766 edition. pp. 192, 211–16.

4. Lester G. Crocker, in his *Jean-Jacques Rousseau—The Prophetic Voice*, vol. II (New York: Macmillan, 1973), p. 151, wrote:

   > He was the only major *philosophe* in the Enlightenment to take such an enlightened attitude, although he does speak of the ancient Hebrews as "the vilest of all peoples." Voltaire hated and reviled the Chosen People, who had given the world *l'infame* of Christianity. None of the other *philosophes* included the Jews in their plans for a modern state and an open society. They looked on that mysterious group with natural aversion for the alien tinged with the scorn of popular folklore.

5. I. Kant, *Critique of Judgment*, trans. Bernards, p. 322.

6. Maimonides, *Guide of the Perplexed*, II, 25.

7. Spinoza, *Theological-Political Tractate*, ch. 2.

8. I. Kant, *Religion Within the Limits of Reason Alone*, trans. Greene & Hudson, sec. ed. (1960), p. 100.

9. *Ibid.*, p. 126.

10. *Ibid.*, p. 116.

11. *Ibid.*, p. 142.

12. *Ibid.*, p. 116.

13 *Ibid.*, p. 118.

14. *Ethics of the Fathers*, pp. 1, 3.

15. *Ibid.*, 4, 1.

16. I. Kant, *Religion Within the Limits of Reason Alone*, p. 116.

17. *Ibid.*, p. 116.

18. *Ibid.*, p. 118.

19. *Ibid.*, p. 142.

20. *Ibid.*, p. 122.

21. *Ibid.*, p. 132.

22. *Ibid* pp. 183–85.

23. *Ibid.*, XXXIV.

24. In "Emunot Vedeot" III, 2, Saadia distinguished between "mizvot of obedience" and "mizvot of reason," adding that the former, too, are designed to further man's moral growth. Maimonides, in "Guide of the Perplexed" III, 32, maintained that all the *mizvot* serve either the physical and spiritual well-being of the individual or the welfare of the community.

25. Emil L. Fackenheim, in "Encounters between Judaism and Modern Philosophy," Philadelphia, J.P.S. 1973 discussed the challenge of Kant in his brilliant chapter "Abraham and the Kantians." His reply to Kant's criticism of God-given laws as heteronomous is as follows: The Jew regards the laws of the Torah as marks of God's love, to which he responds by obedience in love. So, his performance of the divine

command is an immediate expression of the love of God, whether it be a ritualistic *mizvah* or an ethical obligation. This view of Fackenheim's is consistent with the Hasidic tradition, which interpreted the requirement "for its own sake" (*Lishmo*) as meaning that every commandment must be performed for the sake of "adhering to" the Divine Being (*leshem devekut*). It differs from the rationalistic and legalistic traditions. Thus Maimonides acknowledged the supreme importance of the principle of moral autonomy by distinguishing between *mizvot* that reflect God's "first intention," and those that reflect His "secondary intention." Maimonides would have agreed with Kant [against Kierkegaard] that there can be no "theological suspension of the ethical." The legalist did not always require *Kavanah*, the right intention.

26. Leo Baeck's interpretation of Steinheim's view as quoted in Graupe's *Steinheim and Kant*, in Leo Baeck Institute *Yearbook* V, p. 140.
27. Especially in the Palestinian Targum. The references are analyzed in '*Targum and Testament*' by Martin McNamara, (Grand Rapids, Mich.: Wm. W. Eerdmans Publ. Co. 1972), pp. 131–39.
28. A. Geiger, *Urschrift* (Breslau, 1857).
29. Sanhedrin 108a.
30. Jerusalem Sanhedrin, XI, 5.
31. *Gesammelte Schriften*, vol. I, p. 325.
32. N. Glatzer in Leo Baeck Institute *Yearbook* V, p. 126.
33. The historian Graetz in his "Konstruktion d. jüdischen Historie," printed in four installments in Frankel's "Zeitschrift für die religiösen Interessen des Judentums" Bd. III (1846), wrote as follows:

For Judaism is not a faith of individuals but of the community as a whole, and the promises of reward for *mizvot* were not intended for the individual but for the national body. The well-being and peace of the Jewish polity is dependent upon the observance of the *mizvot*. In the same way, the individual is not promised a portion in the World to Come as a reward for obedience. Immortality is none of its concern and life in the hereafter is no more a central dogma than "transsubstantiation," and who knows if this weakness is not also its strength.

We repeat and say—Judaism is not a faith for individuals at all, but of the community as a whole. This means that in an exact sense, *Judaism is not a religion at all* [my italics]—if by religion be understood man's relation to his Creator and his concern for his personal destiny—but in essence it is a political constitution.

The Hebrew translation of this essay appears in *Darchai Hahistoria Hayehudit* (Jerusalem, Mossad Bialick, 1969), p. 61.

This quotation illustrates the Jewish-nationalistic mentality, which agreed so often with the Christian critique of the Jewish religion.
34. Emil Schürer, *A History of the Jewish People* English translation of

second edition (New York: Scribner's, 1891), 31,5, vol. 4, p. 291 f. for references.

35. Josephus, *Contra Apionem*. Philo, *Mission to Caligula*. Tacitus, *History*, V, 2. Cicero, *Pro Flacco*, chap. XXVIII. Gill, *Notices of the Jews and their Country by the Classic Writers of Antiquity*, Second Edition (London; 1872).

36. Tossefta, Sanhedrin, 13.

37. A. Geiger, in *Judaism and Its History*, vol. I, ch. 1 (New York, 1911) wrote:

> Is not the Jewish people likewise endowed with such a genius, with a religious genius? Nevertheless, Israel is the people of revelation; the favored organs of which came from that people; it is as though the rays of light had been dispersed, and were concentrated into a flame by those gifted with higher endowments. It is the revelation which lay dormant in the whole people and was concentrated in individuals.

38. Judah Halevi, *The Kuzari*, IV, 16; IV, 17; V, 19; IV, 3; IV, 23. (New York: Schocken Books, 1964).

39. M. Lazarus, *The Ethics of Judaism*, trans. Henrietta Szold (Philadelphia: J.P.S., 1900), p. x.

40. *Ibid.*, vol. I, p. 106.

41. *Ibid.*, vol. I, p. 116.

42. *Ibid.*, p. 156.

43. *Ibid.*, p. 165.

44. *Ibid.*, p. 170.

45. *Ibid.*, p. 172.

46. *Ibid.*, vol. I, p. 167.

47. *Ibid.*, vol. II, p. 46.

48. Lazarus, *Ethics*, vol. II, p. 52.

49. *Ibid.*, vol. I, p. 131.

50. *Ibid.*, vol. II, p. 61.

51. *Ibid.*, vol. II, p. 71.

52. *Ibid.*, vol. I, p. 41.

53. *Ibid.*, p. 96.

54. H. Cohen, *Religion of Reason, out of the Sources of Judaism*, trans. S. Kaplan (New York: Frederick Ungar Publishing Co., 1973), p. 10.

55. *Ibid.*, p. 159.

56. *Ibid.*, p. 34.

57. F. Rosenzweig, *The Star of Redemption*, trans. Hallo (New York, 1970), p. 3.

58. *Ibid.*, p. 147.

59. Cohen, *Religion of Reason* . . . p. 150.

60. *Ibid.*, p. 22.

61. *Ibid.*, p. 169.

62. *Ibid.*, p. 161.

63. *Ibid.*, p. 16.
64. *Ibid.*, p. 160.
65. *Ibid.*, p. 25.
66. *Ibid.*, p. 26.
67. *Ibid.*, p. 145.
68. *Ibid.*, p. 268.
69. *Ibid.*, p. 340.
70. *Ibid.*, p. 344.
71. *Ibid.*, p. 346.
72. *Ibid.*, p. 362.
73. H. Cohen, *Jüdische Schriften*, vol. II (Berlin, 1927), p. 322.
74. *Ibid.*, p. 322.
75. *Ibid.*, p. 323.
76. *Ibid.*, p. 325.
77. *Ibid.*, p. 333.
78. *Ibid.*, p. 331.
79. *Ibid.*, p. 335.
80. *Ibid.,.*p. 336.
81. *Ibid.*, p. 337.
82. *Ibid.*, p. 209.
83. Alexander Altmann, *Leo Baeck and the Jewish Mystical Tradition* (New York: Leo Baeck Institute, 1973), p. 5.
84. *Judaism and Christianity* (Philadelphia: J.P.S., 1958), p. 189.
85. *Ibid.*, p. 190.
86. *Ibid.*, p. 191.
87. *Ibid.*, p. 196.
88. *Ibid.*, p. 198.
89. *Ibid.*, p. 202.
90. *Ibid.*, p. 211.
91. A. Altmann, "Leo Baeck and the Jewish Mystical Tradition" (New York: Leo Baeck Institute, 1973), pp. 15, 21.
92. *This People, The Meaning of Jewish Existence*, trans. A. H. Friedlander (Philadelphia: J.P.S., 1965).
93. *Ibid.*, p. 21.
94. Baeck, *This People* . . . , p. 27.

III. *In the Perspective of German Romanticism*

1. Friedrich Schlegel characterized romantic literature as that "which treats sentimental material in a phantastic form." Since, to the romantics, "thinking is only a dream of feeling," what matters is the surge of feeling. Leo Baeck accepted this definition in his discussion of Christianity as a

"romantic religion" (Leo Baeck, "Judaism and Christianity," Philadelphia, 1958, p. 1895).

Our interest, in this chapter, lies in the blending of individuality and the national collectivity.

2. J. Bronowski and B. Mazlish, *The Western Intellectual Tradition* (New York), 1960, p. 280.

3. Abbé Gregoire, *Essai sur la regeneration physique, morale et politique des Juifs* (Paris, 1789).

4. Ezekiel Kaufman, in *Goleh Venaichar* (Tel Aviv, 1930), pp. 70, 71, summarized in this way the decision of the Paris Sanhedrin. Portado regarded it "as a covenant between our religion and our fatherland." Rabbi Zitsenheim, who presided at the plenary sessions, concluded that "it signed a social pact between the people of God and the nations that accepted it."

5. Diogene Tama, *Collection des proces verbaux et decis du grand Sanhedrin,"* (Paris, 1808).

6. Friedrich D. E. Schleiermacher, *Reden über die Religion*, II edition, 1806. New edition by R. Otto, 1926.

7. J. G. Fichte, *Reden an die deutsche Nation*, 1808.

8. H. D. Schmidt, *Anti-Western and Anti-Jewish Tradition in German Historical Thought*, printed in *Yearbook* IV of the Leo Baeck Institute, (London, 1959).

9. Fichte described the German people as an *Urvolk*, possessing an *Ursprache*, not a hybrid, "bastardized" language. The nationalist ideologists, Ernst Moritz Arndt and Father Jahn, extolled "purity of blood" as the most precious guarantee of German supremacy. (Hans Kohn, *The Mind of Germany*, Scribner's, New York, 1960, pp. 69–88). Erich Kahler characterized German nationalism as follows: "German nationalism has always contained this overtone of bitterness and resentment, resentment against the rest of the world and resentment against the universalistic impulse born in the literature and thought of the late eighteenth century." (Erich Kahler, *The Germans* [Princeton: Princeton University Press, 1974], p.261).

10. *Auch eine Philosophie d. Geschichte zur Bildung d. Menschheit*, (1774).

11. *Ideen zur Philosophie d. Geschichte d. Menschheit* in Herder's *Werke*, ed. Mathias, vol. IV, p. 30.

12. *Ibid.*, p. 34.

13. *Ibid.*, p. 39.

14. *Ibid.*, p. 40.

15. *Ibid.*, IV part, Ch. 5.

16. *Ibid.*, IV part, Ch. 5.

17. Zechariah Frankel's letter of resignation from the Rabbinical Conference in Frankfurt, dated July 18, 1945, as well as the response of the Reform majority, is printed in W. Gunther Plaut's *The Rise of Reform*

Judaism (New York, 1963, p. 87f.) The many variations in emphasis, running the entire spectrum from consistent universalism to mild traditionalism, are described and illustrated in Jakob J. Petuchowski's *Prayerbook Reform in Europe* (New York, 1968).

18. Excerpts from the original description of the concept of "science of Judaism," by Immanuel Wolf, are printed in W. Gunther Plaut's *The Rise of Reform Judaism*, pp. 107–10. Of the greatest importance was Leopold Zunz's epoch-making book *Die Gottesdienstliche Vorträge d. Judentums*, which was first printed in 1832. In his introduction, Zunz declared that the restriction of Jewish civil rights and the neglect of "the science of Judaism" were intimately related. A. Geiger's essay on *The Science of Judaism* is included in Max Wiener's *Abraham Geiger and Liberal Judaism* (Philadelphia, 1962, p. 149f).

19. Abraham Geiger, who combatted the notion of the indispensability of the Hebrew language in Jewish worship, did not deny the role of national feeling in the formation of Judaism.

   However, in his view, Judaism has outgrown the phase of national existence. "Let us, therefore, look back with joy on our former life as a nation, as being an essential transitional era in our history."

   What the modern Jew retains, in addition to the principles of his faith, is a living participation in the "genius" of his people. He interprets the biblical doctine of revelation, in the light of this inborn genius. "This is the revelation which lay dormant in the people as a whole and then found a unifying focal point in certain individuals." (Quoted in Max Wiener, *Abraham Geiger and Liberal Judaism*, pp. 151, 152, 181).

20. N. Rothenstreich, *The Bruno Bauer Controversy* (London: Leo Baeck Institute *Yearbook* IV, 1959).

21. See Gershon Scholem's *Major Trends in Jewish Mysticism* and Martin Buber's introductions to the two volumes, *Tales of Hassidism*, for twentieth-century views of Kabbalah and Hasidism. A nineteenth-century appreciative interpretation of Kabbalah is contained in A. Frank's *The Kabbalah*, recently reissued by Arno Press, New York. Abraham Geiger, a leading founder of Reform, wrote: "Christianity is the true mother of mysticism and romanticism. Judaism, on the other hand, is lucid, concrete, vital and affirmative." (Quoted in Max Wiener, *Abraham Geiger and Liberal Judaism*, p. 152).

22. L. Zunz, *Gesammelte Schriften* II, pp. 172–73.

23. L. Zunz's letter to Geiger in latter's *Nachgelassene Schriften* V, p. 184.

24. Samuel Cohen, *Zunz and Reform Judaism*, in Hebrew Union College Annual, vol. XXXI, 1960, p. 251f.

25. Z. Frankel, *Zeitschrift für die religiösen Interessen des Judentums*, II, 15.

26. I. Heinemann, *Taamai Hamizvot Besafrut Yisroel*, II vol. pp. 161–94. Frankel's emphasis on the national base of the Jewish religion and on the continuity of revelation in the life of the people was probably occasioned

by the Karaite tendencies among the Reformers and their anti-nationalism. See Jakob J. Petuchowski's *Karaite Tendencies in an early Reform Haggadah*, H.U.C.A. vol. XXXI, p. 223f.

27. Samuel David Luzzato, *Vikuah al Hakabbalah*, Goricia, 1852.

28. Solomon Schechter, *Studies in Judaism*, Meridian books, 1958. See essays titled *Chassidim* and *Nachmanides*.

29. Samuel David Luzzato, *Yesodai HaTorah*, *Mehkorai Hayahadut*, *Igrot Shadal*—all in Hebrew.

30. Moses Maimonides, *Guide of the Perplexed*, III, 32 and 26–51. On the distinction between laws of primary and secondary intention see III, 32, p. 529 in S. Pines' translation, U. of Chicago Press, 1963.

31. Letter to M. Letteris of 18,1. '38. Quoted in M. Wiener's *Jüdische Religion im Zeitalter d. Emanzipation* (Berlin; 1939).

32. *Gesammelte Schriften*, V, 546.

33. Salo W. Baron, *Proceedings of the American Academy for Jewish Research*, 1951, p. 35. I. Heinemann, *Taamai Hamizvot*, II vol. pp. Ch. 4.

34. S. R. Hirsch, *The Nineteen Letters of Ben Uziel*, transl. by B. Drachman (New York; 1899, Letter Three).

35. *Ibid.*, Letter Four.

36. *Ibid.*, Letter Nine.

37. *Ibid.*, Letter Fifteen.

38. *Ibid.*, Letter Nine.

39. *Ibid.*, Letter Eighteen.

40. The notion that Hebrew was the original language of mankind is stated in the commentary of Rashi on Genesis 20:1. In the Book of Jubilees (XII, 26,26), Abraham was taught Hebrew, "the language of creation," by the revealing angel. In the Kabbalah, the Hebrew letters, forming part of the Holy Name, became the "elements of creation." It is doubtful that Hirsch was familiar with the revival of the Kabbalistic belief in the continuing role of the sacred letters in the Hasidic movement. Letters issue from the "upper realms of the Pleroma," which the Zaddik can recombine—such as rearranging the letters of *nega*, an affliction, to those of *oneg*, a delight. (See *Degel Mahne Ephraim*, Beshalah, *Kether Shem Tov*, collections of sayings of Baal Shem Tov, Talpiot edition, p. 193). R. Levi Yizhak in *Kedushat Levi*, "Kedushah Sheniya," ed. Warsaw, 1890, p. 12, maintains that the shape of the Hebrew letters reflects the manner in which the divine flow comes down to the lower worlds.

41. In his long essay, *Jüdische Welt und Lebensanschauungen* (in *Gesammelte Schriften*, vol. V, pp. 143–208), Hirsch set out to derive a philosophy of life out of the Hebrew language and the sacred literature. Hebrew was not, to him, a reflection of the Jewish national genius, for the language was bestowed on the people as "the creation of the Spirit of spirits," in order to mold the Jewish national spirit (p. 146). There is no basic root for the verb, to *possess*, in Hebrew, but the verb, to *be*, is spoken with

reverence, for it is associated with the name of God. And *he was* is related to *hagah* ("he thought") yielding the idea, "He (the Lord) thinks, therefore, I am"—quite a change from the Cartesian formulation (p. 149). Since the awareness of God's Presence in all phenomena was so axiomatic, to the Jew, the Torah did not set out to "prove" God's existence. Heaven and earth were perceived directly as "creaturely"—the Hebrew word *Bara*—suggesting that the realm of existence was externalized, or made manifest. (p. 159)

In this way, Hirsch attempted to found his world view and the ethic of knowing one's station in life (p. 155).

42. I. Heinemann remarked on the "coolness" of Hirsch to the "land of Israel." This attitude was understandable in the Reformers, who consciously and clearly gave up an important aspect of their heritage. But it was seemingly out of character in an Orthodox rabbi who maintained the sanctity of every tittle of the law. We recall that Graetz's *Palestinocentrism* became a burning issue in 1880, during the Graetz-Treitschke controversy (I. Heinemann, *Taamai Hamizvot*, Jerusalem, 1956, vol. II, p. 158).

43. S. R. Hirsch, *Commentary on Genesis XIII*, 3. Translated by Isaac Levy (London, 1963).

iv. *Are the Jews "Ahistorical"?*

1. To be sure, St. Augustine's dissociation of "The City of God" from "The City of Man" implied an inner withdrawal from the fate of the Empire. Doubtless his mood was shared by many Christians.
2. Hegel, *Encyclopedia*, sec. 237, in *Werke*, Stuttgart, 1927–1939, vol. VI, p. 409.
3. *Werke,* vol. VI, p. XXI.
4. *Werke*, vol. VI, p. 160.
5. Walter Kaufmann, *Hegel: Reinterpretation, Texts and Commentary*, New York 1965, p. 369.
6. A. Harnack, *What Is Christianity?* trans. by Saunders (London; 1900), p. 306.
7. Sidney Hook, *From Hegel to Marx* (New York; Reynall & Hitchcock, 1936), p. 97.
8. *Ibid.*, p. 105.
9. L. Feuerbach, *The Essence of Christianity*, trans. George Eliot, Harper Torchbooks, 1957, p. 298, par. 10, in Appendix.
10. J. F. C. Schiller, *Briefe über die ästhetische Erziehung des Menschen*, 1795, Letter 6.
11. S. Formstecher, *Religion d. Geistes*, 1841, pp. 66 and 280–81.

12. *Ibid.*, pp. 230–32.

13. *Ibid.*, p. 234–52.

14. *Ibid.*, p. 280.

15. *Ibid.*, p. 365.

16. Samuel Hirsch, *Religiöse Philosophie der Juden*, 1842, para. 62–66.

17. M. Wiener, *Jüdische Religion im Zeitalter d. Emanzipation* (Berlin; 1933), pp. 140–42.

18. Samuel Hirsch, *Religiöse Philosophie der Juden*, 1842, "Samuel Hirsch and Hegel," by Emil L. Fackenheim in *Studies in Nineteenth Century Jewish Intellectual History* (Cambridge: Harvard University Press, 1964).

19. The interpretation of the inner logic of Kabbalah that is here assumed is contained in my Hebrew essay, *Lehaiker Hegyon Hakabbalah*, printed in *Sefer Hashono Liyehudai America* (New York, 1947).

20. Krochmal, *Moreh Nebuhai Hazeman*, edited by L. Zunz, Lemberg, 1863, Gate 6. The unity of fear, joy, and love in piety is affirmed in *The Kuzari*, II, 49.

21. Krochmal, *Moreh*, Gate 6.

22. On the various meanings of the term, *devekut*, adherence, see my essay, *Ish Hamistorin* in *Talpiot*, New York 1946 (Hebrew), where five types of mystical and pietistic adherence to the Divine are described.

23. Martin Buber, in his article *What Is Right and What Is Not in Krochmal* (included in Buber's volume, *Israel and the World* [New York, 1965]), points out that Krochmal is wrong if he asserts that Jews *possess* the Absolute Spirit, but right if he means that we have set ourselves the *task* of possessing it in thought and exemplifying it in action. This ambiguity marks the unfinished work of Krochmal. The interpretation of Krochmal that is here presented adopts the second alternative. I expounded the meaning and implications of this conception in my article, *Religion as Quest*, in *The Journal of Ecumenical Studies* (Philadelphia, 1972).

24. Abraham Geiger, a younger contemporary of Krochmal, interpreted religion as an infinite journey. "Yea, longing after the Highest and Noblest, attachment to the Whole, soaring up to the Infinite, despite our finiteness and limitedness—This is Religion. Herein also consists the guarantee of the Highest and Infinite, because we long to soar up to it . . ." (A. Geiger, *Judaism and Its History*, transl. Maurice Mayer [London, 1865], p. 18).

25. N. Krochmal, *Moreh*, Gate VI.

26. Bahya Ibn Pakuda, *Hovot Halevovot*, 1;2.

27. Krochmal, *Moreh*, Gate VI.

28. *Ibid.*, Gate VII.

29. *Ibid.*

30. Erich Kahler, *The Meaning of History* (New York: 1964, pp. 171–186). He distinguished between "historism"—studying cultural phenomena in

the context of history—and "historicism"—the completely relativistic approach to national values and norms of conduct.

31. Jacob Taubes, "Nahman Krochmal and Modern Historicism," in *Judaism—A Quarterly*, 1963, pp. 150–164.
32. Krochmal, *Moreh*, Gate VII.
33. Hegel, *Werke*, vol. VIII, p. 449.
34. Krochmal, Moreh, Gate XII.
35. *Ibid.*, Gate X.

v. *On the Crossroad between Liberalism and Nationalism*

1. Bruno Bauer, *Die Juden-frage*, Braunschweig, 1843. Nathan Rothenstreich, *For and Against Emancipation; The Bruno Bauer Controversy*, in Leo Baeck Institute Yearbook IV, 1959; *Hashkofotov HoAnti-yehudiot shel Bruno Bauer*, by Zvi Rosen in *Tsiyon*, (Hebrew) year 33, 1968.
2. It is interesting that the author of the *Letter of Aristeas* employs this term in describing the effect of Jewish law. *Letters of Aristeas*, Charles' edition, p. 139.
3. *Tosefta*, Sanhedrin, 13.
4. Bruno Bauer, who started as a liberal extremist in the 1840s, became a conservative nationalist in later life. His anti-Jewish posture in the 1860s was based on sheer racism. See his article *Das Judentum in der Fremde*, a reprint (Berlin, 1863). Nathan Rothenstreich discussed this change in an article in *Hebrew Union College Annual*, vol. XXV, 1954.
5. K. Marx, *Early Writings*, ed. T. Bottomore (London, 1963).

   Whether or not Karl Marx was antisemitic has been disputed. It cannot be doubted, however, that many of the statements in his two essays *On the Jewish Question* were utilized widely by antisemites. He used the terms *Judentum* and *mercenary spirit* interchangeably, which demonstrates the pervasive character of antisemitic rhetoric among radical intellectuals.

   Marx, unlike Bauer, was not opposed to the complete enfranchisement of the Jews of Prussia. In 1843 he composed a petition in behalf of the Jews of Cologne. Some of his most offensive epithets against the Jews were taken almost verbatim from the writings of the herald of Socialist Zionism, Moses Hess.

   D. McLellan, *Karl Marx—His Life and Thought* (New York, 1973), p. 86.
6. Sh. Z. Shazar, "Orai Dorot," *Jerusalem*, 1971, pp. 320–333.
7. Max Weber, *The Sociology of Religion*, translated by E. Fischoff, with an Introduction by T. Parsons (Boston: Beacon Press), p. 109.
8. *Ibid.*, p. 112.
9. Ellis Rivkin, *The Shaping of Jewish History* (New York, 1971), ch VI.

10. Weber, *Sociology*, p. 250.
11. Joachim C. Fest, *Hitler*, p. 113 (New York, 1974). Hitler's enthusiastic acceptance of this notion will be found in *Mein Kampf*, p. 208. See Karl Dietrich Bracher, *The German Dictatorship* (New York, 1970), p. 89; and Robert Payne, *The Life and Death of Adolf Hitler* (New York, 1973), p. 128.
12. Werner Sombart, *The Jews and Modern Capitalism*, translation by M. Epstein, Introduction to the American Edition by Bert F. Hoselitz. Collier Books, 1962.
13. *Ibid.*, p. 236.
14. *Ibid.*, p. 235.
15. *Ibid.*, p. 127.
16. *Ibid.*, p. 137.
17. *Ibid.*, p. 251.
18. *Ibid.*, p. 247.
19. *Ibid.*, p. 312.
20. *Ibid.*, p. 274.
21. *Ibid.*, p. 303.
22. Ellis Rivkin in *The Shaping of Jewish History*, p. 146, pointed out that the Marranos did indeed play a most important role in the promotion of the commercial revolution. Some of the Marranos returned to Judaism, particularly those in Holland and Turkey. For a while Don Joseph Nasi held out the possibility of an alliance between Jews in Turkey and Marranos in western Europe. He stressed, however, that "professing Jews were excluded totally from settling in the areas of commercial, financial and industrial innovation." Emphatically, he asserts, "Jews were *not* the first great entrepreneurs, and Judaism was *not* the breeding ground of the capitalistic spirit." (*Ibid.*, p. 140.)

    But all facets of life are interrelated. The religion and way of life of any group will affect its enterprise. It is well to compare R. H. Tawney's *Religion and the Rise of Capitalism*, 1927, with the works of Weber and Sombart. The English scholar pointed out the role of religious dissenters in a society that deprives them of political power. They focus all their energies in the economic sphere. "The recognition accorded by Puritan ethics to the economic virtues, in an age when such virtues were rarer than they are today, gave a timely stimulus to economic efficiency. But it naturally, if unintentionally, modified the traditional attitude towards social obligations." (Tawney, *Religion*, 1937 edition, p. 210.)
23. W. Sombart, *Die Zukunft d. Juden* (Leipzig, 1912).
Ismar Schorsch, *Jewish Reactions to German Antisemitism* (New York, 1972), p. 196.
24. Sh. Dubnow, *Divrai Yemai Am Olam* (Hebrew), vol. X., p. 259.
25. *Darchai Hahistoria Hayehudit*, edited by Sh. Etinger, Jerusalem, 1969, p. 62.

26. See Shemuel Etinger, "Yahaduth vetoldoth Hayehudim betefisoto shel Graetz," in "Darchai Hahistoria Hayehudit," Jerusalem, 1969, p. 19.
27. Graetz's 1939 entry into his diary, dated Rosh Hashono, 5509. His letter to Hess is dated October, 1861.
28. *Zeitschrift für die religiösen Interessen des Judentums*, Bd. III, S. 90.
29. Zohar, Mantua edition, II vol. p. 77—"The Holy One, blessed be He, Torah and Israel are one."
30. As early as 1844, in his diary, he contrasted the wretched stolidity of the Germans with the effervescence of the French, the pride of the Italians, and the national spirit of the English. See Graetz, *Darchai*, p. 252.
31. *Darchai* p. 209.
32. Graetz, *Darchai*, "Halifat Michtavim," Letters 12 and 14.
33. *Ibid.*, p. 182.
34. *Ibid.*, p. 124.
35. Samson Raphael Hirsch, the militant founder of neo-Orthodoxy, recognized this trend in Graetz's thought in 1839, when the first volume of Graetz's *History of the Jews* appeared. That volume dealt with the formation of Mishnah and Talmud. Hirsch called attention to Graetz's attempt to derive the teaching of each sage from his personal temperament and the socio-economic events of his day, as if the sages were not bearers of the tradition, but its creators. In Hirsch's view, Graetz reduced the Talmud to a chronicle of temperamental idiosyncrasies and historical contingencies. S. R. Hirsch, *Gesammelte Schriften*, vol. V, p. 322f.
36. Heinrich von Treitschke's essay "On our Jews," appeared in the November, 1879 issue of *Preussische Jahrbücher*. Graetz's response, in "Schlessische Presse," appeared in December, 1879. Treitschke's reply to Graetz was in the December, 1879, issue of *Preussische Jahrbücher*.

   Selections from the four letters involved are found in Sh. Etinger's *Darchai HaHistoria Hayehudit*, pp. 213–234. An abridged English translation of Graetz's *History* was published in Philadelphia, 1891–92.
37. *Darchai.*
38. *Ibid.*
39. Goethe, *Wilhelm Meister's Wanderjahre*, Bk. III, ch. 11.
40. *Darchai*, pp. 211–234.
41. *Ibid.*, pp. 234–275.
42. In contrast to racists like Wagner and Chamberlain, Treitschke praised the composer Felix Mendelssohn's "Germanism":

    A German from tip to toe. Among foreigners he was never fully understood by Frenchmen, only by Bretons of Germanic kin-race. Since this musician, known and beloved throughout the whole of Germany, commenced wielding his baton in Berlin, Düsseldorf, Frankfurt and Leipzig, music, which had degenerated into sheer entertainment, regained esteem as the highest of arts.

(Quoted in *Mendelssohn's Letters* (New York: Pantheon Books Inc, 1945), p. 12.)

43. J. Agus, *Modern Philosophies of Judaism*, Behrman House, 1971, p. 52.

44. It is interesting to compare Treitschke's position with that of the English philosopher of liberalism, John Stuart Mill. For Treitschke described himself as a national liberal.

　　Mill wrote: "Of all the vulgar modes of escaping from the consideration of the effect of social and moral influences on the human mind, the most vulgar is that of attributing the diversities of conduct and character to inherent national differences." *Political Economy*, vol. I, p. 390.

45. *Monatsschrift für Geschichte und Wissenschaft des Judentums* (Breslau: 1917). *Graetzen's Philosophie der Jüdischen Geschichte*, by H. Cohen, pp. 356–366.

46. *Ibid.*, p. 361.

47. *Ibid.*, p. 362.

48. *Ibid.*, p. 366.

49. *Ibid.*, p. 366.

50. Theodor Mommsen, *Auch ein Wort über unser Judenthum* (Berlin, 1880), p. 7.

51. Letter 14, in *Darchai*, p. 164.

52. Ismar Schorsch summarized the Jewish reaction to the Graetz-Treitschke dispute as follows:

　　"Many Jews were dismayed at the lack of discretion exhibited by Heinrich Graetz. It is remarkable that in all the ink spilled over Treitschke's attack against Graetz, not a single important Jewish spokesman defended the Jewish historian, a fact that rankled Graetz deeply." (Schorsch, *Jewish Reactions.*)

53. See Chapter I, note 52.

54. *Das Judentum in Gegenwart und Zukunft*, by Edouard v. Hartmann (Leipzig: Verlag Wilhelm Friedrich, 1885).

55. *Ibid.*, p. 54.

56. Schopenhauer, *Parerga*, part II, p. 132.

57. Hartmann, *Das Judentum in Gegenwart und Zukunft*, p. 194.

58. Proverbs 3, 6. Berochot 63a.

59. M. Buber, *Reden über das Judentum* (Frankfurt, 1923), pp. 8, 13, 15.

60. H. Steinthal, *Über Juden und Judentum* (Berlin, 1906).

VI. *The Jews as Socialists Saw Them*

1. Robert Conquest, *The Great Terror* (New York, 1968), p. 76. "But Stalin was deeper and more complex than Hitler. His view of humanity was cynical, and if he too turned to antisemitism, it was a matter of policy rather than dogma."

2. See J. S. Hertz, ed. *Doyres Bundisten*, 3 volumes. Yiddish, 1956–1969. A. Menes, *The Jewish People, Past and Present*, vol. 2 (1948), pp. 355–368. R. Abramowitz, *ibid.*, pp. 369–398.
3. See E. Silberner, *Sozialisten zur Judenfrage* (1962). Leon Poliakov, *Histoire de l'Antisemitisme*, vol. 3 (1968), pp. 380–384. In his later years, Fourier was intrigued by the Zionist ideal and the vision of communes, or, as he called them, "phalansteres." *Encyclopedia Judaica*, 6,1448.
4. See L. Thomas, *Alphonse Toussenel, Socialist, National, Antisemite* (1941). Z. Szajkowski, *Jewish Social Studies*, vol. 9 (1947), pp. 33–47. It is interesting to note the association of antisemitism with a generalized xenophobia. Toussenel attacked Jews, along with Protestants, the English, the Dutch, and the Swiss, as "birds of prey." *Encyclopedia Judaica*, 15, 1291.
5. Engels, F. *Anti-Dühring*. First published in London in 1878. Quotations are from New York edition, International Publishers.
6. Theodor Herzl, *Tagebücher*, vol. I (Leipzig, 1881), p. 135.
7. Peter Gay, *The Dilemma of Democratic Socialism, Eduard Bernstein's Challenge to Marx* (New York, 1952), p. 100.
8. Quoted in *Ibid.*, p. 158. Karl G. Popper maintained that Bernstein's socialist philosophy "gives up Marxism altogether; it is nothing but the advocacy of a strictly democratic and nonviolent workers' movement." (Karl G. Popper, *The Open Society and its Enemies*, II vol., Marx and Hegel, p. 339.)
9. Engels, *Anti-Dühring*, p. 128.
10. *Ibid.*, p. 352.
11. Karl Kautsky, *Are the Jews a Race?* (New York, 1926, International Publishers), p. 179.
12. *Ibid.*, p. 176.
13. *Ibid.*, p. 159.
14. *Ibid.*, p. 141.
15. Kautsky referred in particular to the work of Ignaz Zollschan, *Das Rassenproblem* (1910).
16. Kautsky, *Are the Jews a Race?*, p. 246.
17. St. Simon, *Nouveau Christianisme* (Paris, 1825), p. 116.
18. F. E. Manuel, *The New World of Henri St. Simon* (Cambridge: Harvard University Press, 1956), p. 359.
19. *Ibid.*, p. 347.
20. Emile Durkheim, *Socialism and St. Simon* (Antioch Press, 1958), p. 237.
21. *Ibid.*, p. 191.
22. *Ibid.*, p. 197.
23. E. Durkheim, *The Elementary Forms of the Religious Life* (New York; 1965), p. 215.
24. Victor M. Glasberg, "Intent and Consequences: The 'Jewish Question' in the French Socialist Movement of the Late Nineteenth Century," in

Jewish Social Studies (January, 1974), pp. 360–671. He concludes, "But the main spokesmen of the *anti-juif* school—the very men accused of leading the anti-semitic camp within the socialist movement—cannot be called antisemites."

25. J. L. Talmon, *Israel among the Nations* (New York, 1971), p. 13.
26. Pierre-Joseph Proudhon, "Oeuvres completes de P. J. Proudhon," vol. 2. Silberner, "Hasocialism Hamaarovi," Jerusalem (1955), p. 70.
27. Karl G. Popper, *The Open Society and Its Enemies* (Princeton, 1971), p. 159.
28. *Ibid.*, p. 159.
29. *Ibid.*, p. 211.
30. *Ibid.*, p. 154.
31. I. Schorsch, *Jewish Reactions to German Antisemitism* (New York, 1972).
32. Donald L. Niewyk, *Socialist, Antisemite and Jew* (Baton Rouge, Louisiana, 1971), Louisiana State Press, p. 19.
33. Jacob Burckhardt, *Briefe an Fr. von Preen, 1864–1893* (Stuttgart, 1922), pp. 144, 188.
34. Record of the Society of the Hebrew Socialists of London, May 20, 1876, cited in Ber Borochov's *Nationalism and the Class-Struggle*, ed. M. Cohen (New York, 1937).
35. *Ibid.*, p. 171.
36. Theodor Herzl, *Diaries*, vol. 3, p. 1090.
37. In commenting on Marx's *Das Kapital*, Hess wrote, "The Talmudic-halachic categories of thought, impressed in his blood, as an inherited quality . . ." (*Encyclopedia Ivrit*, XVIII), p. 844.
38. The letters of Graetz to Hess are printed in *Darchai Hahistoria Hayehudit* (published by Mossad Bialick, 1969), pp. 366–373.
39. Gershon Greenberg, "The Reformers' First Attack upon Hess, Rome and Jerusalem: An Unpublished Manuscript of Samuel Hirsch" (*Jewish Social Studies*) (1973), Nos. 3 and 4, p. 175.
40. Graetz, *Darchai*. Letter of Graetz to Hess, from Breslau, dated December 30, 1964.
41. B. Borochov, *Nationalism*, p. 150.
42. *Ibid.*
43. *Ibid.*
44. *Ibid.*, p. 195.
45. *Ibid.*, p. 196.
46. *Ibid.*, p. 128.
47. Quoted by M. Buber, *Paths in Utopia*, trans. R. F. C. Hull (Boston: Beacon Press, 1958), p. 55.
48. *Ibid.*, p. 48.
49. *Ibid.*, p. 55.
50. *Ibid.*, p. 56.
51. *Ibid.*, p. 133.

52. *Ibid.*, p. 148.
53. *Ibid.*, p. 142.
54. *Ibid.*, p. 149.
55. The scroll of the "War of the Sons of Light with the Sons of Darkness" is described in Millar Burrows's *The Dead Sea Scrolls* (New York: 1955). Predictions of an Armageddon preceding the advent of the Messiah are found in Judaism as well as in Christianity. Revelations 26:16. Ezekiel 38. "Midrashai Geula—Pirkai Hoapocalypsia Hayehudit." by Y. Ibn Shemuel, Jerusalem, 1954 (Hebrew).
56. J. L. Talmon, *Israel Among the Nations* (New York, 1970), p. 19.
57. Even the neo-Orthodox rabbi, Samson Raphael Hirsch, spoke of the year 1848 as one of the hours when "God entered into history," bestowing upon mankind a fresh outpouring of "inner revelation." (I. Heinemann, *Taamni Hamitzvot*, pp. 95, 264.) The messianic rhetoric of Zunz and others is described by N. Glatzer in Leo Baeck Institute, J. L. Talmon states, "There was hardly a revolution—that year of revolutions—in which Jews were not prominent or at least very active."
58. Hastings's *Encyclopedia of Religion and Ethics*, vol. 3, p. 842.
59. Friedrich Nietzsche, *The Genealogy of Morals*, translated by L. Golffing, Anchor Book, pp. 167–168.
60. Avoda Zara 3a.
61. See Abraham Newman's "Josippon, History and Pietism" in Newman's *Landmarks and Goals* (Philadelphia, 1953).
62. Pesahim 87b.
63. Judah Halevi, *The Kusari*, II, 44.
64. Persons of Jewish descent, such as Rosa Luxemburg (1870–1919) and Kurt Eisner (1867–1919) had no roots in Jewish life. They and other revolutionaries of Jewish or semi-Jewish descent surfaced during the upheavals of 1917–1920 more as symbols of the rejection of the old order than as leaders of the people.
65. *Encyclopedia Britannica*, 1968, vol. 10, p. 565.
66. Sh. Dubnow, *The Jews in Russia and Poland*, 1918, Vol. II, p. 222.
67. A. Tscherikower, *Yivo*, vol. III, 1939 (Yiddish). Lucy Davidowitz, *The Golden Treasure* (New York, 1967), p. 406.
68. Th. Herzl, *Diaries*, ed. M. Lowenthal (London, 1958), p. 395.
69. Louis Fischer, *The Life of Lenin* (New York, 1964), p. 39.
70. Sh. Dubnow, *Divrai yemai am olam* (Hebrew) vol. X, p. 222.
71. Fischer, *Life of Lenin*, p. 515.

VII. *The Zionist Response to Racist Nihilism*

1. A. Schopenhauer, *The World as Will and Idea*, translated by Payne (New York: Dover Publications, 1958), vol. I, p. 232.

2. *Ibid.*, vol. II, p. 167.
3. *Ibid.*, vol. I, p. 254.
4. *Ibid.*, vol. I, p. 329.
5. *Ibid.*, vol. I, p. 380.
6. *Ibid.*, vol. II, p. 170.
7. *Ibid.*, vol. II, p. 444.
8. *Ibid.*, vol. II, p. 644.
9. A. Schopenhauer, *Parega u. Paralipomena*, first German edition, *Werke*, 5.136.
10. A. Schopenhauer, *The Basis of Morality*, translated by Bullock (London, 1903), p. 237.
11. A. Schopenhauer, *Parerga u. Paralipomena*, II. *Werke*, 5.281.
12. A. Schopenhauer, *The Basis of Morality*, Bullock translation (London, 1903), pp. 213, 214.
13. *Sanhedrin*, 37a.
14. A. Schopenhauer, *The Basis of Morality*, p. 221.
15. L. Poliakov, *History of Antisemitism*, p. 247.
16. Quoted in Leon Stein, *The Racial Thinking of Richard Wagner* (New York, 1950), p. 33.
17. Wagner's mythology is found in his "Die Nibelungen," "Das Judentum in der Musik," "Religion und Kunst," "Christentum u. Heroismus," all in his *Gesammelte Schriften*.
18. F. W. Nietzsche, *The Antichrist* (New York, 1920), A. A. Knopf, translated H. L. Mencken, p. 182.
19. *Ibid.*, p. 54.
20. *Ibid.*
21. *Ibid.*, p. 79.
22. *Ibid.*, pp. 89, 90.
23. *Ibid.*, p. 90.
24. *Ibid.*, p. 80.
25. F. W. Nietzsche, *The Genealogy of Morals*, translated by F. Golffing (Doubleday, 1956), p. 167.
26. *Ibid.*, p. 169.
27. F. W. Nietzsche, *The Birth of Tragedy*, Golffing translation (1956), p. 77.
28. *Ibid.*, p. 120.
29. Werner Meisen, *Hitler's Mein Kampf* (Munich, 1966), p. 81.
29. P. de Lagarde, *Deutsche Schriften*, vierte Auflage (München-Berlin, 1940). Vorrede by Karl August Fischer, München, Juni, 1934.
31. *Ibid.*, p. 89.
32. *Ibid.*, p. 90.
33. *Ibid.*, p. 291.
34. *Ibid.*, p. 152.
35. *Ibid.*, p. 154.
36. *Ibid.*, p. 368.
37. *Ibid.*, p. 370.

38. *Ibid.*, p. 414.
39. Lagarde's anti-biblicism was all-embracing. The genius of Jesus consisted in his "not wanting to be a Jew"; Lutheranism was burdened by "the rotten remains of Christianity"; and Catholicism was "the born enemy of all states and nations." He even suggested that Jews might be exiled to Madagascar, a proposal that the Nazis took up seriously in the years 1938–1941. (L. Poliakov, *Le Breviare de la haine*, pp. 50–54. F. Stern, *The Politics of Cultural Despair* [Berkeley, 1961].)
40. M. Nordau, *Entartung* (first published in Berlin: C. Duncker, 1893). English translation, *Degeneration* (D. Appleton & Co., 1895), ninth edition, 1902, p. 373.
41. *Ibid.*, II, p. 363.
42. M. Ben-Horin, "Max Nordau," *Conference of Social Studies* (New York, 1956), pp. 238–245.
43. Nordau, *Degeneration,* II, p. 121.
44. *Ibid.*, p. 96.
45. *Kol Kitvai Micha Yosef* (Ben Gurion), Stybel edition, 20 volumes (Tel-Aviv, 1921–1925).
46. Whether or not A'had Ha'am himself was a vitalist is a matter of controversy. See *A'had Ha'am* (Hebrew) by Arye Simon and Joseph Heller (Jerusalem, 1957), p. 145. Also, the monograph, "Bisus Haleumut Bechitvai A'had Ha'am," p. 52. My view is based on an analysis of the implications of his argument and on the reason for its popular appeal.
47. A'had Ha'am, *Al Poroshat Derochim* (Berlin, 1930), vol. 1, p. 109.
48. *Ibid.*, vol. I, "Divrai Sholom," p. 113.
49. *Ibid.*, Torah Shebilev," p. 96.
50. "Shelilat Hagolut," in *Al Poroshat Derochim*, vol. IV.
51. A'had Ha'am, *Iggroth A'had Ha'am*, vol. 2, p. 68.
52. *Kol Kithvai A'had Ha'am*, pp. 161, 162.
53. *Ibid.*, "Al Shtai Haseipprim," p. 376.
54. A'had Ha'am, *Al Poroshat Derochim*, vol. II (Berlin, 1921), "Hamussar Haleumi," p. 85.
55. Sabbath 30a.
56. "Al Shetai Haseipim." *Al Poroshat Derochim*, IV, p. 42. Much has been made, in both Jewish and Christian literature, of this difference in formulation between Hillel and Jesus. Actually, in the "Testaments of the Twelve Patriarchs" we find a positive formulation. The kernel of truth in this claim is that in Judaism the virtue of fidelity to religious law is stressed, while in Christianity, the supreme virtue is love. But, taken as wholes, both traditions enjoin the two aspects of the good life—Jewish law encompasses the duty "to love thy neighbor as thyself" and Christian love is in practice structured and guided by the various traditions prevailing within the Christian world.
57. *Ibid.* (Berlin, 1921), vol. II, "Shinuy Ha'arachin," p. 70.

58. *Ibid.*, p. 72.

59. *Ibid.* (Berlin, 1930), Introduction to the Second Edition, XVII.

60. *Ibid.*, Tehiyah Uveriah, vol. III, p. 93.

61. *Ibid.*, "Torah Mizion," vol. IV, p. 127.

62. J. Agus, *The Vision and the Way*, an interpretation of Jewish ethics (New York: Frederick Ungar Publishing Co., 1969).

VIII. *If God Be the* Élan Vital

1. Henri Bergson, *Creative Evolution*, English translation, New York 1911, p. 266.

2. *Ibid.*, p. 299.

3. Henri Bergson, *Matter and Memory*, English translation, 1911, p. 296.

4. Henri Bergson, *Creative Evolution*, p. 271.

5. Quoted by Ben-Ami Scharfstein in *Roots of Bergson's Philosophy*, p. 119.

6. *Ibid.*, p. 116.

7. Henri Bergson, *Time and Free Will* (New York, Macmillan, 1910), p. 240.

8. Henri Bergson, "Life and Consciousness," *Hibbert Journal*, October, 1911.

9. Gilbert Maire, *Bergson, mon maitre*, p. 222.

10. Ben-Ami Scharfstein, *Roots of Bergson's Philosophy* (New York: Columbia University Press, 1943), p. 101.

11. Quoted by Jacques Maritain, *Ransoming the Time*, p. 101, note.

12. Joseph Salvador, "Paris, Rome et Jerusalem," *Ou la Question Religieuse au XIXeme Siecle* (Paris, 1860).

13. Henri Bergson, *Time and Free Will*, p. 227.

14. *Ibid.*, p. 231.

15. Georges Sorel, *Reflections on Violence* (Collier Books, 1967), p. 123, note.

16. *Ibid.*, p. 126.

17. *Ibid.*, p. 122.

18. *Ibid.*, p. 249.

19. Henri Bergson, *The Two Sources of Morality and Religion* (New York, 1935).

20. Emile Durkheim, *The Elementary Forms of the Religious Life*, translated by Joseph W. Swain (London, 1916), pp. 296, 416.

21. *Ibid.*, p. 419.

22. *Ibid.*, p. 416.

23. *Ibid.*, p. 425.

24. *Ibid.*, p. 426.

25. Henri Bergson, *Two Sources*, p. 286.

26. *Ibid.*, p. 223.

27. *Ibid.*, p. 229.
28. *Ibid.*, p. 243.
29. *Ibid.*
30. Jacques Maritain, *Bergsonian Philosophy and Thomism*, translated by Audison (New York: Philosophical Library, 1955).
31. *Ibid.*, p. 287.
32. *Ibid.*, p. 345.
33. Henri Bergson, *Two Sources*, p. 228.
34. Immanuel Kant, *Critique of Judgment*, Bernard Translation, p. 322.
35. Jacob Agus, *Banner of Jerusalem* (New York, 1946), p. 181.
36. Maimonides, *Guide of the Perplexed* II, 45.
37. *Ibid.*, III, 51.
38. Maimonides, *Hilchot Melochim* XI, end in uncensored version.
39. Henri Bergson, *Two Sources*, p. 229.
40. Teilhard de Chardin, *The Phenomenon of Man* (Harper Torchbooks, 1961), p. 224.
41. *Ibid.*, p. 221.
42. *Ibid.*, p. 260.
43. *Ibid.*, p. 262.
44. *Ibid.*, p. 298.
45. Oswald Spengler, "Preussentum u. Sozialismus," included in *Politische Schriften*, p. 45.
46. *Ibid.*, pp. 53–55.
47. Oswald Spengler, *Hour of Decision*, p. 225. H. Stuart Hughes, *Oswald Spengler*, revised edition (New York: Scribner's, 1962), p. 130.
48. Oswald Spengler, *The Decline of the West*, I, p. 151.
49. Oswald Spengler, *Reden u. Aufsätze*, pp. 73–75.
50. *Ibid.*, pp. 292, 293.
51. N. Glatzer, *Franz Rosenzweig—His Life and Thought* (Schocken, 1953), p. 25.
52. *Ibid.*
53. Letter to Rudolf Ehrenberg, dated October 31, 1913, in Franz Rosenzweig, *Briefe* (Schocken, 1935), p. 73.
54. N. Glatzer, *Franz Rosenzweig*, p. 33.
55. *Ibid.*, p. 78.
56. *Ibid.*, p. 129.
57. Franz Rosenzweig, *Star of Redemption*, Hallo translation (New York), p. 52.
58. *Ibid.*, p. 106.
59. *Ibid.*, p. 107.
60. Franz Rosenzweig, *Briefe*, p. 265.
61. In his letter to his parents, dated April 10, 1917, Rosenzweig described his German plan as an expression of his "power" and his Jewish plan as an outgrowth of his "energy." We must not underestimate the fact that the

two plans were produced in the same few weeks. N. Glatzer, op. cit., p. 52. *Briefe*, p. 185.
62. Franz Rosenzweig, *Star*, p. 63.
63. Franz Rosenzweig, *Briefe*, p. 520.
64. Franz Rosenzweig, *Kleinere Schriften* (Berlin, 1937), p. 114.
65. Franz Rosenzweig, *Briefe*, p. 386.
66. Franz Rosenzweig, *Star*, p. 181.
67. *Ibid.*, p. 199.
68. *Ibid.*, p. 396.
69. *Ibid.*, p. 339.
70. *Ibid.*, p. 341.
71. *Ibid.*, p. 408.
72. Quoted in N. Glatzer, *Rosenzweig*, p. 335.
73. Franz Rosenzweig, *Star*, p. 413.
74. M. Brod, *Heidentum, Christentum, Judentum* (Munich, 1921). Published in an English translation by University of Alabama Press in 1970.
75. Franz Rosenzweig, *Briefe*, p. 359.

IX. *Biblical Criticism and the Changing Image of the Jew*

1. Leon Poliakov, *The Aryan Myth* (New York, 1974), p. 330.
2. Benno Jacob, "Das Judenthum und die Ergebnisse der Assyriologie," *Allgemeine Zeitung des Judenthum's* (1902). Jacob J. Finkelstein, "Bible and Babel," *Commentary*, XXVI (1958). F. Delitsch, *Babel u. Bibel: Ein Vortrag* (Stuttgart, 1909). A thorough examination of the Shabbatu-Sabbath problem is found in Julius Lewy's "The Week and the Oldest West Asiatic Calendar," *H.U.C.A.* vol. XVIII (1942–1943) pp. 1–152.
3. F. Delitsch, *Die grosse Täuschung*, Stuttgart, 2 volumes (1922).
4. *Ibid.*, p. 76.
5. *Ibid.*, p. 149.
6. *Ibid.*, p. 144.
7. *Ibid.*, p. 145.
8. J. H. Breasted, *Dawn of Conscience* (New York, 1934).
9. Quoted in Solomon Goldman's *The Book of Books: An Introduction* (New York: Harper & Bros., 1948), p. 71.
10. *Ibid.*, p. 72.
11. F. W. Nietzsche, *The Antichrist*, trans. H. L. Mencken (Alfred A. Knopf, 1918), p. 79.
12. Emil Schürer, *A History of the Jewish People in the Time of Jesus Christ*, Second Edition, translated by Taylor & Christie (New York: Scribner's, 1891), vol. IV, 28, pp. 93, 94, 120, 125. Italics are the author's.
13. Solomon Schechter, "The Law and Recent Criticism," *Jewish Quarterly Review*, vol. III (London, 1891). Reprinted by Arno Press in a

volume *Judaism and Christianity*, edited by Jacob B. Agus (New York: Arno Press, 1973).

14. Israel Abrahams, "Prof. Schürer on 'Life under the Jewish Law,'" *Jewish Quarterly Review*, vol. XI (London, 1899). Reprinted in Jacob B. Agus's anthology, *Judaism and Christianity* (New York: Arno Press, 1973).

15. Prof. Louis Ginzberg, a preeminent authority, put it this way: "The Rabbis, who after all ought not to be entirely ignored in judging or rather in sentencing Judaism, are at least as severe in their censure of legalism as the church fathers in their denunciation of antinomianism." *Hebrew Union College Annual*, vol. I. p. 320.

16. R. Travers Herford, *The Pharisees* (London, 1924), p. 137.

17. *Ibid.*, p. 146.

18. I. Abrahams, *Life*, p. 635.

19. R. T. Herford, *Talmud and Apocrypha*, first published in 1933. Reprinted by *K'tav*, 1971, p. 308. Actually, as the monumental exposition of Philonic thought by Wolfson has demonstrated, Philo was linked to the Talmudic-Midrashic literature by the entire texture of his thought. Furthermore, Philo describes himself as an heir to a long tradition of interpretation. H. A. Wolfson, *Philo*, 2 volumes (Cambridge: Harvard University Press, 1974).

20. H. A. Wolfson, *Philo*, vol. I, p. 85.

21. M. Friedlander, "The 'Pauline' Emancipation from the Law: A Product of the Pre-Christian Jewish Diaspora," *Jewish Quarterly Review* (London, 1902), vol. XIV; reprinted in Agus's *Judaism and Christianity* (New York: Arno Press, 1973).

22. George F. Moore, "Christian Writers on Judaism," *Harvard Theological Review*, vol. XIV, No. 3 (Cambridge, 1921), p. 252. Reprinted in J. Agus's anthology, *Judaism and Christianity* (New York: Arno Press, 1973).

23. George F. Moore, *Judaism*, vol. I, p. 296.

24. *Ibid.*, II. pp. 9, 10.

25. *Ibid.*, II, p. 78.

26. *Ibid.*, II, p. 95.

27. Shabbat 17a. Solomon Zeitlin, *The Rise and Fall of the Jewish State*, II volume (Philadelphia, 1968), p. 358.

28. Gittin 19a; Sanhedrin 51b; Hagigah 10a.

29. Sanhedrin 106b.

30. Avodah Zara 10b.

31. Hullin 7a; Sabbat, 31a.

32. Hagigah 15b.

33. George F. Moore, *Judaism*, vol. I, p. 258.

34. Yebamot, 46a.

35. Tos. Sanhedrin, ch. 13.

36. Louis Ginzberg, *On Jewish Law and Lore* (Philadelphia, 1955), pp. 77–124.

37. Solomon Zeitlin, *The Rise and Fall of the Jewish State*, 2 volumes. Louis Finkelstein, *The Pharisees*, 2 volumes.

38. Ephraim A. Urbach, *Hazal, Pirkai Emunot Vedeot* (Jerusalem: The Magnes Press, Hebrew University, 1969), p. 8.

39. Louis Ginzberg, "Attitude of the Synagogue toward the Apocalyptic-eschatological Writers," *Journal of Biblical Literature*, vol. 41, 1922.

40. Max Güdemann, *Jüdische Apologetik*, Glogau, 1906, VIII and X.

41. J. Wellhausen, *Israelitische und Jüdische Geschichte*, Chapter IV. Güdemann, *Jüdische Apologetik*, p. 63.

42. J. Wellhausen, *Israelitische*, p. 189.

43. Max Güdemann, *Jüdische*, pp. 3, 165, 174.

44. Through the various *Midrashim* deriving from the Tannaitic period are difficult to disentangle, scholars generally speak of the two schools of hermeneutics—the spiritual one of Rabbi Yishmoel and the literal one of Rabbi Akiva. A. Marmorstein concluded, after a lengthy study, "that in Judea and later in Galilee, there were two different theological systems, the one understanding the early religious documents more literally, the other more spiritually. . . ." (A. Marmorstein, "Essays in Anthropomorphism," p. 26, K'tav, 1968, in volume called *The Doctrine of Merits in Old Rabbinic Literature*.)

   A. J. Heschel, in his study of the doctrine of revelation, *Torah min Hashomaim Beaspaklaria shel Hayahdut*, 2 volumes (Hebrew), demonstrates the great divergence between these two schools in regard to basic theological concepts (vol. I, p. XLI).

   The literalist Akiva used his hermeneutical method in order to bring about great innovations in Jewish practice.

   A well-known legend talks of Moses visiting the academy of R. Akiva and discovering that the doctrines and laws taught there were far different from those that were familiar to him. He is consoled by the reassurance that all the new laws were really implied in his own Torah (Menahot 29b).

   From Philo, we know that Alexandrian Jewry was divided into many religious groups. His allegorical method was intended to reconcile the literalists with the spiritualists.

45. Max Güdemann, "Spirit and Letter in Judaism and Christianity," *Jewish Quarterly Review*, vols. V and VI (London, 1895).

46. J. Wellhausen, *Israelitische*, p. 389. This passage is discussed by Martin Schreiner, *Die jüngsten Urteile über das Judentum* (Berlin, 1902).

47. E. Meyer, *Entstehung des Judentums*, p. 222. Quoted in Martin Schreiner's *Die jüngsten*, pp. 99, 105, 106.

48. Ernest Renan, *The Life of Jesus*, translation, newly revised from the 23rd edition (Boston: Roberts Bros., 1896).

49. Ernest Renan, *Oeuvres* I, p. 242.
50. Ernest Renan, *Life*, p. 123.
51. *Ibid.*, p. 229.
52. *Ibid.*, p. 219.
53. *Ibid.*, p. 240.
54. *Ibid.*, p. 242.
55. *Ibid.*, p. 326.
56. *Ibid.*, p. 242.
57. Ernest Renan, *Judentum u. Christentum*, authorized translation (Basel: Bernheim, 1883), p. 15.
58. *Ibid.*, p. 20.
59. *Ibid.*, p. 20.
60. F. C. Grant, *Ancient Judaism and the New Testament* (New York, 1959), p. 144.
61. *Ibid.*, p. 13.
62. *Ibid.*, p. 7.
63. *Ibid.*, p. 11.
64. A. Harnack, *What Is Christianity?* (1800–1900) translated by Saunders, II edition, revised (New York: Putnam, 1901), p. 67.
65. *Ibid.*, p. 67.
66. *Ibid.*, p. 75.
67. *Ibid.*, p. 79.
68. Felix Perles, "What Jews May Learn from Harnack," *Jewish Quarterly Review* (O.S.) XIV, pp. 517–543.
69. *Ibid.*, p. 521.
70. A. Harnack, *The Essence*, p. 138.
71. *Ibid.*, p. 154.
72. *Ibid.*, p. 156.
73. *Ibid.*, p. 151.
74. *Ibid.*, p. 52.
75. *Ibid.*, p. 52.
76. *Ibid.*, p. 188.
77. *Ibid.*, p. 255.
78. *Ibid.*, p. 315.
79. *Ibid.*, p. 302.
80. Felix Perles, "What Jews May Learn from Harnack," *Jewish Quarterly Review* (O.S.) XIV, pp. 521, 524, 524.
81. *Ibid.*, pp. 520, 525.
82. H. Cohen, *Jüdische Schriften*, II vol. (Berlin, 1924), p. 345.
83. *Ibid.*, p. 375.
84. *Ibid.*, p. 144.
85. *Ibid.*, p. 147.
86. H. Steinthal, *Über Juden und Judentum*, herausgegeben von G. Karpeles (Berlin, 1906), pp. 12, 15, 67.

87. Uriel Tal, *Yahadut ve Nazrut bareich Hasheni*, 1870–1914, p. 154.
88. *Ibid.*, IV volume (Munich, 1965), p. 6.
89. Shabbat 104a.
90. Strack–Billerbeck, *Kommentar*, p. 15.·
91. Taanit 25a.
92. Strack–Billerbeck, *Kommentar*, p. 500.
93. *Ibid.*, vol. I, p. 473.
94. The scope and depth of this phrase are explained in the chapter under this heading in my book, *Dialogue and Tradition* (New York: Abelard–Schuman, 1971).
95. George F. Moore, *Judaism*, vol. I, pp. 292–294.
96. "Vikuah de R. Yehiel miParis," Salo W. Baron, *A Social and Religious History of the Jews*, second edition, vol. XI, pp. 82, 276, 277.
97. *Hilchot Melochim*, X, 14, in the unexpurgated Constantinople edition.
98. *Allgemeine Zeitung des Judentums*, 1871, pp. 178–180, 380–382. A. Geiger, *Das Judentum u. seine Geschichte*, Appendix, III vol. (Breslau, 1871). Ismar Schorsch, *Jewish Reactions to German Antisemitism, 1870–1917*, (New York, 1972), p. 28.
99. See München Manuscript of Babylonian Talmud, Tractate Yebamot, where the words, "ela behama" (only cattle) are added to the oft-quoted phrase—"ye are called, Man, but the nations of the world are not so designated," where the term *Man* is used in an ideal sense.
100. Maimonides' letter to Rav Hisdai, "Kovetz Toshuvot Horambam veigrotov." "Veda mah Shetashiv," H. Bloch (New York, 1962), p. 18.
101. Sh. Etinger, Introduction to Uriel Tal, *Hayehudim*.
102. S. Formstecher, *Der Geist d. Religion* (Frankfurt, 1841); 2.451.
103. Jacques Maritain, *A Christian Looks at the Jewish Question,* first published by Longmans, Green & Co., 1939. Reprinted by Arno Press, New York, 1973, p. 25.
104. *Ibid.*, p. 27.
105. *Ibid.*, p. 29.
106. *Ibid.*, p. 32.
107. *Ibid.*, p. 35.
108. Quoted by Jules Isaac, *The Teaching of Contempt* (New York, 1964), p. 49.
109. Augustin Cardinal Bea, *The Church and the Jewish People* (New York: Harper & Row, 1966), p. 66.
110. *Ibid.*, p. 69.
111. *Ibid.*, p. 78.
112. *Ibid.*, p. 85.
113. *Ibid.*, p. 68.
114. Acts 5:38, referring to the trial of Peter by the Sanhedrin, "If this counsel of work be of men, it will come to naught, but if it be of God, ye cannot overthrow it, lest haply ye be found even to fight against God."

115. Karl Barth, *Commentary on the Epistle to the Romans*, I, 16, translated from VI edition by E. C. Hoskyns (London: Oxford University Press, 1933), p. 35.

116. *Ibid.*, I, pp. 19–21.

117. *Ibid.*, X, 16–20, p. 389.

118. *Ibid.*, X, 16–20, p. 391.

119. *Ibid.*, IX, 3–5, p. 338.

120. *Ibid.*, IX, 31, p. 366.

121. *Ibid.*, p. 462.

122. *Ibid.*, p. 452.

123. *Ibid.*, p. 434.

124. *Ibid.*, p. 432.

125. *Ibid.*, p. 451.

126. Nazir 23b.

127. Rolf Hochuth, *The Representative*, translated by R. D. Macdonald (London, 1963), p. 235.

128. Karl Barth, *The Only Way* (New York: Philosophical Library, 1947), p. 78.

129. Karl Barth, *Church Dogmatics*, vol. IV, Doctrine of Reconciliation, p. 877.

130. *Ibid.*

131. *Ibid.*, p. 878.

132. For the mystical overtones of the Chosen People and the meta-myth, see the references in Chapter I, note 52.

133. E. Kaufman, *Toldot Haemunah Hayisrealit*, 8 vols. A condensed version is contained in Moshe Greenberg's one-volume edition. E. Kaufman's *Goleh Venaicher*, 4 volumes (Tel Aviv, 1929) contains his analysis of the Zionist philosophy.

134. Martin Buber, *The Kingship of God* (Harper Torchbooks, 1967), pp. 59–65.

135. *Ibid.*, p. 65.

136. *Ibid.*, p. 97.

137. *Ibid.*, p. 108.

138. *Ibid.*, p. 109.

139. *Ibid.*, p. 148.

140. *Ibid.*, p. 149.

141. M. Buber, *Moses* (Harper Torchbooks, 1958), p. 16.

142. *Ibid.*, p. 41.

143. *Ibid.*, p. 54.

144. *Ibid.*, p. 85.

145. *Ibid.*, p. 200.

146. *Ibid.*, p. 130.

147. Martin Buber, *The Prophetic Faith* (Harper Torchbooks, 1960), p. 215.

148. *Ibid.*, p. 232.

149. *Ibid.*, p. 195.
150. *Ibid.*, pp. 164, 165.
151. *Ibid.*, p. 234.
152. Martin Buber, *Good and Evil* (New York: Scribner's, 1952), p. 41.
153. Martin Buber, *The Origin and Meaning of Hassidism* (Harper Torchbooks), p. 242.
154. *Ibid.*, pp. 109, 110.
155. Quoted in note to *Origin and Meaning of Hasidism*, p. 249.

x. *Jewish Self-Image in the Postwar World*

1. G. Haupt and J. J. Morie, *Les Bolshevistes par eux mêmes* (Paris, 1968).
2. John S. Curtis, *An Appraisal of the Protocols of Zion* (New York, 1942).
3. General Jewish Council, *Father Coughlin, His Facts and Arguments* (New York, 1963).
4. Joachim C. Fest, *Hitler* (New York, 1974), p. 133.
Alfred Rosenberg, *Der Mythus des 20. Jahrhunderts* 99th–102 Auflage, p. 214.
5. A. Hitler, *Mein Kampf*, translated by Ralph Manheim (Boston, 1943). Sentry edition, p. 654.
6. Robert Conquest, *The Great Terror* (New York, 1968), p. 76. On p. 498, he writes, "Stalin's execution of the main Yiddish writers in the 'Crimean Affair' of 1952 is among the most extraordinary of all State acts."
   The "Crimean Affair" was a proposal which had arisen in the Jewish Anti-Fascist Committee, after the war, to resettle Jews in the Crimean peninsula.
7. Lucy S. Davidowicz, *The War Against the Jews, 1939–1975* (New York: Holt, Rinehart & Winston, 1975), pp. 255–260.
8. Some Orthodox rabbis pointed to the "sin" of Zionism as the reason for the horrendous suffering of their people—Jews must wait passively for the Messiah. R. Yael Taitelbaum, *Vayael Moshe* (Brooklyn, 1959).
   Others discovered such "sins" as overbold feminine attire. R. Schemuel Grainiman, *Hofez Hayim al Hatorah* (New York, 1943), p. 242, in an open letter written in 1924.
9. A. Menes, *The Jewish People, Past and Present*, volume IV (New York, 1955), pp. 334–391.
10. Richard S. Levy, *The Downfall of the Antisemitic Political Parties in Imperial Germany* (New Haven: Yale University Press, 1975).
11. Richard S. Levy in *The Downfall* points out that even the Jewish Defense organizations had no conception of the revolutionary, radical nature of the post-war antisemites. p. 264.

> After information filtered into the ghetto about the mass shootings in the out of doors, about the operations of mobile death vans, about gassing installations in desolate camps, the first response everywhere was disbelief grounded in shock. Even the wanton and unconstrained killings and cruelties committed by the Germans had not prepared the Jews to grasp the facts of systematic mass murder.

Lucy S. Davidowicz, *The War*, p. 349.

12. E. Vermeil, "The Origin, Nature and Development of German Nationalist Ideology in 19th and 20th centuries" in *The Third Reich*. A study published under the auspices of the international council for philosophy and humanistic studies, with the assistance of UNESCO (New York, 1955).
13. Erich Kahler, *The Germans* (Princeton University Press, 1974), p. 277.
14. *Ibid.*
15. Erich Kahler's essay, "The Germans and the Jews" in *Studies of the Leo Baeck Institute* (New York: Frederick Ungar Publishing Co., 1967).
16. Joachim C. Fest, *Hitler* (New York: Harcourt, Brace and Jovanovich, 1974), p. 211.
17. Erich Kahler, *The Germans*, p. 287.
Joachim C. Fest, *Hitler*, p. 56.
18. Joachim C. Fest, *Hitler*, p. 499.
19. O. Spengler, *Jahre d. Entscheidung* (München, 1933).
20. *Ibid.*, p. 8.
21. *Ibid.*, p. 12.
22. *Ibid.*, p. 14.
23. *Ibid.*, p. 44.
24. *Ibid.*, p. 49.
25. *Ibid.*, pp 52 and XII.
26. *Ibid.*, p. 66.
27. *Ibid.*, p. 133.
28. *Ibid.*, pp. 58, 146.
29. *Ibid.*, p. VII.
30. *Ibid.*, p. 161.
31. The German army was not unaware of the plans of the S.S. and the Einsatzgruppen with regard to the Polish population. General Franz Halder's notes contain the notation: "cleaning out: Jewry, intelligentsia, clergy, nobility."
Lucy S. Davidowicz, *The War,* p. 115, summarizes: They were instructed to prepare lists of top Polish leaders and also of those on the middle level of leadership—teachers, clergy, nobility, legionnaires. Those listed were clearly foredoomed."
32. K. D. Bracher, *The German Dictatorship* (New York, 1971), p. 407. The author summarizes Hitler's program on the basis of his recorded tapes. "The 180 million Russians, on the other hand, would have to die out.

They were to be prohibited from procreating; their schools were to be closed, to prevent the development of an educated class. . . ." See also Wm. L. Shirer's *The Rise and Fall of the Third Reich*, pp. 937–995.

33. Joachim C. Fest, *Hitler*, p. 383.
34. K. D. Bracher, *The German Dictatorship*, p. 42.
35. *Ibid.*, p. 45.
36. *Ibid.*, p. 81.
37. *Ibid.*, p. 183.
38. A. Hitler, *Mein Kampf*, p. 42.
39. Charles S. Liebman, "Diaspora Influence on Israel: The Ben Gurion-Blaustein 'Exchange' and its Aftermath." *Jewish Social Studies*, vol. XXXV, p. 271.
40. J. L. Talmon, *The Unique and the Universal* (New York, 1965), p. 72.
41. Herzl Fishman, *American Protestantism and a Jewish State* (Detroit, 1973), p. 178.
41a. J. L. Talmon, *The Unique and the Universal*, p. 121.
42. Jewish reactions to Toynbee were on the same large scale as those which followed the comments on the Jews of Bruno Bauer, Heinrich Treitschke and Adolf Harnack, only more so. It is indeed difficult to find a parallel to the storm of resentment and criticism aroused by Toynbee's work.
43. A. J. Toynbee, *A Study of History* (New York, 1954), vol. VIII, p. 272.
44. Joachim C. Fest, *Hitler* (New York, 1974), p. 506.
45. A. J. Toynbee, *Experiences* (New York, 1969), p. 136. "To believe that one's own tribe is God's Chosen People is the error of nationalism. Other peoples besides the Jews have fallen into it."
46. A. J. Toynbee, *A Study of History*, vol. XII, 1961, p. 419n.
47. Toynbee takes note of this criticism in his *Reconsiderations*, vol. XII, p. 412. In answer, he cites the massive archeological discoveries in Palestine, which place the biblical faith in its civilizational context. In his view, Christianity arose out of the suppressed Canaanite elements in the Jewish religion. See his critique of Albright who rationalizes the presumed massacre of the Canaanites. (*Ibid.*, p. 419) as representing the "right" of a "young" nation to remove an "old" and corrupt nation from the scene.
48. Martin Wight, in Annex to vol. VII, *A Study of History*, p. 738.
49. Genesis Rabba, 12,15.
50. Matt. 18,8; Jude 1,7.
51. Shabbat 33a.
52. Rosh Hashono 17a.
53. Tosefta, Sanhedrin 13.
54. Hullin, 13b.
55. Shabbat 30a.
56. Rosh Hashono 17a.
57. To be sure, this verse was not interpreted in an irenic way by the traditional commentators, Rashi and Mezudat David, But, Abraham

Ibn Ezra and David Kimhi explain that it foretells that there will be no mass conversions to Judaism, prior to the coming of the Messiah. The modern, liberal interpretation is probably closer to the original intent of Micah, who accepted Isaiah's prophecy and added his own codicil.

58. The best known antisemitic collection of this type is that of Eisenmenger, which served as the basis of popular diatribes. But even the monumental *Kommentar zum Neuen Testament aus Talmud und Midrash* by Strack-Billerbeck, 4th edition, 1926, is, for all its vast erudition, saturated with contempt, in its interpretive passages, as we have maintained in the previous chapter.

59. For example, the *lex talionis* was changed to call for monetary compensation. Baba Kama, 83b. Maimonides' *Guide* III, 41. Other examples are the case of the rebellious son, Deuteronomy 21,18 Sanhedrin 71b, and the case of the heretical city, Deuteronomy 13,13, Sanhedrin 111a and 112b.

60. The continuity of the impetus of classical prophecy in the rabbinic Aggada, in medieval philosophy and mysticism, down to our own day is outlined in my essay, "The Prophet in Modern Hebrew Literature," which was first printed in Hebrew Union College Annual of 1957, reprinted in my *Dialogue and Tradition*, 1971. More extensively, this thesis underlies the entire argument in my book, *The Evolution of Jewish Thought* (New York: Arno Press).

61. *A Study of History*, XII, p. 214.

62. *Ibid.*, p. 216.

63. *Ibid.*, p. 217.

64. Oscar K. Rabinowitz, *Arnold Toynbee on Judaism and Zionism* (London, 1974), p. 221. Toynbee's books are *The Murderous Tyranny of the Turks*, preface by Viscount Bryce (London, 1917) and *Turkey: A Past and a Future* (New York, 1917).

65. L. Stein, *The Balfour Declaration*, p. 322.

66. Rabinowitz, *Arnold Toynbee*, p. 232. "Syria and Palestine Handbook," No. 60. Toynbee, "Turkey: A Past and a Future," p. 6.

67. A. J. Toynbee, *Experiences*, p. 266. "Israeli colonialism since the establishment of the state of Israel is one of the two blackest cases in the whole history of colonialism in the modern age; and its blackness is thrown into relief by its date . . . a crime that was also a moral anachronism."

68. Vol. VIII, p. 277.

69. *Reconsiderations*, vol. XII, p. 621, in which Toynbee takes note of Stecchini's criticism.

70. The relevance of anti-colonialism to the plight of Israel is acknowledged by the Israeli historian, J. L. Talmon in his book, *The Unique and the Universal* (New York, 1965), p. 266. "The Jews in Israel are in the ambiguous position of the last white settlers in Asia and Africa, after the

European imperialists and colonizers had made their exit from the two continents."

71. Toynbee, *Study*, vol. XII, p. 624n.
72. J. L. Talmon, *The Unique and the Universal*, p. 123.
73. *Ibid.*
74. Berochot 35b.

Selected Bibliography

This bibliography supplements the information given within the text and in the notes.

Arendt, Hannah. *The Origins of Totalitarianism*. Rev. ed., New York: Harcourt, Brace, 1966.

Ayinn, Sidney. "Kant on Judaism." Philadelphia: *Jewish Quarterly Review 59*. 1968.

Barzilai, I. *Shlomo Yehudah Rapoport (Shir) and His Contemporaries*. Tel Aviv, Israel: Masada Press, 1969.

Cassirer, Ernst. *The Philosophy of the Enlightenment*. Translated by Fritz C. A. Koellin and James P. Pettegrove. Boston: Beacon Press, 1955.

Cohn, Norman. *Warrant for Genocide: The Myth of the Jewish World Conspiracy and the Protocols of the Elders of Zion*. London: Eyre and Spottiswoode, 1967.

Dorpalen, Andreas. *Heinrich von Treitschke*. New Haven: Yale University Press, 1957.

Geiger, Ludwig. *Abraham Geiger, Leben und Lebenswerk*. Berlin: 1919.

Katz, Jacob. *Out of the Ghetto: The Social Background of Jewish Emancipation, 1770–1870*. Cambridge, Massachusetts: Harvard University Press, 1973.

Kaufman, Yehezkiel. "Antisemitic Stereotypes in Zionism. The National Rejection of Diaspora Jewry." New York: *Commentary*, VII, pp. 239–45, 1949.

Krieger, Leonard. *The German Idea of Freedom: History of a Political Tradition*. Boston: 1957.

Leschnitzer, Adolf. *The Magic Background of Modern Antisemitism: an Analysis of the German-Jewish relationship*. New York: International Universities Press, 1956.

Lewkowitz, Albert. *Das Judentum und die geistigen Strömungen des neunzehnten Jahrhunderts*. Breslau: 1935.

Liebeschütz, Hans. *Das Judentum im deutschen Geschichtsbild von Hegel bis Max Weber*. Tübingen: J. C. B. Mohr (Leo Baeck Institute) 1967.

Longee, Robert W. *Paul de Lagarde (1827–1891)*. Cambridge, Massachusetts: Harvard University Press, 1962.

Markham, F. M. H., editor and translator. *Selected Writings of Saint-Simon*. Oxford: B. Blackwell, 1952.

Marrus, Michael R. *The Politics of Assimilation: A Study of the French-Jewish Community at the Time of the Dreyfus Affair*. London: Oxford University Press, 1971.

Massing, Paul. *Rehearsal for Destruction: A Study of Political Antisemitism in Imperial Germany*. New York: Howard Fertig, 1949.

Meyer, Michael A. *Great Debate on Antisemitism: Jewish Reaction to New Hostility in Germany, 1879–1881*. New York: Leo Baeck Jahrbuch, 11, 1966.

Mosse, George L. *The Crisis of German Ideology: Intellectual Origins of the Third Reich*. New York: Grosset and Dunlap, 1964.

Pulzer, Peter G. *The Rise of Political Antisemitism in Germany and Austria: 1867–1918*. New York: John Wiley, 1964.

Rich, Norman. *Hitler's War Aims: Ideology, the Nazi State and the Course of Its Expansion*, 2 volumes. New York: W. W. Norton, 1973.

Rotenstreich, Nathan. *Jewish Philosophy in Modern Times: From Mendelssohn to Rosenzweig*. New York: Holt, Rinehart and Winston, 1968.

————. *Hegel's Image of Judaism*. New York: Jewish Social Studies 15, 1953.

Silberner, Edmund. "French Socialism and the Jewish Question, 1865–1914." Historica Judaica, XVI (1954), pp. 3–38.

Snell, John L. *The Nazi Revolution: Germany's Guilt or Germany's Fate*. Boston: D. C. Heath and Co., 1959.

Sterling, Elinore. *Er ist wie Du: aus der Frühgeschichte Deutschlands (1815–1850)*. München: Chr. Kaiser, 1956.

Stern, Fritz, *Gold and Iron: Bismarck, Bleichröder, and the Building of the German Empire*. New York: Alfred A. Knopf, 1977.

————. *The Politics of Cultural Despair: A Study in the Rise of the Germanic Ideology*. Berkeley: University of California Press, 1961.

Vermeil, Edmond. *Germany in the Twentieth Century: A Political and Cultural History of the Weimar Republic and the Third Reich*. New York: Praeger, 1956.

Waxman, Myer. *A History of Jewish Literature, from the close of the Bible to Our Own Day*. 4 volumes. New York: Bloch Publishing Co., 1941.

Index

ABOUT THE AUTHOR

JACOB B. AGUS is Rabbi of Beth-El Congregation, a Conservative synagogue in Baltimore, and was for twelve years editorial consultant to the Encyclopedia Britannica for articles on Judaism and Jewish history. He has taught at Temple and at Dropsie Universities. Dr. Agus is also the author of *The Evolution of Jewish Thought, Modern Philosophies of Judaism,* and *The Vision and the Way: An Interpretation of Jewish Ethics,* among other books.